Join, or Die – Philosophical Foundations of Federalism

Join, or Die –
Philosophical Foundations
of Federalism

Edited by
Dietmar H. Heidemann and Katja Stoppenbrink

DE GRUYTER

ISBN 978-3-11-060967-7
e-ISBN (PDF) 978-3-11-042210-8
e-ISBN (EPUB) 978-3-11-042212-2

Library of Congress Cataloging-in-Publication Data
A CIP catalog record for this book has been applied for at the Library of Congress.

Bibliographic information published by the Deutsche Nationalbibliothek
The Deutsche Nationalbibliothek lists this publication in the Deutsche Nationalbibliografie;
detailed bibliographic data are available on the Internet at http://dnb.dnb.de.

© 2018 Walter de Gruyter GmbH, Berlin/Boston
This volume is text- and page-identical with the hardback published in 2016.
Cover image: "Join, or Die" (attributed to Benjamin Franklin); Public Domain
Printing and binding: Hubert & Co. GmbH & Co. KG, Göttingen

♾ Printed on acid-free paper
Printed in Germany

www.degruyter.com

Contents

Nineteenth Century Reception and Criticism of Federalist Ideas

Contemporary and Systematic Approaches to Federalism

Katja Stoppenbrink & Dietmar H. Heidemann
Introduction

A political cartoon. When in 1754 French colonists in North America attempted to establish a line of fortifications from the shores of Lake Erie and along the Ohio river up until their southern settlement in Louisiana British colonists feared they might become confined to the territories east of this imaginary line from north to south so that any further territorial expansion towards the west would become practically unfeasible for the British. The chief bone of contention was Fort Duquesne situated at the confluence of the Monongahela and Allegheny rivers in Pittsburgh, Pennsylvania, the source of the Ohio river. On April 17, 1754, Fort Duquesne fell to the French. This setback for the British colonies prompted Benjamin Franklin, then a delegate to the colonial assembly of Pennsylvania, to write a commentary for his[1] local newspaper, the *Pennsylvania Gazette*, which was straightaway reprinted in other colonies' newspapers.[2]

In this article of May 9, 1754, Franklin articulates the demand for a genuine political union of the British colonies. His aim is to establish a unified high command to be able to counter acts of aggression as those by the French. The point of his claims is to join forces and implement a common defense and security strategy both at the policy and at the operative level. He describes the British colonies' problem as follows:

> The Confidence of the French in this Undertaking seems well-grounded on the present disunited State of the British Colonies, and the extreme Difficulty of bringing so many different Governments and Assemblies to agree in any speedy and effectual Measures for our common Defence and Security [...]

The underlying motivation is to safeguard economic activity since the French "kill, seize and imprison our Traders, and confiscate their Effects at Pleasure [...] murder and scalp our Farmers [...]". If they are not hindered, according to Franklin's warning, this "must end in the Destruction of the British Interest, Trade and Plantations in America".[3] As an eye catcher, he adds what has

---

1 Franklin became a co-publisher on October 2, 1729, see http://www.loc.gov/rr/news/circulars/pagazette.txt (retrieved 2016/01/19).
2 See Overhoff (2006, 184). The Pennsylvania Gazette can be accessed here https://lccn.loc.gov/sn84026371 and online upon subscription http://www.accessible-archives.com/collections/the-pennsylvania-gazette/ (both retrieved 2016/01/19).
3 All quotations are taken from Franklin's aforementioned article.

since been labelled "America's first political cartoon".[4] On this sketch a number of British North American colonies, namely (from left to right) South and North Carolina, Virginia, Maryland, Pennsylvania, New Jersey, New York and the New England colonies Massachusetts, New Hampshire, Connecticut and Rhode Island, are represented as pieces of a fragmented snake. It is implied that the snake will not survive if the pieces are not bound together to form a 'whole'. The corresponding slogan (or rather: exhortation) is "Join, or Die".

Fig. 1

Franklin thus acts as a self-proclaimed spokesman of the British colonies in North America. At first it seems his proposal is followed and put into practice: In the weeks after Franklin's article the need for intercolonial cooperation is urgently felt and what comes to be known as the Albany Congress is convened on June 19, 1754. Seven colonies send their commissioners. Among these Franklin is appointed to represent Pennsylvania, and he further writes some "short hints to-

---

4 See Overhoff (2006, 185): "eine von ihm selbst entworfene politische Karikatur [...]" and (ibid.) "Amerikas erster politischer Cartoon".

wards a Scheme for uniting the Northern Colonies"[5]. However, he proposes to implement a union by way of a top-down directive, an act of the British Parliament. Accordingly, in the plan adopted by the Albany Congress, the "Albany Plan of Union", a so-called "Grand Council" is envisaged to be constituted by representatives of the colonial governments (apart from those of Georgia and Delaware) while a "Governour General" is designed to be appointed by the British Government and to preside over the unified intercolonial government thus to be installed.

The Albany Plan is ambivalent. While the overall authority of the British government over the North American colonies is not called into question, the Grand Council is to have 'relative' authority over intercolonial and Indian-colonial affairs and even to levy colonial taxes. In spite or rather because of this mixed tendency between colonial autonomy and independence on the one hand, reinforcement of British colonial power on the other, the Albany Plan fails.

Albeit dismissed in 1754, Franklin's idea to establish a union of the British colonies in North America so as to allow for a common government to handle what then would be 'external' relations of the union is out in the world; its renewal lies ahead. In 1777, after the Declaration of Independence in the previous year, the first former colony and new-born independent *state* ratifies[6] the Articles of Confederation and Perpetual Union. Like a showcase the years to come highlight the advantages and disadvantages of a confederation as opposed to a federal state. Entering into force in 1789, the United States Constitution finally replaces the 'general government' of the Articles and introduces a strong(er) federal government.

Montesquieu is the first author to discuss the advantages of a 'federal state' under the rubric of a "république fédérative"[7]. The expression 'federalism'

---

5 See Franklin's letter and enclosure "[T]o James Alexander and Cadwallader Colden with Short Hints towards a Scheme for Uniting the Northern Colonies" written from "N York June 8. 1754"; http://franklinpapers.org/franklin/framedVolumes.jsp?vol=5&page=353a (retrieved 2016/01/19).

6 Virginia, December 16, 1777.

7 Montesquieu, *De l'Esprit des Lois*, Book 9, Chapter 1 (1951, 369 [1758]): "une manière de constitution qui a tous les avantages intérieurs du gouvernement républicain, et la force extérieure du monarchique [...] la république fédérative. Cette forme de gouvernement est une convention par laquelle plusieurs Corps politiques consentent à devenir citoyens d'un État plus grand qu'ils veulent former. C'est une société de sociétiés, qui en font une nouvelle, qui peut s'agrandir par de nouveaux associés qui se sont unis". He continues that "[C]et État [...] [C]omposé de petites républiques, [...] jouit de la bonté du gouvernement intérieur de chacune; et, à l'égard du dehors, il a, par la force de l'association, tous les avantages des grandes monarchies." Ibid. (1951, 370).

(French: *fédéralisme*[8]) has come into existence as a neologism[9] in the French revolution and has spread in its aftermath[10]. In his *Philosophical Sketch* of 1795 Kant develops a teleological political philosophy towards *Perpetual Peace*. Adapting the contemporary form of a peace treaty Kant proposes in the second of his three "Definitive Articles" that "[T]he law of nations shall be founded on a federation of free states"[11].

However, it is easy to detect and describe pre-federal phenomena *avant la lettre*. Of course political units have been able to cooperate and to unite through

---

8 According to Koselleck (1972, 637 fn. 285) the term 'fédéralisme' was in "1772 von Robespierre zuerst verwendet". The year is obviously erroneous and should read '1792' when Robespierre (1758–1794) started to polemize against 'federalism' as a threat to the unity and indivisibility of the Republic in his speeches. See, e.g., Robespierre (1957, 578f. [1793]) in a speech of 18 June 1793 on the "Conventions nationales" in the constitution: "Un peuple qui a deux espèces de représentans cesse d'être un peuple |unique. Une double représentation est le germe du fédéralisme et de la guerre civile."

9 Koselleck (1972, 638).

10 See Koselleck (1972, 637 fn. 285) and (2006, 486 [1994]) for an abbreviated version of the Chateaubriand quote from the French writer's questionable *Voyage en Amérique* (1838, 170 [1826]), "Les Indiens de l'Amérique septentrionale connoissent les monarchies et les républiques représentatives; le fédéralisme étoit une des formes politiques les plus communes employées par eux". With this quote Koselleck alludes to the dual territorial and 'ethnic' or 'communitarian' aspects of federalism and points to the fact that in the French revolution with the defeat of the 'federalist' Girondins faction and its aftermath, 'fédéralisme' is predominantly used pejoratively in France. Cf. French constitutional law scholar Beaud who starts off with the observation "qu'il n'existe pas en France de tradition fédérale" (²2009, 2) in order to develop a theory of the federation understood as "union 'librement consentie' entre États" (ibid., 116f.). "Là où une telle liberté de formation n'existe pas, il n'y a pas de veritable Fédération" (ibid., 118).

11 "Das Völkerrecht soll auf einen Föderalism freier Staaten gegründet sein" (*Zum Ewigen Frieden. Ein philosophischer Entwurf* AA 8:354; English translation by the editors). Kant discusses forerunner ideas by French thinkers such as Charles-Irénée ["l'abbé"] Castel de Saint-Pierre (1658–1743) with his *Projet pour rendre la paix perpétuelle en Europe* (1712; see http://catalogue.bnf.fr/ark:/12148/cb30204145x, retrieved 2016/03/03) and Jean-Jacques Rousseau (1712–1778) and calls for states "[...] aus dem gesetzlosen Zustande der Wilden hinaus zu gehen und in einen Völkerbund zu treten; wo jeder, auch der kleinste Staat seine Sicherheit und Rechte nicht von eigener Macht, oder eigener rechtlichen Beurtheilung, sondern allein von diesem großen Völkerbunde (*Foedus Amphictyonum*), von einer vereinigten Macht und von der Entscheidung nach Gesetzen des vereinigten Willens erwarten könnte. So schwärmerisch diese Idee auch zu sein scheint und als eine solche an einem Abbé von St. Pierre oder Rousseau verlacht worden (vielleicht, weil sie solche in der Ausführung zu nahe glaubten) [...]" (*Idee einer Geschichte in weltbürgerlicher Absicht* AA 8:24). Kant is cited by the corresponding volume in the standard "Akademie" edition of Kant's works: Kants gesammelte Schriften, edited by the Königlich Preußischen Akademie der Wissenschaften (Berlin 1902–[here 1912/23]).

all of recorded human history. The ancient Greek alliances and leagues of *poleis*[12] are but one example—even though the Swiss *Eidgenossenschaft* and the North American federation with their origins in medieval and modern times respectively may be the first historically more 'tangible' political co-operations of the type of a federation. The Roman *foedus*, the etymological origin of all composites and variants of 'federal', was instrumentalised as an imperial subjugation treaty on pain of religious penalties.[13] Historically and empirically, a *foedus* was taken to be regulated by 'international law'; there was the *foedus* among equals (*foedus aequum*) and the *foedus iniquum* characterized by a subjugation clause.[14]

Judging from the mere depiction of the dissected snake, Franklin's cartoon may at first sight be read as signifying an 'organicist' or 'holistic' understanding of a federal entity: the sub-units would accordingly be taken to be organs or sub-ordinated parts of a body which itself would only be able to function as a whole.

By this picture we are reminded of the pre-federal political-theological conception proposed by Johannes Althusius (1563[?]-1638) who, as a leading Calvinist thinker, emphasized the 'corporative' nature of *consociationes*.[15] In his "consocial federalism" (Hueglin/Fenna in their comparative work) or "consocialism" (Friedrich[16]) the ambivalent politically secular and teleologically religious nature of his commonwealth is founded upon both free consent by all to join a consociation (starting from the level of the family) *and* the idea of a special obligation of the faithful towards God.[17] The *telos* of a consociation is to enable its members to lead a life pleasing to God. The *consociationes* form a whole, their members are conceived of as parts of a body.[18]

However, this corporative, organicist picture is misguided with respect to the North American federative process since an essential feature of this modern federalist conception is the sustainable, long-term autonomy of the sub-units which in themselves have the quality of 'sovereign states' and merely 'join forces' on a contractual basis and transfer well-defined powers to a central governmental unit with a limited attribution of powers. According to this contractarian concep-

---

12 See, e.g., Beck (1997); Ward and MacDonald (2009) offer interpretations of Herodotus and Thucydides to explore what they consider "Nascent Federalism"—which then collapses into imperialism.

13 Baldus (2002; 2004).

14 Baldus (2002; 2004). Ziegler (1994, 49) points out that the *foedus iniquum* is not a Roman term but a scholarly concept not used in the historical sources.

15 See, e.g., Hüglin [Hueglin] (1991; 1999).

16 In his edition of Althusius's *Politica Methodice Digesta* (1932, lxxxviii).

17 Elazar (1997) points to the biblical features of Althusius's conception which therefore is a paradigm example for the covenant tradition of federalism argued for by Elazar.

18 Koch (2009, 78).

tion of a federal structure the sub-units coming together each have the characteristics of a state, and the central unit will also acquire state-making properties itself (*E pluribus unum*) while the sub-units retain their 'state quality'[19]. Even if the actual genesis of a federal state may not be mistaken for its claim for legitimacy, it is hard to see how the legitimacy of a *federation* (used here as an umbrella term to include confederations, federal states and related institutional arrangements) can be derived from the idea of a pre-existing, 'naturally united' body existing *in potentia* awaiting its actualization by a process of federation.

Both on conceptual and ontological grounds, a question pertaining to the idea of state continuity remains: How is state continuity to be conceived of with respect to federal and to federated states? Legal theories on the continuance or succession of a state through constitutional renewal rely on different ontological presuppositions relevant for the question of whether or not constitutional change means continuity rather than foundation of a 'new' state. Even if *arguendo* we take transtemporal identity of states through radical constitutional change to be possible, this assumed continuity would not *necessarily* include the federation-making properties.

If we go back to Franklin's drawing, the snake is in so far an inadequate visualization as the claim to a pre-existing snake torn apart and to be re-united does not account for the situation of the colonies—which at the time of Franklin's article still form part of the British Crown. From the moment in which the colonies do not directly accept legislation adopted by the British Parliament anymore it could be claimed that the structure uniting Britain and the colonies is a federal structure in which the colonies have each acquired state-making properties (legislative, administrative, judicial powers) but in some domains accept the authority of a central unit (Britain) which itself now has the character of a federal state. Now Franklin's call for action can be interpreted as a revolutionary appeal to 'exchange' the 'old' central unit (Britain) for a new central unit still to be created. The structural problem (what to do with the 'old' central unit in Europe?) highlighted by this certainly daring and historically inappropriate reading of Franklin's 1754 article in the *Pennsylvania Gazette* may point to the reason why the Albany Plan of Union was doomed to failure. The role of the British colonial power remained unclear, the colonies feared to lose their relative autonomy. The situation could only be resolved by a clear-cut move towards independence from Britain and the creation of a 'new' federation by the Articles of Confederation and Perpetual Union in 1777. The subsequent period was then marked by quarrels over the *kind* of federation to be implemented, federalists

---

19 In German federal constitutional lingo: *Eigenstaatlichkeit der Länder.* Cf. Herbst (2014, 74).

and so-called anti-federalists (who, inappropriately denominated, did not argue against *any* federation but strove for a kind of *con*-federation) disputed about the nature of what then would be the Constitution of the *United States* [our emphasis; the eds.] of America.

Some conceptual clarification and desiderata for research. Leaving aside Franklin and the intricate ontological underpinnings of the protracted unification process of the former British colonies in North America, we have to turn to the task of conceptual clarification and introduce at least some provisional taxonomic categories.[20] Roughly, today's world can be divided into two groups of states: *federal states* and *unitary states.* Although theoretically and empirically the picture is much more colorful, with quite a few options in between, these two forms of the organization of states can be taken to be ideal-types allowing for classification in the sense that states can either be said to be closer to one or the other type or to combine elements of the two.

Another theoretical dividing line which historically and practically is of great relevance is the one between *federal states* and *confederations* which on a certain understanding can both be subsumed under the concept of a federation understood as an umbrella term. Thus, a unitary state may become a member unit of a federation in the sense of a confederation. Present-day European Union (EU) is neither considered a confederation (in German: *Staatenbund*) nor a federal state (*Bundesstaat*) but a federation *sui generis* with many features of an ideal type federal state; in its case law[21] the German constitutional court (*Bundesverfassungsgericht*; BVerfG) has used the term *Staatenverbund* to capture the particular characteristics of the European Union and its special nature of 'an association of sovereign states'.

In the history of ideas and in political science the definition and genesis of federalism, the advantages and problems of each organizational form of a state, confederation, federal or unitary state have been investigated in many ways. However, 'federalism' is an elusive concept in so far as there is a plethora of different phenomena to be subsumed under this umbrella. This makes it a fertile ground for manifold analytic and empirical approaches in the historical, political and social sciences as well as in law. However, in these prolific multidiscipli-

---

20 Cf. for a taxonomy Føllesdal (2014).
21 Most recently see the judgment of the Second Senate of 30 June 2009 – 2 BvE 2/08 on the "Act Approving the Treaty of Lisbon" which is found compatible with the German Basic Law while the accompanying law is judged unconstitutional "to the extent that legislative bodies have not been accorded sufficient rights of participation"; http://www.bundesverfassungsger icht.de/SharedDocs/Entscheidungen/EN/2009/06/es20090630_2bve000208en.html (2016/ 02/22).

nary studies the philosophical foundations of federalism often go unnoticed and unappreciated.[22] Philosophical analysis sheds light on the reasons for and against federalism, especially the legitimacy conditions of 'shared' political authority and the vertical division of powers. The justification of dual or multiple political authority in a multilevel federal order, the nature of demands for allegiance and loyalty and the related concerns of legitimacy, democratic participation and distribution of powers as well as, e. g., more technical issues of distributive justice including levying of taxes and fiscal redistribution in a federal order all refer back to underlying theories of political philosophy and can most adequately be addressed if the philosophical perspective is not ignored. Modern federalist thought cannot—*pace* Rousseau—be detached from philosophical social contract theory. On this reading, federative and confederative agreements can in a 'bottom up' approach be regarded as freely negotiated associations of states the legitimacy of which is based on individual self-determination. Although often the focus is primarily put on the tensions between decision-making in a multi-level political order, protection of individual rights and democratic sovereignty, federalism and democratic theory are closely interwoven; an eventual 'democratic deficit'[23] has important repercussions on the legitimacy of a federal arrangement.

Departing from this diagnosis the aim of this book is to counterbalance this focus and, first, to present original research into historical reasoning in political philosophy which may be regarded as a justification or—at least—a precursor of federalist thought. Secondly, this is complemented with philosophical research into present-day organizational and justificatory issues of federal or federative orders, notably the principle of subsidiarity, its interpretive dimensions and its suitability to remove or lower tensions between the principle of democratic sovereignty of sub-units or member states and binding higher-order decision-making by central governments or international human rights jurisdictions.

We wish to help fill the lacunae in philosophical research on federalism and respond to a renewed interest in questions of federalism both from a theoretic point of view as well as from a political concern for a possible *finalité* of the European Union by shedding light on philosophical foundations from both a his-

---

22 See, e. g., Deuerlein (1972) who in his title claims to offer a work covering "[D]ie historischen und philosophischen Grundlagen des föderativen Prinzips" and then presents a predominantly historical outline of federal structures in the history of Germany. More recently the four volume compendium edited by Härtel contains more than one hundred contributions from a variety of disciplines while as few as three are from philosophers: see Höffe, Lübbe and Nida-Rümelin (2012).

23 See, e. g., Føllesdal/Hix (2006) for an examination of contemporary EU institutions.

torical and a systematic perspective. Instead of proposing an attempt at some overarching conceptual analysis—which, depending on the methodological background theory one may hold, will at any rate be doomed to failure—the approach pursued here is, admittedly, marked by its fragmentary character and piecemeal fashion. The idea is to explore principal philosophical tributaries flowing into the large delta of federalism, mainly Kant and *The Federalist*. Far from any claim to comprehensiveness, some upstream pre- and proto-federal conceptions are added, as well as selected examples of 'downstream' criticism and reception.

In what follows we introduce to the structure of the book and present a short summary of each of the contributions. The book commences with a survey of early modern roots of federalist thought. Two central building blocks of the book are dedicated to Kant and federalism and to the *Federalist Papers*, each with three contributions. A further historical section examines nineteenth century reception and criticism of federalist ideas with a special focus on Hegel and John Stuart Mill. Finally, in a systematic approach contemporary applications of and challenges to the concept of federalism—especially its operationalization in the political and legal sphere—are illuminated and fathomed out.

Early modern roots of federalist thought. Early modern forerunners of federalist thought are explored in the two contributions by Bernd Ludwig (Göttingen, Germany) on Thomas Hobbes (1588–1679) and Lukas K. Sosoe (Luxembourg) on Gottfried Wilhelm Leibniz (1646–1716).

Ludwig examines the spiritual presuppositions of secular politics in Hobbes's conception of the "Common-Wealth Ecclesiasticall and Civill". He does so in light of the frontispiece of Hobbes' major work where it reads "Leviathan. Or: the *Matter, Forme, and Power of a Common-Wealth Ecclesiasticall and Civill*". The Hobbesian *Common-Wealth* is a model case of the early modern idea of federation, a political structure, though, that stands under the strong impression of the religious wars of the seventeenth century. Ludwig shows that the unity of politics and religion is, for Hobbes, the unity of state and church. In view of this insight he intertwines central aspects of Hobbes's theory, i.e., political anthropology, state of nature, natural right, religion and politics. According to Ludwig's diagnosis, Hobbes neither aimed at a theological foundation of the state nor did he want to undermine Christianity. In the end Ludwig is more than sceptical whether the idea of the "Common-Wealth Ecclesiasticall and Civill" was, and maybe even still is, a promising one, and whether it offers a solid foundation of the modern (federal) state.

The aim of Sosoe's article is to demonstrate that Leibniz is one of the forerunners of a European cosmopolitan idea. In a first step he delineates Leibniz's idea of a universal republic, which is a political ideal, also called by him *Optima*

Respublica or *Respublica Christiana* or *Civitas Dei*. He then pays special attention to the theological and metaphysical foundations of Leibniz's cosmopolitanism, to his *Civitas Dei* based on natural right embracing the whole world and to the place of the Christian republic within this cosmopolitan structure. In this context, Leibniz's *Mars Christianissimus*, which contains a very severe criticism of France's imperialism in Europe and a defense of the German princes based on the Westphalian Treaty, plays a significant role. Sosoe dedicates the last part of his contribution to Leibniz's position on European federalism and to his debate with Abbé de Saint-Pierre. This debate has the advantage to reveal clearly Leibniz's idea of European federalism. It will become clear that these three parts are all based on Leibniz's metaphysical and theological premises. This explains why many commentators of Leibniz's political ideas contend that his whole metaphysics was at the service of his unified global international political order and, specifically, at the service of his *Civitas Dei*.

Thus, the Hobbesian *Common-Wealth* may be characterised as *pre*-federal, not yet of a federal nature, whereas Leibniz's proposal for a European federation could be termed *proto*-federal, a first instantiation of modern-day federalism.

Kant and federalism. Robert Hanna (Boulder/Colorado, US, now Curitiba, Brazil), Dietmar H. Heidemann (Luxembourg) and Heiner Klemme (Halle/ Saale, Germany) offer analyses of federalist thought in Immanuel Kant (1724 – 1804) or rather, as in the case of Hanna, an innovative interpretation of what might be termed 'Kantian federalism'.

Starting from general considerations on coercion, political authority, defensive or preventive moral force and state Hanna explores Kant's philosophy as a source of what he calls *existential cosmopolitan anarchism*. According to Hanna, the thesis of philosophical anarchism says that there is no adequate rational justification for political authority, the State, or any other State-like institution. Thus the thesis of political anarchism says that we should construct a world in which there are no States or other State-like institutions. He argues that Kant's political theory, as formulated in the *Metaphysics of Morals*, is sharply out of step with the central ideas of his own moral philosophy. The doctrine of right of the *Metaphysics of Morals*, in Hanna's opinion, presents a fairly run-of-the-mill and explicitly anti-revolutionary, hence politically mainstream and safe, version of classical individualist liberalism, plus constitutional monarchy and/or parliamentarianism, plus a peace-securing internationalism, in the social-contract tradition of Hobbes, Locke, Grotius, and Rousseau. On Hanna's account, the cosmopolitan, existentialist version of anarchism, i. e., *existential Kantian cosmopolitan anarchism*, very naturally flows from Kant's moral philosophy, his philosophy of religion, and his political anthropology.

In his contribution Heidemann shows that Kant's foundation of federalism is teleological. Kant conceives of federalism as a natural consequence of the finite cognitive make-up of the human being that can, in the end, secure its freedom solely under cosmopolitan conditions, that is to say, within a federalist political framework as the purposeful outcome of human political history. Kant sketches this teleological conception in the *Idea of a Universal History with a Cosmopolitan Aim* (1784). It is only in the *Critique of teleological Judgment* that he elaborates in detail what might be called 'political teleology', the view that the antagonism between individuals and furthermore states is the means by which nature evokes individual states and eventually an international political federation of states.

In his article Klemme discusses the problem of the so-called unjust confederate (*ungerechter Bundesgenosse*). The problem springs from Kant's consideration of the *Metaphysics of Morals* (§§ 59 – 60) on the right a state has against the "unjust enemy" and concerns the associated question of what right a confederation has against an *unjust confederate*, i. e., a confederate state that is unjust not with respect to other confederate states but to states that are not confederates. Klemme debates this important problem of any federalist political structure from the point of view of international right in Kant and focuses on the more specific questions concerning the juridical relation between just and unjust confederate, and furthermore what exactly the injustice of the unjust confederate consists in.

The "Federalist Papers". Legal scholar and philosopher of law Beatrice Brunhöber (Berlin, Germany) then turns to the *Federalist Papers* the authors of which, Alexander Hamilton (1757[?] – 1804), James Madison (1751– 1836) and John Jay (1745 – 1829), might—against the usual ascriptions—be termed the intellectual 'founding fathers' of the US Constitution. Brunhöber demonstrates that *The Federalist* (as the *Federalist Papers* are usually being referred to) is at the origin of an innovative interpretation of political representation. The composite of "representative democracy" is a term introduced by Alexander Hamilton. Representation and democracy, in the tradition of Aristotle and Rousseau hitherto deemed incompatible, are shown to be compatible. Thus, democracy understood as and implemented by representative government is suited even for a large territory and a large number of people. Brunhöber carefully carves out how according to *The Federalist* for a democratic representative government to avoid despotism is to implement a thorough separation of powers. This does not only account for the different powers horizontally but also vertically, and favors a multilevel federal state. A federal structure thus helps prevent an undue accumulation of power and—indirectly, by means of vertical separation of powers—serves to guarantee citizens' individual freedom.

Analysis and discussion of *The Federalist* and its context is continued with two contributions on the role of political emotions and political virtues by philosophers Norbert Campagna (Luxembourg) and Heinz-Gerd Schmitz (Köln/Cologne, Germany).

Campagna starts off with an observation by French anarchist Pierre-Joseph Proudhon (1809–1865) who claims that in a federal order the central unit is not a government but an agent of the sub-units. For Campagna such an instrumental analysis of federalism originates in an analysis of fear as the decisive political emotion. He sets off to examine the function of fear as a motivating factor for arguments on cooperation and federal unification in the making of the US Constitution. Fear asks for controls and checks to be implemented, however, it is a Janus-faced emotion. The controls may be put into place both *from* fear but also *because of* fear. In the latter case it is fear which needs to be checked. In his convincing four-partite analysis Campagna shows how fear was a multidimensional phenomenon and catalyst of US institutional arrangements. From the perspective of a federated state there was fear of fellow citizens, of potential foreign invaders, of the other federated entities and even of political ideas including a fear of republicanism in its more demanding interpretations—putatively put forward by the central unit the progressive stance of which then needed to be curbed. The underlying assumption is that the role of emotions in the political sphere can hardly be overestimated. Campagna claims that the US founding fathers had a pessimistic view of human nature and therefore preferred a federal state with its multi-level checks and balances. It is claimed that, had their anthropological convictions been more optimistic, they might have opted for a unitary state.

This is in line with the analysis Schmitz offers: On his reading federalism with its vertical division of powers is first and foremost a remedy to the infirmity of political virtue. In his tripartite contribution Schmitz first expounds an Aristotelian conception of political virtue. Building on these conceptual premises he goes on to show that the authors of the *Federalist Papers* resorted to federalism as a constitutional construction to compensate the demise of political virtue. However, the *Federalist Papers* are concerned with a federal state among other (foreign) states. The argument from virtue does not apply to a single universal state, not even a federal world state, as can be shown with recourse to Kant. In the *Perpetual Peace* Kant offers four objections against a universal state. It is impracticable in two respects, it is inconsistent and it presents a slippery slope towards despotism. Thus Kant pleads for a *federation* of individual states however not a world state or *civitas gentium*. Schmitz finally demonstrates how federal structures conflict with the Kantian conception of sovereignty of the people. Even a partial 'waiver' of sovereignty is excluded.

Nineteenth century reception and criticism of federalist ideas. In a further section the reception and criticism of federalist ideas in the nineteenth century are explored. First, Michael Wolff (Bielefeld, Germany) examines Georg Wilhelm Friedrich Hegel (1770–1831) as a critic of Kant and his cosmopolitan and universalistic conception of a federation. Then, Katja Stoppenbrink (Münster, Germany; formerly Luxembourg) sheds light on federalist thinking in John Stuart Mill (1806–1873).

Wolff provides a careful analysis of Hegel's views on federalism in the *Philosophy of Right* and related writings, in particular of his criticism of Kant's idea of "Völkerbund" in the *Perpetual Peace*. On the backdrop of a discussion of the classical theory of the state of nature and war (including Hobbes) he points out that Hegel's critique is not polemic but reveals systematic difficulties of the idea of a federal political structure. Although major discrepancies between Hegel and Kant cannot be ignored, Wolff is capable of showing that there is a much too often overlooked consensus between the two thinkers with respect to international right and federalism.

Stoppenbrink takes a closer look into the political philosophy of John Stuart Mill who is a fervent advocate of representative democracy in the line of the *Federalist Papers*. However, following Alexis de Tocqueville and his *Democracy in America* (two volumes 1835 and 1840), Mill fears the 'tyranny of the majority', a *topos* not unusual in early modern commentators on democracy and to be read as 'working classes' in Mill's case. Here, the emphasis is placed on an often overlooked chapter of Mill's *Considerations on Representative Government* (1861) in which he expounds his views "[O]f Federal Representative Governments" (Chapter XVII). Stoppenbrink explains that Mill offers a defense of a certain conception of a federal state, again along the lines of the *Federalist Papers* and, although not explicitly, the eyewitness account of the American political practice of the time given by Tocqueville. Mill argues in favor of bicameralism and a judicial control of constitutionality to watch over the vertical attribution of powers. For him, a constitutional court is the 'logical' counterpart and prerequisite of the implementation of a federal order. As Stoppenbrink argues, in a certain sense in Mill judicial operationalization of the rule of law becomes a by-product of federalism.

The analysis and criticism of philosophical foundations and important philosophical contributions to the history of federalist ideas—however incomplete—is concluded here. The editors certainly would have liked to include critical examinations of other important discussions of federalism, such as for instance the less well-known pleas for an Italian federation ("United States of Italy") embedded in a European federalism as proposed by the philosophical and political writers of the Italian Risorgimento Carlo Cattaneo (1801–1869)[24] or Guiseppe Ferrari (1811–1876)[25]. Equally, the 'bottom up' anti-authoritarian or even anarchistic federalist socialism argued for by Mikhail Bakunin (1814–1876) in his *Federalism, Socialism, and Anti-Theologism* (1867) as a follower of Pierre-Joseph Proudhon and his *Principle of Federation* (*Du Principe fédératif et de la nécessité de reconstituer le Parti de la Révolution*; 1863) are representative of nineteenth century philosophical approaches to federalism.

We equally acknowledge the important theoretical work on federalism undertaken in the second half of the twentieth century in the English-speaking world, William Riker and Daniel Elazar probably being the most prominent representatives of these scholars. Their research is the object of a considerable number of recent publications on federal thought, highlighting the interconnectedness and mutual fruitful influences of federal theory and practice and in the aftermath giving rise to numerous comparative and empirical studies (e. g. Burgess 2006; Hueglin/Fenna 2006; Watts 2008).

Still, our aim is not to give a full account of the intellectual history and philosophical foundations of federalism. Far from raising an unattainable claim for completeness we wish to highlight and thereby select philosophically relevant stages in the formation of present-day federalist thinking. In a final section we therefore turn to key notions and problems of contemporary forms of federalism.

Contemporary and systematic approaches to federalism. Contributions by Volker Gerhardt (Berlin, Germany) and Andreas Føllesdal (Tromsø and Oslo, Norway) examine central legal and political principles and resulting problems facing contemporary institutional settings in pursuit of a federal character or—at least—some federal elements. They focus on the meaning and import of the principle of subsidiarity (Gerhardt) for a supranational entity such as the European Union and the doctrine of the margin of appreciation (Føllesdal) in the jurisprudence of the European Court of Human Rights, a court instituted in Strasbourg as an institutional novelty in 1959 in the institutional framework of the Council of Europe and made permanent in 1998. Unlike the US Supreme Court in the aftermath of the *Federalist Papers* and unlike the proposal of a judicial control of attribution of powers, the Strasbourg court is charged with the interpretation and

---

24 See for an account of Cattaneo's philosophy, political thought and life Bobbio (1971) and, e. g., Armani (1997), Sabetti (2013). Cattaneo's philosophical writings have been published in an anthology entitled *Stati Uniti d'Italia* by Norberto Bobbio in 1945; for a new edition see: Cattaneo/Bobbio (2010).
25 Ferrari (1851). See also Bruch (2005), Ziblatt (2006).

realization of the European human rights regime introduced by the European Convention on Human Rights.

In his contribution Gerhardt commences his examination of the relationship of 'federalness' and subsidiarity in several grand strides with a historical and systematic outline opening into two central theses and several arguments for the 'constitutive role' of these principles. For Gerhardt the Kantian cosmopolitan alternative of a centralized universal republic on the one hand and a federation of free (republican) states on the other hand is but hypothetical. Under real-world conditions—and this, for instance, ties in with the analysis offered by Schmitz—a world republic is both undesirable and undesired. Gerhardt's first claim is that both *de facto* and *de jure* today's states are interconnected in so many ways and bound by such a multitude of international legal instruments that there is no need any longer for a single supranational institutional entity at a global scale. Secondly, given the antagonistic interplay of few international actors Gerhardt makes a case for the historical necessity of the European Union. Gerhardt's argument for intra-European and other federalism is multi-faceted: (i) there is the *formal* aspect of recognition of and respect for the equality of the partners, (ii) the federal structures preserve and accentuate cultural diversity (ethnic, religious, linguistic, regional and other identities), (iii) there is a corre-lative nexus of 'federalness' and subsidiarity which reduces the burden of each sub-unit while promoting the social and political flourishing of the union and (iv) allowing for the greatest possible self-determination of each of the partners such that, in Gerhardt's terms, "the 'subsidiarist' is the *material federalist*".

Just as the very first text by Brunhöber on the import of the *Federalist Papers*, the final contribution of this book broadens the outlook to take up a philosoph-ically informed legal perspective again and examines the tensions in a multilevel legal and political order created by an international human rights convention and corresponding adjudication. Føllesdal reflects upon the complex and often rather 'technical' balancing processes undertaken by the Strasbourg-based European Court of Human Rights (ECtHR) which is assigned the role to watch over compliance by Council of Europe member states with the European Convention on Human Rights (ECHR). EU member states have to be parties to the ECHR and, more recently, the EU itself is supposed to accede. In 2014, however, the Court of Justice of the European Union (CJEU; based in Luxembourg) rejected the draft of the accession treaty—the apple of discord exactly being the question of judicial review of EU and CJEU decisions by the ECtHR. This is but a variant—but a practically very important and prominent one—of the general dilemma be-tween state sovereignty and the requirements of human rights protection im-posed by an international human rights regime, here the ECHR. ECtHR jurisdic-tion and a new protocol amending the ECHR (N°15) explicitly mention the principle of subsidiarity and refer to member states' 'margin of appreciation' in assessing their compliance with the convention.

Føllesdal's first claim is that the margin of appreciation can be defended but needs to be specified in order to alleviate its vagueness and achieve its objectives. He goes on to introduce the distinction of a state-centric and a person-centered version of the principle of subsidiarity and discusses the role of trust in the rule of law in a federal setting: A person-centered reading of the principle of subsidiarity seems favorable for several reasons, since it does not give the 'last word' to the state's interests. Human rights guarantees and judicial review have a particular bearing in a federation with qualified majority voting. Here, international or supranational adjudication is an additional instrument of control of member state governments where citizens feel it is no longer 'their' government enacting binding decisions and exercising political authority. A centralized human rights court can thus create trust and dispel fears in a multilevel federal arrangement with more and more majoritarian decision-making. Føllesdal argues that on the basis of a person-centered understanding of the principle of subsidiarity the margin of appreciation should be specified according to the likelihood that local authorities and courts will appropriately respect human rights. Thus, in some subject matters, with respect to rights related to political participation and the democratic decision making process, international human rights courts should not grant *any* margin of appreciation at all, in others they should not grant a *wide* margin (e. g. when minority interests such as freedom of religion are at stake).

In lieu of a conclusion. The federalist world is pluralist. Philosophical foundations of federalism are multifarious. Federalism is both a *product* and a *process* concept of political organization, it is a normative idea, a historically versatile phenomenon, an umbrella term which covers very many and very different institutional arrangements. It is interesting to note a basic tendency in federalist thought to find dichotomous conceptual attributes and theoretical approaches to explain federal phenomena: symmetric vs. asymmetric[26] federalism, cooperative vs. uncooperative[27] federalism, treaty vs. constitutional federalism, views based on religious presuppositions (derived from 'revelation') compete with completely secular(ized) explanations (e. g. based on 'reason'), the idea of a 'given', organic, corporative or covenant nature competing with consensual, contractual or otherwise constructivist foundations of a federal order, teleological with process-driv-

---

26 I.e., the attributions of power differ between sub-units.
27 In the same vein goes the distinction of a 'separate' or 'interlocking' federalism. (Cf. the introductory taxonomy in Føllesdal 2014.)

en or ateleological conceptions of federalism, etc. Upon closer conceptual or empirical examination these claims for exclusive disjunctions may not be sustainable and give way to more nuanced distinctions. However, there is up until this day no single, unifying, overarching 'theory of federalism'. Accordingly, the philosophical foundations of federalism are found to be manifold.

Depending on whether we are faced with a 'coming together'[28] (associative) or a 'holding together' (dissociative) type of federation the *ratio unionis* differs. Federative processes of the first type are moved either by the idea to promote common welfare, to better guarantee individual freedoms, to allow for better defense and, ultimately, sustainable peace or an instrumental combination of any or all of these. With the second type, decentralizing a formerly centralized state to form a federation of states—be it in the form of a federal state with a strong central unit or a mere (con-) federation of independent states with a less powerful central unit—the focus is to further (democratic) self-determination[29] by the

---

28 The 'coming together/holding together' distinction has been introduced by Stepan (1999) and is used, e. g., in Føllesdal (2014) and his contribution to this book. The 'associative/dissociative' terminology is equally widely used (cf., e. g., Bauböck 2003, 140 n. 12). However, the predicate 'dissociative' puts the emphasis on centrifugal forces and fails to capture the integrating tendency of attempts of 'holding together'. Bauböck prefers to refer to a 'devolutionary' federalism instead (ibid., 124). The distinction 'integrative vs. devolutionary federalism' (Lenaerts 1990, 206–208) does not sufficiently discriminate between the types of federalism since the intention or purpose of 'holding together' is to 'integrate' and avoid dissolution, secession or the like.

29 This latter effect may *e contrario* be exemplified by the anti-democratic forced centralization imposed in the German Weimar Republic on July 20, 1932, when in the so-called *Preußenschlag* (Prussian *coup d'état*) the then president of the central level of the *Reich*, Hindenburg, issued an emergency decree under Article 48 of the Weimar Constitution to replace the social-democratic managing minority government of the Republic (*Freistaat*) of Prussia by a *Reichskommissar*. This paved the way for the dissolution of Germany's federal order after Hitler's accession to power in 1933 ('*Gleichschaltung der Länder mit dem Reich*'). The justificatory strategy allowed for by the constitution was to enforce and reestablish 'law and order', this being a pretext to get rid of the center-left Prussian government (Walter (2007); see, e. g., Deuerlein (1972, 190–193) for an analysis of the "Preußenschlag" from a federal perspective). However, above all, this incident throws into relief the weakness of the federal order established under Weimar. Deuerlein (1972, 193) concludes "daß das Fehlen eines Macht verteilenden und damit Macht hemmenden Prinzips [...] den Durchbruch der politischen Kräfte begünstigte, die Unität mit Uniformität verwechselten [...]". The social-democratic government takes recourse to the constitutional court of the Weimar Republic, the *Staatsgerichtshof*. In these proceedings, in which the anti-federal thinker Carl Schmitt pleads the cause of the right-wing government of the *Reich* (federal level), the measure is in part held unconstitutional (October 25, 1932). However, the court ruling is only implemented symbolically and cannot rebuild trust in the rule of law and the federal character of the constitution. For Schmitt, the 'divided' or 'shared sovereignty' presupposed

then sub-units hitherto integrated into a unitary state. Apart from the aspect of democratic legitimacy, this serves a sense of belonging and attachment since the sub-units may both conceptually and often also empirically be regarded as the institutional substrata of cultural, linguistic, social, economic and political identities.

Furthermore, the field of federal thinking is divided between rights-based and consequentialist approaches. We can distinguish an overall consequentialist reasoning (welfare, common defense, etc.) from a broadly liberty-preserving, rights-based reasoning in favor of federalism. Härtel (2012, 5, marginal no. 5) describes federalism as an "Organisationsform der Freiheit" whereby it remains an open question whether individual liberty is meant or rather the preservation of autonomy and marge de manœuvre of a state in the form of a sub-unit. Either reading is conceivable. Härtel's formula "Autonomiesicherung durch Autonomieabgabe" (ibid., 4, marginal no. 3) is state-oriented, while in the liberal rights-oriented Kantian tradition the very purpose of the state is to enable and protect the exercise of individual liberty. In the current age of international human rights treaties the person-oriented purpose of federalism as an 'order of freedom' comes to the fore. Judicial review of fundamental or human rights violations by courts at the federal, supranational or international level benefits and protects the individual invoking her rights and acts as a counterbalance to and constraint on state sovereignty.

The political stances toward federalism and the federal prospects of the project of European unification have changed significantly between 2014 and early 2016 when the European Commission's president Jean-Claude Juncker[30] has unexpectedly become a sceptic with regard to the future of the European Union, in particular the rights of free movement of workers and subsequently also the internal market and common currency. When in 2014 most of the contributions to this book were first presented, the outlook on Europe's future was an utterly different one: Political actors themselves argued for and examined a pos-

---

by federal arrangements is even conceptually impossible, a *contradictio in adiecto*. His disciple, conceptual historian Reinhart Koselleck (2006 [1994], 503) proposed just this model for the European integration process: "Unser Handlungsspielraum ist nicht unendlich offen. Föderale Möglichkeiten müssen ergriffen werden."

30 See the European Commission President's New Year's press conference on January 15, 2016 http://europa.eu/newsroom/rapid-failover/mex-16-85_en.pdf. For an example of the corresponding news coverage see http://www.zeit.de/politik/ausland/2016-01/jean-claude-juncker-schengen-euro (both 2016/01/16).

sible federalist perspective for the European Union.[31] More recently, in the case of Juncker, even one of the most fervent defenders of EU cooperation and integration has voiced a rigorous admonition that "[W]aiting at an internal border would cost every lorry 55 euros for every hour." Sacrificing freedom of movement and the Schengen Agreement of 1985 for a reintroduction of border controls comes at a heavy financial cost and—to take up but slightly adapt Franklin's article in the *Pennsylvania Gazette*—'must end in the Destruction of the European Interest, Trade and Prosperity in Europe'. Thus, it seems, apart from individual rights and liberties, defense and security, there is always an aspect of economic welfare involved in 'federalism'. This adds a consequentialist underpinning to what is otherwise a 'liberty-preserving' framework of delegation of authority and powers. In contrast with a unitary state, a federation in the form of a federal state helps to safeguard the sub-units' political, cultural or other identities while, in contrast with a set of independent states, a federation—*inter alia*—helps to save transaction costs. However, to put it in Koselleck's words ([1994] 2006, 503), it seems that "[W]as immer Europa sein mag, es gibt ein föderales Minimum, das nicht nur wirtschaftlich, sondern auch politisch erreicht werden muß, und das wir wahren müssen, wenn wir auf diesem Kontinent weiterleben wollen."[32]

Acknowledgements

Contributions to this volume go for a large part back to a conference organized by the Institute of Philosophy of the University of Luxembourg in May 2014. The editors would like to thank all authors that they have agreed to submit their conference presentations and we wish to extend our gratitude to those who, without having had the opportunity to present their texts at the conference, consented to their publication in this volume. The conference and the book form part of the research program "Philosophical Foundations of Federalism (R 4.5)" of the research priority "European Governance" of the University of Luxembourg. We also wish to thank Oliver Motz and Sebastian Orlander (both Luxembourg), Ru-

---

31 See for a high-level seminar in April 2014 involving government officials in the context of a Franco-German joint research initiative: http://www.strategie.gouv.fr/sites/strategie.gouv.fr/files/archives/BMF-Programm-Druckversion.pdf (2016/01/19). Cf. also the then Belgian prime minister Reynders (2012).

32 "Whatever Europe may be, there is a federal minimum to be achieved and preserved not only economically but also politically if we wish to continue to live on this continent" (our translation, the eds.).

dolf Owen Müllan and Manon Westphal (both Münster) for their helpful comments and support in the editing process of this book. Of course all remaining deficiencies are ours.

Bibliography

Armani, Giuseppe (1997): Carlo Cattaneo: una biografia. Il padre del federalismo italiano, Milano.

Baldus, Christian (2002): Vestigia pacis: Der römische Friedensvertrag als Struktur und Ereignis, in: Historia 51, pp. 298–348.

Baldus, Christian (2004): Vestigia pacis. The Roman peace treaty: structure or event?, in: Randall Lesaffer (ed.), Peace Treaties and International Law in European History. From the late Middle Ages to World War One, Cambridge, pp. 103–146.

Bauböck, Rainer (2003): Im Missverständnis vereint? Asymmetrie in multinationalen Föderationen, in: Monika Mokre, Gilbert Weiss und Rainer Bauböck (Hg.), Europas Identitäten: Mythen, Konflikte, Konstruktionen, Frankfurt/New York, pp. 117–143.

Beaud, Olivier (²2009): Théorie de la Fédération, Paris.

Beck, Hans (1997): Polis und Koinon. Untersuchungen zur Geschichte und Struktur der griechischen Bundesstaaten im 4. Jhdt. v. Chr. (Historia Einzelschriften 114), Stuttgart.

Bobbio, Norberto (1971): Una filosofia militante: studi su Carlo Cattaneo, Torino.

Bruch, Anne (2005): Italien auf dem Weg zum Nationalstaat. Giuseppe Ferraris Vorstellungen einer föderal-demokratischen Ordnung (Beiträge zur deutschen und europäischen Geschichte 33), Hamburg.

Burgess, Michael (2006): Comparative Federalism: Theory and Practice, New York.

Cattaneo, Carlo/Bobbio, Norberto (2010): Stati Uniti d'Italia. Scritti sul federalismo democratico, Rome.

Chateaubriand, François-René vicomte de (1838 [1826]): Oeuvres, Tome IV, Voyage en Amérique, suivi des Natchez, Paris.

Deuerlein, Ernst (1972): Föderalismus. Die historischen und philosophischen Grundlagen des föderativen Prinzips, München.

Elazar, Daniel J. (1997): Althusius and Federalism as Grand Design, in: Giuseppe Duso, Werner Krawietz and Dieter Wyduckel (eds.), Konsens und Konsoziation in der politischen Theorie des frühen Föderalismus, in: Rechtstheorie Beiheft 16, Berlin, pp. 209–218.

Ferrari, Giuseppe (1851): La Federazione repubblicana, Capolago.

Føllesdal, Andreas (2014): Federalism, in: Edward N. Zalta (ed.), The Stanford Encyclopedia of Philosophy (Spring 2014 Edition), http://plato.stanford.edu/archives/spr2014/entries/federalism/ (2016/01/15).

Føllesdal, Andreas/Hix, Simon (2006): Why There is a Democratic Deficit in the EU: A Response to Majone and Moravcsik, Journal of Common Market Studies 44, 533–562.

Friedrich, Carl Joachim (1932): Introduction, in: Politica Methodice Digesta of Johannes Althusius [1603], reprinted [with minor abridgements] from the Third Edition of 1614, ed. by C. J. Friedrich, Cambridge, Mass., pp. xiii–cxl.

Härtel, Ines (2012): Alte und neue Föderalismuswelten, in: idem (ed.): Handbuch Föderalismus—Föderalismus als demokratische Rechtsordnung und Rechtskultur in Deutschland, Europa und der Welt. Band I: Grundlagen des Föderalismus und der deutsche Bundesstaat, Berlin/Heidelberg, pp. 3–22.

Herbst, Tobias (2014): Gesetzgebungskompetenzen im Bundesstaat. Eine Rekonstruktion der Rechtsprechung des Bundesverfassungsgerichts, Tübingen.

Höffe, Otfried (2012): § 104: Föderalismus als Strukturprinzip einer Weltordnung, in: Ines Härtel (ed.): Handbuch Föderalismus—Föderalismus als demokratische Rechtsordnung und Rechtskultur in Deutschland, Europa und der Welt. Band IV: Föderalismus in Europa und der Welt, Berlin/Heidelberg, pp. 875–887.

Hüglin, Thomas O. (1991): Sozietaler Föderalismus. Die politische Theorie des Johannes Althusius, Berlin & New York.

Hueglin, Thomas O. (1999): Early Modern Concepts for a Late Modern World. Althusius on Community and Federalism, Waterloo, Ontario.

Hueglin, Thomas O./Fenna, Alan (2006): Comparative Federalism: A Systematic Inquiry, Peterborough.

Koch, Bettina (2009): Johannes Althusius: Between Secular Federalism and the Religious State, in: Ann Ward & Lee Ward (eds.): The Ashgate Research Companion to Federalism, Farnham, Surrey & Burlington, Vt., pp. 75–90.

Koselleck, Reinhart (1972): 'Bund, Bündnis, Föderalismus, Bundesstaat', in: Otto Brunner, Werner Conze and Reinhart Koselleck (eds.): Geschichtliche Grundbegriffe: historisches Lexikon zur politisch-sozialen Sprache in Deutschland: A-D, Bd. 1, Stuttgart, pp. 582–671.

Koselleck, Reinhart (2006 [1994]): Diesseits des Nationalstaats. Föderale Strukturen der deutschen Geschichte, in: idem: Begriffsgeschichten. Studien zur Semantik und Pragmatik der politischen und sozialen Sprache, Frankfurt am Main, pp. 486–503.

Lenaerts, Koen (1990): Constitutionalism and the Many Faces of Federalism, in: The American Journal of Comparative Law (AJCL) 38, pp. 205–263.

Lübbe, Hermann (2012): Raumordnungen in der zivilisatorischen Evolution. Über die Reichweite des Föderalismusbegriffs, in: Ines Härtel (ed.): Handbuch Föderalismus— Föderalismus als demokratische Rechtsordnung und Rechtskultur in Deutschland, Europa und der Welt. Band I: Grundlagen des Föderalismus und der deutsche Bundesstaat, Berlin/Heidelberg, pp. 23–38.

Montesquieu, Charles Louis de Secondat, baron de La Brède et de Montesquieu (1951 [1748]): De l'Esprit des Lois, in: Œuvres completes, vol. II, Paris, pp. 227–995.

Nida-Rümelin, Julian (2012): § 5 Philosophische Grundlagen des Förderalismus, in: Ines Härtel (ed.): Handbuch Föderalismus—Föderalismus als demokratische Rechtsordnung und Rechtskultur in Deutschland, Europa und der Welt. Band I: Grundlagen des Föderalismus und der deutsche Bundesstaat, Berlin/Heidelberg, pp. 145–164.

Overhoff, Jürgen (2006): Benjamin Franklin. Erfinder, Freigeist, Staatenlenker, Stuttgart.

Reynders, Didier (2012): Slowly but surely on the path towards a federal European Union, http://diplomatie.belgium.be/en/Newsroom/news/press_releases/foreign_affairs/2012/07/ni_200712_open_forum_reynders.jsp (published 2012/07/20; retrieved 2016/01/19).

Robespierre, Maximilien (1957 [1793]): Œuvres de Maximilien Robespierre, tome IX, Discours, Quatrième Partie, Septembre 1792–27 Juillet 1793, edited by Marc Bouloiseau, Jean Dautry, Georges Lefebvre and Albert Soboui, Paris.

Sabetti, Filippo (2013): Civilization and Self-Government: The Political Thought of Carlo Cattaneo, Maryland.

Stepan, Alfred C. (1999): Federalism and Democracy: Beyond the U.S. Model, Journal of Democracy 10, pp. 19–34.

Walter, Franz (2007): Putsch am 20. Juli 1932. Wie der Mythos Preußen zerschlagen wurde, in: Der Spiegel, http://www.spiegel.de/politik/deutschland/putsch-am-20-juli-1932-wie-der-mythos-preussen-zerschlagen-wurde-a-495275-3.html (first published 19 July 2007; retrieved 15 February 2016).

Ward, Ann/MacDonald, Sara (2009): Nascent Federalism and its Limits in Ancient Greece: Herodotus and Thucydides, in: Ann Ward and Lee Ward (eds.): The Ashgate Research Companion to Federalism, Farnham, Surrey (England) and Burlington, Vt. (USA), pp. 15–30.

Watts, Ronald L. (³2008): Comparing Federal Systems, Montreal.

Ziblatt, Daniel (2006): Structuring the State. The Formation of Italy and Germany and the Puzzle of Federalism, Princeton.

Ziegler, Karl-Heinz (²2007 [1994]): Völkerrechtsgeschichte: Ein Studienbuch, München.

Early Modern Roots of Federalist Thought

Bernd Ludwig
Gibt es spirituelle Voraussetzungen säkularer Politik? Thomas Hobbes über das „Common-Wealth Ecclesiasticall and Civill"

1 Säkulare Politik

Die Philosophie des siebzehnten Jahrhunderts steht nicht unwesentlich im Zeichen der religiösen Bekenntniskriege in der Folge der Europäischen Reformation: Angesichts der neuen Pluralität unterschiedlicher Kirchen, die alle ihrerseits an dem universalistischen Anspruch des Christentums festhalten, verkehrt sich die ursprünglich einheitsstiftende Kraft des Monotheismus in ihr Gegenteil, und die unterschiedlichen Bekenntnisse werden zu mächtigen Instrumenten der Gefolgschaftssicherung der einander bekämpfenden politischen Parteien. Es gehört zur Erfolgsgeschichte der Rechts- und Staatsphilosophie der Neuzeit, dass sie den theoretischen Grundriss jener Form politischer Organisation entwickelt hat, die den damit heraufbeschworenen religiösen Bürgerkrieg in Europa zunächst erfolgreich eingehegt und am Ende dann sogar eliminiert hat: den modernen Staat.

Für die Engländer stellte sich das Problem seinerzeit unter anderem als das Problem der konkurrierenden anglikanisch, presbyterianisch oder römisch eingekleideten Ansprüche auf den Thron. Die Lösung, die Thomas Hobbes 1651 im *Leviathan* vorträgt, scheint auf den ersten Blick sehr einfach zu sein: Allein der Sieg im religiösen Bürgerkrieg beendet den religiösen Streit. Der politische Souverän bestimmt sodann die Staatsreligion *ad libitum* und beendet die Bekenntniskriege per Dekret. Der Klerus steht damit allein im Dienste des Staates und abweichende Bekenntnisse werden nicht geduldet.

Bereits ein Blick auf das berühmte Titelkupfer des *Leviathan* von 1651 scheint das zu bestätigen: Man sieht eine ikonografische Karikatur der mittelalterlichen Lehre von den Zwei Schwertern, welche letzteren sich nämlich nun *beide* in der Hand des *einen, weltlichen* Souveräns befinden, und darunter ist zu lesen: „Leviathan. Or: the *Matter, Forme, and Power of a Common-Wealth Ecclasiasticall and Civill*". Hier ist die Einheit von Politik und Religion in der Gestalt der Einheit von Staat und Kirche Programm, ja es steht sogar das „Ecclasiasticall commonwealth", das *kirchliche* Gemeinwesen, an erster Stelle, vor dem *bürgerlichen:* Der Staat ist Kirche, so die vermeintliche Botschaft, die Kirche ist Staat und deren Einheit ist der Leviathan, mit dessen Macht sich (wie das über allem stehende Zitat aus *Hiob* 41.24 betont) keine irdische messen kann.

Wie ist nun aber das Verhältnis der beiden Attribute des Commonwealths genau zu denken? Bezeichnete das „Ecclasiasticall", das später dann im Text auch durch ein „Christian" ersetzt wird, bloß eine *species* des Civil Commonwealth (neben möglicherweise jüdischen, muslimischen oder gar agnostischen Gemeinwesen), dann wäre die Abfolge von „ecclesiasticall" und „civill" auf dem Titelblatt ein wenig befremdlich und es wäre zudem schlecht damit zu vereinbaren, dass Hobbes im dritten Teil „Of a Christian Common-Wealth" klarstellt, dass 1) der Staat *in specie* ein Christlicher zu sein hat, und dass 2) der Gehorsam gegen den Leviathan jener ist, der einem wahren, d. h.: einem nicht von den interessierten Lehren irgendeiner partikularen Kirche irregeleiteten, Christen kraft seines Bekenntnisses zur Gotteskindschaft Jesu Christi üben muss. Zudem identifiziert Hobbes das Grundprinzip seiner eigenen philosophischen Moral mit einem moralischen Grundsatz des *Christentums,* wie wir gleich sehen werden.

Aber zugleich *begründet* er diese Moral und das Recht des Staates – auch das werden wir noch sehen – ganz und gar ohne jeden Rekurs auf ein göttliches Gesetz und ohne Gott als Gesetzgeber, also gleichsam *gegen* die Tradition des seinerzeit bemühten Christlichen Naturrechts (u. a. *das* hat ihm des Ruf des „Devil from Malmesbury" eingebracht). Warum ist dann aber sein Commonwealth gleichwohl *„ecclasiasticall* and *civil",* ein *„Christian* Common-Wealth"?

Schauen wir es uns kurz im Detail an: Hobbes rekonstruiert die Normen des Naturrechts, indem er einen Katalog von neunzehn so genannten *natural laws,* natürlichen Gesetzen vorlegt. Diese bilden seines Erachtens den Kernbestand der „morall philosophy", und *deren* Grundprinzip, so betont er selbst zu Beginn der Darstellung derselben, ist tatsächlich

> [...] that Law of the Gospell; Whatsoever you require that others should do to you, that do ye to them. And that Law of all men, *Quod tibi fieri non vis, alteri ne feceris. (Lev.* XIV, 5[1])

Und am Ende seiner Aufzählung der Naturgesetze bietet Hobbes diese Formel erneut als Zusammenfassung seiner Morallehre an.

Die *Alten* hatten die Moral auf die Natur gegründet, die *Christen* auf den Willen Gottes. Für Hobbes hatten beide zwar *inhaltlich* bereits im Wesentlichen die

---

1 Ich zitiere den *Leviathan* nach der Ausgabe von Richard Tuck (Thomas Hobbes (1991), *Leviathan Student Edition.* Cambridge: Cambridge University Press), gebe die Nachweise aber ausgabenunabhängig mit Kapitel und Absatzzahl an. Alle andern Hobbes-Zitate aus der Molesworth-Ausgabe von 1839 ff. (EW = Thomas Hobbes (1839), *The English Works of Thomas Hobbes.* Molesworth, William (ed.). London: Bohn.) OL = Thomae Hobbes (1839) *Opera Philosophica quae Latine Scripsit.* Gulielmi Molesworth (ed.). Londini: Bohn.) mit Band und Seitenzahl.

richtigen Tugenden bestimmt, aber sie hatten nicht den Grund erkannt, aus dem sie sich wie — Hobbes zu zeigen beansprucht — allesamt *philosophisch*, d. i. unter Verzicht auf jeden besonderen Glaubensinhalt, sei dieser nun heidnisch-antik oder christlich-mittelalterlich, begründen lassen.

2 Politischer Kontraktualismus

Im Einklang mit der naturrechtlichen Tradition betont Hobbes, dass die sogenannten „natürlichen Gesetze" ewig und unveränderbar sind. Er nennt sie moralische Regeln oder Tugenden („moral rules", „moral vertues") und die Wissenschaft von ihnen „Moralphilosophie":

> [...] Morall Philosophy is nothing else but the Science of what is Good, and Evill, in the conversation, and Society of man-kind. (*Lev.* XV, 40)

Als solche sind diese Regeln nun aber *gerade nicht* im strikten Sinne *präskriptiv*, also keine *Gesetze*, sondern nur *evaluativ*, darin vergleichbar etwa den Vorschriften des Arztes, die man um der eigenen Gesundheit willen annehmen *kann*, deren Befolgung der Arzt aber darum noch nicht *erzwingen* darf (*Lev.* XLII, 104). Sie sind weder Maximen bloß-*individueller* Klugheit noch sind sie – wie in der Tradition des Christlichen Naturrechts – verbindliche *göttliche* Normen, sondern vielmehr *Konstitutionsprinzipien* einer bestimmten Form menschlicher Praxis: Die Konstitutionsprinzipien des bürgerlichen Zustandes. Nur in einem solchen Zustand nämlich können die einzelnen Menschen *selbstbestimmt*, d.h., jeder als ‚master of his own life' (vgl. *Lev.* XXI, 6), leben, denn nur dort ist der eine nicht der Gewalt des anderen ausgeliefert. Ein solcher Frieden unter Menschen muss den Artikeln gemäß *gestiftet* werden und mit diesen die öffentliche Unterscheidung von Recht und Unrecht. Denn der *natürliche* Zustand der Menschen ist der Kriegszustand eines sogenannten „Recht auf alles", in dem die Begriffe von Recht und Unrecht „keinen Platz" haben. Ich möchte hier nicht im Detail auf die Grundlagen der Hobbesschen Naturzustandslehre eingehen,[2] doch einer ihrer Aspekte ist für das Folgende zentral: Die Unmöglichkeit des natürlichen Friedens unter den Menschen gilt Hobbes als eine unmittelbare Folge der *differentia specifica* von Mensch und Tier: eine Folge der *Vernunftbegabung*. Während das Tier durch aktuelle sinnliche Wahrnehmungen bestimmt wird, wird der Mensch auch durch rationale Antizipationen der Folgen seiner Handlungen bestimmt, d.h., nicht nur durch aktuell-veranlasste „desires and aversions", sondern auch durch

---

2 Für Details siehe: Ludwig (1998).

solche, die durch Kalkulation von zu erwartenden „Apparent or Seeming Good[s]" (*Lev.* VI, 57) erzeugt werden. Damit gewinnt die Zukunft Herrschaft über die Gegenwart, denn die Sorge um die *morgige* Sicherheit bestimmt bereits *heute* das Handeln. Und weil die für die Herstellung von Sicherheit erforderte Macht ein rein komparatives Gut ist, wird das naturzuständliche Leben notwendig zum Konkurrenzkampf um Macht, zum „perpetuall and restlesse desire of Power after power" (*Lev.* XI, 2): Die Bedürfnisse wachsen über sämtliche natürlichen Grenzen hinaus und der Mensch wird dem Menschen damit *vernünftigerweise* zum Feind, denn es gibt keine *natürlichen* Schranken individueller Machtausübung. Kurz: Anders als für die vernunftlosen Tiere mit ihren *natürlicherweise* beschränkten Bedürfnissen ist für die vorausblickenden Menschen die Verfolgung des eigenen Glücks im natürlichen Zustand der Menschen miteinander unmöglich — so die Konsequenz der Hobbesschen Psychologie — und eine *künstliche* Stiftung des Friedens somit *notwendig* ein Gut für *jeden* Menschen: „all men agree on this that peace is good" (*Lev.* XV, 40). Die natürlichen Gesetze, die „articles of peace" zeigen auf, wie dieser Frieden hergestellt werden kann. Diese „rules of reason" fordern dafür unter anderem und in erster Linie die Abgrenzung der individuellen Handlungssphären vermittels der Einführung der *sprachlichen* Unterscheidung von Recht und Unrecht sowie einer machthabenden Instanz, die vermittels eines Sanktionssystems diese *künstlichen* Rechtsbegriffe, die „consequences of speech in contracting", mit den *natürlichen* Handlungsantrieben, den „consequences of passions" (vgl. dazu die Gliederung der Wissenschaften in *Lev.* IX) synchronisiert. Und das ist möglich vermittels eines „terrour of some punishment" seitens des Leviathan, der dem widerrechtlichen Handeln jegliche Attraktivität raubt (*Lev.* XV, 3). *Vor* der Etablierung eines dadurch ausgezeichneten „Civil Commonwealth" ist, wie erwähnt, die Rede von Recht und Unrecht leer („has no place"; *Lev.* XIII, 13). Denn *alle* menschliche Verpflichtung ist Selbstverpflichtung durch das Gesetz eines von *ihnen selbst* autorisierten Gesetzgebers: „There being no obligation on any man that arises not from some Act of his own" (*Lev.* XII, 10).

> For the Lawes of Nature, which consist in Equity, Justice, Gratitude, and other morall Vertues on these depending, in the condition of meer Nature (as I have said before in the end of the 15th Chapter,) are not properly Lawes, but qualities that dispose men to peace, and to obedience. When a Common-wealth is once settled, then are they actually Lawes, and not before; as being then the commands of the Common-wealth; and therefore also Civill Lawes: For it is the Soveraign Power that obliges men to obey them. (*Lev.* XXVI, 8)

Kurz: Rechtliche Verbindlichkeit und damit die Unterscheidung von Recht und Unrecht wird nicht durch Ausfaltung und Ausdifferenzierung eines göttlichen Gesetzes gestiftet, sondern allein durch die Menschen selbst, welche die durch ihre *Vernunft* als konstitutive Prinzipien des Friedens *erkannten Regeln* („otherwise[!]

called Laws [!] of Nature", *Lev.* XIII, 14, „but improperly", *Lev.* XV, 41) durch die *vertragliche Autorisierung* eines machthabenden, weltlichen Gesetzgebers zu *legitimen Befehlen*, d. h., zu *Gesetzen* im strengen Wortsinne, *machen:*

> For though it be naturally reasonable; yet it is by the Soveraigne Power that it is Law (*Lev.* XXVI, 22)

In der lateinischen Übersetzung von 1668 steht an dieser Stelle das berühmte „*Auctoritas, non veritas facit legem*".[3] Der *Leviathan* ist mit dieser, von Hobbes wieder und wieder vorgetragenen, Einsicht gleichsam die Geburtsurkunde des modernen politischen Kontraktualismus.

3 Politisches Christentum

Diese konsequente Ablösung der Autorität der *natürlichen* Gesetze (und damit des Naturrechts) vom *göttlichen* Gesetz, d. h., vom Göttlichen *Befehl,* war für Hobbes' Zeitgenossen ein veritabler Skandal, wie etwa noch ein Brief von James Tyrrell an John Locke zeigt:

> [...] the not taking God into this hypothesis has been the great reason of Mr Hobbeses mistake that the laws of nature are not properly Laws nor do oblige mankind to their observation when out of a civil state or commonwealth.[4]

Für Hobbes selbst war es allerdings kein „mistake", sondern eine, angesichts des zu lösenden politischen Problems, essentielle Voraussetzung, denn es gibt keine *universelle*, jedem Einzelnen zuteilwerdende Offenbarung, die uns über den göttlichen Gesetzeswillen Auskunft geben könnte. Und jene *besonderen* Offenbarungen, auf die sich Einzelne mitunter berufen, können keine universalen Ansprüche begründen:

---

3 Entscheidend ist dabei, dass auch für Hobbes – nicht anders als für die Naturrechtliche Tradition (s. prägend Thomas, *summa theol.* II.1 qu. 90 ff.) – Gesetze *sensu stricto* Anordnungen eines machthabenden Oberhauptes sind (*Lev.* XXV, 4): Das *Unvernünftige* wird erst dadurch auch zum *Ungerechten* (bzw. zur Sünde), dass seine Unterlassung durch den (von Sanktionsdrohungen begleiteten) *Willensakt* eines dazu Befugten *geboten* wird (*obligatio est necessitatio imposita justae poenae metu*, Leibniz (1999, 2151)). – Somit treten in der Hobbesschen Naturrechtslehre die menschliche *Vernunft* und der *Wille* des vertraglich geschaffenen Souveräns an jene Stellen, die im christlichen Naturrecht von *ratio* und *voluntas dei* besetzt waren – und deren *Zusammenspiel* daher bereits im Naturzustand Normativität *sensu stricto* zukam.
4 Tyrrell an Locke im Sommer 1690; zit. nach Peter Laslett (1988, 80).

> For to say that God hath spoken to him in the Holy Scripture, is not to say God hath spoken to him immediately, but by mediation of the Prophets, or of the Apostles, or of the Church [...]. To say he hath spoken to him in a Dream, is no more then to say he hath dreamt that God spake to him. (*Lev.* XXXII, 6)

Kurz: Das *Wort* (und insbesondere der *Wille*) Gottes ist denen, die bei Sinnen sind, immer nur durch die Vermittlung *anderer* Menschen zugänglich. Mit dem Ausruf: „Que d'hommes entre dieu et moi" wird Rousseaus Savoyardischer Vikar diese Einsicht 100 Jahre später griffig zusammenfassen. Denn nicht erst bei der Interpretation der dafür einschlägigen heiligen Schriften treten diese Menschen zwischen Gott und den einzelnen, sondern bereits bei der Auszeichnung einzelner Textkorpora als „Heilige Schriften" verlässt der Einzelne sich unausweichlich auf die Auskunft seiner Kirche, denn den Schriften selbst sieht man bekanntermaßen nicht an, ob sie göttlichen Ursprungs sind oder nicht (und wenn man es dennoch *selbst* erkennen zu können glaubt, dann doch nur, weil man bereits von *anderen* mit einschlägigen Kriterien versorgt wurde). Und obgleich Presbyterianer und Anglikaner sich sogar gemeinsam auf die *King-James-Bible* von 1611 als ihren heiligen Text einigen konnten: Der Versuch der Anglikaner, ihr Common-Prayer Book den Schotten als unverzichtbares Medium der rechten Gottesverehrung aufzudrängen, bot 1638 Anlass zu einem Aufstand und führte schließlich zum Bürgerkrieg. Die Berufung auf den *Willen* Gottes – so die Hobbessche Grundüberzeugung – verschärft die politischen Konflikte, statt sie zu lösen, denn sie ist naturgemäß und unvermeidlich durch ein kontingentes *Bekenntnis* vermittelt, das seinerseits zugleich diese Kontingenz leugnet – und erst dadurch seine eigentümliche, jeden Kompromiss verabscheuende, Hartnäckigkeit gewinnt.

Daher beginnt er die zweite Hälfte des *Leviathan* mit der rückblickenden – und gerne übersehenen – methodologischen Bemerkung:

> I have derived the Rights of Soveraigne Power, and the duty of Subjects hitherto, from the Principles of Nature onely; such as Experience has found true, or Consent (concerning the use of words) has made so; that is to say, from the nature of Men, known to us by Experience, and from Definitions (of such words as are Essentiall to all Politicall reasoning) universally agreed on. (Lev. XXXII, 1)

Die (bislang entfaltete) Hobbessche Lehre vom Civil Commonwealth soll demnach ausschließlich zweierlei voraussetzen: Eine *erfahrungsbasierte Lehre* vom Menschen und die *Existenz eines politischen Diskurses*, in dem über Machtansprüche in den dafür unverzichtbaren Begriffen von Recht und Unrecht gestritten wird. *Dieser* Diskurs wird in der „Civill Philosophy" unter Hinzunahme der Lehre vom Menschen auf seine Voraussetzungen befragt, mit dem Resultat, dass man *Herrschaftsansprüche* der souveränen Gewalt grundsätzlich nicht mittels *Rechtsan-*

sprüchen infrage stellen kann, weil die von allen Streitenden zugestandenen Rechtsbegriffe – wie die Analyse im zweiten Buch („of the form and power of a commonwealth") im Detail zeigt – grundsätzlich nur Bedeutung haben *können*, wenn sie auf die wechselseitigen Beziehungen *zwischen Bürgern*, die einer souveränen Herrschaft *unterworfen sind,* angewandt werden: „Where there is no common [!] power, there is no law, where no law no injustice!" (*Lev.* XIII, 13). Werden die rechtlichen Termini hingegen auf das Verhältnis *zwischen* Souverän und Bürger angewandt, führen sie in einen Progress der Souveräne (Lev. XXIX, 9) und sind daher nichts als *rhetorische* Waffen ohne jeden normativen Gehalt – sie signalisieren allenfalls den Rückfall in den Naturzustand (*Lev.* XXVIII, 13).

Erst in der nachfolgenden zweiten Hälfte des *Leviathan* (im 3. und 4. Buch) will Hobbes neben der Vernunft, dem offenbarungsunabhängigen *natürlichen* Wort Gottes, auch noch dessen *prophetisches* Wort, also die Christliche Offenbarung, befragen und damit dann auch vom „ecclasiasticall Commonwealth" handeln.

Nun wirkt es zunächst befremdlich, wenn ein Autor einerseits die Staatsphilosophie, wie wir sahen, ganz ausdrücklich *ohne* jedes religiöses Fundament errichtet, aber gleichwohl im Titel des Buches das projektierte Staatswesen als ein bürgerliches *wie kirchliches* apostrophiert und zudem die zweite Hälfte, also gut 250 moderne Druckseiten, theologischen und kirchenpolitischen Frage widmet. In der Hobbes-Literatur erheben sich daher immer wieder Stimmen, die in Hobbes doch wieder einen verkappten Theoretiker des Christlichen Naturrechts entdecken wollen: Dass das Wort „Gott" mit seinen über 1000 Vorkommnissen im *Leviathan* alle anderen Substantive weit übertrifft, scheint diese Auffassung zu stützen.

Aber dieser Schluss ist vorschnell, und er wird weder der Architektonik des *Leviathan* noch dem philosophischen und politischen Scharfblick Hobbes' gerecht, denn die Betonung der *christlichen* Dimension des „Civil Commonwealth" hat bei Hobbes eine grundsätzlich andere Bedeutung als in den Vorläufertheorien – und vielen vermeintlich moderneren.

Auch wenn für Hobbes die Theologie kein Teil der Philosophie ist (God „is no fit subject of our philosophy", so *EW* V, 435) und Religion kein direktes Erzeugnis der Vernunft, so ist für ihn Religion gleichwohl ein *Naturbedürfnis* des Menschen, und ein solches ist sie – paradoxerweise – gerade aufgrund von dessen spezifischer *Vernunftbegabung.* Die Vernunft schaut nämlich nicht nur in die *Zukunft* und macht – wie wir bereits sahen – durch die die Entgrenzung der Bedürfnisse eine *künstliche* Etablierung des Friedens für das menschliche Miteinander unverzichtbar. Vernunft sucht mit der gleichen Unvermeidlichkeit nun auch nach dem Unbedingten in der *Vergangenheit.* Für Hobbes ist das religiöse Bedürfnis daher eine notwendige Begleiterscheinung der menschlichen Vernunfttätigkeit (*Lev.* XII, 2f.), gleichsam ein Vernunftbedürfnis, weil es aus der nie endenden Suche nach Ursachen hervorgeht:

> For he that from any effect he seeth come to pass, should reason to the next and immediate cause thereof, and from thence to the cause of that cause, and plunge himself profoundly in the pursuit of causes; shall at last come to this, that there must be (as even the heathen philosophers confessed) one first mover; that is, a first, and an eternal cause of all things; which is that which men mean by the name of God. (*Lev.* XII, 6)

Es ist wichtig, diesen philosophischen Gemeinplatz hier als eine genuin vernunfttheoretische *Begründung* einer *natürlichen Religiosität* des Menschen, der *seeds of religion,* zu erkennen, die sie als direktes, *gleichursprüngliches* Komplement seiner *natürlichen Zukunftsorientiertheit* ausweist. Die Religion füllt gleichsam eine beunruhigende Leerstelle im rationalistischen *Selbstverständnis* des Menschen aus, sie ist somit kein kontingentes, bloß sozialgeschichtliches Faktum, über welches uns die Erfahrung unterrichtet. Mit der Frage nach der letzten Ursache ist für Hobbes der Grund für die Religion gelegt, und damit kann er behaupten,

> [The first seeds or principles of religion] can never be so abolished out of humane nature, but that new Religions may againe be made to spring out of them, by the culture of such men, as for such purpose are in reputation. (*Lev.* XII, 23)

Das *spirituelle Bedürfnis* ist dem Menschen somit als Zwilling der *Sorge um die eigene Zukunft* gleichsam in die Wiege gelegt, es ist so unlösbar wie diese mit seiner Vernunft verknüpft und kann (wie ein *weltliches Bedürfnis*) jederzeit *geweckt* werden – und *wird* es eben auch: Nicht zuletzt von interessierten Kreisen, die es in den Dienst ihres politischen Machtstrebens stellen wollen (*„such men, as for such purpose are in reputation"*) und dann mit einem – als solchem *kontingenten* – Inhalt füllen.

Der Text des *Leviathan* gibt wenig Gründe zu der Annahme, dass Hobbes durch die eingangs angesprochene Verbindung von staatlicher und kirchlicher Macht in erster Linie die religiösen *Bindungskräfte* für den Leviathan nutzbar machen will, wie es uns heutzutage vertraut zu sein scheint (s. *Lev.* XIV, 31). Belehrt durch die Gewaltexzesse, die in der Neuzeit im Namen der Religion angezettelt wurden, diagnostiziert er ein anderes Problem, das der Bürgerkrieg deutlich vor Augen gestellt hat: Der religiöse Mensch steht im *Spannungsfeld* staatlicher und religiöser Verpflichtung, und zwar immer dann, wenn das Bekenntnis etwas fordert, was der weltliche Souverän verbietet *vice versa*. In gut englischer Tradition wird dieser Konflikt in dem Anspruch des Papstes deutlich, der aus der Ferne von den britischen Katholiken Loyalität im Kampf gegen die anglikanische Krone einfordert. Hier gibt es angesichts der Unauslöschlichkeit der *semina religionis*, der „Keime der Religion", der Hobbesschen Psychologie zufolge nur *ein* Remedium: Weil die Sprengkraft der in Aussicht gestellten *unendlichen* Himmelslöhne und

Höllenstrafen stärker auf das menschliche Handeln Einfluss nehmen kann, als alles, was *endliche*, weltliche Herrscher aufzubieten vermögen, um sich der Gefolgschaft ihrer Bürger zu versichern, dürfen religiöse Forderungen gar nicht erst mit denen der weltlichen Macht konfligieren *können*. Es bedarf also seinerseits einer geeigneten Religion im Staat, um der stets drohenden spirituellen Herausforderung die Spitze zu nehmen. Und zu Hobbes' großer Erleichterung ist gerade das Christentum eine Religion, die *genau das* leisten kann. Dafür muss er dessen Heilige Schriften allerdings in einer recht eigenwilligen Weise auslegen.

Hobbes' praktisch-religiöse Botschaft im *Leviathan* ist trotz des gewaltigen Textumfanges der Bücher III und IV kurz und prägnant:

> The (Unum Necessarium) onely Article of Faith, which the Scripture maketh simply Necessary to Salvation, is this, that JESUS IS THE CHRIST. (*Lev.* XLIII, 11; vgl. *OL* III, 568)

Wer seinen Verstand gebrauchen kann (so, wie es die erste Hälfte des *Leviathan* lehrt) und zudem diese *eine* zusätzliche Botschaft (der zweiten Hälfte des Werkes) in sein Herz eingeschrieben hat, wird ein treuer Bürger des Leviathan sein: Er wird dank eigener Einsicht auf die natürlichen Gesetze, die „articles of peace" vertrauen, und angesichts des hinzukommenden ‚Glaubensartikels' wird er sich in seinem Gehorsam gegenüber diesen Gesetzen auch und *gerade* von denjenigen nicht irre machen lassen, die behaupten, der irdische Staat könne oder solle ihm noch *mehr* bieten als den *irdischen* Frieden – den der Bürger schließlich hat. In einem Satz:

> God disposes men to Piety, Justice, Mercy, Truth, Faith, and all manner of Vertue, both Morall, and Intellectuall, by doctrine, example, and by severall occasions, naturall, and ordinary. (*Lev.* XXXVI, 14)

Die *Bereitschaft*, die natürlichen Gesetze zu befolgen, *könnte* durchaus unter Christen angesichts der angenommenen göttlichen Strafandrohung besonders ausgeprägt sein, aber das interessiert Hobbes im Grunde wenig, denn seines Erachtens kann man darauf angesichts der Streitlust der Christen untereinander ohnehin nicht bauen. Es geht ihm an dieser Stelle um etwas gänzlich anderes: Wer hier und jetzt auf Erden, also *nach* dem Tod des Erlösers und *vor* dessen Wiederkunft, *im Namen Gottes* gegen den Staat antritt, der kann – so interpretiert Hobbes den s. E. zentralen „Article of faith" der *Heiligen Schrift* – kein anderer sein als der Antichrist höchstpersönlich. „Jesus *was* the Christ" steht bei Hobbes für die einfache Wahrheit, dass man *als Christ*, gleich welchen Bekenntnisses, *in dieser Welt* aus den Armen des Leviathan nur noch in die Fänge des Bösen fliehen kann. In dieser letztgenannten, von Hobbes mehrfach benutzten Perfekt-Formulierung („Jesus *was* the Christ") kommt deutlicher als in dem – biblischen – Satz „Jesus *is* the Christ" (wie wir ihn etwa in *Joh.* XX, 31 der *King-James Bible* finden) zum Ausdruck, dass der Erlöser seine irdische Mission bereits erfüllt hat. Es wird daher kein *anderer* mehr kommen vor dem Ende der Zeiten. Wer *hier und jetzt* im Namen Gottes antritt, um dessen Reich zu etablieren, kann daher nur betrügen wollen, der ist womöglich sogar gerade jener Antichrist, vor dem die Heilige Schrift in Math. 24.5 ff. uns warnt. Der Papst wäre dafür also *prima facie* durchaus ein möglicher Kandidat (so hatte es ja Luther 100 Jahre zuvor gesehen), denn er will den Engländern vorschreiben, welchem König sie um Gottes willen Gehorsam schenken müssen und welchem nicht. Weil allerdings der „Bischop of Rome" zumindest die Gotteskindschaft Christi nicht leugnet, ist er für Hobbes wohl doch nicht mehr als der Geist des versunkenen römischen Reiches, der tot und gekrönt noch auf dessen Grabstein hockt (*Lev.* XLVII, 22).

Die Herrschaft Gottes – so Hobbes' politischer Kern des Christentums – bedeutet das imaginäre Ende der *politischen* Phase in der Geschichte der Menschheit, und es liegt gerade *nicht* an den Menschen, dieses Ende herbeizuführen – oder auch nur den genauen Termin zu erraten. Vielmehr haben sie die Zeit bis dorthin mit der Etablierung *irdischer* Gerechtigkeit auszufüllen:

> [...] we are not to renounce our Senses, and Experience; nor (that which is the undoubted Word of God) our naturall Reason. For they are the talents which he hath put into our hands to negotiate, till the coming again of our blessed Saviour; and therefore [to be] employed in the purchase of Justice, Peace, and true Religion. (*Lev.* XXXII, 2)

Auf eine *göttliche* Ordnung der Welt sollen die Menschen zwar *hoffen*. Sie dürfen aber nicht versuchen, sie selbst zu etablieren, ja sie sollen nicht einmal mit ihr *rechnen*, denn wenn sie schließlich einmal kommen sollte, so würde dann doch *alles* anders, als sie es mit ihrer endlichen Vernunft antizipieren können – was schließlich jeder Christ im Text der *Offenbarung* nachlesen kann:

> And he that sat upon the throne said, Behold, I make all things new (*Offenb.* 21.5).

Es bedarf im Hobbesschen Commonwealth also *allein deshalb* unausweichlich einer Religion wie der christlichen, weil allein eine solche diejenigen ruhig zu stellen vermag, welche ohne sie in Versuchung geraten könnten, im Namen einer (vermeintlich) *geoffenbarten Wahrheit* ihre *menschliche Vernunft* zu verraten: Ausschließlich eine Religion, welche um der Gerechtigkeit willen die weltliche Herrschaft von der Sorge um das jenseitige Heil befreit (*Lev.* XXXII, 2), kann dem unauslöschlichen spirituellen Bedürfnis der Menschen, den sprießenden „seeds of religion", des politischen Stachels berauben – und nur wo *das* gelingt, so Hobbes, haben Recht und Frieden überhaupt eine Chance. Möglicherweise ist dies eine der beunruhigendsten Einsichten der frühen europäischen Aufklärung. Jedenfalls hat Hobbes' Versuch der Einhegung der spirituellen *Sprengkräfte* durch das „comonwealth ecclasiasticall" nicht das Geringste zu tun mit der intellektuellen Selbstaufgabe des „Wenn es keinen Gott gibt, ist alles erlaubt!" politischambitionierter Theologien: Denn diese riskieren gerade durch das Spiel mit dem Feuer spiritueller *Bindekräfte,* einen jeden politischen Konflikt in einen kollektiven Kampf um die letzten Dinge und damit in einen Krieg auf Leben und Tod zu verwandeln. Geradezu prophetisch heißt es im letzten Absatz des Haupttextes:

> it is not the Romane Clergy onely, that pretends the Kingdome of God to be of this World.

Ich denke, hier haben wir es mit einer Einsicht zu tun, deren zeitlose Aktualität erst seit Ende des vorigen Jahrhunderts wieder ins abendländische Bewusstsein zu rücken beginnt. Dazu gleich!

Hier ist es zunächst wichtig noch einmal zu betonen, dass Hobbes' Hoffnung auf das Christentum nicht bloß der kontingenten Tatsache geschuldet ist, dass die seinerzeit in Europa blutig streitenden Parteien allesamt das Neue Testament im Marschgepäck trugen und daher am Ende des Bürgerkriegs voraussichtlich irgendein dem Anspruch nach *christlicher* Staat stehen wird. Der Satz 'Jesus is/was the Christ' – und das ist der erinnernswerte, systematische Ertrag dieser philosophischen Analyse des Verhältnisses von Religion und Politik – ist grundsätzlich durch jeden anderen 'article of faith' ersetzbar, der dreierlei leistet: Dass er dem nach spiritueller Erlösung Suchenden 1) eine Erlösungshoffnung gibt, ihm 2) zugleich deutlich macht, dass infragestehender Erlösung nur würdig ist, wer hier auf Erden durch Gehorsam gegen den Souverän den Frieden befördert und 3) die Errichtung eines erlösungsverheißenden 'Kingdome of God' gefälligst Gott selbst überlässt. Thomas Hobbes brauchte sich über mögliche Alternativen zum Christentum noch keine Gedanken zu machen, denn jene Parteien, die um ihn herum mit der Bibel in der Hand um die Souveränität in den einzelnen Staaten kämpften, sollten sich seiner Überzeugung nach auf den geeigneten 'article' leicht einigen können. Aber selbst das war möglicherweise schon zu viel verlangt, denn sicherlich ist eine Auslegung der Heiligen Schriften des Christentums, deren Kern sich im „Jesus *was* the Christ" erschöpft, aus der Sicht der einzelnen Bekenntnisse fragwürdig – und für alle jene politischen Strategen, die sich ihrer zur spirituellen Aufrüstung bedienen wollen, naturgemäß unannehmbar. Doch bekanntermaßen – das ist ja gerade problemkonstitutiv – kann man die heiligen Texte des Christentums auf vielerlei Weise lesen. Warum dann nicht auch so, wie Thomas Hobbes es vorschlug?

4 Friedenswille und Heilserwartung

Der *Leviathan* des vielgescholtenen „Devil from Malmesbury" war also genauso weit davon entfernt, dem Staat eine theologische Grundlegung zu verschaffen, wie davon, mit seiner Bibelkritik die Grundlagen des Christentums zu untergraben. Er war vielmehr – wie wir jetzt erkennen können – ein *staatsphilosophisches* Angebot an das historische Christentum, dem dieses sich bekanntlich verweigert hat. Die Erwartung des Thomas Hobbes, dass es nämlich durch die Botschaft „Jesus *was* the Christ" und „his Kingdome is not of *this* world" alle unversöhnlichen religiösen Gegensätze – wenn auch nicht auflöst, so doch zumindest – aus dem *politischen* Raum fernhält, diese Erwartung hat es bis heute nicht erfüllt: Politische Missionen werden von christlichen Regimes auch im 21. Jahrhundert mitunter noch als Kreuzzüge inszeniert. Aber zumindest in Blick auf die konfessionellen Konflikte innerhalb Europas ist das Christentum den Hobbesschen Erwartungen schon in einem hohen Maße gerecht geworden – möglicherweise aber auch nur, weil hier die *spirituelle politische* Energie generell erlahmt ist.[5] Diese Entwicklung ist allerdings nicht nur den Christen selbst zugute gekommen, sondern *allen jenen*, die Politik im Namen einer diesseitigen Gerechtigkeit betrieben sehen wollen.

Sollte Hobbes' Analyse auch nur im Ansatz in die richtige Richtung weisen, dann wäre dies in Hinblick auf eine *globale* Friedensordnung allerdings eine derzeit höchst beunruhigende Tatsache – und zwar beunruhigend ausgerechnet für die, die *mit* Hobbes darauf bestehen, dass Politik eine durch und durch *diesseitige* Angelegenheit ist, deren Sorge der äußeren Gerechtigkeit eines irdischen Friedens gilt und gerade *nicht* dem Seelenheil und einer immerwährenden Erlösung (von was nun auch immer), denn diese ist dem menschlichen Zugriff entzogen. Sollte säkulare Politik tatsächlich 1) nur in einem spirituell entlasteten Raum auf Dauer gestellt werden können, und setzte 2) die spirituelle Entlastung tatsächlich die *positive Besetzung* des spirituellen Raumes durch *solche* Religionen voraus, die, wenn sie überhaupt ein Reich Gottes suchen, zumindest dessen Herbeiführung einfach diesem ihrem Gott selbst überlassen, dann wären freilich alle Versuche, das eine ohne das andere zu etablieren, notwendig zum Scheitern verurteilt. Hoffnung macht uns Hobbes damit vermutlich nicht.

Dem Optimismus der meisten modernen liberalen Konzeptionen politischer Gerechtigkeit liegt die Annahme zugrunde, dass die historisch gewonnene Überzeugung, Religionskriege seien nicht endgültig zu gewinnen, zunehmend in das allgemeine Bewusstsein übergeht – was in letzter Konsequenz dann zwangsläufig zu einer Art Privatisierung des Spirituellen führt. Doch diese

---

5 Dazu etwa: Graf (2014).

Überzeugung kann nur dort politisch *wirksam* werden, wo entweder den *religiösen Gehalten selbst* bereits im Geiste der Hobbesschen „true religion" der politische Stachel gezogen ist, oder wo Bekenntnisse ihre Herrschaft über den Menschen vollständig und auf Dauer verloren haben. Angesichts der offenkundigen (und von Hobbes auch theoretisch eingefangenen) Tatsache, dass ein globaler, dauerhafter Bedeutungsverlust von Religion nicht in Aussicht steht, sollten wir uns über diese zweite Option derzeit genauso wenig Gedanken machen, wie seinerzeit Hobbes: Das Problem hat also *nur dann* eine Lösung, wenn die gelebten Bekenntnisse den politischen Raum *durch ihre spirituelle Botschaft* entlasten, wenn es also zum *Inhalt,* ja – als „unum necessarium" der Erlösung – geradezu zum *inhaltlichen Kern* der jeweiligen Bekenntnisse gehört, dass sie die spirituelle Energie in solche Bahnen leiten, wo sie eine gerechte, d. h. den Frieden sichernde, politische Ordnung nicht sprengt. Das historische Christentum hat diese Bedingung nicht immer erfüllt (und bietet, besonders in seiner römischen Spielart, öffentlich wenig Anlass zu der Annahme, dass dieses Versäumnis *intern* als ein Makel wahrgenommen wird), und wenn andere Religionen sie derzeit nicht erfüllen, dann lässt auch das keine apodiktischen Prognosen zu.

Die Hobbessche Diagnose ist für uns heute vor allem deshalb so irritierend und desillusionierend, weil sie die Anwälte säkularer, liberaler Politik in der Situation einer prinzipiellen Schizophrenie zurücklässt. Schon in der Person des Thomas Hobbes findet dies deutlichen Ausdruck. Es gibt kaum einen neueren Autor, der das öffentliche Bekenntnis zur Staatsreligion und die Anpassung an deren äußeren Kult so kompromisslos – und dabei aus zutiefst lauteren Motiven – gefordert hätte wie Hobbes: Funktionsbedingung des säkularen Staates ist, dass der Souverän, d. i. die von den Bürgern autorisierte Regierung, Auswahl und Interpretation der Heiligen Schriften sowie die Form des äußeren religiösen Kults bestimmt. Und niemand sonst hat die Befugnis, einzelnen Bürgern Vorschriften zu machen, die mit einem Prestige der *Verbindlichkeit* (welchen Ursprungs auch immer) daherkommen. Der Klerus ist demzufolge der politischen Macht vollständig untergeordnet und der Bürger zu bedingungslosem äußerlichen Gehorsam gegenüber dem staatlichen Religionsprogramm verpflichtet. Zugleich ist sich Hobbes selbst in aller Schärfe dessen bewusst, dass eine öffentliche Religion nicht notwendig ins Herz der Bürger dringt: „Beleef, and Unbeleef never follow mens Commands" (*Lev.* XVII, 11; vgl. XXXVII, 13; XL, 2; XLII, 80). Sie ist und bleibt damit ein *politisches* Angebot, dem um des Friedens willen allerdings kein konkurrierendes Angebot an die Seite treten darf. Um ihre *politische* Wirksamkeit zu beweisen, muss diese öffentliche Religion demnach gar nicht – und das weiß niemand besser als Hobbes selbst – die Seele des Einzelnen gefangen nehmen (wie auch sollte das *erzwungen* werden können?), solange sie nur wirksam *verhindert*, dass irgendein *anderes* politisch-spirituelles Angebot dieses tut, und damit den

Friedenswillen dem Heilsbegehren opfert. Der *Agnostiker* ist im anglikanischen England also nur *deshalb* zu fürchten (so könnte man die Hobbessche Position pointieren), weil er, falls die „seeds of religion" bei ihm wider Erwarten (und wodurch auch immer) doch einmal zum Keimen gebracht werden, zum *Katholiken* werden könnte.[6] Den Religiös-Gestimmten muss gleichsam verbindlich ein Weg spirituellen Engagements aufgezeigt werden, der die politische Ordnung nicht sprengt. Nicht mehr, aber auch nicht weniger bedarf es, um den Frieden spirituell abzusichern. Die religiös Unmusikalischen (um Max Webers Stenogramm zu benutzen) hingegen müssen um des irdischen Friedens willen lernen, das öffentliche Ansinnen des *äußeren* Kults eines tauglichen, durch staatliches Dekret zur *Religion* erklärten *Aberglaubens* (*Lev.* VI, 36) unverzagt zu ertragen – und der Leviathan muss im Gegenzug die kultischen (und doktrinalen) Zumutungen für die Agnostiker unter seinen Bürgern in Grenzen halten, um sich deren Gefolgschaft nicht zu verscherzen. Säkulare Politik *bleibt* somit immer eine heikle Aufgabe.

Thomas Hobbes gehörte in der Tat zu jenen Heroen, die sich zutrauen, um des Friedens willen die Spannung zwischen privater Bekenntnisabstinenz und öffentlicher Ergebenheit bis zum Ende ihres Lebens auszuhalten. Zwischenzeitlich allerdings, als er während seines Frankreich-Exils mit dem Tode kämpfte und somit erwartete, sich durch diesen zeitnah dem Zugriff jeder irdischen Gerechtigkeit endgültig zu entziehen, brach es – wie sein Biograph berichtet – dann doch aus ihm heraus:

> When Mr T. Hobbes was sick in France, the divines came to him, and tormented him (both Roman Catholic, Church of England and Geneva). Said he to them 'Let me alone, or else I will detect all your cheats from Aaron to yourselves!' (Aubrey 1898, 375 f.)

---

6 Erst in der lateinischen Version des *Leviathan* von 1668 (nachdem Hobbes mit bedrohlichen Häresie-Vorwürfen konfrontiert war) finden wir die Behauptung, Atheisten könnten keine Staatsbürger sein (*OL* III, 542). Dass Hobbes' berühmter „Foole" auch 1651 bereits Gerechtigkeit *und* somit auch die Gottesexistenz im Herzen leugnete (*Lev.* XV, 4), hieß ja noch nicht, dass auch umgekehrt der Gottesleugner *notwendig* die Gerechtigkeit leugnet. – Andererseits ist zu beachten, dass *für Hobbes* mit Atheisten (im modernen Wortsinne), die öffentlich deklarieren, die Nichtexistenz Gottes ließe sich beweisen, im Unterschied zu Agnostikern, Epikureern (die davon ausgehen, dass die Götter existieren, den Gedanken allerdings ertragen, dass diese sich nicht um die Menschen kümmern) und den *Hobbesschen* Christen kein Frieden möglich sein wird, *weil* die strikt atheistische Position (für Hobbes) nicht nur vernunftwidrig ist, sondern zudem ein politische Strategie zur Folge hätte, die den Frieden verfehlt, weil sie den *vernunftbedingten* „seeds of religion" der Menschen nicht Rechnung trägt (s.o.): Im *politischen Streit* steht ein strikter Atheismus in gleichberechtigter Konkurrenz mit allen Religionen, die ihren Anspruch auf *universelle Seelenführerschaft* durchsetzen wollen.

Bibliographie

Aubrey, John (1898): Brief Lives, Andrew Clarke (ed.), Oxford.

Graf, Friedrich Wilhelm (2014): Götter global. Wie die Welt zum Supermarkt der Religionen wird, München.

Hobbes, Thomas (1991): Leviathan Student Edition, Cambridge.

Ludwig, Bernd (1998): Die Wiederentdeckung des Epikureischen Naturrechts. Zu Thomas Hobbes' Philosophischer Entwicklung von De Cive zum Leviathan im Pariser Exil 1640 – 1651, Frankfurt.

Leibniz, Gottfried Wilhelm (1999): Sämtliche Schriften und Briefe, hg. von der Berlin Brandenburgischen Akademie der Wissenschaften und der Akademie der Wissenschaften in Göttingen, Reihe VI (Philosophische Schriften), Band 4.

Laslett, Peter (1988): Introduction, in: ders. (Hg.): John Locke, Two Treatises of Government (Student Edition), Cambridge.

Lukas K. Sosoe
Leibniz and European Cosmopolitanism

Introduction

It might be surprising to many to present Leibniz as a political thinker, and more precisely, as one of the forerunners of a European cosmopolitan idea, that of European federalism. Leibniz is known as a great metaphysician, as well as a philosopher and a diplomat, but not as a great political thinker of European and world scale. One only needs to choose the series of books dedicated to the history of Western political ideas to realize Leibniz's absence. Not merely historians of modern European philosophy, but even political philosophers ignore Leibniz's contribution to political philosophy, as a pioneer of the idea of the European Union. Leibniz's name does not figure in German academic anthologies: absent, for example, from the fifth edition of the *Klassiker des politischen Denkens* (1979)[1] from Plato to Max Weber, celebrated by the review *Neue politische Literatur* in the 1970s as "ein gelungenes Schulwerk", characterized by the book review in the *Zeit* as a work expounding the "Gesamtbild einer Geschichte abendländicher Staatstheorie" and edited by political scientists like Hans Maier, Heinz Rausch and Horst Denzer. The chapter "The Federalists" of the same book mentions only the American founding fathers: Hamilton, Jefferson and other Federalists. No Europeans besides Immanuel Kant and the authors of the great idea of the Respublica Christiana of the Medieval and early Modern philosophy, are mentioned.

There may be many reasons for this. One of them owes to the huge volume of Leibniz's philosophical work and the scattered character of most of his philosophical thinking, in addition to his status as a diplomat and politician, which overshadows his political philosophical writings. The separation of Leibniz's political thought from his metaphysical theory stands as another reason. And finally, an important number of Leibniz's political writings could be easily found in journals on the history of international relations or theology than in journals on philosophy.

The purpose of this contribution is to sketch Leibniz's place in the history of political ideas on European federalism. We will not be able to give an exhaustive account of his political ideas in general, but we believe it to be possible to highlight his contribution to the idea of the European Union underlying the basic

---

1 Maier, Rausch and Denzer (^{5}1979 [1968]).

concepts of his political thought[2] by showing both the central role played by Leibniz in European political and federal thought as an important figure on the long list of the greatest pioneers of European federalism and the direct impact of his political ideas on great thinkers from Wolff to Kant and beyond.

In a word Leibniz proves as important as Crucé, Dubois, Guillaume Postel, Podebrady, Abbé de Saint-Pierre and even Wolff in his concern for a European federalism. With his program of a universal republic, Leibniz establishes himself as an important benchmark on the way to Wolff's universal republic and Kant's idea of *Perpetual Peace*.

In what follows, we will sketch in a first step Leibniz's idea of a universal republic, which is a political ideal, also called by him, *Optima Respublica* or *Respublica Christiana* or *Civitas Dei*. Secondly, special attention will be paid to the theological and metaphysical foundations of Leibniz's cosmopolitanism, to his *Civitas Dei* based on natural right embracing the whole world and to the place of the Christian republic within this cosmopolitan structure, i.e. a republic in accordance with the teachings of Jesus Christ. In this context, Leibniz's *Mars Christianissimus*, which contains a very severe criticism of France's imperialism in Europe and a defense of the German princes based on the Westphalian Treaty, plays a significant role. The last part will be dedicated to Leibniz's position on European federalism and to his debate with Abbé de Saint-Pierre. This debate has the advantage to reveal clearly Leibniz's idea of European federalism. It will become clear that these three parts are all based on Leibniz's metaphysical and theological premises. This explains why many commentators of Leibniz's political ideas contend that his whole metaphysics was at the service of his unified global international political order and, specifically, at the service of his *Civitas Dei*.[3]

1 The hierarchical unity of the Civitas Dei

Leibniz's political thought can be summarized thus: harmony, reconciliation and conciliation. Without the search for harmony and conciliation, Leibniz's philosophy would amount to that which Bertrand Russell takes it to be: a sheer op-

---

2 For a more comprehensive presentation of the basic notions of Leibniz's political thought, see Riley (1988, 1–44); see also Goyard-Fabre (1994, Part I, 105–120).
3 "Leibniz stellte die universalistische Metaphysik in den Dienst der Politik und entwarf eine Weltrechtsphilosophie [...] Leibniz' Rechtsmetaphysik spielte in dieser Hinsicht bei der Entwicklung des modernen politischen Universalismus eine Gründerrolle" (Cheneval 2002, 53). See also Goyard-Fabre (2011, 31–48).

portunistic discourse at the service of changing European political powers.[4] Through harmony and conciliation, Leibniz succeeds in laying down the metaphysical and theological foundation of the unity of this thought made of "apparent conflicting ideas" taking from each kind of thought that which proves soundest and synthesizing it with the seemingly incommensurable truths of other systems, in this way fusing "Platonism, Cartesianism, Christian voluntarism, Hobbesian mechanism" etc. into a system of thought.[5] That is why the search for the "harmonie universelle" or universal harmony is the key concept which lends Leibniz's philosophy a unified shape and can be seen as the core of his thought.[6] One understands why Leibniz sought to develop a universal jurisprudence. By "universal jurisprudence" we mean that Leibniz intended the establishment of a World Republic, a hierarchical system of law common to God as the perfect being and man.

> God and man exist in a society of a universal republic of spirits, the noblest part of the universe [...] in which universal right is the same for God and for men.[7]

The cosmological and cosmopolitan character of Leibniz's political philosophy appears from the start. It stands as a metaphysical theory based on God and the order of creation.

Leibniz welcomes every idea necessary to sustain this political philosophical program. One of the best illustrations is his work: *Civitas Dei*, the City of God where God is considered the supreme power, the monarch. Since God is the monarch of the universal city, his word is the natural law and theology a part of jurisprudence. The Christian Church hence possesses a legal and political significance. Whereas believers or Christians are the citizens of God's Republic (*Republica Dei*), pagans are declared rebels who must be fought (*ubi infideles quasi rebelles sunt*).[8] In this political theory of universal monarchy, morality can only be understood as a legal concept and the relation between man and God as a political relation hierarchically ordained. That is why for Leibniz,

> [...] it is best to derive human justice, as from a spring, from the divine in order to make it complete. Surely the idea of just, no less that the idea of the true and the good, relates to

---

4 Russell (1964, 202).
5 Riley (1988), in: Leibniz (1988, 2).
6 Holz (1996, 5).
7 Riley (1988).
8 *De Arte Combinatoria*, Leibniz (1866, 190).

God. [...] and the rules which are common certainly enter in to the sciences and ought to be considered in universal jurisprudence. (Leibniz, 1706)[9]

Leibniz's metaphysics is entirely written in political concepts. It appears from the above cited text that there is no difference between God's and human justice. The difference proves one of degree. It can be considered on three levels: 1) On the level of the relation between Man and God, 2) on the level of the natural law of the entire human race and 3) on the level of the State.

The State, according to Leibniz, represents the lowest stage of the universal legal public order. It is subordinated to the World and the human race. Leibniz speaks of "omnia societati universali sub Rectore Deo" instead of the World, and this reveals the cosmological and cosmopolitan character of his conception of Law. That means that the whole world is God's city and the legal rules of this city his Laws.

Second, the metaphysically grounded structure of Law has a goal, namely the common good (*publice utile*), because it is subordinated to the direction of God's will insofar as God as Monarch of the whole universe wants for Man the best possible good.

Third, when Leibniz refers the State to the universal structure of Law, he does not heed the fate and the multiplicity of concrete States. For him, individuals do not matter in this context. The fact of their existence is neglected or underestimated when compared to the world legal divine order. The project of the *Civitas Dei* or of the universal cosmopolitan republic prevails over the individual States in which God is the Sovereign and legislator. Leibniz is convinced "que le monde est une espèce de cité aussi bien ordonné(e) que possible, dont le Seigneur a en main la sagesse et la puissance souveraine" (Leibniz 1679, 523)[10] for the common good of the spirits. By spirits, Leibniz means all reasonable beings, all monads or simple substances living in the City where God reigns as Monarch. The *Civitas Dei* is a society created, conserved and governed by God. It proves a cosmopolitan State based on reason. As Leibniz states it in the *Discours de métaphysique*:

Il ne faut pas seulement considérer Dieu comme le principe et la cause de toutes les substances et de tous les Estres, mais encore comme chef de toutes les personnes ou substances intelligentes, et comme Monarque absolu de la plus parfaite cité ou République, telle

---

9 "Opinions on the Principles of Pufendorf" in: Riley (1988, 64–75).
10 *Dialogue entre un habile politique et un ecclésiastique d'une piété inconnue* (1679–1682, 523).

qu'elle est, celle de l'univers composée de tous les esprits ensemble, Dieu lui-même étant aussi bien le plus accompli de tous les Esprits.[11]

In these, one finds the main lines of Leibniz's political philosophy which can then easily be summarized by underlining the *Civitas Dei*'s main characteristics. The *Civitas Dei* is metaphysical-theologically conceived as the normative ideal of the perfect State and Monarch, the latter God himself. All human beings and societies have to submit themselves to this Monarch's power, which is not to be identified with command but with justice. Every rational being necessarily belongs as citizen to the City of God. We have also mentioned the City's cosmopolitan nature. The main question is how and where Leibniz's European federal order fits in this overarching world society. Where is the place of a federal Europe in the world political structure and which kind of role does Leibniz assign Europe to play therein? And, finally, as the whole political philosophy is based on God, what is the function of religion and, specifically, the Christian religion in world politics and in relation to non-Christians in the world?

2 Leibniz's theory of international relations

Leibniz's political philosophy cannot be thoroughly presented without mentioning his writings on international relations, especially the relations between European states. For that, we need to know more of Leibniz's conception of natural right.

In writing on international affairs, Leibniz gives a concise definition of natural right and the relation between natural right, *Civitas Dei* and international Law.

In a paper on Abbé de Saint-Pierre's project of perpetual peace in Europe, Leibniz writes:

> When I was quite young, I became acquainted with a book entitled *Le Nouveau Cynée* whose unknown author advised sovereigns to govern their states in peace, and to let disputes be judged by an established tribunal, but I no longer know how to find this book [...][12]

---

11 Leibniz (2004, § 35, 88). Leibniz also speaks of "République générale des Esprits dont le chef est Dieu" (*Essais de Théodicée*, § 120).
12 *Observations on the Abbé Saint-Pierre's for Perpetual peace* [1715]; in Leibniz (1988, 178 – 183).

This indicates his early interests for European and world political problems given that the book *Le nouveau Cynée* speaks of peace and unity in Europe, which Leibniz's *Codex Juris Gentium*[13] will further develop.

Contrary to almost all philosophers in his lifetime, Leibniz shows in the definition of political philosophy's main categories that there proves no separation or distinction between Law, religion and theology. "Tout est lié", he contends, not only in the City of God but also in international relations, the ultimate ends of which remain peace and happiness for the realization of which Europe possesses a special mission.

One of the objectives of the *Codex Juris Gentium* (hereafter *CJG*) is, as stated in the Preface, to understand the law of nations. Nevertheless, Leibniz takes the opportunity to clarify again a few basic notions from his political philosophy like justice and law, which, he laments, even after having been treated by so many illustrious authors, have not been made sufficiently clear.[14]

> Right is a kind of moral possibility and obligation a moral necessity. By moral, I mean that which is equivalent to "natural" for a good man [...] A good man is one who loves everybody, in so far as reason permits [...] Justice, then [...] will be most conveniently defined [...] as the charity of the wise man, that is charity which follows the dictates of wisdom. (*CJG* 170–171)

Needless to say how strange and peculiar these definitions are compared to Hobbes's or Pufendorf's and even to Grotius's. Leibniz's definition has little to do with the natural right tradition. The reader will already have noticed it with the main features of the *Civitas Dei*. Most of Leibniz's writings make no difference between law, a legal duty and a moral duty. Here begin the difficulties in understanding Leibniz's concepts of practical philosophy. Far from Locke's distinguishing two great maxims in moral philosophy, namely justice and charity, Leibniz's conflation of the two comes out in the following definition:

> Charity is universal benevolence and benevolence the habit of loving or willing the good. Love signifies rejoicing in the happiness of another [...] into one's own. (*Idem*)

At first glance, the reader is drawn into utilitarian considerations. Then, as D'Holbach says:

---

13 Leibniz (1988, 165–176). All the references to the *Codex Juris Gentium* are abbreviated.
14 Our quotations are taken from Patrick Riley's translation of the Preface of the *Codex Juris Gentium*, in *Leibniz. Political writings* and abbreviated as *CJG* and quoted in the text.

L'homme vertueux est celui dont les actions tendent constamment au bien-être de ses semblables. La vertu n'est que l'art de se rendre heureux soi-même de la félicité des autres.[15]

Yet Leibniz's conception of happiness ends at a theological idea of God's perfection, an idea which no utilitarian would defend. Thus Leibniz says that "divine love exceeds all other loves because God can be loved with greater result since nothing is happier than God and nothing more beautiful and more worthy can be conceived." (*CJG* 171) Leibniz contends that, as God possesses the supreme power and supreme wisdom, his happiness becomes and even creates our own. At last, he concludes that wisdom is the science of happiness.

The clearness of this chain of definitions proves far from self-evident. This is not, however, the place to analyse in detail the relationships between wisdom, happiness, benevolence, perfection, utility and charity. All these concepts lead to Leibniz's conception of law and justice; the latter is the Love of God from which natural right flows. Furthermore, simple right is born out of the principle of conservation of peace. This stands as the principle of avoidance of misery, and higher right tends toward happiness. But to prove the truth of this conceptual edifice, Leibniz contends, we must assume the immortality of the soul and the existence of God as ruler of the universe, a perfect monarch who imposes all natural laws, rewards just actions and punishes wrong ones. "The divine providence and power cause all right to become fact and assure that no one is injured except by himself, that no good action goes unrewarded, and no sin unpunished." (*CJG* 174) Indeed, this is the teaching of Jesus Christ.

Leibniz's definition of natural law follows from theological grounds. Accordingly, it leads us to a universal political order based on divine providence. Although it also contains the description and analysis of the political situation in Europe, such as the alliances and treaties between princes, the *Codex Juris Gentium*, at least in its preface, proposes little more than the description and explanation of divine monarchy. On this ground, justice is called universal and includes all other virtues, even duties towards oneself, such as "not to abuse our own body or our own property". These kinds of abuses, which stand beyond the power of human laws, "are still prohibited by natural law, that is the eternal law of divine monarchy, since we owe ourselves and everything we have to God." (*CJG* 174) It appears that without God's supreme power directing the universe, punishing wrongs and rewarding good actions, there can be no moral and political order. Leibniz establishes this order on a theologically founded natural right

---

15 D'Holbach (1966, Chap. XVI, 405).

theory, which is of interest to the state and of a much greater interest to the universe. (*CJG idem*)

All that is needed for the development of cosmopolitism has already been given. And Leibniz's theologically, even christologically founded cosmopolitism serves as a theoretical realm in which European federalism finds its legitimate place. Before we come back to this topic, a few more stories need to be told on Leibniz's international relations or divine monarchy.

3 Leibniz: international relations or divine monarch

Leibniz takes it for granted that the Christian religion reveals God's will and should likewise be the fount of the world social and political order, as much of the individual states as of European federalism. The tight link between the City of God, the theory of natural right, and revelation gives the impression that Leibniz's political thought finds its ground in a kind of theology of revelation. This would mean that the ultimate justification of the Divine city rests on faith in the teachings of Christ and the Christian religion. At this point, further clarification is necessary, which we cannot undertake here. Nonetheless, it should be noted that Leibniz confers, without any justification, a precedence to Christianity over other world religions and justifies its extension through war against those religions and cultures in the world as we will see later. For present purposes, it suffices to bring forward a few passages to show the kind of dogmatic certainty with which Leibniz affirms the so-called truths of the Christian religion and their superiority over other religions'.

> Les anciens philosophes ont fort peu connu ces importantes vérités: Jésus Christ seul les a divinement exprimées et d'une manière si claire et si familière que les esprits les plus grossiers les ont conçues [...] il nous a donné à connaître le royaume des cieux ou cette parfaite république des esprits qui mérite le titre de cité de Dieu et dont il nous a découvert les admirables lois.[16]

Jesus Christ's teaching not only overrides that of other religions. For Leibniz, there is no doubt that Jesus stands as the founder of the purest and most enlightened religion:

---

16 Leibniz (2004, 217).

[...] les sages d'autres nations en ont peut-être autant quelquefois, mais ils n'ont pas eu le bonheur de se faire suivre assez et de faire passer le dogme en loi [...] jusqu'à ce que Jésus Christ leva le voile, et sans avoir la force en main, enseigna avec toute la force d'un législateur que les âmes immortelles passent dans une autre vie, où elles doivent recevoir le salaire de leurs actions [...] Jésus Christ acheva de faire passer la religion naturelle en loi, et de lui donner l'autorité d'un dogme public.[17]

This finds its basis in what here seems a revelation, as Leibniz observed that the theory of natural right is "jus naturae et gentium traditum secundum disciplinam christianorum id ex Christi documentis"[18] and that "the learned have rightly held [...] that the law of nature and of the nations should follow the teachings of Christianity [...] the divine things of the wise, according to the teaching of Christ." (*CJG* 174)

Besides the concept of natural right so defined, Leibniz also recognizes what he calls voluntary right "derived from custom or made by superior"; in the state, civil law receives its force from the one who holds the supreme power. Outside the state, the supreme power is the voluntary law of nations originating from the tacit consent of peoples. In addition to this international law of nations, Leibniz contends that "Christians have another common tie, the divine positive law contained in the sacred Scriptures [...] the sacred canons accepted in the whole Church and, later, in the West, the pontifical legislation to which kings and peoples submit themselves." (*CJG id.*) This Christian universalism overshadows the rational structure of other peoples' natural right and allows Leibniz to restrict his cosmopolitism to European Christian nations, to the "common republic of Christian nations", the heads of which remain the Pope in sacred matters and the emperor in temporal matters. Thus, Leibniz's cosmopolitism ends at a Europeanism in which two different theories are at play: one is rational and general and valid for all; the second based on positive legal structure derived from Christian revelation, *gentium christianarum respublica*, in other words, a Christian republic which is, at the same time, for Leibniz, the justification of the European Christian federal order with the right to wage wars against non-Christian peoples, Turks, Muslims and non-European peoples. The question proves how this Europeanism can be situated, "harmonized" or "conciliated" within Leibniz's universal political theory, i.e. in Leibniz's cosmopolitanism.

A partial and tentative answer to this question may be found in the *Codex Juris Gentium* where Leibniz develops his conception of war and peace. It may help 1) in understanding why and how Leibniz's universal republic can go

---

17 Leibniz (1969, Preface, 26 f.).
18 *CJG*, Preface, 8.

hand in hand with his strong Europeanism or European federalism and 2) in cap-
turing its fundamental intuition.

Leibniz deems it not unreasonable to believe, like Hobbes, that war between
states and peoples is and will be perpetual. Wars are destructive and do not hon-
our the belligerents, most of all a war waged between civilized nations. In this
sense, Louis XIV's expansionist politics in Europe should be severely con-
demned. Leibniz himself did so in his *Mars Christianissimus*. Leibniz is not, however, a pacifist for maintaining such. Indeed, it is preferable that the state be
ready for war if needed or that they make tactical alliances against an assault
coming from an enemy. Thus, it remains prudent and realistic to ready oneself,
for, as Leibniz writes:

> Quand les Français prêchent la paix, c'est à peu près le sermon que le renard allant en
> pèlerinage à Saint Jacques et publiant une amnistie générale entre les animaux, faisait à
> une troupe de poules qu'il rencontra sur son chemin. Ils ont sans doute fort bonne
> grâce de parler de paix perpétuelle, eux qui ne connaissent aucune autre que celle d'un
> esclavage générale à la turque.[19]

Nevertheless, Leibniz insists on the validity of a minimal justice demanding that
one not injure anyone, of a superior justice corresponding to charity, and of a
universal justice useful for all mankind. Yet the validity of the rules of justice
does not stand in opposition to the idea that, if one wants peace, one should
be ready for war. "Tout homme de bien," says Leibniz, "demeure d'accord
qu'on ne doit jamais faire guerre que lorsqu'il est nécessaire" (1866, 110). Therefore, states which follow peace should be armed, unless they are united by common interest. In that case they must make alliances with each other. Against
France's expansion the just war is that which the just man should undertake
to restore peace. (Truyol y Serra 1984, 68)[20]

4 Peace for Europe

The political situation in Europe after the Thirty Years War was one of total desolation, misery, hunger and political anarchy. In this situation, which kind of
peace was there for reconstruction? With a common interest in both, European
states needed more than ever to become closer and work together. As a Christian

---

19 Leibniz (1866, 254).
20 Leibniz, *Raison touchant à la guerre ou l'accomodement avec la France* (1625). See also
Truyol y Serra (1984).

philosopher, jurist and diplomat, Leibniz felt the necessity to take concrete measures for the reconstruction of Europe: 1) reconstruction of Christianity's lost unity, 2) reconstruction by pacification of political relations between European countries by exporting the violence outside Europe, and 3) construction of the project of a European union.

1.) Leibniz never accepted the Church's division following the Reformation. As one can notice in his correspondence with Bossuet, he strives for the unity of Catholics and Protestants by downplaying insofar as possible the dogmatic aspects of the church's division and by putting his effort into the unity of Christianity and the integrity of the Holy Roman Empire's constitutive nations with the Pope and the Emperor as the spiritual and secular heads respectively. But numerous tensions and rivalries plagued the empire. Accordingly, the solution lay in exporting tensions and wars outside Europe; its states, for the sake of peace, should then conquer other parts of the world in order, among other ends, to spread the Christian religion and, at the same time, to satisfy their thirst for power and expansion.

2.) Indeed, Leibniz makes concrete proposals about the way political structures in a 17th century Christian Europe devastated by wars could reorganize themselves through the imposition of the *pax christiana* on the world. Starting with the acknowledgement of an imbalance between forces at the European level, Leibniz made every effort possible to analyze methodically the situation and, to that end, made suggestions, where his diplomatic talents constantly shone through. Through metaphysically and religiously based argument, he legitimates France's conquest of Egypt, and this not without defending the Habsburgs against France. In a highly satirical and somewhat amusing writing, *Mars Christianissimus* (Most Christian War God, 1683), he suggests that France wage war against the Turks instead of conquering Christian nations like Holland and other European nations. In this same writing, Leibniz voices the idea of an alliance between German Protestant princes against the power of Catholic France under Louis XIV. And beyond Louis XIV, he pleads for a new European political balance. For Leibniz, the political unbalance in Europe owes to the "House of France", to which the Peace of Westphalia (1648) and the Treaty of the Pyrenees (1659) have granted too many advantages. These treaties, intended to protect stability in Europe or the "political balance of Europe", have instead led to a state of disharmony that fails to respect other states' sovereignty. According to Leibniz, the "policy of balance" proves in fact a policy that is "unbalanced"[21]. Before this balance, it is important to rethink the overall issue of interstate relationships, to replace, on one hand, strategies of division by those of unity and, on the other, strategies dictated by passion by those of reason.

Leibniz's solution consists in "exporting" the tensions and rivalries between European houses to other parts of the world. The justification of this imperialistic solution lies in the superiority of the European Christian religion and culture. First of all, Leibniz recommends to Louis XIV to conquer Egypt; by doing so, he will strengthen his kingdom and weaken the Turk instead of waging war against Holland, a Christian country:

> Je veux parler, Sire, de la conquête de l'Egypte. De toutes les contrées du globe, l'Egypte est la mieux située pour acquérir l'empire du monde et des mers: la population dont elle est susceptible, et son incroyable fertilité, l'appellent à cette élévation. Jadis, mère des sciences et sanctuaire des prodiges de la nature, aujourd'hui elle est le repaire de la perfidie mahométane, pourquoi faut-il que les chrétiens aient perdu cette terre sanctifiée, lien de l'Asie et de l'Afrique, digue interposée entre la mer Rouge et la Méditerranée, grenier de l'Orient, entrepôt des trésors de l'Europe et de l'Inde?[22]

Leibniz finds two justifications for Egypt's conquest. The first consists in hindering France's expansion wars in Europe. The second reason lies in spreading the *pax christiana* all over the world.[23] The conquest of Egypt is a 'bellum sacrum', a holy war against the pagans for the utility of mankind. Economically and politically, Europe's greatest threat, the Turks, will be discarded. By giving up its expansion in favor of the Christian nations and by waging war against the infidels, France and the Habsburgs will share mastery of the world and will be able to contribute both to the Christian religion's expansion and to peace and prosperity in Europe.

3.) In a third step, Leibniz designs a project for political Union for the prosperity of Europe, although he himself favored universal monarchy. At the time, he still admired Louis XIV and would have entrusted him with the general direction of European state affairs: at the least, the charge of arbitrating disputes and litigations. When confronted, however, with Louis XIV's expansionist politics, wholly at odds with a politics of concordat, he gave up his first draft of the project of the

---

21 History will confirm that assertion: after its victories, France saw the creation of coalitions against her; these eventually isolated the former and shifted the situation (Treaty of Aix-la-Chapelle, Nijmegen and Ryswick).
22 Leibniz (1840, 3 f.).
23 See Kaplan (1995, 91–95).

Union and concentrated his effort on German unification. For Leibniz, Germany "is the kernel of Europe" (*CJG* § 87). Leibniz further wrote in a strong nationalist mood that there is only Germany which is "personne civile" (*CJG* § 88) capable of giving Europe its unity. It therefore proves vital that it become a highly centralized State. It must become a true federal State legally harmonizing or conciliating the diversity of German states in political unity: the Empire.

In his capacity as diplomat and also philosopher, Leibniz suggests to each power a solution to satisfy its thirst for expansion in the world. To Leibniz, that division amounts to what those powers must do to ensure peace in Europe: the carving up of the world outside Europe. Thus, England and Denmark have to occupy North America; Spain, South America; Holland, East Indies; and France, with divine providence, is designated as the Christian warrior in the Middle East. To that end, it finds itself bound to attack Africa and Egypt. Likewise, West and East India must be dominated. Human beings must wage war against wolves and wild animals prior to domestication, to which barbarians and infidels are likened.[24]

It is only at this price that Europe can realize its dream of peace. At the same time, Leibniz develops a cultural plan consisting in the creation of learned societies to help to complete on the cultural level his imperialistic program. For peace and development and all the interests of mankind, learned Societies are indispensable to achieving the ideal of *Civitas Dei*. In this sense, Leibniz fully shares the scientific optimism of Bacon's *Novum Organum*.

As Goyard-Fabre expresses it,

> to rebuild Europe's shredded political unity, is a task that, in Leibniz's philosophy, does not come under the classic issue of 'The One and the Multiple'; it must be considered metaphysically, that is to say according to the vertical reference to the almighty divine's eminent perfection of which universal harmony and jurisprudence are the expression.[25]

This implies the transformation of the circumstances of justice, imposed by the House of France, to use Hume's expression, into circumstances of peace, based on law—law offering possibilities of regulation outside of the state of non-right, the state of nature. But law means understanding, and understanding means that we are only one step away from establishing its mechanisms: a union of all European states. Then what stands as the basis of the union recommended by Leibniz?

---

24 Leibniz, Bedenken welcher Gestalt *Securitas publica* (1670–1671, I, 167).
25 Goyard-Fabre (2011, 41).

In his work *Securitas publica*, impressive as it remains relevant even today, Leibniz suggests an association of sovereigns (§ 32), presided by a rotative Emperor, its objective being a "permanent alliance" (*concilium perpetuum*) with the function of the arbitration in order to avoid an absolutist government. That is why a federation of sovereign national states would be the suitable political strategy. The federation of sovereign states will assure the political unity necessary; every state needs to defend its interests against other political powers but also to respect the freedom and plurality of the States under the imperial administration. This kind of federation of national sovereign states is far from what Abbé de Saint-Pierre is proposing which is totally different from the perpetual council aiming at "the common interest of States" (Leibniz 1670 – 1671, § 24)[26] in the same Empire. Thus introducing a theme which he discussed unsuccessfully with Abbé de Saint-Pierre, Leibniz insists on the creation of peace in the union, on the safeguard of each people's and culture's difference. The advocated union must, at the same time, guarantee the diversity of its components. With this, he anticipates by two to three hundred years the "aborted" project of a European constitution wherein the question of unity in diversity is raised[27]—which, unfortunately, is no longer to be found in the Lisbon Treaty. Far from being an obstacle, that diversity is well accepted and perceived and remains, to Leibniz, the stepping stone towards the opening up of other sociopolitical and cultural horizons: towards the cultural wealth of each state, each nation having its own particular genius.

5 Leibniz and Abbé de Saint-Pierre: The impossible dialogue

One cannot entirely discuss Leibniz's foundation of European federalism without taking into account the correspondence between l'Abbé de Saint- Pierre and Leibniz about the *Mémoire pour rendre la paix perpétuelle en Europe* (1712), which helps him to clarify some points of his European federal dream. Leibniz cannot be indifferent to that project. Vanishing though his dream is to resuscitate the Holy Roman Empire with the Pope and the Emperor as heads of the Empire of universal Christendom, he answered Abbé de Saint-Pierre. His answer reveals how realistic and practical Leibniz could be in political matters but also his po-

---

26 Cf. *Entretiens de Philarète et d'Eugène:* that text, beyond its circumstances, has an ideological dimension.
27 Duhamel (2003, 158).

sition against the federation of individual sovereign States based on a contractual model.

L'Abbé de Saint-Pierre published from 1712–1717 his *Projet de paix perpétuelle* wherein he puts forth an idea of European Union founded on the contractual tradition. This intends to replace the imperial order by a federation of sovereign states with a central government. This project of a Union bases itself on a dual political power, the major goal of which is to secure peace in Europe, as indicated by the title. He sent it to Leibniz not only to seek his opinion but to use his influence to help the former convince European princes.

In his first reaction to Saint-Pierre, Leibniz expresses an apparent scepticism full of civility. But, as we know, his theory lies in imperial Christian order. "Men lack the will to deliver themselves from an infinity of evils", he wrote to Abbé de Saint-Pierre: "If five or six persons wanted to, they could end the great schism in the West and put the church in good order".[28] To put an end to wars, "it would be necessary that Henri IV, together with some great princes favour your project. The evil is that it is difficult to suggest it to great princes."[29]

But this finds itself only the apparent reason. Indeed, the main reason proves that, in his *Codex Juris Gentium*, Leibniz carried out a general inventory and evaluation of international relations and all agreements made under the history of the Empire. This history is, for Leibniz, the princes' concrete rights, especially those of the Holy Roman Empire's princes.[30] It amounts to more than a merely normative discourse like Saint-Pierre's project, which remains, for Leibniz, wholly cut off from concrete legal life and historical reality, from the psychological and strategic considerations of European princes.

In a small text, *Observation on the Abbé de Saint-Pierre's project for perpetual peace* written in 1715, Leibniz insists on the fact that Saint-Pierre's project has no originality. Leibniz shows clearly his position by questioning the project's originality in reference to Crucé's *Cyneas*.[31] Leibniz maintains his position against

---

28 Letter to the Abbé de Saint-Pierre (1715), in: Leibniz (1988, 176).
29 *Op. cit., idem.*
30 See Cheneval (2002, 112 f.).
31 "Everyone knows," Leibniz adds, "that Cyneas was the confidante of King Pyrrhus, who advised him to rest, (content with what he has) at once, because that would also have been his goal, as he confesses to him, if he had conquered Sicily, Calabria, Rome an Carthage." Emeric Crucé's work particularly deserves mention. He is the author of a work entitled *The New Cyneas*, *Cyneas* (1623) being the name of a collection of publications about the project for peace in Europe and around the world. *The New Cyneas* is full of stories about the Romans, Albanians, Turks and British, about priests, the rich, and thieves, about philosophers, kings and their advisers... It is a diplomatic program intended for monarchs and princes. The preface unveils this program: "It is necessary before everything else to uproot the most common vice and the one

Saint-Pierre's idea of confederation. For him, Saint-Pierre's project of perpetual peace is somehow naïve. The European political situation does not allow to see any dream of perpetual peace. The project is a utopia, the political price of which would be very high. It will lead to the loss of freedom, happiness, and justice of the citizens and each confederate member state will follow its own economic and political interests and loose sight of the common ones which can be favored only by the Empire of the German principalities the union of which is indispensable for a new equilibrium in Europe.

With his Realpolitik Leibniz thinks that Saint-Pierre's project is against the very idea of international law and international politics. In his opinion, Saint-Pierre's project of European federation transgresses the idea of international politics understood as a legitimate "struggle for power" to survive and safeguard one's sovereignty. Unless the sovereignty of other States is guaranteed, the achievement of a confederation would not only be totally irrational, but also an impossibility in a state of total disequilibrium, devastation, and desolation. In any case, it would not be the best action to be taken.

For Leibniz, the European federal state has to avoid absolutism. It must contribute to the rise of a strong nation indispensable for political equilibrium in Europe. It must be powerful enough to oppose the two potential aggressors, from the East, Louis XIV's France, and from the South, the Muslim Ottoman Empire. For that a treaty is needed between different nations of the Empire if the search for equilibrium must become a reality, a real peace depending on that equilibrium, if we don't want to confuse the *Pax Ludovica* or the French peace with that which Europe really needs.

Leibniz's position is not only similar to a Hobbesian account of security in the natural condition of man but also to the contemporary security solution adopted during the cold war in Europe. The dictate of reason in Hobbes's natural condition of man is "that every man, ought to endeavour peace, as far as he has hope of obtaining it; and when he cannot obtain it, that he may seek, and use all helps and advantages of war".[32] Leibniz is also for peace but not at any price and at any condition. It seems to him that the most rational course of action in the situation in which the German states find themselves at that time, needs war

---

which is the source of all others, namely, inhumanity". To do so, Crucé underlines, that what matters first and foremost is to enlighten minds and, secondly, because human society is "one body, of which all the members are in sympathy" with one another, to bring them closer: only then will they reach happiness—the French, Europeans, and lastly, all Christians. For this union, faith in intelligence and reason is necessary and sufficient: not only will it effectively stop the act of resorting to violence, it will smoother the instinct of war itself in humanity.

32 Hobbes (1976, 190).

to restore acceptable conditions, that means fair conditions of peace. It is also the kind of action taken during the cold war: the balance of terror. Only a good balance of terror has produced a deterrence effect on the world power. Without the Union of the states of the Holy German Empire there can be no peace, or the only peace possible would be that of the House of France. So the Saint-Pierre Project would suppress one side of the scale. And this is against the idea of Harmony. That is why it is necessary to restore, even at the price of war, the precondition of peace: political equilibrium of European political powers.

Leibniz's concept of peace is very different from that of Kant. Peace is a negative concept for Leibniz. It means the absence of war (*pax absentia belli*) and is contingent on treaties (*pactum pacis*) among states or parties and achievable only through an international legal order (*jus Gentium*) which confers its legitimacy to the just war against the infidels, non-European, especially Turks, and perhaps France (*Bellum justum*) (Rodan 2007, 124).[33]

Should the federation be absolutely realized, the unity of the Empire should be conserved as a member of the confederation.

> Since Saint-Pierre has given us two plans for Christian society, Leibniz argues, one in which the Emperor with the Empire make up one member and one in which the Empire is destroyed and in which the emperor would have a voice only as a hereditary sovereign (in Austria) and in which the elector would have each one vote, I must be for the former plan and Justice itself would prefer this plan, following the very principle of M. l'Abbé de Saint-Pierre, that the Christian society must leave things in their present state.[34]

Should the federation be inevitable, the Empire must remain as it is. Otherwise, Leibniz goes quite far in the direction of Saint-Pierre's Project, which he apparently took rather seriously as a diplomat and as a politician. As regards Saint-Pierre's proposal of a European tribunal, Leibniz observed that it possesses no guaranty. Perpetual peace between States requires a guaranty without which any agreement would prove mere words for powerful princes. He took up the European confederation's fourth article, which provides for administrative and even military sanctions against member States unwilling or unable to comply with the rules. This article in Saint-Pierre's project reads:

---

33 Concha Roldán, Pax perpetua y federacion europea. La Critica de Leibniz a Saint-Pierre, in: II (FFI2010–15914), "Filosofía de la historia y valores en la Europa del siglo XXI" (FFI2008–04279/FISO) y "Enlightenment and Global History" (ENGLOBE: Marie Curie Inicial Training Network: FP7-PEPLE-2007–1–1-ITN), 124.

34 Leibniz, *Observations sur le projet de l'Abbé de saint Pierre*, op. cit., 181.

> By the fourth shall be specified the conditions under which any Confederate who may break this Treaty shall be put to the ban of Europe and proscribed as a public enemy: namely, if he shall have refused to execute the decisions of the Grand Alliance, if he shall have made preparations for war, if he shall have made a treaty hostile to the ends of the Federation, if he shall have taken up arms to resist it or to attack any one of the confederate.[35]

Instead of planning to declare war against the State inclined to violate the federal clauses, Leibniz makes the proposal to establish a European Federal Court in Rome over which the Pope should preside and play judge between Christian princes. He pleads for resuming the old ecclesiastic authority, as well as for excommunication "making Kings and Kingdoms tremble". Similarly, he stands for a federal financial guaranty, for a European central bank, because certain nations will be powerful enough not to respect the European tribunal. Thus, to reinforce Saint-Pierre's proposal, he wrote:

> It will be necessary that all these gentlemen contribute a *caution bourgeoise* or a deposit in the bank of tribunal, a King of France, for example, hundred millions *écus* and a King of Great Britain in proportion, so that the sentence of the tribunal could be executed on their money, in case they prove refractory.[36]

The interest of the guaranty would be returned to the princes; in cases of refraction, the princes would, however, lose them.

Both contrary to Kant's later hyper-optimistic and somewhat metaphysical solution, wherein the reference to providence or nature replaces the guaranty of perpetual peace, and against Saint-Pierre's proposal of judicial sanctions without the power of enforcement against powerful member states, Leibniz suggests a highly practical and pragmatic solution two years before his death. Leibniz's suggestion is a politician's diplomatic decision, a strategic decision. Leibniz neither waits for nature's prowess to drive human beings willy-nilly to peace nor for a punitive expedition of tribunal doomed to failure in the face of powerful states. Leibniz chooses the path of efficiency: a European central bank, as the use of force or war remains uncertain in terms of time and resources. For Leibniz, a financially backed agreement comes to the best guaranty of peace.

Although Leibniz sends this letter to Saint-Pierre to show his good will to review the project, he still believes it rather unoriginal and classifies it on a long list of similar proposals. For Leibniz, it stands as one more project among many

---

35 Rousseau (2013, tome 3, 574).
36 Letter II to Grimarest: Passages concerning the Abbé de Saint-Pierre's Project of Perpetual Peace (June 1712), in: Leibniz (1988, 183 f.).

others on peace in Europe; yet it proves nothing but a romance. "But since it is permitted to write romances," he confesses in the same letter to Grimarest, "why should we find bad the fiction which would recall the age of gold for us."

6 Conclusion

A history of transcendental philosophy without Kant would be not imaginable. It is not exaggerated to say that the same holds for Leibniz concerning the philosophical foundation of the European Union. No account on the philosophical foundation of European federalism will be finished without mentioning Leibniz's philosophical endeavour. At quite different periods of his life, Leibniz seeks solutions as to how Europe's unity could be achieved through a union or a federal system. From the metaphysically grounded ideal of *Civitas Dei* to the Letter to Grimarest about Saint-Pierre's project two years before his death, Leibniz never ceases to insist on European unity in his writing. He finds in this unity the ferment for the development of the whole world and human emancipation. Peace is needed for that. And, for Leibniz, it will come from Europe. Yet still Leibniz remains a cosmopolitan philosopher. His Eurocentric attitude has to be considered as a stage on the way to a world society even if, from a normative point of view, it remains unacceptable. It is not an end in itself but just as his argument for just war one of the means to a global political order, the last stage of which will be dominated by learned societies. In this sense, a more systematic contribution will certainly be necessary to account for the many, sometimes contradictory, aspects, of Leibniz's immense legacy in political philosophy in general and especially for Europe, an Europe contributing to peace and harmony in the world.

Bibliography

Cheneval, Francis (2002): Philosophie in weltbürgerlicher Bedeutung. Über die Entstehung und die philosophischen Grundlagen des supranationalen und kosmopolitischen Denkens der Moderne, Basel.

Crucé, Emeric (1623): Le Nouveau Cynée ou Discours d'Etat: Représentant les occasions et moyens d'établir une paix générale et liberté du commerce par tout le monde, eds. (2004) Alain Fenet and Astrid Guillaume, Rennes.

Duhamel, Olivier (2003): Pour l'Europe. Le texte integral de la constitution expliqué et commenté, Paris.

Goyard-Fabre, Simone (1994): La Construction de la paix ou le travail de Sisyphe, Paris.

Goyard-Fabre, Simone (2011): L'européanisme des pionniers, in: Gary Overvold, Philippe Poirier and Lukas Sosoe (eds.): Regards croisés sur la constitution avortée de l'UE, Paris.

Hobbes, Thomas (1976): Leviathan, London.

D'Holbach, Paul Heinrich Dietrich (1966 [1770]): Le système de la nature, Hildesheim.

Holz, Hans Heinz (ed.) (1996): Sitzungsberichte der Leibniz-Sozietät, Bd. 13, Berlin.

Kaplan, J. Zenz (1995): Das Naturrecht und die Idee des ewigen Friedens, Bochum.

Leibniz, Gottfried Wilhelm (1679): Dialogue entre un habile politique et un ecclésiatique d'une piété reconnue, in: Foucher II, 520–554 (Ausgetauschter Anfang, Vorausedition zur Reihe VI, philosophischer Schriften, in: Ausgabe der Akademie der Wissenschaften der DDR, bearbeitet von der Leibniz-Forschungsstelle der Universität Münster, Manuskript ad usum collegium, Münster (1982–).

Leibniz, Gottfried Wilhelm (1840): Mémoire de Leibniz à Louis XIV, sur la conquête de l'Egypte, M. De Hoffmanns (ed.), Paris.

Leibniz, Gottfried Wilhelm (1866): Die Werke von Leibniz: Historisch-politische und staatswissenschaftliche Schriften, Hannover.

Leibniz, Gottfried Wilhelm (1670–1771): See (1923) Bedenken, welcher Gestalt securitas publica interna et externa und status praessens im Reich iezigen Umbeständen nach auf festem Fuß zu stellen, in: Paul Ritter (ed.): Gottfried Wilhelm Leibniz, Sämtliche Schriften und Briefe, Darmstadt: Preussische Akademie der Wissenschaften.

Leibniz, Gottfried Wilhelm (1969): Essais de théodicée, Brunschwig, Jacques J., Paris.

Leibniz, Gottfried Wilhelm (1988): Leibniz. Political Writings, Patrick Riley (ed.), Cambridge.

Leibniz, Gottfried Wilhelm (2004): Discours de métaphysique, édition établie, Michel Fichant (ed.), Paris.

Maier, Hans/Rausch, Heinz/Denzer, Horst (eds.) (⁵1979 [1968]): Klassiker des politischen Denkens, Vol. I. Von Plato bis Hobbes, Vol. II Von Locke bis Weber, München.

Overvold, Gary/Poirier, Philippe/Sosoe, Lukas (eds.) (2011): Regards croisés sur la constitution avortée de l'UE, Paris.

Roldán, Concha: Pax perpetua y federacion europea. La Critica de Leibniz a Saint-Pierre, in: II" (FFI2010–15914): "Filosofía de la historia y valores en la Europa del siglo XXI" (FFI2008–04279/FISO) y "Enlightenment and Global History" (ENGLOBE: Marie Curie Inicial Training Network: FP7-PEPLE-2007–1–1-ITN).

Rousseau, Jean-Jacques (2013): Projet de paix perpétuelle, Polysynodie de l'Abbé de Saint-Pierre, in: Œuvres Complètes, Paris.

Russell, Bertrand (1964): A Critical Exposition of the Philosophy of Leibniz, London.

Truyol y Serra, Antonio (1984): Die Lehre vom gerechten Krieg bei Grotius und bei Leibniz und ihre Bedeutung für die Gegenwart, in: Studia Leibniziana XVI/1, pp. 60–72.

Kant and Federalism

Robert Hanna

Radical Enlightenment: Existential Kantian Cosmopolitan Anarchism, With a Concluding Quasi-Federalist Postscript

Our age is the genuine age of **criticism**, to which everything must submit. **Religion** through its holiness, and **legislation** through its **majesty** commonly seek to exempt themselves from it. But in this way they excite a just suspicion against themselves, and cannot lay claim that unfeigned respect that reason grants only to that which has been able to withstand its free and public examination. (*CPR* A xi n.)

Enlightenment is the human being's emergence from his own self-incurred immaturity. Immaturity is the inability to make use of one's own understanding without direction from another. This immaturity is *self-incurred* when its cause lies not in lack of understanding but in lack of resolution and courage to use it without direction from another. *Sapere aude!* Have the courage to use your *own* understanding! is thus the motto of Enlightenment. (*WE*, AA 8: 35)

That kings should philosophize or philosophers become kings is not to be expected, but is also not to be wished for, since possession of power unavoidably corrupts the free judgment of reason. (*PP*, AA 8: 369)

"Is there a special group of people with the right to use threats of violence to force everyone else to obey their commands, even when their commands are wrong?" .... The modern state claims a kind of authority that obliges all other agents to obey the state's commands and entitles the state to deploy violence and threats of violence to enforce those commands, independently of whether the commands are just, reasonable, or beneficial. [T]hat sort of authority, "political authority," is an illusion. No state is legitimate, and no individual has political obligations. This leads to the conclusion that at a minimum, the vast majority of government activities are unjust. Government agents should refuse to enforce unjust laws, and individuals should feel free to break such laws whenever they can safely do so. (M. Huemer[1])

For convenience, I refer to Kant's works infratextually in parentheses. The citations include both an abbreviation of the English title and the corresponding volume and page numbers in the standard "Akademie" edition of Kant's works: *Kants gesammelte Schriften*, edited by the Königlich Preussischen (now Deutschen) Akademie der Wissenschaften (Berlin: G. Reimer [now de Gruyter], 1902–). I generally follow the standard English translations, but have occasionally modified them where appropriate. For references to the first *Critique*, I follow the common practice of giving page numbers from the A (1781) and B (1787) German editions only. See the bibliography at the end of the article for the relevant abbreviations and English translations.

1 Huemer (2013, 332–334).

1 Introduction

By *political authority* I mean:

> the existence of a special group of people (a.k.a. *government*), with the power to coerce, and the right to command other people and to coerce them to obey those commands as a duty, no matter what the content of these commands might be, and in particular, even if these commands and/or the coercion are morally impermissible.

By *coercion* I mean:

> either (i) using violence (e.g. injuring, torturing, or killing) or the threat of violence, in order to manipulate people according to certain purposes of the coercer (primary coercion), or (ii) inflicting appreciable, salient harm (e.g. imprisonment, termination of employment, large monetary penalties) or deploying the threat of appreciable, salient harm, even if these are not in themselves violent, in order to manipulate people according to certain purposes of the coercer (secondary coercion).

But whether primary or secondary, coercion should be carefully distinguished from what I will call *minimally effective defensive or preventive moral force*:

> using either the smallest sufficiently effective level of violence or threat of violence, or inflicting or deploying the smallest sufficiently effective threat of appreciable, salient harm, in order to defend against, or prevent, someone's being immorally primarily or secondarily coerced.

In any case, as I am understanding it, *the problem of political authority* is this:

> Is there an adequate rational justification for the existence of any special group of people (a.k.a. *government*) with the power to coerce, and the right to command other people and to coerce them to obey those commands as a duty, no matter what the content of these commands might be, and in particular, even if these commands and/or the coercion are morally impermissible?

Now by *the State* I mean:

> any social organization that not only claims political authority, but also actually possesses the power to coerce, in order to secure and sustain this authority.

Therefore, by *the problem of political authority* I also mean:

Is there an adequate rational justification for the existence of the State or any other State-like institution?

What then, if anything, adequately rationally justifies political authority, the State, or any other State-like institution? Is it the divine right of kings? Is it the actual social contract, as per Hobbes, Locke, Rousseau, and the enlightened despots of Europe in the eighteenth and nineteenth centuries? Is it the hypothetical social contract, as per Rawls? Is it actual democracy, or the democratic process? Is it rule consequentialism? In sharp contrast to the justificatory strategies of divine right, the actual or hypothetical social contract, actual or process-based democracy, or consequentialism, the thesis of *philosophical anarchism* says that there is no adequate rational justification for political authority, the State, or any other State-like institution; and, correspondingly, the thesis of political anarchism says that we should construct a world in which there are no States or other State-like institutions.

Ironically, although perhaps altogether understandably, in view of the very real risks of political and religious dissent and unorthodoxy in eighteenth century Europe, Kant's political theory, as formulated in the *Metaphysics of Morals*, part 1, the *Rechtslehre*, in my opinion, is sharply out of step with the central ideas of his own moral philosophy, as formulated in *Groundwork for the Metaphysics of Morals*, the *Critique of Practical Reason*, and the *Lectures on Ethics*, his own philosophy of religion, as formulated in *Religion within the Boundaries of Mere Reason* and "What Does it Mean to Orient Oneself in Thinking?," and his most famous political-anthropological essays, "Idea of a Universal History with a Cosmopolitan Aim," "Toward Perpetual Peace," and "What is Enlightenment?" The *Rechtslehre*, in my opinion, presents a fairly run-of-the-mill and explicitly anti-revolutionary, hence politically mainstream and safe, version of classical individualist liberalism, plus constitutional monarchy and/or parliamentarianism, plus—when we add to it "Idea of a Universal History with a Cosmopolitan Aim" and "Toward Perpetual Peace"—a peace-securing internationalism, in the social-contract tradition of Hobbes, Locke, Grotius, and Rousseau.

But emphatically on the contrary, I think that a highly original, politically radical, and if not revolutionary, then at least robustly State-resistant, State-subversive, and even outright civilly-disobedient *cosmopolitan, existentialist* version of *anarchism* that I call *existential Kantian cosmopolitan anarchism*, very naturally flows from Kant's moral philosophy,[2] his philosophy of religion, and his political anthropology. Roughly, the idea is that if we take Kant's famous injunction *to*

---

2 For an earlier argument for philosophical and political anarchism from Kantian ethical premises, see Wolff (1998, 3–19 [1970]).

have the courage to use your own understanding, and apply this morally courageous act not merely to "the public use of reason" (that is, to intellectual activity,
writing, and speech or self-expression in the broad sense of "free speech"), but
also to our individual choices, our individual agency, our shared social life, and
especially to what Kant quite misleadingly calls "the private use of reason" (that
is, to our social lives as functional role-players, or functionaries, within the State,
including, e. g., citizenship or public office), then the result is existential Kantian
cosmopolitan anarchism. Then and only then, in my opinion, can we understand
the last sentence of "What is Enlightenment?" as it truly ought to be understood,
namely as formulating a vision of *radical* enlightenment:[3]

> When nature has unwrapped, from under this hard shell [of the "crooked timber of human-
> ity" (*IUH*, AA 8: 23)], the seed for which she cares most tenderly, namely the propensity and
> calling to *think* freely, the latter gradually works back upon the mentality of the people
> (which thereby gradually becomes capable of *freedom* in acting) and eventually even
> upon the principles of *government*, which finds it profitable to itself to treat the human
> being, *who is now more than a machine*, in keeping with his dignity. (*WE*, AA 8: 41–42)

To be sure, neither the term 'existentialism' nor the term 'anarchism' existed until
the nineteenth and twentieth centuries. But insofar as existentialism was substantially anticipated by certain lines of thought in Pascal's seventeenth century
writings,[4] and insofar as the very idea of cosmopolitanism was already a well-es-
tablished notion in political philosophy by the time Kant came to write about it,[5]
and insofar as philosophical anarchism was substantially anticipated by certain
lines of thought in William Godwin's eighteenth century writings,[6] it seems clear
that Kant belongs to an emergent existential cosmopolitan anarchist tradition in
seventeenth and eighteenth century philosophy. In any case, insofar as it is at
once existentialist, Kantian, cosmopolitanist, and anarchist, this essay constitutes the beginnings of a project in radical *Kantian* enlightenment.[7]

---

3 In his excellent but also highly controversial *Radical Enlightenment: Philosophy and the Making of Modernity 1650–1750* (2001), and its two sequel volumes, Jonathan Israel traces the origins of the very idea of a radical enlightenment project back to Spinoza, pantheism, and metaphysical monism. I certainly agree with Israel that Spinozism is at least *one* important source of
the radical enlightenment tradition. Kant's own contribution to the controversy about Spinozism is presented in "What Does it Mean to Orient Oneself in Thinking?" (1998).
4 See, e. g., Clarke (2012, esp. section 6).
5 See, e. g., Kleingeld and Brown (2013, section 1).
6 See, e. g., Philp (2013, esp. section 3).
7 My radical Kantian enlightenment project is thus a new-&-improved version of what Samuel
Fleischacker aptly calls "the maximalist strand of Kantian enlightenment"; see his *What is En-*

2 Existential Kantian cosmopolitan anarchism defined

What, more precisely, do I mean by "existential Kantian cosmopolitan anarchism"?

1. By *existential*,[8] I mean the primitive motivational, or "internalist," normative ground of the philosophical and political doctrine I want to defend. This is the fundamental, innate need we have for a wholehearted, freely-willed life that is not essentially based on egoistic, hedonistic, or consequentialist (e. g., utilitarian) interests, that is, a life in which *self-transcendence* is possible. At the same time, however, we must also fully assume the natural presence—the facticity—of all such instrumental interests in our "human, all too human" lives. In a word, the existential ideal of a rational human wholehearted autonomous life is the ideal of non-instrumental *authenticity*, in a world of instrumental aims and needs.

2. By *Kantian*, I mean the primitive objective, or "externalist," normative ground of the philosophical and political doctrine I want to defend, which is the recognition that the fundamental, innate need we have for a wholehearted, freely-willed, non-egoistic, non-hedonistic, non-consequentialist life—which I call *the desire for self-transcendence*[9]—can be sufficiently rationally justified only in so far as it is also a life of what I call *principled authenticity*. By 'principled authenticity' I mean reasons-based wholehearted autonomy, or having a good will in Kant's sense, inherently guided by respect for the dignity of all real persons,[10] under the Categorical Imperative.

3. By *cosmopolitan*,[11] I mean that this philosophical and political doctrine recognizes States (e. g., nation-States) as actual brute past and contemporary facts; but it also requires our choosing and acting in such a way that we reject in thought, and perhaps also reject and resist in words and/or actions, any im-

---

lightenment? (2013, 7). By contrast, Fleischacker himself defends a version of "minimalist [Kantian] enlightenment," (Fleischacker 2013, 169 – 193).

8 See also, e. g., Crowell (2012). In order to address the classical "formalism," "rigorism," and "universalism" worries about Kant's ethics, I work out a broadly existential approach to Kantian ethics in Hanna (2015b).

9 See Hanna and Maiese (2009, ch. 3); and Hanna (2015a, ch. 3).

10 By "real person," I mean *an essentially embodied person*, or a rational minded animal, as opposed to either disembodied persons (e. g., souls) or collective persons (e. g., business corporations). On essential embodiment, see Hanna and Maiese (2009, esp. chs. 1 – 2). I work out a general theory of real personhood in *Deep Freedom and Real Persons*, chs. 6 – 7.

11 See also, e. g., Kleingeld and Brown (2013, esp. section 2).

moral commands, limitations, restrictions, and prejudices present in any contemporary States—especially including the one (or ones, in my case, Canada and the USA) we happen to be actual citizens or members of—and regard ourselves instead as citizens or members of a single moral world-community of real persons, The Real Realm of Ends.

It is particularly to be noted that the conjunction of 1., 2., and 3. is only accidentally consistent with, and very frequently sharply at odds with, both the general theory and also the specific practices of contemporary large-scale capitalism, especially in its globalizing manifestations.

4. Finally, by *anarchism*,[12] I mean that this philosophical and political doctrine fully recognizes that there is no adequate rational justification for political authority, and correspondingly also no adequate rational justification for the existence of States or any other State-like institutions, and that the sole adequate rational justification for the continued existence of any aspects or proper parts of actual contemporary States or other State-like institutions, is that they fully satisfy the moral requirements under 1., 2., and 3. Otherwise, resistance, subversion, or even outright civil disobedience—strictly constrained, however, by using at most minimally effective defensive or preventive moral force—is at the very least permissible, and possibly also required.

It is also particularly to be noted that the conjunction of 1. through 4. rules out the possibility that "the single moral world-community of real persons, The Real Realm of Ends," mentioned under 3., could ever permissibly take the form of either a league of States or a world-State, assuming that these also claim political authority and actually possess the power to coerce.

On the other hand, however, my idea is not the non-revolutionary Marxist idea that States and other State-like institutions will somehow wither away in the face of the gradual actualization or realization of The Real Realm of Ends, nor is it the revolutionary Marxist idea that States and State-like institutions must be destroyed in a single all-encompassing campaign of violent social change. On the contrary, my idea is instead the very different thought that existing or real-world States and other State-like institutions will be gradually detoxified and devolved by us into something less and less State-like. Or in other words, existential Kantian cosmopolitan anarchism is *devolutionary* anarchism, not *revolutionary* anarchism. As regards the use or threat of physical force, what is at most permissible for the existential Kantian cosmopolitan anarchist is minimally effective defensive or preventive moral force, *never* coercion, and *never* terrorism.

---

12 See also, e.g., Kropotkin (1910), and Bookchin (1995).

In effectively detoxifying and devolving States and other State-like institutions, we will gradually deconstruct, purge, and neutralize all their immoral political and social toxins, including, in my opinion: protected State-borders and State-boundaries; State-centralized or more locally institutionalized identity-politics and xenophobia; State-centralized or more locally institutionalized patriotism; wars of aggression or pre-emption; the military development and/or use of doomsday weaponry; police-statism and totalitarianism, including State-centralized or more locally institutionalized mechanisms of thought-control, censorship, and witch-hunting; State-driven terrorism; State-driven espionage; Constitutional idolatry, permitting such moral abominations as the private possession of firearms and other lethal weapons, capital punishment, the denial of universal healthcare, and the destruction or degradation of the environment; and above all, State-centralized or more locally institutionalized racial, religious, sexual, or age-based forms of discrimination, persecution, or—the nadir of all State-driven evil—genocide.

What would remain after such a gradual detoxification and devolution of all existing or real-world States and other State-like institutions is a living, organismic, fundamentally healthy, garden-like, world-encompassing, complex dynamic pattern of post-States. Such a global nexus of post-States would at once instantiate multiple overlapping non-coercive, non-compulsive[13] social institutions or structures for bottom-up mutual aid, care, empowerment, and support (e. g., intimate partnerships and families), and also incorporate multiple overlapping non-coercive, non-compulsive social institutions or structures for top-down communal aid, care, empowerment, and support (e. g., hospitals and universal health-care systems). Hence it would be neither a league-of-nations, nor a world-State, nor any sort of global capitalist system, whether Statist or anti-Statist. Just to give it a name, I will call this vital, world-encompassing, complex dynamic pattern of post-States *The Kosmopolis*, with a capital 'K' to distinguish it sharply from league-of-nations-oriented and/or world-State-oriented conceptions of cosmopolitanism, and also from global capitalist conceptions of cosmo-

---

13 By *non-compulsive* I mean "that which avoids, or constitutes the opposite of, the malign psychological effects of living within and under the control of States and other State-like institutions." The Existentialist analysis of *inauthenticity*, and the Marxist analysis of *alienation*, can then be brought under the general critical analysis of the *compulsiveness* of States and State-like institutions. The fact of the compulsiveness of States and other State-like institutions also verifies, in the special case of those who directly belong to governments, or are officers of governments, or are administrators or officers of other State-like institutions, the truth of Kant's observation that "possession of power unavoidably corrupts the free judgment of reason" (*PP*, AA 8: 369).

politanism—and, equally importantly, to remind us of the ancient Greek term *Kosmos* and 'Kantian' alike.

3 Existential Kantian cosmopolitan anarchism further explicated

Let me now spell out the basic ideas of existential Kantian cosmopolitan anarchism again somewhat more fully.

According to existential Kantian ethics,[14] the highest or supreme good is a *good will* in Kant's sense (*GMM*, AA 4: 393; *CPrR*, AA 5: 110). And a good will in Kant's sense is the self-consciously experienced realization, at least partially and to some degree, of our innate capacity for autonomy, i.e., our innate capacity for free moral self-legislation, insofar as it is also inherently combined with an innate capacity for wholeheartedness, in this fully natural and thoroughly nonideal actual world. Otherwise put, self-consciously-experienced-autonomy-with-wholeheartedness-in-this-fully-natural-and-thoroughly-nonideal-actual-world is nothing more and nothing less than a rational human minded animal or real human person who is choosing and acting freely, on principle, hence according to reasons, and with a passionate and yet Stoic commitment, for the sake of the Categorical Imperative, "the moral law." The self-conscious experience of our own at-least-partially-realized capacity for autonomy carries with it a deep happiness, or "self-fulfillment" (*Selbstzufriedenheit*) (*CPrR*, AA 5: 117), aptly characterized by Kant—who clearly has the Stoic notion of *ataraxia* in mind—as a "negative satisfaction in one's own existence." This, in turn, strongly anticipates what the Existentialists later called *authenticity*. It consists, in the ideal case, of the self-conscious experience of the perfect coherence and self-sufficiency of all one's own desires, beliefs, cognitions, inferences, intentions, motivating reasons, and choices in the act of autonomous willing. To choose and act in this way to any extent is, to that extent, to have thereby achieved principled authenticity—i.e., principled wholehearted autonomy, or a "good will" in Kant's sense—at least partially and to some degree. Or otherwise put, to choose and act in this way is to have reached or exceeded the highest possible bar, standard, or ideal of rational normativity for rational human minded animals, and indeed for any other actual or possible creatures essentially like us, whether or not they are human.

---

14 See Hanna (2015b).

This fundamental axiological thesis about the good will can be directly compared and contrasted with that of *ethical egoism*, which says that the highest good is individual self-interest (whether this self-interest is specifically narcissistic/self-loving, selfish/self-inflating, or hedonistic/pleasure-seeking, or not), and also with that of *act consequentialism*, which says that the highest good is choosing and acting with good results. Now ethical egoism (including but not restricted to hedonism) and act consequentialism can both be consistently combined with classical *eudaimonism*, which says that the highest good is human happiness—whether fundamentally self-interested and therefore individual shallow happiness for the ethical egoist, or, for the act consequentialist, good results that increase overall shallow happiness for as many people or other shallow-happiness-capable creatures as possible. Deep happiness, however, is not only irrelevant to ethical egoism (including hedonism) and act consequentialism, but even inimical to them, since the achievement or pursuit of deep happiness generally runs contrary to the achievement or pursuit of shallow happiness. Or in other words, and more plainly put, if you are trying with all your heart to be a principled authentic person, you frequently miss the boat on what would generally be regarded as "common sense" and "prudence." So existential Kantian ethics is sharply distinct from ethical egoism, hedonism, act consequentialism, and classical eudaimonism alike.

Now real persons exist in the fully natural and thoroughly nonideal actual world, alongside non-living material things, forces, and processes, other living organisms, and non-rational minded animals; and various sorts of structured intersubjective and social relationships between real persons also exist in this world. But it is what Gilbert Ryle aptly called a *category mistake* to infer from the existence of real persons and structured, intersubjective, mutual and communal social relationships between them, to the thesis that The State-in-itself, i. e., the supposed Really Real ground of human social existence and political authority, either exists or does not exist, or has a knowable essence or nature of some sort.

More precisely, The State-in-itself, the supposed Really Real ground and source of human social existence and political authority, with the power and the right to command and to coerce people to obey its commands as a duty, even if these commands and/or the coercion are impermissible according to basic existential Kantian moral principles, is nothing but a noumenal or transcendental abstraction in the Kantian sense, a mere "thought-entity" or *Verstandeswesen*. So too the God of Divine Command Ethics, the supposed Really Real ground of worldly, creaturely existence and morality, namely a super-human entity with the power and the right to command and to coerce people to obey its commands as a duty, even if these commands and/or the coercion are impermissible according to basic existential Kantian moral principles, is a mere *Verstan-deswesen*. If Kant's radical agnosticism about things-in-themselves or noumena is correct, then it follows that the existence or non-existence of The State-in-it-self, just like God the Divine Commander, is knowably unknowable, and its na-ture, were it to exist, is also knowably unknowable.

Now the non-existence of the mythical State-in-itself is the mythical Hobbe-sian "state of nature," and it is just as philosophically fallacious to think that if God were to fail to exist (the dark night of atheism), then everything would be permitted in a moral sense (the chaos of nihilism), as it is to think that if the State-in-itself were to fail to exist (the dark night of the Hobbesian state of na-ture), then everything would be permitted in a political sense (the chaos of "the war of all against all"). Correspondingly, it is just as philosophically falla-cious to use the mythical bogeyman of "the war of all against all" as a sufficient reason for believing in the necessity of a State-in-itself, as it is to use the myth-ical bogeyman of nihilism as a sufficient reason for believing in the necessity of God's existence. Theism is to Statism, as atheism is to the belief in a Hobbesian state of nature lurking behind the paper-thin façade of civil society. All are equal-ly rationally unsupported and illusory.

Therefore, since there is no knowable Really Real ground or source of human social existence and political authority, or of States, then there is no such thing as a sufficient rational justification of either political authority or States. Or as Michael Huemer crisply puts it, "that sort of authority, 'political au-thority', is an illusion."—Not merely a psychological illusion, however, but more fundamentally a philosophical illusion, and even more specifically, a noumenal or transcendental illusion.

That is one Kantian argument for philosophical anarchism. Later, in section 4, I will present another Kantian argument for philosophical anarchism, this time specifically from Kantian ethics, that I call *the core Kantian argument for philosophical anarchism*.

In any case, according to existential Kantian cosmopolitan anarchism, The Realm of Ends is the total ideal moral community of rational minded animals or real persons, each of whom respects one another and themselves as creatures with dignity (absolute objective intrinsic non-denumerable moral value), and also considers all the others and themselves equally in relation to the Categorical Imperative/moral law, and, finally, each possesses a good will. The good will, as I have said, is the highest or supreme good. The sole and complete good, i.e., the best life for any rational human minded animal or real human person, is a life of deep individual happiness, and also deep communal or social happiness, that is intrinsically controlled and structured by a good will in the Kantian sense. Now The Realm of Ends and the sole and complete good are only regulative ideals, never real-world facts. What I call, by sharp contrast, The *Real* Realm of Ends is what is really possible for us in this fully natural and thoroughly nonideal actual world. Otherwise put, The Real Realm of Ends is the "human, all too human" actualization or realization of The Realm of Ends, to whatever degree or extent this is really possible, by means of our wholehearted autonomous constructive activity.

So every time an agent truly chooses or acts for the sake of the Categorical Imperative/moral law, she thereby actualizes or realizes moral worth, and she thereby experiences autonomous self-fulfillment, at least partially or to some degree. But if she also thereby achieves some individual deep happiness and also some communal or social deep happiness, then she also realizes a proper part of the sole and complete good, and partially actualizes or realizes The Realm of Ends in this "human, all too human" world, at least partially or to some degree. Given "the crooked timber of humanity" in this thoroughly nonideal world—which is a timber that "can never be made straight" (*IUH*, AA 8: 23) and which is a world in which, it seems, as they say, no good deed ever goes unpunished—then the sole and complete good is not humanly possible to any degree or any extent unless

(i) we satisfy the moral constraints of what I call *existential Kantian moral theology*,[15] and unless

(ii) we recognize that proofs of The State-in-itself's existence or non-existence (the Hobbesian state-of-nature), and knowledge of The State-in-itself's nature as a supposed Really Real ground of human social existence and source of political authority, and therefore any rational justification of its political authority, are all knowably unknowable (Kant's radical agnosticism), and unless

(iii) we prove ourselves to be morally worthy of happiness, by collectively constructing/realizing The Real Realm of Ends on this earth and in this fully natural and thoroughly nonideal world, in the form of a world-wide vital dynamic pattern of post-states, The Kosmopolis, as if we were already liberated from the morally impermissible and rationally unjustifiable commands, limitations, prejudices, and restrictions of actual States and other State-like institutions (existential Kantian cosmopolitan anarchism), hence

---

15 See Hanna (2014, 26–69).

(iv) it is at the very least always permissible, and, other things being equal, sometimes also obligatory, that we refuse to accept, and are also prepared to resist, subvert, or even overtly civilly disobey—using, however, at most minimally effective defensive or preventive moral force—any actual State or State-like institution, precisely insofar as it is not morally consistent and coherent with collectively constructing The Real Realm of Ends on this earth and in this fully natural and thoroughly nonideal actual world, as The Kosmopolis ("the arts of resistance"[16]).

Now as I see it, the four classical problems with anarchism are

(i) its lack of well-worked-out ethical foundations,

(ii) its tendency to collapse into destructive ludic mayhem,[17] revolutionism, and terrorism,

(iii) how it handles the all-important issue of the use of physical force and threats of physical force within an anarchist social framework, and

(iv) its lack of a workable theory of how, once anarchism has been widely accepted, "to make the trains run on time": that is, the lack of any workable theory of how to sustain all the morally good things in our actual-world political and social existence, while also expunging all the morally reprehensible things in actual-world States and other State-like institutions.

But, at least prospectively, existential Kantian cosmpolitan anarchism clearly responds adequately and effectively to problems (i) to (iv).

First, existential Kantian cosmopolitan anarchism is committed to the basic principles of Kantian ethics and to moral realism about those principles: according to the existential Kantian cosmopolitan anarchist, such principles really do objectively exist, and they are humanly knowable by means of rational intuition.[18]

---

16 See, e.g., Scott (1990) and Scott (2009).

17 But I also think there's nothing wrong with a certain measured amount of *constructive, morally-constrained, non-violent* ludic mayhem, if it's properly aimed at exposing, resisting, or subverting the moral evils of actual-world nation-states or other coercive and compulsive social institutions. See, e.g., Vigo's 1933 film, *Zéro de Conduite*; Simonsson's and Nilsson's 2010 film, *Sound of Noise*; and Scott (2012) *Two Cheers for Anarchism*.

18 See Hanna (2015b, esp. chs. 1–2). Huemer's *Problem of Political Authority* (2013), by contrast, appeals only to common-sense moral intuitions, and remains officially neutral about moral realism and ethical intuitionism. But in fact, Huemer is elsewhere committed to moral realism and ethical intuitionism; see Huemer (2008). For my alternative view about the nature of intuitions, *Kantian Intuitionism*, see Hanna (2015, chs. 6–8).

Second, according to existential Kantian cosmopolitan anarchism, destructive ludic mayhem, revolutionism, and terrorism are all strictly inconsistent with respecting the dignity of real persons, and with choosing and acting for the sake of the Categorical Imperative. Thus destructive ludic mayhem, revolutionism, and terrorism are all strictly morally impermissible.

Third, according to existential Kantian cosmopolitan anarchism, the use of physical force or the threat of physical force within an anarchist social framework is morally permissible *only* for the purposes of

(i) minimally effective defense against or prevention of, primary coercion directed against oneself, especially life-threatening primary coercion,

(ii) minimally effectively protecting others, especially innocent and weak others, from primary coercion, especially life-threatening primary coercion, and

(iii) minimally effective defense against or prevention of direct violations of rational human dignity.

In other words, as I mentioned in section **2**, where the use or threat of physical force is concerned, only minimally effective defensive or preventive moral force is permissible for existential Kantian cosmopolitan anarchists, never coercion, and never terrorism.[19]

Fourth, existential Kantian cosmopolitan anarchism's "detoxification" and "devolution" model of the deconstruction of actual-world nation-states and other state-like institutions—whereby all and only the morally good-making, environmentally-sound, non-coercive, non-compulsive bottom-up and top-down social institutions or structures are all left in place, and all and only the morally, physically, and psychologically toxic features of actual States and State-like institutions are purged and/or phased-out—also clearly and effectively responds to problem (iv).

Within the scope of "morally good-making, environmentally-sound, non-coercive, non-compulsive bottom-up and top-down social institutions or structures" I mean to include, e. g., flourishing families and intimate adult partnerships of all kinds[20]; hospitals and universal healthcare; schools and colleges; humanistic and scientific communities of free inquiry, which I call *post-universities*; fine arts and everyday arts, and crafts; private and public entertainment;

---

19 See also Hanna (2015b, chs. 3 – 5), for the moral foundations of this constraint.
20 I mean: heterosexual or non-heterosexual—including lesbian, gay, bisexual, transgendered, or whatever; and monogamous or polyamorous.

sports and games; small-scale, eco-sensitive agriculture, public forestry, and public park-cultivation; small-scale capitalism with universal social security; and trains that run on time. As such, existential Kantian cosmopolitan anarchism is neither anarcho-*capitalist*, insofar as unconstrained large-scale capitalism is immoral, nor anarcho-*socialist*, insofar as authoritarian and/or totalitarian socialism is also immoral. At the same time, however, existential Kantian cosmopolitan anarchism is perfectly compatible with any and all morally permissible forms of petit bourgeois capitalism and social welfare.

In any case, it should therefore be obvious by now that the version of political anarchism that I am proposing is thoroughly devolutionary and constructive (moral-community-growing) and not revolutionary, terrorist, or destructive (bomb-throwing). That the version of political anarchism that I am proposing is deep, and not shallow or lifestyle (radical chic). And that the version of political anarchism that I am proposing is realistic, and not excessively idealistic or utopian (cloud cuckoo-land). Indeed, political anarchism as I am understanding it is the permanent necessary social condition of achieving principled authenticity and constructing the real-world moral community of The Real Realm of Ends on earth, via our detoxifying and devolutionary construction of the Kosmopolis. And thereby, in effect, we prune back and weed out real-world States and other State-like institutions, until finally they are nothing but mulch for the world-wide growth of morally good-making, environmentally-sound, non-coercive, non-compulsive bottom-up and top-down social institutions or structures. In this way, we endlessly create and cultivate the post-state, fundamentally healthy, world-wide garden of our deepest individual and collective rational human aspirations. This is not the pre-lapsarian, mythical, paradisal, Adam-and-Eve-privately-owned garden of Eden, however: instead, it is nothing more and nothing less than the post-lapsarian, real-world, mixed-use, communal garden of home-planet earth.

Bounded in a nutshell, then, here are the five simplified imperatives of this devolutionary, constructive, deep, realistic, existential Kantian cosmopolitan anarchism:

1. *Think for yourself.*

2. *Criticize political and institutional authority.*

3. *Recognize and reject political and institutional bullshit.*[21]

---

21 Of course, I mean "bullshit" in the strictly philosophical sense of that term. See, e. g., Frankfurt (1988).

4. Treat everyone else with at least minimal moral respect, but never allow yourself to be tyrannized by the majority.

5. Take responsibility for constructing The Real Realm of Ends on earth.

4 The core Kantian argument for philosophical anarchism, and beyond

As I mentioned in section 1, by *political authority* I mean:

> the existence of a special group of people (a.k.a. *government*), with the power to coerce, and the right to command other people and to coerce them to obey those commands as a duty, no matter what the content of these commands might be, and in particular, even if these commands and/or the coercion are morally impermissible.

And again, by *coercion* I mean:

> either (i) using violence (e.g. injuring, torturing, or killing) or the threat of violence, in order to manipulate people according to certain purposes of the coercer (primary coercion), or (ii) inflicting appreciable, salient harm (e.g. imprisonment, termination of employment, large monetary penalties) or deploying the threat of appreciable, salient harm, even if these are not in themselves violent, in order to manipulate people according to certain purposes of the coercer (secondary coercion).

Therefore, again, as I am understanding it, *the problem of political authority* is this:

> Is there an adequate rational justification for the existence of any special group of people (a.k.a. *government*) with the power to coerce, and the right to command other people and to coerce them to obey those commands as a duty, no matter what the content of these commands might be, and in particular, even if these commands and/or the coercion are morally impermissible?

And again, by *the State* I mean:

> any social organization that not only claims political authority, but also actually possesses the power to coerce, in order to secure and sustain this authority.

Therefore, as before, by *the problem of political authority* I also mean:

Is there an adequate rational justification for the existence of the State or any other State-like institution?

This problem applies directly to *all* kinds of political authority, States, and State-like institutions, from pharaohs, kings, and popes, to constitutional monarchies, communist States, capitalist liberal democracies, provincial or city governments, military organizations, business corporations, and universities—basically, any institution with its own army or police-force. But of course the problem is not just philosophical, it is all too horribly real. Since the nineteenth century, States, especially nation-States, and other State-like institutions have explicitly claimed to possess political authority, and then have proceeded to use the power to coerce, especially the power of primary coercion, frequently of the most awful, cruel, and monstrous kinds, thereby repressing, detaining, imprisoning, enslaving, torturing, starving, maiming, or killing literally hundreds of millions of people, in order to secure their acceptance of these authoritarian claims. Even allowing for all the other moral and natural evils that afflict humankind, it seems very likely that there has never been a single greater cause of evil, misery, suffering, and death in the history of the world than the coercive force of States and other State-like institutions.

As I also noted in section 1, the thesis of philosophical anarchism says that there is no adequate rational justification for political authority, States, or any other State-like institutions, and the thesis of political anarchism says that we should construct a world in which there are no States or other State-like institutions. On the one hand, it is rationally coherent and permissible to defend philosophical anarchism without also defending political anarchism. But on the other hand, it is hard to see how one could rationally justify political anarchism except by way of philosophical anarchism. So philosophical anarchism is the rational key to anarchism more generally, although of course political anarchism is ultimately where all the real-world action is.

Although I want to defend both philosophical anarchism and also political anarchism, from an existential Kantian cosmopolitan point of view, this is not the place to take on the strenuous task of fully justifying political anarchism. Instead, here is what I take to be a self-evidently sound five-step argument for philosophical anarchism, the core Kantian argument for philosophical anarchism:

(1) We adopt, as basic moral principles, by means of which we can judge the permissibility or impermissibility of any human choice, action, practical policy, or other practical principle, the set of basic Kantian moral principles.

(2) Precisely insofar as it is morally impermissible for ordinary individual real persons or groups of real persons to command other people and coerce them to obey those commands as a duty, then by the same token, it must also be morally impermissible for special groups of people inside States or other State-like institutions, i.e., *governments*, to command other people and coerce them to obey those commands as a duty.

(3) Therefore, precisely insofar as it is morally impermissible for ordinary individual real persons or groups of ordinary real persons to command other people and coerce them to obey those commands as a duty, even if governments have the power to command other people and coerce them to obey those commands, nevertheless governments do not have the right to command other people and coerce them to obey those commands as a duty.

(4) But all governments claim political authority in precisely this sense.

(5) Therefore, there is no adequate rational justification for political authority, States, or other State-like institutions, and philosophical anarchism is true.

Or in other and fewer words, because there is no adequate rational justification, according to the set of basic Kantian moral principles, for an ordinary individual real person's, or any group of ordinary real persons', immorally commanding other people and coercing them to obey those commands as a duty, yet the very idea of political authority entails that special groups of people within States or State-like institutions, namely governments, have not only the power to coerce, but also the right to command other people and to coerce them to obey those commands as a duty, even when the commands and/or coercion are immoral, then it follows that there is no adequate rational justification for political authority, States, or any other State-like institutions—therefore, philosophical anarchism is true. Or in still other and even fewer words: human governments have no moral right to do to other people what ordinary real human persons have no moral right to do to other people, according to the set of basic Kantian moral principles; yet all human governments falsely claim this supposed moral right; hence philosophical anarchism is true. **QED**

A very striking feature of the core Kantian argument for philosophical anarchism is that it has exactly the same form as what I will call *the core Kantian argument against Divine Command Ethics*, with appropriate substitutions made in boldface:

Because there is no adequate rational justification, according to the set of basic Kantian moral principles, for an ordinary individual real person's, or any group of ordinary real persons', immorally commanding other people and coercing them to obey those commands as a duty, yet the very idea of **Divine Command Ethics** entails that **an all-powerful, all-knowing, and all-good being, namely God, has not only the supreme power to cause people to do things,** but also the right to command other people and to **cause** them to obey those commands as a duty, even when the commands and/or **causing** are immoral **by rational human standards**, then it follows that there is no adequate rational justification for **Divine Command Ethics**—therefore, **the denial of Divine Command Ethics** is true. Or in still other and even fewer words, **divine beings** have no moral right to do to people what ordinary real human persons have no moral right to do to other people, according to the set of basic Kantian moral principles; yet all versions of **Divine Command Ethics** falsely claim this supposed moral right; hence **the denial of Divine Command Ethics** is true. **QED**

By the immediately preceding argument, the falsity of Divine Command Ethics is rationally obvious. Reduced to its essentials, Divine Command Ethics fallaciously says that God's commands are good and right, just because God says that they are good and right, and also has the power to impose these commands on people, no matter what the moral content of these commands might be. Now Statism fallaciously says that a government's commands are good and right, just because governments say that they are good and right, and also have the power to impose these commands on people, no matter what the moral content of these commands might be. Hence *God* plays exactly the same functional and logical role in Divine Command Ethics as *governments* do in Statism. Therefore the truth of philosophical anarchism is as rationally obvious as the falsity of Divine Command Ethics.

If only it were so simple! Another fundamental task for the existential Kantian cosmopolitan philosophical anarchist is to explain how, paradoxically, there is almost universal belief in the political authority of governments, States, and other State-like institutions, even in the face of (what I take to be) the rationally self-evident soundness of the core Kantian argument for philosophical anarchism.

One possible explanation for the almost universal failure to recognize the truth of philosophical anarchism is that most people, including most political philosophers, are subject to a complex and powerful psychological illusion—the illusion of political authority—that interferes with and undermines the proper employment of their rational capacities, and thus makes it extremely difficult for them to recognize what is otherwise rationally self-evident. And I do think that this is indeed the case. One everyday example of this complex and powerful psychological illusion is the more or less spine-chilling spectatorial horror we feel when we watch post-apocalyptic movies, directed to the mythic Hobbesian "war of all against all" (often reminiscent of Hollywood depictions of the Wild West, only even more chaotic and gory) that is depicted as following from the breakdown of State-order, yet often (except when this is specifically a part of the movie's content) feel no disgust or horror whatsoever about the horrendous State-system that must have led to the fictional apocalypse.

But I also think that there is a deeper Kantian explanation, namely, that most people, especially including most political philosophers, are subject to a complex and powerful philosophical illusion—the noumenal or transcendental illusion of The State-in-itself and its equally illusory dialectical contrary, the Hobbesian state-of-nature—that makes it extremely difficult for them to see the self-evident truth of philosophical anarchism.

Here, then, is where Kant's radical agnosticism can be smoothly extended and added to the five-step core Kantian argument for philosophical anarchism, as follows:

(6) Nevertheless, there is almost universal belief in the political authority of governments, States, and other State-like institutions.

(7) Part of the explanation for the almost universal failure to recognize that there is no adequate rational justification for political authority is that most people, including most political philosophers, are subject to a complex and powerful psychological illusion—the illusion of political authority—that makes it extremely difficult for them to recognize the self-evident truth of philosophical anarchism.

(8) The psychological illusion of political authority can, to a significant extent, be dismantled by a careful critical diagnosis of its basic elements,[22] together with a bracing regimen of what Scott very aptly calls "anarchist calisthenics,"[23] i.e., frequent rehearsals, under non-dangerous physical and social conditions, of the art of avoiding and undermining mindless, pointless obedience to the commands of States or other State-like institutions.

---

22 See, e.g., Huemer (2013, ch. 6).
23 Scott (2012).

(9) But the deeper Kantian explanation is that most people, including most political philosophers, are subject to the philosophical, and more specifically noumenal and transcendental illusion that it is possible to know the existence or non-existence and nature of The State-in-itself, the supposed ultimate ground or source of the right to command people and to coerce them to accept its commands as a duty, even if these commands and/or the coercion are impermissible according to basic Kantian moral principles.

(10) Kant's radical agnosticism undermines this philosophical illusion, and makes it possible to see the rationally self-evident truth of philosophical anarchism.

This argument-strategy, in turn, has a special advantage over other existing arguments for philosophical anarchism that proceed by, **first**, enumerating, criticizing, and rejecting a finite number of candidates (say, divine right of kings, social contract theory, democracy, and rule consequentialism) for providing sufficient rational justification for political authority, then, **second**, critically attacking the psychological illusion of political authority, and then, **third**, concluding that philosophical anarchism is true.[24] Such an argument-by-cases cannot, in principle, rule out the possibility that there is some *other* candidate, as yet unexamined, that will provide sufficient rational justification for political authority. So, apparently, there is always room for a reasonable doubt that political authority *cannot* be sufficiently rationally justified, and correspondingly room for a reasonable hope that political authority *can* be justified: hence the argument for philosophical anarchism falls short of decisive proof.

This critical reply to the argument-by-cases for philosophical anarchism is importantly analogous to *theodicy*-based replies to arguments for atheism from the existence of natural and moral evil. Suppose that one has enumerated, criticized, and then rejected a finite number of candidates for providing sufficient rational justification for the compatibility of evil and theism, and then concludes that atheism is true. Nevertheless, says the theodicy-based reply, this argument-by-cases cannot, in principle, rule out the possibility that there is some *other* candidate, as yet unexamined, that will provide sufficient rational justification for the existence of natural and moral evil in a world created and governed by an all-powerful (omnipotent), all-knowing (ominiscient), and all-good (omnibenevolent) God. So, apparently, there is always room for a reasonable doubt that the compatibility of evil and a "3-O" God *cannot* be sufficiently rationally justified, and correspondingly room for a reasonable hope that the compatibility

---

24 This is the argument-strategy of, e. g., Huemer (2013).

of evil and a 3-O God *can* be justified: hence the argument for atheism falls short of decisive proof.

In view of this important analogy, let us call this objection to the argument-by-cases for philosophical anarchism, *the Statist-theodicy objection*.

But if, as Kant's radical agnosticism shows, just as it is impossible to know the existence or non-existence and nature of a 3-O God, so too it is impossible to know the existence or non-existence and nature of The State-in-itself, the supposed ultimate ground or source of the right of a government to command and to coerce people to accept its commands as a duty, even if these commands and/or the coercion are impermissible according to basic Kantian moral principles. Then unless the philosophical defender of political authority can actually specify *another* minimally plausible candidate for providing a rational justification for it, there is no reason whatsoever to believe in the possibility of there being such a thing. So the Statist-theodicy objection fails, and there is decisive proof for philosophical anarchism.

It is perhaps needless to say that the radical Kantian enlightenment project which emerges from the philosophical, moral, and political convergence of Kant, Kierkegaard,[25] and Kropotkin[26] that I have spelled out so far in this essay might come as somewhat of a surprise to you. But it gets even worse. Not only do I believe-*that* existential Kantian cosmopolitan anarchism is true, I also believe-*in* it.[27] And now generalizing my cognitive and emotional situation to any other actual or possible defender of existential Kantian cosmopolitan anarchism, this leads to another problem for the ethical anarchist.

5 The plight of the ethical anarchist in a world of States

In *Religion within the Boundaries of Mere Reason*, Kant distinguishes between

(i) an "ethical-civil community," under non-coercive laws of virtue, guaranteeing the possibility of autonomy (i.e., moral laws), and

---

25 See, e.g., Kierkegaard (2000).
26 See, e.g., Kropotkin (1972).
27 For more on the distinction between believing-that and believing-in, see Hanna (2014).

(ii) a "juridico-civil community," under coercive political laws, guaranteeing at most the possibility of external freedom, i.e., mere freedom of action (as opposed to deep freedom of the will), i.e., a kind of freedom that is consistent with our also being nothing but psychological turnspits or wind-up toys. (*Rel*, AA 6:94–95)

The ethical-civil community is of course the same as The Realm of Ends, in real time and space, hence it is the same as The Real Realm of Ends, and the juridico-civil community is of course the same as the State or any other State-like institution.

According to Kant, the ethical-civil community has a "form and constitution essentially distinct from those of the [juridico-civil community]" (*Rel*, AA 6:94).

Nevertheless, supposedly, "without the foundation of a political community, [the ethical-civil community] could never be brought into existence by human beings" (*Rel*, AA 6:94).

Moreover, even though the members of an ethical-civil community must "freely commit themselves to enter into this state, [and] not allow the political power to command over them how to order (or not order) such a constitution internally," still "nothing [can] be included which contradicts the duty of its members as *citizens of the state*—even though, if the ethical bond is of the genuine sort, this condition need not cause anxiety" (*Rel*, AA 6:96).

"Need not cause anxiety"! What Kant is saying here, on the face of it, is utterly incoherent. If the ethical-civil community has an essentially different form and constitution from that of the juridico-civil community, then no coercive laws or commands of the political state can be allowed to control personal and social life in the ethical-civil community. Hence the existence of a juridico-civil community, precisely to the extent that its coercive laws and commands are in force, is in direct opposition to the existence of an ethical-civil community, and cannot possibly be required as a necessary condition of the founding of an ethical-civil community.

Indeed, given the continued existence of a juridico-civil or political community (i.e., the State), the existence of an ethical-civil community (i.e., The Real Realm of Ends) becomes morally impossible. This is because the political community requires its citizens to obey its coercive laws and commands, even when these are rationally unjustified and immoral. Hence to the extent that this obedience occurs, the citizens of the political state must think and act like robots or wind-up toys, and impose upon themselves a self-stultifying rational immaturity and inauthenticity, contrary to their own project of enlightenment and autonomous freedom. At least in the Hobbesian state of nature, the individual thinks and acts for himself, even if egoistically and wickedly. So at least he is still alive-and-kicking, thinking, and transcendentally free. But in the political community, he turns off his ability to think or act for himself, and becomes a drone or puppet of the State, thereby making his enlightenment and achievement of moral autonomy morally impossible.

Therefore, a necessary condition of the real possibility of the creation of an ethical community is that its members must *reject* the juridico-civil community, and *exit* such a community just as, according to Kant, in order to enter the juridico-civil community, the person must reject the Hobbesian state of nature, and exit the Hobbesian state of nature. Kant himself even describes the existence of the juridico-civil community as an "ethical state of nature," which must be rejected and exited in order to enter the ethical-civil community, because the "the ethical state of nature [is] a public feuding between the principles of virtue and a state of inner immorality which the natural human being ought to endeavor to leave behind as soon as possible" (*Rel*, AA 6:97). Or as he puts it most explicitly, in capital letters, in the title of part III, division one, section II of the *Religion*:

THE HUMAN BEING OUGHT TO LEAVE THE ETHICAL STATE OF NATURE IN ORDER TO BECOME A MEMBER OF AN ETHICAL COMMUNITY. (*Rel*, AA 6:96)

In other words, what Kant's view clearly implicitly entails is *ethical anarchism*, e.g., existential Kantian cosmopolitan anarchism, although at the same time he officially and explicitly endorses Statism.

Now either Kant is simply being philosophically insincere or even philosophically mendacious, or else he really is deeply psychologically conflicted and confused on this fundamental point.

The charitable interpretation is the latter, and I am prepared to hold that it is really possible that Kant's commitment to the Hobbesian myth of the state of nature as the war of all against all, and correspondingly his commitment to the belief that this war of all against all is the necessary result of any human community that fails to enter into a juridico-civil condition, and become a State, is so psychologically powerful that he cannot self-consciously accept the valid consequence of his own argument, i.e., ethical anarchism. And then he simply flips back into Statism in order to avoid facing up to the cognitive and emotional dissonance between his fear-driven explicit commitment to Statism on the one hand, and his rational implicit commitment to ethical anarchism on the other.

In any case, the true upshot of Kant's theory of the ethical-civil community (i.e., of The Real Realm of Ends) in relation to the juridico-civil community (i.e., to the State), when taken together with his theories of enlightenment and autonomous freedom, is ethical anarchism, e.g., existential Kantian cosmopolitan anarchism, whether or not he was psychologically capable of facing up to this, and whether or not he was personally brave enough to face up to it explicitly in print.

And of course, to be fair, had Kant actually published this ethical anarchist result, or had refused to knuckle under to censorship, he would have been publicly excoriated, summarily dismissed from his professorship, and jailed, or worse. After all, as it was, in 1794 he had already been required not to teach or publish anything else pertaining to religion, under pain of scandal, dismissal, jail, or worse.[28] This fact, in turn, should be placed alongside the further fact that Kant's radical agnosticism about religion is only (and perhaps even less than) half of the complete story about his philosophical radicalism.

So perhaps the less charitable interpretation is not so very implausible or unfriendly to Kant. After all, how many of us are courageous enough to *say or write* explicitly what we really think about States and other State-like institutions, and face scandal, dismissal from our jobs, jail, or worse, far less *acting upon* what we really think, say, or write? Moreover, it is absolutely true that in the *Religion*, at least, Kant comes *that* close to defending ethical anarchism explicitly; and it is equally absolutely true that ethical anarchism certainly is there, philosophically living and operating just under the surface of many of his published texts, for anyone who is willing to follow Kant's argument right through to the end and to liberate herself intellectually and emotionally from its Statist surface rhetoric.

Quite apart from the self-conflicted state of Kant's own writings on this fundamental point, however, the deeper problem is this:

> If the Hobbesian conception of the state of nature is a myth, then there is no necessity either to enter into, or to remain within, the juridico-civil community. Indeed, since life in the juridico-civil community is inherently inimical to the existence of the ethical-civil community, then it is morally necessary for us both to reject the juridico-civil community and also to exit it in order to pursue the enlightenment project and to live for the sake of autonomy and respect for the dignity of persons and the moral law. But how can the ethical anarchist ever actually survive either (i) inside the State, while still actively rejecting it, or (ii) outside the State, having actively rejected it and exited it?

Let us call this problem *the plight of the ethical anarchist in a world of States.*

I do not pretend to have an adequate solution to this problem, but rather only a few follow-up thoughts about possible partial solutions.

---

28 See, e.g., Wood (1998), and di Giovanni, (1998, pp. xi–xxiv and 41–54 respectively, esp. pp. xv-xxii and 41–50).

One possible route under option (i) is that the ethical anarchist publicly stands up for what he believes, and then accepts the consequences: scandal, dismissal from his job, jail, or worse. But this practically guarantees that he will not survive. The most he could hope for is posthumous vindication.

Another possible route under option (i) is to engage in covert resistance, combined with superficial compliance, utilizing the "weapons of the weak." But this means living a double life, and constantly experiencing the fear of being "outed."

What about option (ii)? In one sense, since virtually every part of the Earth is controlled by some State or another, then moving to a place beyond States is practically impossible. One cannot go anywhere, or remain anywhere, without a passport, proof of citizenship, or a visa, and a social security number, etc.

One can leave the State in which he is currently living, move to another one, or to a series of other States, and live there in exile, having opted out of various coercive laws of that first State. But of course, even if the particular State to which one has moved is a better and less coercively immoral one in certain respects or even overall, nevertheless one is still inside a State. And what about family and loved ones, who live in the first State?

In effect, I have reached the conclusion that the plight of the ethical anarchist in a world of States is hopeless. But perhaps there is still *some* ground for hope, which I will briefly explore in the next and last section.

6 Concluding quasi-federalist postscript

Finally, then, here is another closely related line of thought, by way of a concluding postscript, that could provide some ground for hope for the ethical anarchist. In the Kantian sense, rational hope is believing-in something whose existence or non-existence it is humanly impossible to know, in a way that is also existentially bootstrapping, non-scientifically demonstrative, and morality-affirming.[29] So here is where radically agnostic moral theology and radically enlightened anarchist politics ultimately merge into a single life-project.

In his *Idea for a Universal History with a Cosmopolitan Aim*, Kant develops an explicitly teleological reading of the history of humanity—i. e., rational humanity —that postulates the modern State as a necessary developmental stage on the way to individual and social enlightenment for rational humankind as a not-merely-biologically-defined species.

---

29 See also see Chignell (2013, 197–218; 2014).

Although the very idea of teleology is of course controversial, I do think that Kant is deeply right about the possibility of a teleological history of rational humanity, but also deeply wrong about the teleological necessity of the State. At the same time, however, thinking about Kant's essay prompted me to think about the role of federalism in such a teleological moral history of rational humanity, which in turn led me to what I will call *an idea for a universal history with an existental Kantian cosmopolitan anarchist aim*. It goes like this.

(1) The "original sin of political authority" is that the natural rational human need for mutual aid, and also for the protection of the innocent and weak, in a pre-State condition, plus *fear*, whether justified fear or irrational fear, pushes us into the very idea of the State and its supposed political authority.

(2) But although we do indeed all need mutual aid, and also we do indeed all need to protect the innocent and weak, because of our justified or irrational fear we go too far, and this is a fundamental, tragic error that we have been paying forever since.

(3) In effect, we traded away our basic moral principles, our autonomous freedom, and our respect for rational human dignity, for the social-contractual promise that governments, States, and State-like institutions will (i) provide effective protection against mortal threats, and (ii) guarantee our mutual freedom of action (as opposed to freedom of the will, or autonomy in the Kantian sense), especially our freedom of economic action.

(4) In other words, tragically, because of our justified or irrational fear, we have traded away our own rational humanity for the Mephistophelian (and so often, as a matter of actual political-historical fact, *false*) promise of living like well-serviced State-compatible machinery.

(5) Nevertheless, insofar as there have actually always been various active attempts to challenge, constrain, deconstruct, and detoxify the political authority of the State, or other State-like institutions, by appealing to moral principles with a broadly Kantian justification—e. g., universal human rights, based on the notion of rational human dignity, constitutionally-entrenched "bills of rights," etc.—then there has actually always been a morally healthy devolutionary trend towards Kantian ethical anarchism.

(6) Now, as well-described by Andreas Føllesdal, here is the basic idea behind federalism:

Federalism is the theory or advocacy of [basic Kantian moral] principles for dividing powers between member units and common institutions. Unlike in a unitary state, sovereignty in federal political orders is non-centralized, often constitutionally, between at least two levels so that units at each level have final authority and can be self-governing in some issue area. Citizens thus have political obligations to, or have their rights secured by, two authorities. The division of power between the member unit and center may vary, typically the center has powers regarding defense and foreign policy, but member units may also have international roles. The decision-making bodies of member units may also participate in central decision-making bodies. Much recent philosophical attention is spurred by renewed political interest in federalism, coupled with empirical findings concerning the requisite and legitimate basis for stability and trust among citizens in federal political orders. Philosophical contributions have addressed the dilemmas and opportunities facing Canada, Australia, Europe, Russia, Iraq, Nepal and Nigeria, to mention just a few areas where federal arrangements are seen as interesting solutions to accommodate differences among populations divided by ethnic or cultural cleavages yet seeking a common, often democratic, political order.[30]

(7) In this quotation, taken from the Introduction to Føllesdal's excellent *Stanford Encyclopedia of Philosophy* article on "[F]ederalism," I have made only one editorial change, which is to insert 'basic Kantian moral' for 'federal' in the original text. Of course, this controversial emendation might not be what Føllesdal actually had in mind.[31] But it does set up the final step in my Kantian anarchist teleological history of rational humanity.

(8) Looked at teleologically, the real-world fact of federalism seems to me to be, precisely insofar as it is "the theory or advocacy of [basic Kantian moral] principles for dividing powers between member units and common institutions," a practically necessary and morally healthy devolutionary step in actual human political history between, on the one hand, our fundamental tragic error of believing the myth of political authority and our corresponding creation of States and other State-like institutions, by means of which we voluntarily turn ourselves into more or less well-serviced State-compatible machines, and on the other hand, the guiding moral ideal of an existential Kantian cosmopolitan anarchist post-State world.

---

30 Føllesdal (2014).
31 In conversation, Føllesdal has said to me that "we're probably on the same team." Of course, I wouldn't want to saddle him with a commitment to existential Kantian cosmopolitan anarchism. I think he meant only that, at the end of the day, we have similar views about the moral and rational justification of federalism.

(9) In this way, then, it seems to me that Kantian ethical anarchists could also be *quasi*-federalists. That is, the Kantian ethical anarchist could work in a covert, gradualist, and non-revolutionary way towards The Real Realm of Ends by using federalist means, step-by-step, to devolve and dismantle all States and other State-like institutions, and to replace them with ethically acceptable, non-coercive social structures, institutions, and social relations. And in this way the ethical anarchist could still survive in a world of States, until the post-State world finally emerged. Or at least that is the hope.

(10) And now, with one other editorial addition, we can also re-quote Kant's vision of radical enlightenment:

When [after a long devolutionary federalist process] nature has unwrapped, from under this hard shell [of the "crooked timber of humanity" (*IUH*, AA 8: 23)], the seed for which she cares most tenderly, namely the propensity and calling to *think* freely, the latter gradually works back upon the mentality of the people (which thereby gradually becomes capable of *freedom* in acting) and eventually even upon the principles of *government*, which finds it profitable to itself to treat the human being, *who is now more than a machine*, in keeping with his dignity. (*WE*, AA 8: 41–42)[32]

Bibliography

Bookchin, Murray (1995): Social Anarchism or Lifestyle Anarchism, http://dwardmac.pitzer. edu/Anarchist_Archives/bookchin/soclife.html.

Chignell, Andrew (2013): Rational Hope, Moral Order, and the Revolution of the Will, in: Eric Watkins (ed.): Divine Order, Human Order, and the Order of Nature, Oxford, pp. 197–218.

Chignell, Andrew (2014): What May I Hope?, London.

Clarke, Desmond (2012): Blaise Pascal, in: Edward N. Zalta (ed.): The Stanford Encyclopedia of Philosophy (Fall 2012 Edition), http://plato.stanford.edu/archives/fall2012/entries/pas cal/.

Crowell, Steven (ed.) (2012): The Cambridge Companion to Existentialism, Cambridge.

Fleischacker, Samuel (2013): What is Enlightenment?, London.

32 I am very grateful, first, to the members of my Contemporary Kantian Philosophy working group in political philosophy and the philosophy of religion, at the University of Luxembourg, during 2013 – 2014 (especially Mathias Birrer, Elisabeth Lefort, Oliver Motz, Nora Schleich, Lukas Sosoe, Katja Stoppenbrink, and Katalin Turai), and second, to the participants in the workshop "Philosophical Foundations of Federalism," at the University of Luxembourg, LU, in May 2014, especially Andreas Føllesdal, for their extremely helpful critical comments on earlier versions of this essay, and equally helpful conversations on or around its central topics.

Føllesdal, Andreas (2014): Federalism, in: Edward N. Zalta (ed.): The Stanford Encyclopedia of Philosophy (Spring 2014 Edition), http://plato.stanford.edu/archives/spr2014/entries/federalism/.

Frankfurt, Harry G. (1988): On Bullshit, in: idem: On the Importance of What We Care About, Cambridge, pp. 117–133, http://www.stoa.org.uk/topics/bullshit/pdf/on-bullshit.pdf.

di Giovanni, George (1998): Translator's Introduction, in: idem and Allen W. Wood (eds.): Immanuel Kant: Religion and Rational Theology, Cambridge, pp. 41–54.

Hanna, Robert (2015): Cognition, Content, and the A Priori: A Study in the Philosophy of Mind and Knowledge, Oxford.

Hanna, Robert (2015a): Deep Freedom and Real Persons: A Study in Metaphysics (Unpublished MS, Winter 2015).

Hanna, Robert (2015b): Kantian Ethics and Human Existence (Unpublished MS, Winter 2015 version).

Hanna, Robert (2014): If God's Existence is Unprovable, Then is Everything Permitted?, Kant, Radical Agnosticism, and Morality, in: DIAMETROS 39, pp. 26–69.

Hanna, Robert and Maiese, Michelle (2009): Embodied Minds in Action, Oxford.

Huemer, Michael (2008): Ethical Intuitionism, London.

Huemer, Michael (2013): The Problem of Political Authority, London & New York.

Israel, Jonathan I. (2001): Radical Enlightenment: Philosophy and the Making of Modernity 1650–1750, Oxford.

Kant, Immanuel (1997): CPR | Critique of Pure Reason, trans. Paul Guyer and Allen Wood, Cambridge.

Kant, Immanuel (1996): CPrR | Critique of Practical Reason, trans. Mary J. Gregor, in: Immanuel Kant: Practical Philosophy, Cambridge, pp. 139–271.

Kant, Immanuel (1999): GMM | Groundwork of the Metaphysics of Morals, trans. Mary J. Gregor, in: Immanuel Kant: Practical Philosophy, Cambridge, pp. 43–108.

Kant, Immanuel (2007): IUH | Idea for a Universal History with a Cosmopolitan Aim, trans. Allen Wood, in: Immanuel Kant: Anthropology, History, and Education, Cambridge, pp. 107–120.

Kant, Immanuel (1997): LE | Lectures on Ethics, trans. Peter Heath, Cambridge.

Kant, Immanuel (1999): MM | Metaphysics of Morals, trans. Mary J. Gregor, in: Immanuel Kant: Practical Philosophy, Cambridge, pp. 365–603.

Kant, Immanuel (1999): PP | Toward Perpetual Peace, trans. Mary J. Gregor, in: Immanuel Kant: Practical Philosophy, Cambridge, pp. 317–351.

Kant, Immanuel (1998): Rel | Religion within the Boundaries of Mere Reason, trans. Allen Wood and George di Giovanni, Cambridge.

Kant, Immanuel (1999): WE | An Answer to the Question: "What is Enlightenment?", trans. Mary J. Gregor, in: Immanuel Kant: Practical Philosophy, Cambridge, pp. 17–22.

Kierkegaard, Søren (2000): The Essential Kierkegaard, trans. Howard Hong and Edna Hong, Princeton.

Kleingeld, Pauline and Brown, Eric (2013): Cosmopolitanism, in: Edward N. Zalta (ed.): The Stanford Encyclopedia of Philosophy (Fall 2013 Edition), http://plato.stanford.edu/archives/fall2013/entries/cosmopolitanism/, esp. section 1.

Kropotkin, Peter (1910): Anarchism, in: Encyclopedia Britannica, Edinburgh, also in: http://www.marxists.org/reference/archive/kropotkin-peter/1910/britannica.htm.

Kropotkin, Peter (1972): Mutual Aid: A Factor of Evolution, New York.

Philp, Mark (2013): William Godwin, in: Edward N. Zalta (ed.): The Stanford Encyclopedia of Philosophy (Summer 2013 Edition), http://plato.stanford.edu/archives/sum2013/entries/godwin/

Scott, James C. (2009): The Art of Not Being Governed: An Anarchist History of Upland Southeast Asia, New Haven.

Scott, James C. (1990): Domination and the Arts of Resistance: Hidden Transcripts, New Haven.

Scott, James C. (2012): Two Cheers for Anarchism, Princeton, NJ.

Wolff, Robert Paul (1998 [1970]): In Defense of Anarchism, Berkeley, CA.

Wood, Allen (1998): General Introduction, in: George di Giovanni and Allen Wood (eds.): Immanuel Kant: Religion and Rational Theology, Cambridge, pp. xi–xxiv.

Dietmar H. Heidemann
Letzte Zwecke. Die Grundlegung des Föderalismus in Kants politischer Teleologie

Einleitung

Die Frage nach den philosophischen Grundlagen des Föderalismus ist für Kant keine marginale. Begründet liegt dies nicht in einem vorrangigen Interesse Kants an der politischen Philosophie föderaler Ordnungen, sondern in seiner Konzeption der Idee eines Systems der Philosophie. Für Kant bildet der „Föderalismus freier Staaten" (*Zum Ewigen Frieden* AA 8:354) nicht nur den idealen Endpunkt realgeschichtlicher Entwicklung der Menschengattung, sondern in Einklang mit seinem kosmopolitischen Grundverständnis von Philosophie auch den Schlussstein seines kritischen Theoriegebäudes. Dies ist nicht erst den einschlägigen Schriften vor allem zur Rechts- und politischen Philosophie der 1790er Jahre wie *Über den Gemeinspruch* (1793), dem *Ewigen Frieden* (1795) oder der *Metaphysik der Sitten* (1797/98) zu entnehmen. Die Idee eines philosophischen Systems steht Kant mit der „Architektonik der reinen Vernunft" bereits in der ersten Auflage der *Kritik der reinen Vernunft* (A 832/B 860 ff.) klar vor Augen, wenn auch noch nicht in seiner vollständigen Ausführung. Nur drei Jahre nach dem Erscheinen der ersten *Kritik* legt Kant mit der *Idee einer Geschichte in weltbürgerlicher Absicht* eine Schrift vor, in welcher der „Föderalismus freier Staaten" als Fluchtpunkt seines Systemdenkens bereits entwickelt ist. In dieser Schrift von 1784 entwirft er die Konzeption einer Philosophie der Geschichte als „Erzählung", deren Gegenstand die „menschlichen Handlungen" als „Erscheinungen" der „Freiheit des Willens" (AA 8:17) sind. Aus kosmopolitischer Perspektive sind sie letztlich dazu bestimmt, die Errichtung internationaler föderaler Ordnungsstrukturen mittels eines ihnen naturgemäß innewohnenden Konfliktmechanismus zu befördern. Für Kant ist dies Anlass, in dieser Schrift eine der klassischen geschichtsphilosophischen Grundfragen zu formulieren, nämlich ob Geschichte *zweckmäßig* verläuft und ihr, wenn auch nur „im Großen", eine absichtsvolle Entwicklung und also ein Plan zugrundeliegt (AA 8:27).[1]

---

1 Kants Werke werden zitiert mit Angabe der Band- und Seitenzahlen nach: *Gesammelte Schriften*, Hg.: Bd. 1 – 22 Preussische Akademie der Wissenschaften, Bd. 23 Deutsche Akademie der Wissenschaften zu Berlin, ab Bd. 24 Akademie der Wissenschaften zu Göttingen, Berlin

Die *Idee* ist insofern ein anspruchsvolles Projekt, als Kant schon in dieser Schrift auf das Ganze seiner Philosophie ausgreift, bevor er überhaupt seine drei Hauptwerke sowie manch bedeutende Nebenschrift verfasst hat. Bereits in der *Idee* verdeutlicht er, worauf die konsequente Durchführung einer Metaphysik der Endlichkeit, das heißt eine Theorie endlichen Erkennens und seiner Grenzen hinausläuft, nämlich auf die Verwirklichung der Freiheit innerhalb internationaler föderaler Ordnungsstrukturen unter den Bedingungen des Rechts. Dieses Ziel sei nur historisch zu erreichen durch die Ausbildung der Naturanlagen des Menschen, wie es dann in der *Kritik der Urteilskraft* heißt, mit „Kultur" als dem „letzten Zweck der Natur" (AA 5:429), zu der die Menschengattung sich als politisches Gemeinwesen hinentwickelt. Im Folgenden soll gezeigt werden, dass Kants philosophische Grundlegung des Föderalismus innerhalb eines theoretischen Rahmens erfolgt, der sich als ‚politische Teleologie' bezeichnen lässt. Die politische Teleologie begründet die Existenz bzw. Normativität politischer Strukturen und Institutionen mithilfe von Annahmen über deren *natürliche* Zweckmäßigkeit. Kant begreift den Föderalismus als *natürliche* Konsequenz der kognitiven Verfassung des Menschen als eines endlichen Wesens, dessen Freiheitssicherung zuletzt allein unter kosmopolitischen Bedingungen möglich ist. Diese teleologische Grundlegung des Föderalismus wird zwar erst in der *Kritik der Urteilskraft* in einem komplizierten Gedankengang ausgeführt, ist aber schon in der *Idee einer Geschichte in weltbürgerlicher Absicht* systematisch anlegt. Im ersten Abschnitt dieses Beitrags wird daher zunächst Kants historisierender Anspruch der *Idee* auf eine zweckmäßige Entwicklung der Naturanlagen mit dem Idealziel internationaler politisch-föderaler staatlicher Ordnungsstrukturen erörtert. Wie sich herausstellen wird, holt Kant seinen Anspruch auf eine teleologische Grundlegung solcher Strukturen in dieser Schrift jedoch theoretisch nicht ein. Daher soll im zweiten Abschnitt aus der Perspektive der *Kritik der Urteilskraft* auf die *Idee* von 1784 zurückgeblickt und gezeigt werden, dass Kant explizit eine teleologische Grundlegung des Föderalismus unternimmt, die sich an der geschichtlichen Realisierung letzter Zwecke in und außerhalb der Natur ausrichtet. Der abschließende dritte Abschnitt geht der Frage nach, ob eine solche Konzeption politisch-soziale und insbesondere kriegerische Konfliktszenarien als erforderliche Mittel zur Erreichung einer internationalen föderalen Struktur billigend in Kauf nimmt.[2]

1900 ff. Die *Kritik der reinen Vernunft* wird zitiert nach der Ausgabe von J. Timmermann (Hg.), Hamburg 1998 (= *KrV*, A für die erster Auflage, B für die zweite Auflage).

2 In der Sekundärliteratur zu Kants politischer Philosophie bzw. politischem Kosmopolitismus bleibt der teleologische Hintergrund der Begründung des Föderalismus in der Regel unberücksichtigt (wie zum Beispiel bei Kleingeld (2012) und Höffe (2001)). Allenfalls wird er nur am Rande miterwähnt (wie etwa von Riley (1979, 58)) oder auf Kants angeblich teleologisches Ge-

1 Die zweckmäßige Entwicklung der Naturanlagen in der Geschichte

In den ersten beiden Sätzen der *Idee einer Geschichte in weltbürgerlicher Absicht* behauptet Kant die zweckmäßige und vollständige Entwicklung aller, also sowohl der rationalen als auch der nicht-rationalen, „Naturanlagen" des Menschen in seiner Gattung (AA 8:18). Man könnte gegen diese Lesart einwenden, Kant drücke sich in der *Idee* nicht ausreichend präzise aus und halte im Grunde am atemporalen Status der Vernunft als Quelle logisch-geltungstheoretischer Ansprüche fest. So heißt es auch nur ein Jahr später in den *Prolegomena*, die *Kritik der einen Vernunft* sei ein „System", das „[...] noch nichts als gegeben zum Grunde legt außer die Vernunft selbst und also, ohne sich auf irgend ein Factum zu stützen, die Erkenntniß aus ihren ursprünglichen Keimen zu entwickeln sucht." (AA 4:274) Solche und ähnlich lautende Aussagen, die gegen jegliche empirische oder naturalistische Fundierung des Vernunftvermögens sprechen, lassen sich in den Schriften Kants zahlreich ausfindig machen. Auf der anderen Seite äußert sich Kant aber schon in der *Kritik der reinen Vernunft* dem entgegengesetzt. Sehen wir einmal von Stellen ab, an denen er zum Beispiel davon spricht, die reinen Verstandesbegriffe „bis zu ihren ersten Keimen und Anlagen im menschlichen Verstande verfolgen" zu wollen (*KrV* A 66/B 91), was sich auch als eine bloß metaphorische *façon de parler* begreifen ließe, so scheint eine viel diskutierte Stelle der zweiten Auflage der *Kritik der reinen Vernunft* an einem letztlich genetisch-historischen Verständnis des Vernunftvermögens keinen Zweifel zu lassen. In § 27 der transzendentalen Deduktion unterscheidet Kant zwei Erklärungen der „Übereinstimmung der Erfahrung mit den Begriffen von ihren Gegenständen": „entweder die Erfahrung macht diese Begriffe, oder diese Begriffe machen die Erfahrung möglich" (*KrV* B 167). Hinsichtlich der reinen Verstandesbegriffe komme nur die zweite Option in Frage, von der es dann heißt, sie stelle „gleichsam ein System der Epigenesis der reinen Vernunft" (*KrV* B 167) dar. Eine dritte Option, nämlich „eine Art von Präformationssystem der reinen Vernunft", das reine Begriffe als „von unserem Urheber" „eingepflanzte Anlagen zum Denken" (*KrV* B 167) auffasst, weist Kant dabei als dogmatisch-metaphysische Annahme zurück. Es kann nach Kant also gezeigt werden, wie Begriffe a priori Erfahrung möglich machen. Stellt man nun zusätzlich die Frage nach der Herkunft dieser Begriffe, so

---

schichtsverständnis eingeschränkt (vgl. Brown (2009, 37 ff.)). Dies ist insofern erstaunlich, bildet die Teleologie der dritten *Kritik* doch die systematische Grundlage des Föderalismus, auch wenn sie nicht dessen inhaltliche Ausgestaltung im einzelnen leistet.

lautet die Antwort offenkundig, dass dies durch eine „Epigenesis der reinen Vernunft" zu erklären sei. Was dies nun genau besagt, ist durchaus nicht klar. Auf jeden Fall gilt manchen Kants Verwendung des der Biologie seiner Zeit entstammenden Begriffs der „Epigenesis" als klares Indiz für eine Position, die von einem gattungsgeschichtlich unbestimmten Vernunftvermögen ausgeht, das in seiner historisch-genetischen Fortentwicklung spezifische kognitive Fähigkeiten ausbildet und, wie noch gezeigt wird, in letzter, praktisch-rechtlicher Konsequenz auf die Etablierung internationaler föderaler politischer Strukturen hinausläuft. Auf Kants auch in der Forschung nicht unumstrittenes Verständnis von „Epigenesis" soll an dieser Stelle nicht näher eingegangen werden. Durch die ausdrückliche Erwähnung des Begriffs „Epigenesis" (KrV B 167) scheint der transzendentale Vernunftapriorismus jedoch insofern seine Unschuld zu verlieren, als Kant offenkundig bereit ist, dessen Rigorismus zugunsten einer biologisch-historischen Erklärung der Entwicklung des menschlichen Vernunftvermögens zu revidieren, wodurch er möglichweise den Stand der Wissenschaften seiner Zeit reflektiert.[3]

Eine solche epigenetische Auffassung der reinen Vernunft, so sieht es zumindest aus, macht die *Idee einer Geschichte in weltbürgerlicher Absicht* explizit geltend. Die Argumentation dieser Schrift erfolgt im Grunde in drei Hauptschritten. In den ersten drei der neun Sätze formuliert Kant seine Hauptthese, nämlich dass sich gemäß vorausgesetzter „teleologische[r] Naturlehre" die „Naturanlagen eines Geschöpfes" „vollständig und zweckmäßig auswickeln" müssen (AA 8:18). Für den Menschen gelte dabei, dass „sich diejenigen Naturanlagen, die auf den Gebrauch seiner Vernunft abgezielt sind, nur in der Gattung, nicht aber im Individuum vollständig entwickeln" „sollten" (AA 8:18). Diese vollständige, zweckmäßige Entwicklung der Naturanlagen ist ebenso naturbestimmt wie das Streben des Menschen im Verfolg seiner praktischen Ziele:

> Die Natur thut nämlich nichts überflüssig und ist im Gebrauche der Mittel zu ihren Zwecken nicht verschwenderisch. Da sie dem Menschen Vernunft und darauf sich gründende Freiheit des Willens gab, so war das schon eine klare Anzeige ihrer Absicht in Ansehung seiner Ausstattung. Er sollte nämlich nun nicht durch Instinct geleitet, oder durch anerschaffene Kenntniß versorgt und unterrichtet sein; er sollte vielmehr alles aus sich selbst herausbringen. (AA 8:19)

Die Frage, wie es der Natur gelingt, die Naturanlagen in der Menschengattung sich vollständig und zweckmäßig entwickeln zu lassen, beantworten die Sätze vier bis

---

3 Die allgemeine Bedeutung der „Epigenesis" für Kants Denken wurde zuletzt insbesondere von Mensch (2013, vor allem Kapitel 7 und 156 ff.) betont. Siehe dazu auch die kritischen Differenzierungen von Zammito (2015).

sechs. Das „Mittel", dessen sich nach Kant die Natur bedient, um dies zu erreichen, ist der „Antagonismus [...] in der Gesellschaft, so fern dieser doch am Ende die Ursache einer gesetzmäßigen Ordnung derselben wird." (AA 8:20). Hier ist der Ort, an dem Kant von der „ungesellige[n] Geselligkeit der Menschen" als einer Naturanlage spricht. Die durch Konflikte zwischen den Menschen wachgerufene „Neigung", sich zu vergesellschaften, ist eine natürliche Eigenschaft des Menschen, die die Natur zugleich einsetzt, um die „Talente" (AA 8:20 f.) des Menschen auszubilden. Kant schreibt:

> Dank sei also der Natur für die Unvertragsamkeit, für die mißgünstig wetteifernde Eitelkeit, für die nicht zu befriedigende Begierde zum Haben oder auch zum Herrschen! Ohne sie würden alle vortreffliche Naturanlagen in der Menschheit ewig unentwickelt schlummern. Der Mensch will Eintracht; aber die Natur weiß besser, was für seine Gattung gut ist: sie will Zwietracht. (AA 8:21)[4]

Der Eintritt in eine bürgerliche Gesellschaft unter allgemeinen Bedingungen des Rechts, das heißt insbesondere unter der Bedingung der Freiheit, gilt Kant als das „größte Problem für die Menschengattung" (AA 8:22). In der Einrichtung und Wahrung einer bürgerlichen Verfassung und infolgedessen in der Entstehung internationaler föderaler Strukturen als letztem, kosmopolitischem Zweck erblickt er den eigentlichen Grund der Entwicklung der Naturanlagen, so dass es sogar heißt, die „vollkommen gerechte bürgerliche Verfassung" sei die „höchste Aufgabe der Natur für die Menschengattung" (AA 8:22).

In der geschichtlichen Entwicklung der Menschgattung wird die bürgerliche Gesellschaft als Rechtsgemeinschaft unter dem Gesetz der Freiheit in Kants Konzeption allerdings erst spät erreicht. Ihre Einrichtung bedeutet jedoch nicht zugleich den Endpunkt und damit die vollständige, zweckmäßige Entwicklung der Naturanlagen des Menschen in der Geschichte. Wie Kant in den Sätzen sieben bis neun der *Idee* darlegt, ist die „Errichtung einer vollkommnen bürgerlichen Verfassung [...] von dem Problem eines gesetzmäßigen äußeren Staatenverhältnisses abhängig und kann ohne das letztere nicht aufgelöset werden." (AA 8:24). Denn der auf der Ebene der Individuen bestehende „Antagonismus" kehrt auf der Ebene des Verhältnisses existierender Gesellschaften bzw. Staaten und damit auf der Ebene internationaler zwischenstaatlicher Beziehungen wieder. Er wird aufgelöst durch den das internationale Recht sichernden „Völkerbund" als einer „vereinigten Macht" der Staaten (AA 8:24). Auch dies ist Werk der Natur:

---

4 Den Instrumentalismus der Natur, das heißt die Indienstnahme des zwischenmenschlichen Antagonismus durch die Natur nennt Laberge (2004, 153) nicht zu Unrecht eine „List". Vgl. auch Louden (2000, Kapitel 5).

> Die Natur hat also die Unvertragsamkeit der Menschen, selbst der großen Gesellschaften und Staatskörper dieser Art Geschöpfe wieder zu einem Mittel gebraucht, um in dem unvermeidlichen Antagonism derselben einen Zustand der Ruhe und Sicherheit auszufinden; d.i. sie treibt durch die Kriege, [...] zu dem, was ihnen die Vernunft auch ohne so viel traurige Erfahrung hätte sagen können, nämlich: aus dem gesetzlosen Zustande der Wilden hinaus zu gehen und in einen Völkerbund zu treten (AA 8:24)

Internationale, föderative politische Strukturen sind demnach für Kant Bedingungen der Entwicklung der Naturanlagen des Menschen. Diese Entwicklung vollzieht sich historisch in der Geschichte der Menschengattung, ist dabei jedoch nicht auf das Politische zu restringieren, sondern umfasst ganz grundsätzlich die „Kultur" des Menschen, das heißt die Entwicklung von „Kunst", „Wissenschaft" und „Moralität" (AA 8:24). Daher schlussfolgert Kant, man könne „[...] die Geschichte der Menschengattung im Großen als die Vollziehung eines verborgenen Plans der Natur ansehen, um eine innerlich- und zu diesem Zwecke auch äußerlich-vollkommene Staatsverfassung zu Stande zu bringen, als den einzigen Zustand, in welchem sie alle ihre Anlagen in der Menschheit völlig entwickeln kann." (AA 8:27). Der damit erreichte Zustand sei zugleich „allgemeiner weltbürgerlicher Zustand" (AA 8:28) als Resultat der weltgeschichtlichen Genese der Menschengattung. Kants genetische Vernunftkonzeption hat also schließlich einen kosmopolitischen Ausgang und scheint damit den Rigorismus der Individualvernunft zu überwinden. Eine weitere Stufe historischer Entwicklung ist seiner Auffassung nach offenbar nicht denkbar, so dass die kosmopolitische föderale Ordnung zugleich das Verhältnis darstellt, unter dem auch die zweckmäßige Entwicklung der rationalen Strukturen der Menschengattung ihr Ziel erreicht. Angesichts dieses Zieles hält Kant es zumindest theoretisch für möglich, „die allgemeine Weltgeschichte nach einem Plane der Natur, der auf die vollkommene bürgerliche Vereinigung in der Menschengattung abziele, zu bearbeiten" (AA 8:29).

2 Die Zweckmäßigkeit der Naturanlagen und die teleologische Grundlegung des Föderalismus in der *Kritik der Urteilskraft*

Die teleologische Gesamtdeutung der Geschichte, die Kant im neunten Satz der *Idee* als Konklusion formuliert, nämlich dass man „die Geschichte der Menschengattung im Großen als die Vollziehung eines verborgenen Plans der Natur ansehen" kann (AA 8:28), stellt eine Hypothese dar, deren theoretischer Status in der *Idee einer Geschichte in weltbürgerlicher Absicht* weitgehend ungeklärt bleibt.

Handelt es sich bei dieser Schlussfolgerung um eine Erkenntnis aus theoretischer Vernunft oder um eine teleologische Einsicht gemäß dem Prinzip der Zweckmäßigkeit der Beurteilung der Natur durch die reflektierende Urteilskraft? Auch wenn man nicht unbedingt erwarten sollte, dass historische Prozesse Gegenstand der reflektierenden Naturbetrachtung durch die Urteilskraft sind, ist es die *Kritik der teleologischen Urteilskraft*, die eine Antwort auf diese Frage gibt. Im Folgenden wird gezeigt, dass sich der Gesamtsinn von Kants teleologischer Geschichtsdeutung und der Entstehungsgründe einer internationalen föderalen Staatenordnung erst aus der Perspektive der dritten *Kritik* im Rahmen einer politischen Teleologie erschließt.

Zunächst ist der für Kant auch im Kontext der Geschichts- sowie politischen Philosophie zentrale Begriff des Zweckes zu bestimmen. Die *Kritik der Urteilskraft* definiert „Zweck" als „Begriff von einem Object, sofern er zugleich den Grund der Wirklichkeit dieses Objects enthält", so dass unter „Zweckmäßigkeit" die „Übereinstimmung eines Dinges mit derjenigen Beschaffenheit der Dinge, die nur nach Zwecken möglich ist", verstanden werden muss (*Zweite Einleitung* AA 5:180). Der Begriff der „Zweckmäßigkeit", das heißt die „Zweckmäßigkeit der Natur in ihrer Mannigfaltigkeit" als „Princip der Urtheilskraft" (*Zweite Einleitung* AA 5:180), ist dabei wie folgt zu differenzieren: *Erstens* als allgemeine Zweckmäßigkeit der Natur, *zweitens* als subjektive Zweckmäßigkeit in der Ästhetik sowie *drittens* als objektiv-logische Zweckmäßigkeit in der Teleologie. Die allgemeine Zweckmäßigkeit als Prinzip der reflektierenden Urteilskraft besagt, die Natur in ihrer Mannigfaltigkeit als gemäß allgemeineren und besonderen Begriffen bzw. Gesetzen strukturierte Einheit zu denken. Dagegen bedeutet ästhetische Zweckmäßigkeit das harmonische Spiel von Einbildungskraft und Verstand in der anschaulichen Betrachtung von Formen, wohingegen durch objektive Zweckmäßigkeit Organismen in der Wechselwirkung ihrer Teile als reale Naturzwecke vorgestellt werden.[5] Der Begriff der allgemeinen Zweckmäßigkeit ist dabei grundlegender als die spezifischeren Begriffe der ästhetischen und objektiven Zweckmäßigkeit, da die Urteilskraft in ihrer Reflexion über die Natur davon ausgeht, dass es unter den in der Natur herrschenden besonderen Gesetzen eine nach Gattung und Art eingerichtete Ordnung gebe. Wir müssen dabei den für uns bloß zufälligen Sachverhalt präsupponieren, „daß die Ordnung der Natur nach ihren besonderen Gesetzen bei aller unsere Fassungskraft übersteigenden wenigstens möglichen Mannigfaltigkeit und Ungleichartigkeit doch dieser wirklich angemessen sei" (*Zweite Einleitung* KU AA 5:187). So versucht der Verstand, diese „Ordnung der Natur" in der „Absicht" aufzufinden, „Einheit der Principien in sie

---

5 Vgl. Düsing (1968, 51 ff.) und Heidemann (2010).

hineinzubringen", das heißt diese „Einheit" gemäß einem Zweck zu bestimmen, den die „Urtheilskraft der Natur beilegen muß, weil der Verstand ihr hierüber kein Gesetz vorschreiben kann." Ist diese „Absicht" bzw. der „Zweck" erreicht, zum Beispiel durch die Entdeckung der „Vereinbarkeit zweier oder mehrerer empirischen heterogenen Naturgesetze unter einem sie beide befassenden Princip", stellt sich das Gefühl der Lust ein (*Zweite Einleitung* KU AA 5:187).

Das Prinzip der allgemeinen Zweckmäßigkeit der Natur gilt somit für den subjektiven ebenso wie für den objektiven Fall, in dem an einem empirisch gegebenen Ding Zweckmäßigkeit vorgestellt werden kann. Möglich ist dies entweder rein subjektiv aufgrund der formalen, von Begriffen unabhängigen „Übereinstimmung" seiner Apprehension mit unserem Erkenntnisvermögen, um dadurch Erkenntnis zu erlangen, oder objektiv aufgrund der „Übereinstimmung seiner Form mit der Möglichkeit des Dinges selbst", und zwar gemäß dem Begriff des Dinges, der, wie Kant sagt, „den Grund dieser Form enthält." (*Zweite Einleitung* KU AA 5:192). Folglich macht die allgemeine Zweckmäßigkeit der Natur für die reflektierende Urteilskraft sowohl die subjektiv-ästhetische als auch die objektiv-logische Zweckmäßigkeit erst möglich.

Insofern es in der Philosophie der Geschichte um die Beurteilung kausaler Zusammenhänge von Handlungen und insbesondere um die Frage der organischen Ganzheitlichkeit der Geschichte geht, findet auf sie nicht das Prinzip der ästhetischen Zweckmäßigkeit Anwendung, das auf die Harmonie von Einbildungskraft und Verstand in der anschaulichen Betrachtung von Formen abzielt. Gemäß Kants Systematik hat die Beurteilung der Geschichte gemäß dem Prinzip der objektiven Zweckmäßigkeit zu erfolgen, wonach Organismen in der Wechselwirkung ihrer Teile als reale Naturzwecke vorgestellt werden müssen. Denn Geschichte lässt sich nicht als das bloße Aggregat von sie konstituierenden Handlungen verstehen, sondern muss *organisch* begriffen werden, das heißt als ein zweckmäßiges Ganzes, das als solches zunächst vorauszusetzen ist, bevor es durch seine Teile, die Handlungen, erfüllt wird.

Diese teleologische Geschichtskonzeption der *Kritik der Urteilskraft* liegt der Sache nach bereits der *Idee einer Geschichte in weltbürgerlicher Absicht* zugrunde. Kant führt sie aber erst in den §§ 81–83 der „Methodenlehre der teleologischen Urteilskraft" im Detail aus, indem er wie zuvor in der *Idee* argumentiert, dass sich die Natur des Antagonismus der Menschen bedient, um in der geschichtlichen Entwicklung der Menschengattung die „bürgerliche Gesellschaft" und schließlich „ein weltbürgerliches Ganze, d. i. ein System aller Staaten" (AA 5:432) herzustellen, so dass sich die Naturanlagen des Menschen vollständig und zweckmäßig entwickeln können. Die Hypothese der planvollen Entwicklung der Geschichte mit dem Ziel einer föderalen Staatenordnung erhält somit erst in der *Kritik der Urteilskraft* ihre theoretische Fundierung.[6]

Kants Argumentation in der dritten *Kritik* ist nicht nur deshalb komplexer als in der *Idee*, weil sie hier im Kontext der Theorie der Zweckmäßigkeit als solcher erfolgt, sondern weil er die Einrichtung der bürgerlichen Gesellschaft sowie internationaler föderaler politischer Strukturen spezifisch mit der Lehre vom letzten Zweck der Natur und damit metaphysisch begründet. Diese Argumentation lässt sich wie folgt rekonstruieren. Nachdem Kant in § 81 zunächst das Verhältnis von Mechanismus und teleologischer Naturerklärung thematisiert hat, eröffnet er in § 82 einen Gedankengang, der vom „teleologischen System in den äußeren Verhältnissen organisierter Wesen" zum föderalen Staatensystem als Zweck der Geschichte führt. Den Ausgangspunkt bildet die Überlegung, dass zur inneren Zweckmäßigkeit eines organisierten Wesens die äußere Zweckmäßigkeit hinzukommt. Darunter versteht Kant diejenige Zweckmäßigkeit, derzufolge „ein Ding der Natur einem andern als Mittel zum Zwecke dient", so dass sich fragen lässt: „Wozu ist es da?" (AA 5:425).[7] Auf diese Frage sind im Grunde zwei Antworten möglich: Entweder das Ding ist nicht aufgrund einer absichtsvoll wirkenden Ursache da, so dass es bloßes Produkt des Naturmechanismus ist, oder es gibt einen „absichtliche[n] Grund seines Daseins" (AA 5:426) und dies ist bei organisierten Wesen, deren schon innere Möglichkeit ja auf absichtsvoller Kausalität beruht, der Fall. Das heißt die Existenz selbst eines Dinges, dem äußere Zweckmäßigkeit zukommt, ist als Zweck zu begreifen. Dies lässt sich nun so denken, dass der „Zweck der Existenz" eines organisierten Wesens in diesem selbst liegt und dann sei es nicht bloß einfach Zweck, sondern zugleich „Endzweck", oder sein Zweck

---

6 Deutlicher noch als in der dritten *Kritik* heißt es wenige Jahre später in *Die Religion innerhalb der Grenzen der bloßen Vernunft*: „Wenn man dieser ihre [der Staaten, D.H.] Geschichte blos als das Phänomen der uns großentheils verborgenen inneren Anlagen der Menschheit ansieht, so kann man einen gewissen maschinenmäßigen Gang der Natur nach Zwecken, die nicht ihre (der Völker) Zwecke, sondern Zwecke der Natur sind, gewahr werden. Ein jeder Staat strebt, so lange er einen andern neben sich hat, den er zu bezwingen hoffen darf, sich durch dieses Unterwerfung zu vergrößern, und also zur Universalmonarchie, einer Verfassung, darin alle Freiheit und mit ihr (was die Folge derselben ist) Tugend, Geschmack und Wissenschaft erlöschen müßte. Allein dieses Ungeheuer (in welchem die Gesetze allmählig ihre Kraft verlieren), nachdem es alle benachbarte verschlungen hat, löset sich endlich von selbst auf und theilt sich durch Aufruhr und Zwiespalt in viele kleinere Staaten, die, anstatt zu einem Staatenverein (Republik freier verbündeter Völker) zu streben, wiederum ihrerseits jeder dasselbe Spiel von neuem anfangen, um den Krieg (diese Geißel des menschlichen Geschlechts) ja nicht aufhören zu lassen, der, ob er gleich nicht so unheilbar böse ist, als das Grab der allgemeinen Alleinherrschaft (oder auch ein Völkerbund, um die Despotie in keinem Staate abkommen zu lassen), doch, wie ein Alter sagte, mehr böse Menschen macht, als er deren wegnimmt." (AA 6:34, Anm.).

7 Vgl. hierzu und zum Folgenden Düsing (1968:206–237, bes. 217 ff.).

„ist außer ihm in einem anderen Naturwesen", so dass das Ding zwar zweckmäßig, aber nicht als „Endzweck" existiert (AA 5:426).

Kant entwirft damit ein System der Naturzwecke, dessen Letztpunkt ein Endzweck ist. Dieser aber sei nicht in der Natur aufzufinden, da jedes Ding in der Natur prinzipiell immer auch als Mittel zu anderen Zwecken denkbar ist. So muss der Endzweck außerhalb der Natur liegen, so dass Kant dem System der Naturzwecke mit dem Endzweck einen metaphysischen Fluchtpunkt an die Spitze setzt. In der Natur aber findet sich ein „letzter Zweck", welcher der „letzte Zweck der Schöpfung hier auf Erden" ist: der Mensch (AA 5:426). Kant implementiert an dieser Stelle keine theologischen Überlegungen, sondern argumentiert, dass der Mensch das einzige Wesen auf Erden ist, das „Verstand" hat und „sich einen Begriff von Zwecken machen und aus einem Aggregat von zweckmäßig gebildeten Dingen durch seine Vernunft ein System der Zwecke machen kann". (AA 5:427). Letzter Zweck der Natur ist der Mensch also, weil er die Fähigkeit der Zwecksetzung besitzt, das heißt seine Zwecke selbst festlegen und die dazugehörigen Mittel auswählen kann.

Den für die spätere Begründung der bürgerlichen Gesellschaft bzw. internationalen föderalen staatlichen Ordnung bereits an dieser Stelle entscheidenden argumentativen Angelpunkt bildet das Prinzip der äußeren Zweckmäßigkeit. Denn die Vernunft wendet dieses Prinzip auch auf die Zweck-Mittel-Relation unter Organismen an, um auch hier wieder ein „System aller Naturreiche nach Endursachen zu denken" (AA 5:427). Was Kant an dieser Stelle „System aller Naturreiche nach Endursachen" nennt, wird er am Ende des Argumentationsganges in geschichtsphilosophisch-politischer Hinsicht ganz analog als „System aller Staaten" (AA 5:432) bezeichnen. Denn so wie organisierte Wesen in ihrem äußeren Verhältnis zueinander ein System der Zwecke ausmachen, so machen auch Staaten, die als organisierte Wesen gedacht werden können, in ihrem äußeren Verhältnis zueinander ein System der Zwecke in einer föderalen Vereinigung aus.

Kant macht sich in diesem Zusammenhang selbst den Einwand, dass man im Grunde doch alle Produkte der Natur auch nach bloß mechanischen Ursachen konzipieren und die zweckmäßige Verursachung für entbehrlich halten könnte, so dass zum Beispiel die topographische Beschaffenheit eines Landes einfach da ist, weil sie rein mechanische Ursachen hat, und nicht als Mittel zu irgendeinem Zweck, etwa um den Lauf von Flüssen zu begünstigen, existiert. Folglich wäre auch der Mensch nicht als letzter Zweck der Natur zu denken. Diesen plausiblen Einwand weist er sogleich mit dem Hinweis auf die bereits aufgelöste Antinomie der teleologischen Urteilskraft zurück, derzufolge wir die Natur gemäß dem Prinzip der reflektierenden Urteilskraft auch „nach Endursachen" (AA 5:429) beurteilen sollen, und also bei bloß mechanischen Erklärungen nicht stehen bleiben können.[8]

Der Mensch ist also nicht nur wie alle anderen organisierten Wesen Naturzweck, sondern zugleich letzter Zweck der Natur, „in Beziehung auf welchen alle übrige Naturdinge ein System von Zwecken ausmachen" (AA 5:429). Allerdings ist er dies nicht für die bestimmende, sondern allein für die reflektierende Urteilskraft, wie Kant ausdrücklich betont. Damit ist bereits der entscheidende Hinweis auch für die Zweckmäßigkeitshypothese in der Geschichte gegeben. Denn diese, so werden wir sehen, ist allein nach dem Prinzip der reflektierenden Urteilskraft zu denken und befördert also keine theoretische Erkenntnis der Planmäßigkeit der Geschichte.

Hier ist nun auch die entscheidende systematische Stelle, an der Kant in der *Kritik der Urteilskraft* zum Begriff der Kultur überleitet, durch den er die Geschichtlichkeit der Menschengattung und ihrer Naturanlagen erklärt. Denn dass der Mensch als letzter Zweck der Natur anzusehen ist, bedeutet, dass die Natur überhaupt ihm als Zweck dienlich und also für ihn Mittel sein soll. Wiederum gibt es zwei Optionen: Entweder die Natur befriedigt diesen Zweck, so dass der Zweck im Erreichen der durch die Natur beförderten „Glückseligkeit" bestünde, oder der Mensch als letzter Zweck macht sich die Natur so zueigen, dass sie ihm zur „Tauglichkeit und Geschicklichkeit zu allerlei Zwecken dient". In diesem zweiten Fall besteht der letzte Zweck der Natur in der „Kultur" des Menschen (AA 5:430).

Schon in der *Grundlegung zur Metaphysik des Sitten* kritisiert Kant, dass „Glückseligkeit" nicht „der eigentliche Zweck der Natur" (AA 4:395, vgl. AA 395 – 399) sein kann, nicht zuletzt weil dieser Begriff inhaltlich zu unbestimmt ist. Ähnlich hält er „Glückseligkeit" auch in der dritten *Kritik* für einen untauglichen, weil „schwankenden Begriff", wobei der Mensch „Glückseligkeit" ohnehin nie erreichen könne, „denn seine Natur ist nicht von der Art, irgendwo im Besitze und Genusse aufzuhören und befriedigt zu werden" (AA 5:430). Bestünde der letzte Zweck der Natur in der Glückseligkeit des Menschen, würde der Mensch im Hinblick auf ihre Realisierung in der Gattung ohnehin selbst immer nur Mittel sein, da seine willentlichen Zwecksetzungen stets im Dienst der Glückseligkeit stünden. Da Glückseligkeit einen material bestimmten, aber unerreichbaren letzten Zweck der Natur darstellt, kann sie auch nicht zu dem werden, was sich der Mensch nach Kant überhaupt setzen muss: einen „Endzweck" außerhalb der Natur (AA 5:431).

Der letzte Zweck der Natur lässt sich also nicht materialiter bestimmen. Weil aber gemäß dem System der Zwecke ein solcher letzter Zweck angenommen werden *muss*, kann dieser offenbar nur formal bestimmt werden. Die Bedingung

---

8 Vgl. AA 5:427 – 429.

der formalen Bestimmung des letzten Zweckes der Natur wird erfüllt von der „Tauglichkeit" des Menschen, Zwecke zu setzen und zu deren Verwirklichung die angemessenen Mittel in der Natur aufzusuchen. Letzter Zweck der Natur „in Ansehung der Menschengattung" ist daher für Kant die „Cultur" als die „Hervorbringung der Tauglichkeit eines vernünftigen Wesens zu beliebigen Zwecken überhaupt" (AA 5:431). Unter „Tauglichkeit" ist die Fähigkeit des Menschen zu verstehen, sich die Natur zur Realisierung der von ihm gesetzten Zwecke anzueignen. Indem der Mensch die Natur als Mittel gebraucht, produziert er Gegenstände zu seinen Zwecken, und dies ist in einem weiten Sinne Kultur, deren formale Bedingung eben in der „Tauglichkeit" hierzu besteht.[9]

Die Fähigkeit, die Natur als Mittel der Zweck-Realisierung einzusetzen, liegt nicht einfach im Menschen fertig vor, sondern muss ausgebildet werden. Ebendies geschieht in der Geschichte der Menschengattung durch die Entwicklung der Naturanlagen, die dem Menschen durch die freie Setzung von Zwecken und Wahl der dazugehörigen Mittel die Möglichkeit eröffnet, über sich hinauszugehen. Dabei steht der Mensch nicht außerhalb der Kultur, sondern ist Teil von ihr unter den allgemeinen Bedingungen, die die Natur ihm vorgibt. Kant differenziert hierbei zwischen der Kultur der „Geschicklichkeit" und der Kultur der „Zucht" (AA 5:432). Auf der einen Seite bedarf der Mensch zwar der Geschicklichkeit, um seine Zwecke erreichen zu können, auf der anderen Seite reicht Geschicklichkeit aber nicht aus, um zwischen möglichen Zwecken zu wählen. Dazu erforderlich ist die „Cultur der Zucht" (AA 5:432), wie Kant sagt, durch die der Wille zur Wahl der Zwecke diszipliniert wird.

Entscheidend für die Bestimmung des Verhältnisses von Zweckmäßigkeit und Geschichtlichkeit der Vernunft ist die Geschicklichkeit, deren Möglichkeit Kant in struktureller Analogie zur Einrichtung der bürgerlichen Verfassung wie in der *Idee* aufgrund des Antagonismus der Menschen erklärt: „Die Geschicklichkeit kann in der Menschengattung nicht wohl entwickelt werden, als vermittelst der Ungleichheit unter Menschen" (AA 5:432). Kant ist der Auffassung, dass die Differenziertheit der individuellen Fähigkeiten der Menschen sowie die damit verbundenen Konflikte und Anstrengungen des Lebens die Entwicklung der Naturanlagen überhaupt erst befördert und kulturellen „Fortschritt" bewirkt: „das glänzende Elend ist doch mit der Entwickelung der Naturanlagen in der Menschengattung verbunden, und der Zweck der Natur selbst, wenn es gleich nicht unser Zweck ist, wird doch hiebei erreicht." (AA 5:432). Die Entwicklung der Kultur ist also ohne die Entwicklung der Naturanlagen des Menschen gar nicht denkbar und wird durch diese bedingt. Das heißt Kultur als letzter Zweck der Natur ist nicht

---

9 Vgl. Düsing (1968, 212 ff.).

möglich ohne die Entwicklung der rationalen wie nicht-rationalen Naturanlagen, die die Geschicklichkeit des Menschen, also seine Fähigkeit, sich die Natur als Mittel anzueignen, erst möglich macht.

Als letzter Zweck der Natur gehört die Kultur selbst zur Natur und wird sogar durch die Natur hervorgebracht. Ihren letzten Zweck verwirklicht die Natur aber nur unter einer Bedingung, die zugleich den Punkt darstellt, an dem die Argumentation der *Kritik der Urteilskraft* mit derjenigen der *Idee einer Geschichte in weltbürgerlicher Absicht* zusammenläuft:

> Die formale Bedingung, unter welcher die Natur diese ihre Endabsicht allein erreichen kann, ist diejenige Verfassung im Verhältnisse der Menschen untereinander, wo dem Abbruche der einander wechselseitig widerstreitenden Freiheit gesetzmäßige Gewalt in einem Ganzen, welches bürgerliche Gesellschaft heißt, entgegengesetzt wird; denn nur in ihr kann die größte Entwickelung der Naturanlagen geschehen. Zu derselben wäre aber doch, wenn gleich Menschen sie auszufinden klug und sich ihrem Zwange willig zu unterwerfen weise genug wären, noch ein weltbürgerliches Ganze, d.i. ein System aller Staaten, die auf einander nachtheilig zu wirken in Gefahr sind, erforderlich. (AA 5:432)

Kant ist also offenbar der Auffassung, dass die Naturanlagen in der Menschengattung allein unter der formalen politischen Bedingung einer Freiheit garantierenden rechtlichen Ordnung, nämlich der bürgerlichen Gesellschaft bzw. der kosmopolitischen Föderation der Staaten, zur Entwicklung gebracht werden. Man wird sich fragen müssen, warum er dies annehmen kann. Die Berufung auf die politische Anthropologie hilft hier nicht wirklich weiter, da diese keine naturteleologischen Annahmen im Sinne der *Kritik der Urteilskraft* macht. Auf jeden Fall scheint Kant der Meinung zu sein, dass sich Naturanlagen im gesetzlosen Naturzustand deshalb nicht zweckmäßig entwickeln, weil sie durch den Krieg aller gegen alle gehemmt werden und sich so in den Individuen nicht frei entfalten können. Das heißt nicht, dass Naturanlagen zu ihrer Genese nicht einer gewissen Widerständigkeit bedürfen, um zum Vorschein zu kommen und durch ihre Entwicklung den Fortschritt der Kultur zu bewirken. Wie der vierte Satz der *Idee* erklärt, ist dies sogar ein explizites Erfordernis: „Das Mittel, dessen sich die Natur bedient, die Entwickelung aller ihrer Anlagen zu Stande zu bringen, ist der Antagonism derselben in der Gesellschaft, so fern dieser doch am Ende die Ursache einer gesetzmäßigen Ordnung derselben wird." (AA 8:20) Während in der *Idee* letztlich offen bleibt, worin der Zusammenhang zwischen der Entwicklung der Naturanlagen und der Vergesellschaftung begründet liegt und dort lediglich vorausgesetzt wird, dass sich die Naturanlagen des Menschen in der Gattung vollständig und zweckmäßig entwickeln sollen (AA 8:18f), liefert die *Kritik der Urteilskraft* mit der Theorie des letzten Zwecks der Natur eine nachträgliche teleologische Begründung dieser Annahme.

Wie wir gesehen haben, beruht die Theorie des letzten Zwecks auf dem Begriff der äußeren Zweckmäßigkeit und der sie konstituierenden Zweck-Mittel-Relation. Es ist die der inneren Zweckmäßigkeit koordinierte äußere Zweckmäßigkeit organisierter Wesen, die auf den letzten Zweck der Natur führt. Dieser letzte Zweck der Natur ist, wie dargelegt, der Mensch als Naturwesen, genauer, als Kulturwesen. Im Rahmen des Systems der Zwecke mit dem Menschen als dem letzten Zweck der Natur, ist die Annahme durchaus berechtigt, dass sich die Naturanlagen des Menschen in der Gattung zweckmäßig entwickeln, da er als rationales Wesen nicht nur seine Zwecke, sondern auch die dazu gehörigen, von der Natur vorgegebenen Mittel selbst wählt. Die Zwecksetzungen des Menschen als Kulturwesen, so muss man Kant wohl verstehen, sind dabei natürlicherweise auf die Sicherung seiner Existenz und daher die Vermeidung ihn fundamental bedrohender Konfliktsszenarien ausgerichtet. Diesen Zweck zu realisieren, kann nicht anders gelingen als im Rahmen einer bürgerlichen Verfassung und einer darauf folgenden föderalen Staatengemeinschaft. Als Mittel der Realisierung dieses Zwecks stehen ihm dabei allein seine Naturanlagen zur Verfügung, deren gattungsmäßige Ausbildung und Entwicklung in der Geschichte von Kant als Kultur begriffen wird. Bürgerliche Verfassung und föderale Staatengemeinschaft sind daher nach Kant im Rahmen einer politischen Teleologie nicht bloß als Produkte einer politisch-anthropologischen Grundbestimmung zu begreifen, sondern werden durch die Natur in historischer Genese mittels der Entwicklung von Naturanlagen hervorgebracht.

3 Abschließende Überlegungen: Föderalismus und Teleologie

Die Rolle des Föderalismus in Kants Denken, so hat sich gezeigt, ist ohne die theoretische Einbettung der Idee des „Föderalismus freier Staaten" (*Zum Ewigen Frieden* AA 8:354) in einen teleologischen Gesamtrahmen kaum verständlich zu machen. Nicht erst in der *Kritik der Urteilskraft*, sondern schon in der *Idee* bildet die föderale, kosmopolitische Ordnung den *zweckmäßigen* Schlussstein des Kantischen Systemdenkens, weil sie die rechtlich-politische Existenz gleichermaßen von Bürgern und Staaten unter Freiheitsgesetzen zuletzt sichert. Damit trägt die föderalistische Ordnung des Völkerbundes zur Realisierung politisch-rechtlicher Freiheit bei, um die es Kant in seinem Denken vor allem geht. Wie beide Werke verdeutlichen, macht Kant Geschichte und die durch sie hervorgehende Kultur zum Gegenstand teleologischer Naturbetrachtung gemäß dem Prinzip der Zweckmäßigkeit. Geschichte soll so beurteilt werden als ob es in ihr durch die zweckmäßige Entwicklung aller Naturanlagen in der Menschengattung planvoll zugeht. Das heißt nicht, Geschichte als einen vorherbestimmten, teleologischen Abfolgeprozess menschlicher Handlungen zu supponieren. Ohnehin nimmt Kants Teleologie Zwecke nicht als Realzwecke an, die unabhängig vom menschlichen Erkenntnisvermögen an sich selbst existieren und von der reflektierenden Urteilskraft lediglich entdeckt werden müssen. Zweckmäßigkeit ist allein das Prinzip der reflektierenden Urteilskraft zur Orientierung über bestimmte Arten von Gegenständen, seien es Erkenntnisvermögen in ihrem Verhältnis zueinander, Naturgesetze oder eben auch menschliche Handlungen im systematischen Zusammenhang historischer Prozesse. Dabei versteht Kant Geschichte als Fortschrittsgeschichte. Deutlicher noch als die *Idee* zeigt dies die Erörterung über die „Erneuerte Frage" im zweiten Abschnitt des *Streits der Fakultäten*: „Ob das menschliche Geschlecht im beständigen Fortschreiten zum Besseren sei" (AA 7:79). Diese Frage wird von Kant im Sinne seiner teleologischen Beurteilung der Geschichte grundsätzlich positiv beantwortet. Insofern ist der weltbürgerliche Zustand als „Föderalismus freier Staaten" (AA 8:354) für Kant auch die natürliche Letztkonsequenz historischen Fortschritts.

Als Zustand einer internationalen Rechtsordnung unter Staaten bereift Kant den Föderalismus nicht als Produkt einer Gelegenheitssubsumtion rechtsunsicherer zwischenstaatlicher Verhältnisse unter völkerrechtliche Prinzipien, sondern als Produkt realer historischer Entwicklung zwischenstaatlicher Beziehungen. Das theoretische Modell, mit dem er dabei operiert, ist mereologischer Natur und lässt sich als *bottom-up*-Kontraktualismus bezeichnen. Gemäß diesem Modell wird durch grundlegende Elemente oder Teile eine übergeordnete Struktur errichtet, so dass die Elemente oder Teile als solche nur Bestand haben, wenn die übergeordnete Struktur Bestand hat. Im berühmten zweiten „Definitivartikel" des *Ewigen Frieden* erläutert Kant die Einrichtung föderaler staatlicher Ordnungsstrukturen daher auch in Analogie zur Idee des staatsbürgerlichen Kontraktualismus:

> Völker als Staaten können wie einzelne Menschen beurtheilt werden, die sich in ihrem Naturzustande (d.i. in der Unabhängigkeit von äußern Gesetzen) schon durch ihr Nebeneinandersein lädiren, und deren jeder um seiner Sicherheit willen von dem andern fordern kann und soll, mit ihm in eine der bürgerlichen ähnliche Verfassung zu treten, wo jedem sein Recht gesichert werden kann. (AA 8:354)

Die so etablierten Rechtverhältnisse zwischen Völkern bzw. Staaten sind nach Kant föderaler Natur und damit als „Völkerbund", nicht als „Völkerstaat" zu begreifen. Ohnehin wäre ein föderaler „Völkerstaat" ein „Widerspruch",

> [...] weil ein jeder Staat das Verhältniß eines Oberen (Gesetzgebenden) zu einem Unteren (Gehorchenden, nämlich dem Volk) enthält, viele Völker aber in einem Staate nur ein Volk

ausmachen würden, welches (da wir hier das Recht der Völker gegen einander zu erwägen haben, so fern sie so viel verschiedene Staaten ausmachen und nicht in einem Staat zusammenschmelzen sollen) der Voraussetzung widerspricht. (AA 8:354)

Kant meint, dass eine föderale internationale Ordnung schon allein aus begrifflichen Gründen nicht auf eine weltstaatliche Ordnung hinauslaufen kann, offenbar weil der Begriff ‚Staat' ein Subordinationsverhältnis von Elementen bzw. Teilen unter eine übergeordnete Struktur impliziert. Diese in der Literatur[10] des öfteren in Frage gestellte Argumentation hängt nicht zuletzt vom vorausgesetzten Staatsverständnis ab. Sie ist in diesem Zusammenhang aber nicht entscheidend. Wichtiger für das Problem einer philosophischen Grundlegung des Föderalismus ist die Frage nach der eigentlichen Veranlassung der Staaten, sich zu verbünden. In direkter Analogie zum staatsbürgerlichen Kontraktualismus bewertet Kant das Bestehen nicht-föderativer internationaler Verhältnisse als rechtsfreien Naturzustand. In der *Metaphysik der Sitten* erläutert er dies aus völkerrechtlicher Perspektive wie folgt:

> 1) daß Staaten, im äußeren Verhältniß gegen einander betrachtet, (wie gesetzlose Wilde) von Natur in einem nicht-rechtlichen Zustande sind; 2) daß dieser Zustand ein Zustand des Krieges (des Rechts des Stärkeren), wenn gleich nicht wirklicher Krieg und immerwährende wirkliche Befehdung (Hostilität) ist [...]; 3) daß ein Völkerbund nach der Idee eines ursprünglichen gesellschaftlichen Vertrages nothwendig ist, sich zwar einander nicht in die einheimische Mißhelligkeiten derselben zu mischen, aber doch gegen Angriffe der äußeren zu schützen; 4) daß die Verbindung doch keine souveräne Gewalt (wie in einer bürgerlichen Verfassung), sondern nur eine Genossenschaft (Föderalität) enthalten müsse; eine Verbündung, die zu aller Zeit aufgekündigt werden kann, mithin von Zeit zu Zeit erneuert werden muß, – ein Recht in subsidium eines anderen und ursprünglichen Rechts, den Verfall in den Zustand des wirklichen Krieges derselben untereinander von sich abzuwehren (foedus Amphictyonum). (AA 6:344; vgl. *Zum Ewigen Frieden* AA 8:356)

So wie die Idee des staatsbürgerlichen Kontraktualismus soziale und politische Verhältnisse aus Gründen der Rechtssicherheit und der damit einhergehenden Beendigung prinzipiell feindseliger Beziehungen zwischen Individuen etabliert, resultieren nach der Idee des weltbürgerlichen Kontraktualismus internationale politische Ordnungsstrukturen aus dem Bestreben, Rechtssicherheit zwischen Staaten herzustellen und den Zustand des Krieges zwischen ihnen auch zukünftig zu beenden.[11] *Prima facie* sieht es so aus, als würde Krieg durch die Abwesenheit von Recht in der Beziehung zwischen Individuen bzw. Staaten hervorgerufen mit

---

10 Vgl. etwa Seel (1997) und Kleingeld (2012, 58 ff.).
11 Diese Interpretation ist natürlich nicht unumstritten. Flikschuh (2004,168 ff.) etwa hält eine kontraktualistische Lesart von Kants Kosmopolitismus für verfehlt bzw. reduktionistisch.

dem Ergebnis der Errichtung einer rechtssichernden Ordnung, das heißt des Einzelstaates bzw. Staatenbundes:

> So wie allseitige Gewaltthätigkeit und daraus entspringende Noth endlich ein Volk zur Entschließung bringen mußte, sich dem Zwange, den ihm die Vernunft selbst als Mittel vorschreibt, nämlich dem öffentlicher Gesetze, zu unterwerfen und in eine staatsbürgerliche Verfassung zu treten: so muß auch die Noth aus den beständigen Kriegen, in welchen wiederum Staaten einander zu schmälern oder zu unterjochen suchen, sie zuletzt dahin bringen, selbst wider Willen entweder in eine weltbürgerliche Verfassung zu treten; oder [...] zu einem Zustande zwingen, der zwar kein weltbürgerliches gemeines Wesen unter einem Oberhaupt, aber doch ein rechtlicher Zustand der Föderation nach einem gemeinschaftlich verabredeten Völkerrecht ist. (AA 8:310 f.)

Der explanatorische Mechanismus *Rechtsunsicherheit → Krieg → Staat/Föderation* ist in den einschlägigen Schriften Kants allenthalben anzutreffen. Doch greift dieses Schema im Hinblick auf die in Frage stehende philosophische Grundlegung des Föderalismus zu kurz. Im Kontext seiner politischen Teleologie stellt sich dies anders dar. Dort versteht Kant den Krieg als von der Natur eingesetztes Zwangsmittel zum Zweck der Einrichtung einer föderalen Ordnung. Der „Krieg", so heißt es in der *Kritik der Urteilskraft*,

> [...] so wie er ein unabsichtlicher (durch zügellose Leidenschaften angeregter) Versuch der Menschen, doch tief verborgener, vielleicht absichtlicher der obersten Weisheit ist, Gesetzmäßigkeit mit der Freiheit der Staaten und dadurch Einheit eines moralisch begründeten Systems derselben, wo nicht zu stiften, dennoch vorzubereiten und ungeachtet der schrecklichsten Drangsale, womit er das menschliche Geschlecht belegt, und der vielleicht noch größern, womit die beständige Bereitschaft dazu im Frieden drückt, dennoch eine Triebfeder mehr ist (indessen die Hoffnung zu dem Ruhestande einer Volksglückseligkeit sich immer weiter entfernt) alle Talente, die zur Cultur dienen, bis zum höchsten Grade zu entwickeln. (AA 5:433; vgl. AA 8:24)

Was Kant bereits in der *Idee* im Sinne seiner teleologischen Geschichtskonzeption und im Hinblick auf die These von der vollständigen Entwicklung der menschlichen Naturanlagen in der Gattung behauptet, nämlich: „Der Mensch will Eintracht; aber die Natur weiß besser, was für seine Gattung gut ist: sie will Zwietracht." (AA 8:21), wird in der dritten *Kritik* auf den Föderalismus übertragen. Die Natur setzt den Krieg als Mittel („Triebfeder") zur Realisierung der föderalen, kosmopolitischen Vereinigung der Staaten ein, nicht ohne sich zugleich der „Talente" der einzelnen Menschen zu bedienen. Auch wenn man Kant keine kriegsbilligenden oder -verherrlichenden Motive unterstellen darf, nicht zuletzt weil er den Krieg als ein unter allen Umständen zu vermeidendes Übel der

Menschheit brandmarkt[12], ist diese Auffassung doch höchst problematisch. Schließlich könnte man sich im Sinne einer solchen Argumentation berechtigt sehen, den Krieg angesichts des höheren Guts einer ihm nachfolgenden rechtssichernden föderativen Friedensordnung als ein in Kauf zu nehmendes Übel zu legitimieren, auch wenn man ihn für moralisch verwerflich hält. Es ist nicht erkennbar, wie sich diese Spannung zwischen der geschichtsteleologischen Auffassung des Krieges als Mittel zum Zweck und der Diskreditierung des Krieges als moralisches Übel durch den Hinweis auf die *bloß* teleologische Beurteilung der Geschichte durch die reflektierende Urteilskraft, die im Krieg ja nicht das *reale* Mittel zur Erreichung des *realen* Zwecks einer föderalen weltbürgerlichen Ordnung erblickt, lösen lässt. In der Grundlegung des Föderalismus durch Kants politische Teleologie scheint diese Spannung zunächst unvermeidbar und ist wohl nur im konkreten institutionalisierten Rahmen rechtlich-politischer Friedenssicherung zu lösen.

Bibliographie

Brown, Garrett Wallace (2009): Grounding Cosmopolitanism: From Kant to the Idea of a Cosmopolitan Constitution, Edinburgh.

Düsing, Klaus (1968): Die Teleologie in Kants Weltbegriff (Kant-Studien Ergänzungsheft 96), Bonn.

Flikschuh, Katrin (2004): Kant and Modern Political Philosophy, Cambridge.

Heidemann, Dietmar H. (2010): Allgemeine Zweckmäßigkeit der Natur, in: Tobias Schlicht (Hg.): Zweck und Natur: Historische und systematische Untersuchungen zur Teleologie, München 2010, S. 91–111.

Höffe, Otfried (2001): ‚Königliche Völker': Zu Kants kosmopolitischer Rechts- und Friedenstheorie, Frankfurt am Main.

Kleingeld, Pauline (2012): Kant and Cosmopolitism. The Philosophical Ideal of World Citizenship, Cambridge.

Laberge, Pierre (2004): Von der Garantie des ewigen Friedens, in: Otfried Höffe (Hg.): Immanuel Kant, Zum Ewigen Frieden, 2. Auflage, Berlin, S. 149–170.

Louden, Robert (2000): Kant's Impure Ethics: From Rational Beings to Human Beings, New York.

Mensch, Jennifer (2013): Kant's Organicism. Epigenesis and the Development of Critical Philosophy, London.

Riley, Patrick (1979): Federalism in Kant's Political Philosophy, in: Publius 9, pp. 43–64.

---

12 Siehe u. a. *Metaphysik der Sitten:* „Nun spricht die moralisch-praktische Vernunft in uns ihr unwiderstehliches Veto aus: Es soll kein Krieg sein; weder der, welcher zwischen Mir und Dir im Naturzustande, noch zwischen uns als Staaten, die, obzwar innerlich im gesetzlichen, doch äußerlich (in Verhältniß gegen einander) im gesetzlosen Zustande sind; – denn das ist nicht die Art, wie jedermann sein Recht suchen soll." (AA 6:354). Vgl. AA 8:355–357.

Seel, Gerhard (1997): >Mais il y aurait là contradiction<. Une nouvelle lecture du deuxième article définitif, in: Pierre Laberge e.a. (ed.): L'année 1795. Essai sur la paix, Paris, pp. 160–182.
Zammito, John (2015): Bringing Biology Back In: The Unresolved Issue of „Epigenesis" in Kant, in: Con-Textos Kantianos. International Journal of Philosophy 1, pp. 197–216.

Heiner F. Klemme

Der ungerechte Bundesgenosse. Über die inhaltlichen Grenzen des (Staats- und) Völkerrechts in Kants Rechtslehre

1 Vorbemerkung

In den *Metaphysischen Anfangsgründen der Rechtslehre* (1797) führt Kant im Rahmen des Völkerrechts den Begriff des *„ungerechten Feindes"* ein, dem (wie allen Feinden) gegenüber ein Staat das Recht hat, das Seine zu erhalten. Dieses Recht erstreckt sich jedoch nur auf die „an sich zulässigen Mittel", was bedeutet, dass bestimmte Handlungen zur Durchsetzung des eigenen Interesses durch das Recht selbst verboten sind. Zugleich führt Kant den Begriff einer in einen *„permanenten Staatencongreß"* (AA 6: 350, § 61) mündenden „Bundesgenossenschaft" (AA 6: 349, § 59) ein. Deren Ziel ist die Verteidigung gegen äußere oder innere Angriffe auf ihre Mitglieder in der Absicht, das Recht der Menschen und Staaten zu sichern. Ohne dass Kant diesen Ausdruck verwenden würde, stellt sich die Frage, ob es auch einen *ungerechten* Bundesgenossen geben kann. Bei einem ungerechten Bundesgenossen handelt es sich um einen Staat, der der ungerechte Feind nicht des eigenen, wohl aber eines dritten Staates ist. Was bedeutet dies für das rechtliche Verhältnis, in dem der eigene Staat zu seinem ungerechten Bundesgenossen steht? Worin genau besteht dessen Ungerechtigkeit?

Diese Fragen sollen im Folgenden aus der Perspektive des Verhältnisses von Rechtsform (Rechtszweck) und Rechtsinhalt im Öffentlichen Recht bei Kant beantwortet werden. Im Vorgriff auf unsere Ausführungen ist es hilfreich, bereits an dieser Stelle zwischen sechs verschiedenen Arten von Ungerechtigkeit (moralischer Verwerflichkeit) bei Kant zu unterscheiden: *Erstens* der Ungerechtigkeit gegenüber moralischen Personen im *status civilis*, die sich darin zeigt, dass den Personen (Bürgern, Staaten) das ihnen rechtmäßig Zustehende vorenthalten wird (UNG 1). *Zweitens* der Ungerechtigkeit „an sich", die begangen wird, weil und solange wir uns im *status naturalis* befinden (UNG 2). *Drittens* der Ungerechtigkeit, die sich in Handlungen im *status naturalis* dokumentiert, die einen zukünftigen Frieden unmöglich machen, weil sie das „Vertrauen" (AA 6: 347, § 57) zwischen den Staaten zerstören (UNG 3). *Viertens* der Ungerechtigkeit von Handlungen, die (wie die Leibeigenschaft; vgl. AA: 348, § 58) sich durch ihre unmittelbare Widersprüchlichkeit mit dem Begriff des Moralgesetzes (Sittengesetzes) erklärt. Hierzu zählt beispielsweise der freiwillige oder erzwungene Eintritt in den Sklavenzustand (UNG 4). Und schließlich *fünftens* einer Ungerechtigkeit gegenüber Personen, die in Gesetzen und Maßnahmen besteht, die die Aberkennung oder Vernichtung der moralischen Qualität (Rechtssubjektivität, Personalität) der Menschen zum Ziel hat. In diesem Fall wird gegen das Recht der Menschheit in einer jeden Person verstoßen (UNG 5). Schließlich begeht ein Bürger *sechstens* Unrecht, wenn er Widerstand gegen bestehende staatliche Gesetze leistet (UNG 6).

2 Das Postulat des Öffentlichen Rechts und das Völkerrecht

Kant weist in der *Rechtslehre* auf die Pflicht jedes einzelnen Menschen hin, in „einen rechtlichen Zustand" (AA 6: 307, § 42) zu treten. Er nennt diese Pflicht ein „Postulat", das aus dem „Privatrecht im natürlichen Zustande" hervorgeht, sowie den Zustand, in den der Mensch treten soll, das „öffentliche Recht" (ibid. 307). Das Öffentliche Recht bezeichnet demnach die Bedingung oder den Zustand, unter der oder in dem jeder Mensch das Seine erhalten kann. Nur im Öffentlichen Recht gibt es eine „austheilende Gerechtigkeit" (ibid. 307). Weil aufgrund der kreisförmigen Gestalt der Erde alle Menschen in einem „unvermeidlichen Nebeneinandersein" (ibid. 307) mit allen anderen Menschen stehen, materialisiert sich das Postulat des *Exeundum e statu naturali* als das Gebot, mit allen auf der Erde lebenden Menschen in einen öffentlichen Rechtszustand zu treten. Dabei versteht Kant diesen Rechtszustand als ein „System von Gesetzen für ein Volk, d.i. eine Menge von Menschen, oder für eine Menge von Völkern". Dieses „System der Gesetze" ist eine „*Verfassung* (constitutio)" (AA 6: 311, § 43), die ihren Einheitsgrund und ihre Legitimation im „übereinstimmenden und vereinigten Willen Aller" als der „gesetzgebenden Gewalt" (AA 6: 313 – 314, § 46) findet. Nur wenn wir uns das Gesetz als aus *einem* Willen entsprungen denken, kann es kein Unrecht geben [„denn (*volenti non fit iniuria*)", AA 6: 313, § 46]. Demnach wäre dem Postulat des öffentlichen Rechts genau dann Genüge getan, wenn sich alle auf der Erde lebenden Menschen in eine rechtliche Verfassung begeben würden, in der das Gesetz von der volonté générale gegeben wird. Ihm wäre Genüge getan, wenn alle Menschen in einem einzigen Staat (oder in einem Staat, der im Rahmen einer „Staatsverfassung" mit anderen Staaten verbunden ist; vgl. AA 6: 351, § 61) lebten, in dem das Gesetz als zwangsbewährtes Recht positivrechtliche Wirksamkeit erlangt. Weil wir aber faktisch nicht in einem einzigen Staat leben, ist dies ein Beweis dafür, dass das Postulat des Öffentlichen Rechts noch nicht erfüllt worden ist.

Warum ist die Stiftung einer globalen Verfassung des Öffentlichen Rechts in einem einzigen Staat für die Erfüllung unserer Rechtspflicht unabdingbar? Weil eine Pluralität von Staaten in Analogie zur Pluralität von Einzelwillen verstanden werden muss, die als solche immer im Naturzustand existieren. Der Naturzustand ist ein (potentiell sich durch reale Gewaltanwendung ausdrückender) Kriegszustand, weil die Willkür der Einzelnen noch nicht durch die Herrschaft des allgemeinen und zwangsbewährten Gesetzes überwunden worden ist. Die einzige Möglichkeit der peremtorischen Überwindung des Naturzustandes ist das die (willkürlichen) Einzelwillen von Menschen oder von Staaten überwindende zwangsbewährte Gesetz (positives Recht). Weil aufgrund der Souveränität der Staaten das zwangsbewährte Gesetz nicht zwischen den Staaten existieren kann, das Völkerrecht im engeren Sinne also gar kein Öffentliches Recht ist, befinden sich Staaten untereinander immer im Naturzustand.

Wie kann dieser Zustand überwunden werden? Zunächst besteht die Schwierigkeit darin, im „gesetzlosen Zustande" überhaupt ein Gesetz zu finden, „ohne sich selbst zu widersprechen". Die Lösung dieses Problems lautet: Der (reale) Krieg zwischen Staaten muss „nach solchen Grundsätzen" geführt werden, „nach welchen es immer noch möglich bleibt, aus jenem Naturzustande der Staaten (im äußeren Verhältniß gegen einander) herauszugehen und in einen rechtlichen zu treten." (AA 6: 347, § 57) Kant geht davon aus, dass der einen rechtlichen Zustand zwischen Staaten bezeichnende „ewige Friede (das letzte Ziel des ganzen Völkerrechts) freilich eine unausführbare Idee" ist, nicht aber die „politischen Grundsätze", die auf eine „continuirliche *Annäherung*" (AA 6: 350, § 61) an den ewigen Frieden abzielen. Wir haben die Pflicht, das „Recht der Menschen und Staaten" (ibid.) zu schützen und zu verwirklichen. Und diese Pflicht kann in einem „permanenten Staatencongress" (AA 6: 350, § 61) erfüllt werden, eine Form der „wechselseitigen *Verbindung*" zwischen Staaten, die Kant in der *Rechtslehre* auch die „Bundesgenossenschaft" (AA 6: 349, § 59) nennt. Kant vertritt einen weiten Begriff des Völkerrechts, wonach dieses „nicht bloß ein Verhältniß eines Staates gegen den anderen im Ganzen, sondern auch einzelner Personen des einen gegen einzelne des anderen, imgleichen gegen den ganzen anderen Staat selbst" (AA 6: 343 – 344, § 53) ist. Im Völkerrecht werden Staaten und ihre Bürger aufgrund ihrer natürlichen Freiheit als moralische Personen verstanden (vgl. AA 6: 343, § 53).

Wir haben gesehen: Das Postulat des Öffentlichen Rechts materialisiert sich als die Forderung nach einem globalen Staat. Doch diese Forderung ist bisher nicht nur nicht erfüllt worden, sie wird Kants Auffassung nach faktisch auch niemals erfüllt werden können. Und dies aus zwei Gründen: Einerseits werden die Menschen durch ihre kulturellen, sprachlichen und religiösen Partikularismen getrennt. Sie identifizieren ihren Willen mit Inhalten, die dem positiven Gesetz ihres Staates eine besondere, mit anderen Inhalten unvereinbare Gestalt geben. Und andererseits hält Kant die faktische Verwaltung und Regierung eines Weltstaates für undurchführbar. Als Substitut für den nicht realisierbaren Weltstaat schlägt er einen Bund von Staaten vor, die ihr Verhältnis untereinander rechtlich regeln. Der zwischen souveränen Staaten geschlossene Völkerbund begründet nicht die Einmischung in die inneren Angelegenheiten des anderen Staates, sondern dient dem Schutz vor der Gewalttätigkeit durch einen Drittstaat. Es ist „nur eine *Genossenschaft* (Föderalität) [...]; eine Verbündung, die zu aller Zeit aufgekündigt werden kann, mithin von Zeit zu Zeit erneuert werden muß" (AA 6: 344, § 54). Obwohl der Staatenbund die Souveränität der Einzelstaaten nicht aufhebt, ist er „nach der Idee eines ursprünglichen gesellschaftlichen Vertrags" (ibid.) zu bilden.

Es ist wichtig zu beachten, dass (wie wir gesehen haben) das Völkerrecht kein genuin Öffentliches Recht ist, weil ihm der Zwangscharakter fehlt. Völkerrechtliche Verträge werden von souveränen Staaten geschlossen, und ihre Befolgung setzt den beständigen Willen dieser Staaten voraus, sie einzuhalten. Weil das äußere Verhältnis der Staaten zueinander ein „nicht rechtlicher Zustand" (AA 6: 344, § 54) ist, wird dem Staat, dem gegenüber Kriegshandlungen begangen werden, kein Unrecht zugefügt. In rechtlicher Hinsicht gleicht das Verhältnis der Staaten zueinander dem Verhältnis, in dem Menschen im Naturzustand zueinander stehen. In beiden Fällen kann dem Rechtssubjekt als solchem kein Unrecht zugefügt werden. (Ich werde auf diesen Punkt weiter unten zurückkommen.) Dennoch ist ein derartiger Zustand an sich betrachtet Unrecht (UNG 2), gerade weil die reine Vernunft den öffentlichen Rechtszustand fordert („obzwar dadurch keinem von dem Anderen Unrecht geschieht, doch an sich selbst im höchsten Grade unrecht ist, und aus welchem die Staaten, welche einander benachbart sind, auszugehen verbunden sind", AA 6: 344, § 54). Weil wir die Rechtpflicht haben, den Naturzustand zwischen Menschen zu überwinden, begeben wir uns als Menschen in den *status civilis* und werden zu Staatsbürgern. Weil wir die Rechtspflicht haben, den Naturzustand zwischen Staaten zu überwinden, schließen die Staaten einen Bund, der die Überwindung feindseliger Handlungen zum Ziele hat. Der Völkerbund überwindet den an sich unrechtmäßigen Zustand also gewissermaßen nur provisorisch. Wir sind verpflichtet, den Frieden zwischen den Staaten zu befördern, aber wir werden es niemals schaffen, ihn zu finden. Das faktische Scheitern entbindet uns allerdings so wenig von der Verpflichtung, ihn zu befördern, wie die Verbindlichkeit des Kategorischen Imperativs durch unsere Lügen aufgehoben wird.

Kant greift in seinen Überlegungen zum Öffentlichen Recht auf Rousseaus Begriff des *contrat social* zurück. Der ursprüngliche zwischen den Menschen geschlossene Vertrag stiftet eine bürgerliche Gesellschaft, in der (nach § 46) die gesetzgebende Gewalt mit dem Willen Aller identisch ist. Kant ist jedoch kein Anhänger einer direkten Demokratie, weil er der Auffassung ist, dass der Wille

Aller nur als in Gestalt einer einzigen Person (des Fürsten) repräsentierter Wille als ein einheitlicher gedacht werden kann. In der Rechtsrealität verfehlt die gesetzgebende Gewalt allerdings den gemeinsamen Willen, ohne dass dies ein Recht der Bürger begründen würde, Widerstand gegen die Staatsgewalt auszuüben (UNG 6). Weil die reine Vernunft selbst den Eintritt in den öffentlichen Rechtszustand fordert, ist dieser in jedem Fall (auch im Falle einer despotischen Regierungsform) dem Naturzustand vorzuziehen. Es besteht die Hoffnung auf eine kontinuierlich zum Besseren wirkenden Reform von oben.

> Die Staatsformen sind nur der *Buchstabe* (*littera*) der ursprünglichen Gesetzgebung im bürgerlichen Zustande, und sie mögen also bleiben, so lange sie, als zum Maschinenwesen der Staatsverfassung gehörend, durch alte und lange Gewohnheit (also nur subjectiv) für nothwendig gehalten werden. Aber der Geist jenes ursprünglichen Vertrages (*anima pacti originarii*) enthält die Verbindlichkeit der constituirenden Gewalt, die *Regierungsart* jener Idee angemessen zu machen und so sie, wenn es nicht auf einmal geschehen kann, allmählich und continuirlich dahin zu verändern, daß sie mit der einzig rechtmäßigen Verfassung, nämlich einer reinen Vernunft, *ihrer Wirkung nach* zusammenstimme (AA 6: 340, § 52).

In einer nach Vernunftprinzipien organisierten Verfassung wird die Freiheit „zur Bedingung alles Zwanges" (AA 6: 340, § 52) gemacht, d.h. der Zwang ist nur in Absicht der Ermöglichung von Freiheit erlaubt oder geboten. Staaten sollen von einer despotischen zu einer republikanischen Regierungsart wechseln. Wenn Kant nun fordert, dass das Völkerrecht nach der Idee eines ursprünglichen Vertrags auszurichten ist, obwohl der ursprüngliche Vertrag im engeren Sinne niemals realisiert werden kann (die Realisierung würde bedeuten, dass das Völkerrecht in das Recht eines Weltstaates überführt wird), möchte er die Pflicht aller Staaten zum Ausdruck bringen, das Recht als Mittel zur Realisierung von Freiheit zu gebrauchen. Ohne dass Kant dies ausdrücklich betont, scheint er der Ansicht zu sein, dass das Völkerrecht auch zwischen denjenigen Staaten seinen guten Effekt entfalten kann, unter denen sich eine oder mehrere Despotien befinden. Denn so wie das positive Recht seine verbindende Kraft im Staat nicht dadurch verliert, dass in ihr nach despotischen Prinzipien regiert wird, verliert das Völkerrecht seine verbindende Kraft nicht dadurch, dass es den Willen von innerlich nach despotischen Prinzipien organisierten Staaten bindet. Während Kant eine Republik durch die Begriffe von Freiheit, Gesetz und Gewalt definiert, fehlt in einer Despotie die Freiheit. In ihr herrschen „Gesetz und Gewalt ohne Freiheit".

3 Welche Schranken kennen Recht und Gesetz?

Können wir Kants Verweis auf die fehlende Freiheit in einer Despotie so verstehen, als ob die in ihr herrschenden Prinzipien des Gesetzes und der Gewalt schrankenlos wären? Um diese Frage beantworten zu können, müssen wir das Verhältnis von Rechtsform und Rechtsinhalt klären: Kann es positivrechtliche Rechtsinhalte geben, die nach vernunftrechtlichen Begriffen betrachtet illegitim sind? Diese Frage ist auch für das Verhältnis der an sich souveränen, sich ihren Willen aber durch Verträge bindenden und gebundenen Föderation von Einzelstaaten von Bedeutung: Gibt es Inhalte, die der Form bzw. dem Zweck des Völkerrechts zuwider laufen? Gibt es Rechtsinhalte, deren Legalität in einem Staat B es dem Staat A unmöglich macht, mit dem Staat B einen Bund zu schließen oder diesen zu erhalten? Oder allgemeiner formuliert: Gibt es Grenzen der Legitimität völkerrechtlicher Verträge?

In der *Rechtslehre* thematisiert Kant im Abschnitt über das Völkerrecht unter den Stichwörtern „*Recht im Kriege*" (AA 6: 347, § 57) und „*Recht des Friedens*" (AA 6: 349, § 60) Fragen, die für unsere Frage nach möglichen Inhalten völkerrechtlich verbindlicher Gesetze von zentraler Bedeutung sind:

1. Ein Staat kann von seinen Bürgern keine Handlungen gegenüber anderen Staaten verlangen, durch die die Bürger aufhören, Staatsbürger zu sein. Weil sie durch diese Handlungen ihren staatsbürgerlichen Status verlieren, hört auch der Staat auf, im zwischenstaatlichen Verhältnis als eine Person zu gelten (vgl. AA 6: 347, § 57). Als Beispiele nennt Kant verschiedene „Vertheidigungsmittel" (ibid.) wie Spionage, Meuchelmord oder Giftmischerei. (Ich werde hierauf weiter unten zurückkommen.)

2. Kant spricht vom „Recht eines Staates gegen einen *ungerechten Feind*" (AA 6: 349, § 60). Wenn es einen ungerechten Feind gibt, dann scheint es *ex negativo* auch einen gerechten Feind zu geben. Der ungerechte Feind jedenfalls ist derjenige, „dessen öffentlich (es sei wörtlich oder thätlich) geäußerter Wille eine Maxime verräth, nach welcher, wenn sie zur allgemeinen Regel gemacht würde, kein Friedenszustand unter Völkern möglich, sondern der Naturzustand verewigt werden müsste." (ibid.) (Daraus wäre abzuleiten, dass ein gerechter Feind ein solcher ist, bei dem keine entsprechende Maxime vorliegt.) Kant weist darauf hin (und dies in Übereinstimmung mit § 57), dass der „beeinträchtigte Staat" (AA 6: 349, § 60) das Seine behaupten darf, sich dabei aber nicht aller möglichen Mittel bedienen darf.

Mit Blick auf Kants Begriff eines ungerechten Feindes stellt sich nun die Frage, ob es auch einen ungerechten Bundesgenossen geben kann. Ein ungerechter Bundesgenosse wäre ein Staat, der entweder von seinen Bürgern (oder Bürgern anderer Staaten) ungerechte Handlungen gegen einen fremden Staat und dessen Bürger verlangt. Oder der einen Straf-, Ausrottungs- oder Unterjochungskrieg gegen einen Drittstaat führt (vgl. § 57, AA 6: 347). Im ersteren Fall scheint sich die Ungerechtigkeit des Bundesgenossen in seinem Verhältnis gegenüber seinen Bürgern zu zeigen (und erst in einem abgeleiteten Sinne gegenüber dem fremden Staat). Im zweiten Fall scheint sie sich im Verhältnis zu einem anderen Staat zu zeigen (und erst in einem abgeleiteten Sinne gegenüber seinen Bürgern, von denen verlangt wird, einen an sich ungerechten Krieg zu führen). Für unsere Frage nach den Grenzen möglicher Rechtsinhalte ist zunächst daran zu erinnern, dass Kants Auffassung nach im Naturzustand eine moralische Person (sei es ein Mensch oder ein Staat) einer anderen Person kein Unrecht zufügen kann, gerade weil es Gerechtigkeit nur im *status civilis* gibt. Auf der anderen Seite begehen Personen aber an sich Unrecht, weil sie sich im Naturzustand befinden (UNG 2). Mit seiner These, dass bestimmte Verteidigungsmittel nicht verwendet werden dürfen, möchte Kant nun auf Handlungen aufmerksam machen, die, obwohl sie im Naturzustand begangen werden, dennoch ungerecht sind, weil sie einen zukünftigen bürgerlichen Rechtszustand unmöglich zu machen scheinen. Sie zerstören das „Vertrauen" (AA 6: 347, § 57) in die Friedensfähigkeit des Staates (UNG 3).

Wie soll sich ein Staat, der gerecht sein will, verhalten, wenn er einen Bund mit einem Staat geschlossen hat, der an sich unrechte Handlungen vollzieht? Dies ist die Frage, mit der ich mich im Folgenden beschäftigen möchte. Um sie beantworten zu können, ist es unabdingbar, zunächst die Frage nach dem Verhältnis von Rechtsform und Rechtsinhalt auf der Ebene des Natur- und Staatsrechts (dem eigentlichen Öffentlichen Recht) zu beantworten. Dies schließt die Frage nach dem Geltungsgrund bzw. nach dem verpflichtenden Charakter des Rechts ein.

4 Recht, Freiheit und Verbindlichkeit

Woher nimmt das Recht seine uns verbindende Kraft? Welche Rechte und Rechtspflichten gibt es? Welche positivrechtlichen Inhalte sind mit diesen Rechten und Rechtspflichten vereinbar? Mit der *Rechtslehre* betreten wir einen Kosmos begrifflicher Bestimmungsversuche, die Kant in der Hoffnung vornimmt, die normativen Dimensionen vernünftiger Selbstbestimmung auf den Begriff zu bringen. Kants Philosophie ist „*Vernunfterkenntnis* aus *Begriffen*" (KrV A 713/B 741), und der zentrale Begriff der *Rechtslehre* ist selbstredend der Begriff des Rechts. Kant unterscheidet zwischen dem Rechts*begriff*, dem Rechts*prinzip* und dem allgemeinen Rechts*gesetz*. Der Rechts*begriff* legt fest, was das Recht ist. Das Recht ist der „Inbegriff der Bedingungen, unter denen die Willkür des einen mit der Willkür des andern nach einem allgemeinen Gesetze der Freiheit zusammen vereinigt werden kann" (AA 6: 230). Aus dem freiheitszentrierten Rechtsbegriff folgt das Rechts*prinzip*. Mittels dieses Prinzips kann festgestellt werden, welche Handlungen dem Rechtsbegriff genügen: „Eine jede Handlung ist recht, die oder nach deren Maxime die Freiheit der Willkür eines jeden mit jedermanns Freiheit nach einem allgemeinen Gesetze zusammen bestehen kann'." (ibid.) Das allgemeine Rechts*gesetz* verbindet schließlich das Rechtsprinzip mit dem Begriff der Verbindlichkeit. Das Rechtsgesetz bringt unsere Verpflichtung zum Ausdruck, nach dem Rechtsprinzip zu handeln: „handle äußerlich so, daß der freie Gebrauch deiner Willkür mit der Freiheit von jedermann nach einem allgemeinen Gesetze zusammen bestehen könne." (AA 6: 231) Das Rechtsgesetz ist also das oberste konkrete positivrechtliche Normen stiftende Kriterium. Mit der in ihm zum Ausdruck gebrachten Verbindlichkeit macht Kant deutlich, dass für freie und unter dem Moralgesetz stehende Subjekte die Rechtsförmigkeit ihrer äußeren Handlungen normativ alternativlos ist. Dass es mir als Vernunftwesen nicht freisteht, mich für oder gegen die gesetzliche Bestimmung meiner Willkür zu entscheiden, erläutert Kant durch die selbstbezügliche Struktur unseres Wollens. Sie erklärt die Bedeutung von Recht und Rechtspflicht. Die Vernunft erhebt einen Anspruch uns gegenüber, nämlich nur nach solchen Prinzipien zu handeln, die sich zu einer allgemeinen Gesetzgebung qualifizieren. Kant nennt diesen Anspruch das „*Recht der Menschheit in unserer eigenen Person*" (AA 6: 235). Dass die Vernunft dieses Recht hat, ist eine normative Tatsache. Wir werden uns nach Kant ihrer bewusst, sobald wir Überlegungen darüber anstellen, wie wir unsere Willkürfreiheit gebrauchen wollen.

Weil das Recht einen Anspruch bezeichnet, den wir als Vernunftwesen gegenüber uns selbst erheben, entspricht diesem Recht eine selbstbezügliche Pflicht. Kant nennt sie eine Rechtspflicht. Das Verhältnis von Recht und Rechtspflicht lässt sich auch durch die Unterscheidung zwischen *obligatio* (Verpflichtung, Verbindlichkeit) und *officium* (Pflicht) erläutern. Während die Verbindlichkeit die normative Beziehung ausdrückt, die zwischen dem freien Willen und seinen Gründen besteht, bezeichnet die Pflicht eine konkrete Handlung, die ich aufgrund einer bestehenden und im Gesetz zum Ausdruck gebrachten Verbindlichkeit vollziehen soll. Eine Rechtspflicht fordert also eine Tätigkeit, zu deren Vollzug ich aufgrund des Rechts der Menschheit in mir verbunden bin. Kants Versionen der ulpianischen Formeln drücken dementsprechend selbstbezügliche normative Beziehungen aus. Sie beschreiben die Weise, durch die sich die freie Willkür zum Handeln bestimmen soll.

Die *erste* dieser Rechtspflichten („*honeste vive*") besteht darin, „im Verhältniß zu Anderen seinen Werth als den eines Menschen zu behaupten, welche Pflicht durch den Satz ausgedrückt wird: ‚Mache dich anderen nicht zum bloßen Mittel, sondern sei für sie zugleich Zweck.'" Der erste rechtliche Akt einer Person besteht also nicht darin, das Recht des Anderen anzuerkennen. Die erste Rechtspflicht besteht nach Kant vielmehr darin, sich selbst als Rechtssubjekt vor der Willkürfreiheit der Anderen in Sicherheit zu bringen. Gemäß des Rechtsgrundsatzes *neminem laede* kann eine Person ihre Pflicht also nicht durch Passivität erfüllen. Sie muss selbst aktiv etwas dafür tun. Erst in einem *zweiten* Schritt folgt die aus dem Recht der Menschheit folgende Verbindlichkeit, den anderen Personen deshalb kein Unrecht anzutun, weil sie ebenfalls zur vernünftigen Selbstbestimmung fähige Subjekte sind („*neminem laede*"). Die Abfolge dieser beiden Rechtspflichten ergibt Sinn: Nur wenn ich mich als Rechtssubjekt erkenne und erhalte, kann ich meiner Pflicht nachkommen, andere Personen rechtlich nicht zu lädieren. Die *dritte* Rechtspflicht wird unter einer bestimmten empirischen Bedingung formuliert: Kann ich die Verbindung mit anderen Menschen faktisch nicht vermeiden, dann bin ich dazu verpflichtet, mit ihnen in „eine Gesellschaft" zu treten, „in welcher Jedem das Seine erhalten werden kann (*suum cuique tribue*)" (AA 6: 237). Auch hier wird von jeder einzelnen Person eine Handlung gefordert. Kant ist davon überzeugt, dass wir Menschen aufgrund der kugelförmigen Gestalt der Erde *faktisch* unter dieser Rechtspflicht stehen. Will es mir nun aber nicht gelingen, mit anderen in einen öffentlichen Rechtszustand zu treten, füge ich einem anderen Menschen kein individuelles Unrecht zu, wie Kant in § 42 der *Rechtslehre* mit seiner Unterscheidung zwischen materialem und formalem Unrecht ausführt. Allerdings begehe ich im höchsten Maß Unrecht, wenn ich in diesem Zustand verbleibe (UNG 2). Denn ich erfülle eine auf dem Recht der Menschheit in mir beruhende Pflicht nicht. Die dritte ulpianische Formel drückt eine wechselseitige Zwangspflicht aus, deren Erfüllung die Voraussetzung für die Existenz des zwangsbewährten Rechts im *status civilis* ist.

Mit diesen Überlegungen zu den ulpianischen Formeln ist eine *erste* Hinsicht des Verhältnisses von Vernunft und freier Willkür erklärt: Dem Recht der Menschheit in uns entsprechen drei Rechtspflichten, die Vorbedingungen des Gebrauchs und des Erhalts unserer äußeren Handlungsfreiheit ausdrücken. Diese Pflichten leiten zur *zweiten* Hinsicht über: Weil ich die Pflicht habe, das Recht der Menschheit in mir und in jeder anderen Person zu erhalten, habe ich auch das *Recht*, meine Willkür innerhalb der Grenzen der allgemeinen Freiheitsgesetze zu gebrauchen. Es ist ein Recht, das ich *anderen* Personen gegenüber habe, und das andere Personen mir gegenüber haben. Weil es sich um ein ursprüngliches, nicht erworbenes Recht handelt, nennt es Kant das „*angeborene Recht*": „Freiheit (Unabhängigkeit von eines Anderen nöthigender Willkür), sofern sie mit jedes Anderen Freiheit nach einem allgemeinen Gesetz zusammen bestehen kann, ist dieses einzige, ursprüngliche, jedem Menschen kraft seiner Menschheit zustehende Recht."

Im Recht der Freiheit, im inneren Mein und Dein, individualisiert sich der Anspruch unserer Vernunft auf Selbsterhaltung im Gegenüber einer Pluralität von Personen, die diese Freiheit gefährden. Eine Materialisierung, eine Konkretisierung dieses Anspruchs findet allerdings erst unter den Bedingungen der Existenz des äußeren Mein und Dein statt. Mit dem äußeren Mein und Dein beschreiben wir unsere äußere Handlungsfreiheit aus der Perspektive einer Handlungsweise, durch die wir anderen Personen eine Verbindlichkeit auferlegen können, sich des Gebrauchs einer Sache zu enthalten. Aufgrund meines angeborenen Freiheitsrechts habe ich das Recht, im Rahmen einer allgemeinen Gesetzgebung eine Sache zu erwerben, wodurch die Freiheit anderer Personen begrenzt wird. Rechtlich gefordert ist die Möglichkeit des äußeren Mein und Dein, weil seine Negation eine unzulässige Einschränkung meiner Willkürfreiheit bedeuten würde. Aus ihrer Funktion für die Möglichkeit des äußeren Mein und Dein erläutert sich die *Scharnierfunktion* des Freiheitsrechts im Argumentationsgang der *Rechtslehre:* Es vermittelt zwischen dem Recht der Menschheit in mir (und in jeder Person) auf der einen und der Theorie und Praxis der äußeren Gesetzgebung auf der anderen Seite. Das Freiheitsrecht legt fest, dass alle Einschränkungen meiner Freiheit durch das äußere Mein und Dein begründungsbedürftig sind. Durch das Recht der Freiheit wird erkannt, dass derjenige, der behauptet, ein erworbenes Recht zu haben, hierfür den Nachweis („die Beweisführung (*onus probandi*)", AA 6: 238) führen muss. Wir haben die ursprüngliche Befugnis, uns innerhalb der Grenzen des Gesetzes selbst zum Handeln zu bestimmen. Wer dies bezweifelt oder behauptet, dass ich Unrecht getan habe, muss den Nachweis führen.

Mit diesem Gedanken ist auch schon angedeutet, wie Kant die naheliegende Frage nach der Begründung des Rechts der Freiheit beantwortet. Auch wenn wir von den transzendentalphilosophischen Voraussetzungen von Kants Freiheitsbegriff an dieser Stelle absehen müssen, wird doch deutlich, dass diese Begründung nicht im Rahmen einer Wert*erkenntnis* erfolgt. Es genügt für die faktische politisch-rechtliche Inanspruchnahme der Idee der Freiheit aber auch nicht, dass uns diese im Bewusstsein des „moralischen Imperativs" verbürgt ist, wie Kant in der „Einleitung in die Rechtslehre" ausführt. Wer unter der Idee der Freiheit sich selbst bestimmt, der fragt nach Begründungen für Freiheitseinschränkungen. Aber die faktische Inanspruchnahme dieses Rechts kann argumentativ nicht erzwungen werden, wie Kant in seinen geschichtsphilosophischen Arbeiten deutlich macht. In ihnen führt er aus, dass unser Verlangen nach Freiheit und politischer Selbstbestimmung eine Vorgeschichte hat. Das Verlangen nach einem politischen Gemeinwesen, in dem die Bürger sich selbst das Gesetz geben, muss vielmehr in einem geschichtlichen Prozess reifen, der den Akteuren politische Autonomie als Alternative zu einem rechtlosen und damit armseligen, elenden und kurzen Leben zu begreifen erlaubt. Kant drückt diesen Gedanken in seinem Aufsatz *Idee zu einer* *allgemeinen Geschichte in weltbürgerlicher Absicht* wie folgt aus: Die Vernunft wirkt „nicht instinktmäßig", sondern bedarf der „Versuche, Übung und Unterricht, um von einer Stufe der Einsicht zur anderen allmählich fortzuschreiten" (AA 8: 19).

In seinen geschichtsphilosophischen Arbeiten federt Kant somit den kategorischen Geltungsuniversalismus von Moral und Vernunftrecht auf der Menschheitsebene ab: Das Menschenrecht gilt zwar universell, aber ohne entsprechende „Versuche, Übung und Unterricht" können wir nicht *erwarten*, dass es von allen erkannt und anerkannt wird. Entscheidend für den rechtsgeschichtlich diagnostizierbaren Fortschritt ist der Gedanke eines Rechts, dass man sich in Gestalt des angeborenen Freiheitsrechts selbst nehmen muss.

Es sei der Hinweis gestattet, dass das angeborene Recht der Freiheit kein isolierter Begriff innerhalb von Kants praktischer Philosophie ist. Eine für das Verständnis des Rechts der Freiheit aufschlussreiche Argumentation findet sich im dritten Abschnitt der *Grundlegung zur Metaphysik der Sitten*, in dem sich Kant zur Frage nach der Möglichkeit der in praktischer Absicht gebrauchten Idee der Freiheit äußert. Seine These lautet, dass wir nicht etwa deshalb berechtigt wären, unter der Idee der Freiheit zu handeln, weil die objektive Bedeutung dieser Idee mit den Mitteln der spekulativen Vernunft deduziert worden wäre. Wir sind zu diesem Gebrauch vielmehr in letzter Konsequenz deshalb berechtigt, weil die theoretische Philosophie in Gestalt der Auflösung der dritten Antinomie in der *Kritik der reinen Vernunft* die Unmöglichkeit eines negativen Freiheitsbeweises aufzeigt. In der Kontroverse zwischen Freiheit und Fatalismus verschiebt Kant also die Beweislast: Wir erheben in praktischer Hinsicht den „Rechtsanspruch [...] auf Freiheit des Willens" (AA 4: 456–457), ohne diesen Anspruch in theoretischer Hinsicht förmlich beweisen zu können. Und wir brauchen diesen Anspruch auch nicht zu beweisen, weil wir mit den Mitteln der theoretischen Vernunft beweisen können, dass der Fatalist mit seinem Versuch eines negativen Freiheitsbeweises scheitert. Das reicht für unser praktisches Selbstverständnis und für den praktischen Gebrauch der Idee der Freiheit völlig aus. Es ist dieser Beweis der Unmöglichkeit eines negativen Freiheitsbeweises, der von Kant auch in der *Rechtslehre* in Anspruch genommen wird. Nebenbei bemerkt: Kant vertritt diese Ansicht auch in der Ende 1787 publizierten *Kritik der praktischen Vernunft*:

> Allein die Freiheit einer wirkenden Ursache, vornehmlich in der Sinnenwelt, kann ihrer Möglichkeit nach keineswegs eingesehen werden; glücklich! wenn wir nur, daß kein Beweis ihrer Unmöglichkeit stattfindet, hinreichend versichert werden können, und nun, durchs moralische Gesetz, welches dieselbe postuliert, genötigt, eben dadurch auch berechtigt werden, sie anzunehmen. (AA 5: 94)

In der Tat: Was für ein Glück! Denn würde es beispielsweise Johann Heinrich Schulz in seinem *Versuch einer Anleitung zur Sittenlehre für alle Menschen* (1783) gelungen sein (wovon nach Kant ganz und gar nicht auszugehen ist), einen derartigen Beweis zu liefern, dann wären Kategorischer Imperativ und Rechtsgesetz Begriffsdichtungen. Denn: Ohne Freiheit keine Verbindlichkeit.

5 Rechtsbegriff und Widerstandsverbot

Kants Konzeption des bürgerlichen Zustands geht bekanntlich einher mit dem rechtlichen Verbot, Widerstand gegenüber einer bestehenden Rechtsordnung zu leisten. Ob eine positivrechtliche Norm dem Ideal einer bürgerlichen Gesellschaft und der republikanischen Regierungsart entspricht oder nicht, der Bürger muss gehorchen und auf bessere Zeiten hoffen (UNG 6). Angesichts der Erfahrungen mit totalitaristischen Gewaltherrschaften im 20. und 21. Jahrhundert scheint dies kein wirklich überzeugender Gedanke zu sein. Es stellt sich somit die Frage, ob es Grenzen der Rechtsbefolgung gibt, die Kant vielleicht nicht explizit formuliert, die aber mit einer gewissen Stringenz aus seiner Rechtskonzeption folgen. Meines Erachtens gibt es *drei* Möglichkeiten, diese Frage positiv zu beantworten:

Zur *ersten* Möglichkeit. Positives Recht ist nach Kant Zwangsrecht. Er muss daher zeigen, dass der Staat legitimiert ist, Personen zur Gesetzesbefolgung zu zwingen, obwohl diese Personen ein angeborenes Freiheitsrecht haben. Die Begründung erfolgt über die der positiven Rechtsordnung zugeschriebene Funktion: Weil die reine praktische Vernunft die Erhaltung und Realisierung der Freiheit auch in ihrem rein äußeren Gebrauch gebietet, ist der äußere Zwang gerechtfertigt. Er ist das einzige Mittel zur Realisierung dieses Zweckes (vgl. AA 6: 231, § D). Es scheint paradox zu sein: Ich bin nur deshalb verpflichtet, das positive Gesetz zu befolgen, weil ich ein angeborenes Freiheitsrecht habe. Leiste ich Widerstand gegen eine rechtliche Verfassung, die ich für ungerecht beurteile, verletze ich jedoch die notwendige Voraussetzung, unter der meine äußere Handlungsfreiheit gewährleistet werden kann, nämlich das Gewaltmonopol des Staates.

In welcher Weise sind diese Überlegungen zum Verhältnis von Zwang und Recht für unsere Frage nach einer Schranke für das positive Recht von Bedeutung? Die Antwort lautet: Diese Überlegungen zeigen, dass das Zwangsrecht die äußere Handlungsfreiheit von Personen nicht generell negieren kann. Es muss für jede Person einen Spielraum ihrer Freiheit geben. Denn das zwangsbewährte Gesetz hat nicht die Vernichtung, sondern die Erhaltung der äußeren Freiheit zum Ziel. Besteht der Zweck der Rechtsordnung in der totalen und absoluten Vernichtung dieser Freiheit, handelt es sich um eine Gewaltordnung ohne Freiheit und ohne Gesetz. Was wie eine Rechtsordnung aussieht, ist tatsächlich Barbarei. In diesem Zustand stellt sich die Frage nach der Existenz eines Widerstandsrechts nicht, weil es keine bestehende Rechtsordnung gibt. Obwohl der Eindruck entstehen könnte, als ob Kant wie später Hans Kelsen die Auffassung vertreten würde, dass jeder Inhalt zur positivrechtlichen Norm erhoben werden kann, ist dies gerade nicht der Fall. Es sind Akte der positivrechtlichen Gesetzgebung denkbar, deren Effekt die Aufhebung dieser Rechtsordnung ist. Die einzig rechtmäßige Verfassung der Republik, so schreibt Kant in der *Rechtslehre*, macht „allein die *Freiheit* zum Princip, ja zur Bedingung alles *Zwanges*". Ist diese Bedingung nicht erfüllt, kann es keinen berechtigten Zwang geben. Dies ist auch der Grund, warum ich nach Kant keinen Vertrag in der Absicht schließen kann, meine Freiheit zu verlieren. Durch einen Vertrag kann sich niemand zu einer solchen Abhängigkeit verbinden, dadurch er aufhört, eine Person zu sein; denn nur als Person kann er einen Vertrag machen." (AA 6: 330) Zwingt mich der Staat, einen derartigen Vertrag zu schließen, befinde ich mich ihm gegenüber im Naturzustand. Der Staat hat für mich zu existieren aufgehört. Leiste ich den Inhabern staatlicher Gewalt Widerstand, nehme ich für mich nicht ein (nicht existierendes) Vernunftrecht auf Widerstand gegen eine legitime Autorität in Anspruch. Eine derartige Autorität gibt es nicht mehr.

Zur *zweiten* Möglichkeit. Kant definiert das Recht als „Inbegriff der Bedingungen, unter denen die Willkür des einen mit der Willkür des andern nach einem allgemeinen Gesetze der Freiheit zusammen vereinigt werden kann." (AA 6: 230, § C) Dies ist eine formale, aber keine inhaltlich leere Rechtsdefinition. Sie ist inhaltlich schon deshalb nicht leer, weil es nicht schwer fällt, Alternativen zu ihr zu finden. Diese Alternativen formulieren einen Begriff der Verfassung eines Gemeinwesens, die dem Kantischen Verständnis nach an sich unrechtmäßig ist. Ein schlagendes Beispiel für einen derartigen Begriff der Verfassung findet sich in Ernst Rudolf Hubers *Verfassungsrecht des Großdeutschen Reiches* von 1939. Huber, ein Schüler Carl Schmitts, hebt hervor, dass die „nationalsozialistische Revolution [...] den parlamentarischen Gesetzgebungsstaat vollends zerstört" und an seine Stelle „die neue Verfassungsform des völkischen Führerreichs geschaffen" (2014, 332) hat. Ein zentrales Element der neuen Verfassungsform besteht nach Huber darin, dass sich die „Führung" dieses Staates, die sich im „*Entscheid*" (2014, 339) des Führers materialisiert, zwar „der Gesetzgebung bedienen" kann, „aber nicht notwendig an diese Handlungsform gebunden" (2014, 332) ist. Schon aus diesem Grunde, dem durch und durch politischen Charakters des (so Huber) „völkischen Führerreichs" (2014, 346), befinden sich die Bürger des Reiches Kants Verständnis nach in einem „Zustande äußerlich gesetzloser Freiheit" (AA 6: 307). Nach Kant stiftet diese Verfassung (die in Wahrheit gar keine ist) keinen *status civilis*, weil für sie die Ausübung von Herrschaft jenseits des Gesetzes konstitutiv ist. Weil das „völkische Führerreich" nicht den Vorbehalt der Rechtsförmigkeit staatlichen Handelns und den Primat des positiven Rechts kennt, sind beliebige politische Akte und Maßnahmen schlicht dadurch gerechtfertigt, dass sie gewollt werden –

die Bestrafung Unschuldiger genauso wie die Androhung und der Vollzug grausamer Strafen oder psychische und physische Vernichtung von Personen. Aus diesem Grunde sind die unter diese Verfassung fallenden Menschen nach Kant nicht etwa nur befugt, sondern sie sind auch verpflichtet, dem „Begriff des Rechts" (AA 6: 308 – 309 Anm., § 42) durch Gewalt Gültigkeit zu verschaffen. Das „völkische Führerreich" ist nach Kant ein Reich der Barbarei.

Die *dritte* Möglichkeit ist mit den beiden ersten inhaltlich verschwistert. Allerdings operiert sie nicht mit einer einzig und allein in Begriffen des Rechts formulierten Beweisführung. In ihr geht es um das Verhältnis von Recht und Ethik. Bemerkenswert ist eine Anmerkung in der Religionsschrift, in der Kant darauf hinweist, dass wir ethisch nicht nur nicht verpflichtet sind, staatliche Gesetze zu befolgen, die dem „Sittengesetz unmittelbar zuwider" sind. Wir sollen diese Gesetze auch nicht befolgen. Das Zitat lautet vollständig: „Der Satz ‚man muß Gott mehr gehorchen, als den Menschen' bedeutet nur, daß, wenn die letzten etwas gebieten, was an sich böse (dem Sittengesetz unmittelbar zuwider) ist, ihnen nicht gehorcht werden darf und soll." (AA 6: 99 Anm.) Dieses Zitat ist bemerkenswert, weil es deutlich macht, dass wir aus ethisch-moralischen Gründen einem sittenwidrigen Gesetz nicht Folge leisten dürfen, obwohl wir kein formales Widerstandsrecht haben. Kant argumentiert in der Religionsschrift jedoch nicht im Widerspruch zu der *Rechtslehre*. Vielmehr sind die Argumente der beiden Schriften auf verschiedenen Ebenen angesiedelt: Obwohl es kein Recht auf Widerstand geben kann (dieses müsste ein Zwangsrecht sein), gibt es die ethische Pflicht, sittenwidrige Gesetze nicht zu befolgen. Die Ethik markiert demnach eine Schranke für die positivrechtliche Gesetzgebung.

6 Eine Zwischenbilanz

Die Kantische Rechtsphilosophie sieht im Rahmen ihrer Konzeption des Öffentlichen Rechts drei Fälle vor, in denen die staatliche Herrschaft ihre Legitimität verliert, unter der ihre Anordnungen für den Bürger nicht oder nicht mehr länger verbindlich sind: *Erstens*, wenn der Staat Handlungen von mir verlangt, die mit dem Begriff der Rechtsperson oder der Rechtssubjektivität unvereinbar sind. Kein Gesetz kann verbindlich sein, das Personen zu bloßen Mitteln staatlicher Willkür macht oder die Vernichtung ihrer Rechtsfähigkeit zum Gegenstand hat (UNG 5). *Zweitens* ist jede rein politische Herrschaft rechtlich unverbindlich, weil in ihr der Naturzustand nicht überwunden ist. Die Willkür des Führerentscheids verstößt an sich gegen den Rechtsbegriff (UNG 2). *Drittens* werden bestimmte positivrechtliche Inhalte direkt durch das Moralgesetz ausgeschlossen. Werden diese Inhalte dennoch rechtlich positiviert, ist es den Bürgern untersagt, ihnen Folge zu leisten

(UNG 4). Hierbei berufen sie sich nicht auf ein positivrechtliches Widerstandsrecht. Sie berufen sich direkt auf das Moralgesetz.

7 Der ungerechte Bundesgenosse

Was bedeutet dies alles für unsere Frage nach dem ungerechten Bundesgenossen?
Wenn Kant im Rahmen des Völkerrechts daran erinnert, dass der Mensch

> im Staat immer als mitgesetzgebendes Glied betrachtet werden muß (nicht bloß als Mittel,
> sondern auch zugleich als Zweck an sich selbst), und der also zum Kriegführen nicht allein
> überhaupt, sondern auch zu jeder besondern Kriegserklärung vermittelst seiner Repräsen-
> tanten seine freie Beistimmung geben muß, unter welcher einschränkenden Bedingung al-
> lein der Staat über seinen gefahrvollen Dienst disponiren kann (AA 6: 345–346, § 55),

ist die prinzipielle Perspektive genannt, unter der diese Frage zu beantworten ist.
Es ist dies die Perspektive eines Rechts, dass in Gestalt der drei ursprünglichen
Rechtspflichten von mir verlangt, in einen Rechtszustand zu treten, in dem jedem
das Seine erhalten werden kann. Das Ziel des Rechts kann nicht darin bestehen,
Handlungen zu verlangen, durch die der Handelnde selbst oder der von der
Handlung Betroffene zu einem bloßen Mittel degradiert wird. Bloßes Mittel zu sein
bedeutet, nicht als Person behandelt zu werden, nicht als ein Subjekt, welches
Rechenschaft für seine Freiheitseinschränkungen verlangen kann. Für Freiheitseinschränkungen zumal, die nicht die Vernichtung dieser Freiheit zum Ziel haben
kann. Was bedeutet es nun für einen Staat A, wenn sein Bundesgenosse B von
seinen eigenen Bürgern Handlungen gegenüber einem bündnisfremden Staat C
verlangt, durch die die Bürger des Staates B „unfähig" (AA 6: 347, § 57) werden,
länger Staatsbürger zu sein? Was genau möchte Kant mit dieser Aussage zum
Ausdruck bringen? Vielleicht das Folgende: Es gibt Handlungen, durch die ein
zukünftiger und dauerhafter Friede unmöglich wird, weil sie „das Vertrauen,
welches zur künftigen Gründung eines dauerhaften Friedens erforderlich ist,
vernichten würden" (ibid.) (UNG 3). Die Ungerechtigkeit liegt also nicht in der
Gegenwart, sondern mit Blick auf zukünftige Handlungen begründet, zu deren
Vollzug wir im Sinne des Postulats des Öffentlichen Rechts rechtlich verpflichtet
sind. Das Postulat des öffentlichen Friedens fordert von den Staaten, alles zu
unternehmen, um den Naturzustand zu überwinden. Die real betrachtet einzige
Möglichkeit ist der Abschluss eines Bundes. Der Einsatz „heimtückischer Mittel"
(ibid.) macht es aber unmöglich, Vertrauen zum anderen Staat zu haben. Jeder
Krieg muss demnach nach Grundsätzen geführt werden, „nach welchen es immer
noch möglich bleibt, aus jenem Naturzustande der Staaten (im äußeren Verhältniß
gegen einander) herauszugehen und in einen rechtlichen zu treten." (Ibid.) Der

Einsatz „heimtückischer Mittel" scheint Kants Auffassung nach dem Gegner das Recht zu geben, ebenfalls zu diesen Mitteln zu greifen. Der Verlust des Vertrauens ist umso schlagender, wenn der Staat einen Straf-, Ausrottungs- oder Untergangskrieg geführt hat.

Kants Formulierung in § 57, wonach bestimmte „Vertheidigungsmittel" für einen Staat nicht erlaubt sind, „deren Gebrauch die Unterthanen desselben, Staatsbürger zu sein, unfähig machen würde", ist nicht einfach zu verstehen. Was meint Kant damit? Als Begründung führt er an: „denn alsdann machte er sich selbst zugleich unfähig im Staatenverhältnisse nach dem Völkerrecht für eine Person zu gelten (die gleicher Rechte mit andern theilhaftig wäre)." (AA 6: 347, § 57) Wenn also der Staat seinen Bürgern bestimmte unerlaubte Handlungen befiehlt, hat dies den doppelten Effekt, dass die Bürger keine Staatsbürger mehr sind und der Staat aufhört, nach dem Völkerrecht als eine Person zu gelten. Dies bedeutet: Der fremde Staat kann ebenfalls alle Mittel verwenden, um sich zu verteidigen, weil der andere Staat nicht als Person existiert. Genau dieser Gedanke wurde in §§ 42 und 54 angesprochen: Es gibt eine Art von Unrecht, das an sich besteht (der Naturzustand als Kriegszustand), ohne ein Unrecht gegen eine Person zu sein (UNG 2). Wenn aber der Staat nach dem Völkerrecht nicht mehr als eine Person gelten kann, dann sind die Bürger auch keine Staatsbürger mehr. Sie sind schlicht Feinde nach naturrechtlichem Verständnis. Die Frage stellt sich nun, ob aus der Perspektive der Bürger, von denen der Staat diese illegitimen Handlungen verlangt, auch der eigene Staat seine Legitimität verliert. Er verlangt ja von den Bürgern Handlungen, die sie als moralische Personen nicht wollen können. Wenn der Bürger nicht als „mitgesetzgebendes Glied" (AA 6: 345, § 55) sich betrachten kann, dann hat der Staat nach Rechtsbegriffen für ihn aufgehört zu existieren.

Für das Verhältnis eines Staates A zu seinem Bundesgenossen B kann dies nicht irrelevant sein. Wenn der Staat B an sich ungerechte Mittel ergreift, hat er nicht nur aus der Perspektive des bündnisfremden Staates C aufgehört zu existieren, demgegenüber er sich mit bestimmten illegitimen Mitteln verteidigen oder dem gegenüber er einen Eroberungsfeldzug führt. Der Staat A muss den Bund mit dem Staat B aufkündigen. Verlangt ein Staat von seinen Bürgern Handlungen, durch die sie aufhören, Staatsbürger zu sein, oder führt dieser Staat einen Unterwerfungskrieg gegen einen bündnisfremden Staat, dann muss der Bund mit ihm aufgekündigt werden. Ihm ist nicht zu trauen. Er erfüllt nicht den Zweck, den er entsprechend der Rechtsdefinition zu erfüllen hat, nämlich die Überwindung des *status naturalis*. Durch seine Taten deklariert dieser Staat, sich dem Frieden nicht kontinuierlich annähern zu wollen. Vielleicht ist dies die Bedeutung des Satzes, dass die „Genossenschaft (Föderalität)" eine „Verbündung" ist, „die zu aller Zeit aufgekündigt werden kann, mithin von Zeit zu Zeit erneuert werden muß" (AA 6: 344, § 54).

Bibliographie

Brandt, Reinhard (1982): Das Erlaubnisgesetz, oder: Vernunft und Geschichte in Kants
    Rechtslehre, in: Reinhard Brandt (Hg.): Rechtsphilosophie der Aufklärung. Symposium
    Wolfenbüttel 1981, Berlin, S. 233–285.
Brandt, Reinhard (2012): Sei ein rechtlicher Mensch (honeste vive) – wie das?, in: Mario
    Brandhorst, Andree Hahmann und Bernd Ludwig (Hg.): Sind wir Bürger zweier Welten?
    Freiheit und moralische Verantwortung im transzendentalen Idealismus, Hamburg,
    S. 311–359.
Byrd, B. Sharon und Joachim Hruschka (2010): Kant's Doctrine of Right. A Commentary,
    Cambridge.
Dreier, Horst (2004): Kants Republik, in: JuristenZeitung, Jahrgang 59, Nr. 15/16, S. 745–756.
Fichte, Johann Gottlieb (1971): Grundlage des Naturrechts nach Principien der
    Wissenschaftslehre. [1796] (= Fichtes Werke, hg. von I. H. Fichte, Band III), Berlin.
Horn, Christoph (2014): Nichtideale Normativität. Ein neuer Blick auf Kants politische
    Philosophie, Berlin.
Huber, Ernst Rudolf (2014): Verfassungsrecht des Großdeutschen Reiches (1939) – Auszug, in:
    Herlinde Pauer-Studer und Julian Fink (Hg.): Rechtfertigungen des Unrechts. Berlin,
    S. 245–250.
Kant, Immanuel (1900 ff.): Gesammelte Schriften, hg. von der Königlich-Preussischen
    Akademie der Wissenschaften zu Berlin, Berlin.
Kant, Immanuel (1998): Kritik der reinen Vernunft, hg. von Jens Timmermann, Hamburg.
Kelsen, Hans (2008): Reine Rechtslehre. Studienausgabe der 1. Auflage 1934, hg. von Matthias
    Jestaedt, Tübingen.
Klemme, Heiner F. (1992): Einleitung, in: Immanuel Kant, Über den Gemeinspruch – Zum
    ewigen Frieden, hg. von H. F Klemme, Hamburg, S. VII-LIII.
Klemme, Heiner F. (2001): Das ‚angeborne Recht der Freiheit'. Zum inneren Mein und Dein in
    Kants Rechtslehre, in: Volker Gerhardt u.a (Hg.): Kant und die Berliner Aufklärung. Akten
    des IX. Internationalen Kant-Kongresses, Band 4, Berlin, S. 180–188.
Klemme, Heiner F. (2011): Das rechtsstaatliche Folterverbot aus der Perspektive der
    Philosophie Kants, in: Karsten Altenhain und Nicola Willenberg (Hg.): Die Geschichte der
    Folter nach ihrer Abschaffung, Göttingen, S. 39–53.
Klemme, Heiner F. (2013a): Menschenwürde und Menschenrecht. Variationen eines kantischen
    Themas in systematischer Absicht, in: Frank Brosow und T. Raja Rosenhagen (Hg.):
    Moderne Theorien der Normativität. Zur Wirklichkeit und Wirksamkeit des praktischen
    Sollens, Münster, S. 213–229.
Klemme, Heiner F. (2013b): Das Recht auf Rechte und die Pflicht zur Staatlichkeit. Kants
    Antwort auf Hannah Arendts Menschenrechtskritik, in: Falk Bornmüller, Thomas Hoffmann
    und Arnd Pollmann (Hg.): Menschenrechte und Demokratie. Georg Lohmann zum
    65. Geburtstag, Freiburg, S. 161–182.
Klemme, Heiner F. (2014): Freiheit oder Fatalismus? Kants positive und negative Deduktion der
    Idee der Freiheit in der Grundlegung (und seine Kritik an Christian Garves Antithetik von
    Freiheit und Notwendigkeit), in: Heiko Puls (Hg.): Deduktion oder Faktum? Kants
    Rechtfertigung des Sittengesetzes im dritten Abschnitt der „Grundlegung", Berlin,
    S. 61–103.

Klemme, Heiner F. (2015): ‚als ob er frei wäre'. Kants Rezension von Johann Heinrich Schulz'
    Versuch einer Anleitung zur Sittenlehre für alle Menschen, in: Claudia Jáuregui et al. (Hg.):
    Crítica y Metafísica. Homenaje a Mario Caimi. Hildesheim/Zürich/New York, S. 200–211.
Klemme, Heiner F. (2016, im Erscheinen): Gewissen und Verbindlichkeit. Kants Idee eines
    „inneren Gerichtshofs" zwischen Christian Wolff und Adam Smith, in: Saša Josifović und
    Arthur Kok (Hg.): Der innere Gerichtshof der Vernunft, Leiden.
Meier, Georg Friedrich (1767): Recht der Natur, Halle (Nachdruck mit einem Vorwort von
    Dominik Recknagel, Hildesheim et al, 2014).
Mohr, Georg (2011): Person, Recht und Menschenrecht bei Kant, in: Eckhart Klein und
    Christoph Menke (Hg.): Der Mensch als Person und Rechtsperson, Berlin, S. 33–36.
Pauer-Studer, Herlinde (2014): Einleitung: Rechtfertigungen des Unrechts. Das Rechtsdenken
    im Nationalsozialismus, in: Herlinde Pauer-Studer und Julian Fink (Hg.): Rechtfertigungen
    des Unrechts, Berlin, S. 15–135.
Pauer-Studer, Herlinde und Julian Fink (Hg.): (2014): Rechtfertigungen des Unrechts. Das
    Rechtsdenken im Nationalsozialismus in Originaltexten, Berlin.
Ripstein, Arthur (2009): Force and Freedom. Kant's Legal and Political Philosophy, Cambridge,
    MA.

The *Federalist Papers*

Beatrice Brunhöber

The *Federalist Papers*, Federalism and Democratic Representation

Alexander Hamilton, James Madison and John Jay put forward a trail-blazing claim in the *Federalist Papers:* representation has to be democratic. At the time, this conjunction was considered contradictory. However, with the idea of democratic representation the *Federalist*[1] found a way out of the difficulties besetting the contemporary theory of democracy. Against the background of the Aristotelian idea of pure democracy, it was considered unsustainable—in any case, for a heterogeneous and expansive state—a mere utopia. The question of how the political autonomy of a pluralist society can be sustained within a vast body politic in the long run remains topical to this very day. The *Federalist* gives an answer that is not only theoretically convincing, but has also been borne out as practicable in the reality of the United States Constitution.

1 Representation as pathway to democracy

The invention of democratic representation[2] in the *Federalist Papers* was a novelty in the years of its inception (1787/88).[3] Up to that point, the relation of democracy and representation had been conceived of as dichotomous. The reason for this is to be found in the meaning of the two concepts. In political theory[4], since the middle ages[5] representation had been seen as an instrument by means of which a plurality of people could act collectively within a body politic.

---

1 In the USA the *Federalist Papers* are commonly referred to as the *Federalist*. This was the title of the first publication in book-form (McLean/McLean 1788). On the question of the coherence of the papers see Brunhöber (2010a, chapter 2, III), affirmatively Epstein (1984, 2), White (1987, *passim*), Potter (2002, 7 ff.); negatively Mason (1952, 625 ff.). This paper is based on previous considerations in Brunhöber (2010b).

2 On democratic representation in general see Böckenförde (2004, 12 ff.).

3 While the developments in France and Great Britain were equally as important for the history of the concept, the constitution of the French revolution was only instated in 1791. And English parliamentarianism cannot rightly be characterised as democratic. On this matter see section 2 below.

4 The concept of 'representation' is used with variable meanings in most humanities. Cf. Hofmann (2003, 1 ff.).

5 First by Thomas Aquinas (1943, 20, book 2, section 2, qu. 105, art. 1).

The questions to be solved by representation are: How can an individual or several be empowered to act and decide on behalf of the group? To what extent can these actions and decisions by the representatives be ascribed to the members or the group?[6] Conversely, Aristotle had characterised democracy as the form of government of immediate self-determination of the people, one, however, that he saw as prone to decay.[7] As such, in the early modern period, most notably by Rousseau[8], it was assumed that democracy and representation were incompatible.[9] But if, according to this definition, delegating legislative decisions and executive action is ruled out in a democracy, it can only be realised in a small area with a very homogeneous population: only then can people convene at frequent intervals, and only then is there a chance of agreement.

In the wake of the American Revolution, in the *Federalist Papers*, Alexander Hamilton, James Madison and John Jay suggest combining "a government wholly popular" with "the great principle of representation" in order to make the idea practicable in a body politic with a heterogeneous population. In 1777 Hamilton called the new form of government "representative democracy".[10] However, the *Federalist* settled on the term "republic" to clearly set it off from Aristotelian democracy. In *Federalist* No. 39, Madison defines a republic as

> a government which derives all its powers directly or indirectly from the great body of the people, and is administered by persons holding their offices during pleasure, for a limited period, or during good behaviour.[11]

A republic is defined as a form of government in which all power resides with the people but is enacted by elected representatives.[12] The representatives are determined by means of free, equal, general and regular elections. Thus the concept of 'the people' has been essentially altered: it no longer refers to the lowest class,

---

6 Hofmann/Dreier (1989, 165 ff.).
7 Aristotle (2003, book VI, 1317b 19–48).
8 Rousseau (1966, book III, ch. 15).
9 The after-effects are noticeable to this day. Cf., for instance, Schmitt (1970, 204 ff., 218, 243), Kelsen (1981, 26 ff.), Landshut (1968, 482 ff.), Meyer (2005, 99 ff., 104). See also Leibholz (1967, 78 ff.), Graf von Kielmannsegg (1985, 9 ff.). An objection is Duso (2006, 99).
10 For instance, with regard to the constitution of the state New York of 1777 Hamilton (1961, 254 ff., 255). Buchstein argues that Hamilton invented this concept (1997, 376 ff., 380).
11 Madison, *Federalist* (No. 39 [38], 251). The definition of 'republic' is similar to Kant's (1968b, 341).
12 On the concept of 'republic' in the *Federalist* see Epstein (1984, 120 f.); von Bose (1989, 89 ff.). On the use of the concepts 'democracy' and 'republic' of the time see Adams (1973, 99 ff., 106 ff.); Dahl (2006, 152 ff., 156 f.).

but the totality of free and equal individuals of which society consists.[13] While the representatives have a free mandate, they are nonetheless bound by the constitution.[14] A further essential element that is mentioned by Hamilton is the separation of powers.[15] Just as he did, we, too, would call such a form of government representative democracy.

However, it is highly disputed that the *Federalist's* theory is democratic. How it is to be categorised depends on the interpretation which is, however, marked by extreme changes of direction in the United States.[16] Three interpretations can be distinguished, of which the first two do not categorise the *Federalist* as democratic. The *economic* interpretation from the beginning of the twentieth century emphasises the influence of John Locke, however, in a manner focused on individual property and, as such, sees in the idea of representation a mere means of protecting the upper classes.[17] This is countered by the so-called claim of *republicanism* in the 1960ies. It traces the influence of classical republican ideas to the *Federalist* and sees in its theory an attempt to create an aristocracy influenced by the Aristotelian idea of a mixed government.[18] Since the 1980ies Locke's influence is levelled against this, but this time emphasising his idea of the social contract.[19] Only the last analysis allows a *democratic* interpretation of the *Federalist Papers*. Against the backdrop of the social contract it becomes possible to see representation as a contractual relation between political institutions and the people based on the will of the latter. If one furthermore takes into account the influence of Montesquieu's mixed constitution on the *Federalist's* doctrine of the separation of powers, one can see that this idea, too, is freed from its classical republican context. It no longer, as with Aristotle, serves to prevent the decay inherent in any pure form of government. It serves—in a very modern way—to prevent an accumulation of power that endangers freedom.

For the *Federalist*, representation is the pathway to popular sovereignty.[20] The *Federalist* argues as follows: If man is a free creature, he must govern himself.[21] However, people have not been able to govern themselves, yet.[22] It

---

13 For this reason Madison speaks of the "great body of the people", *Federalist* (No. 39 [38], 251). See Brunhöber (2010a, chapter 4, II. 1. a.).

14 Hamilton, *Federalist* (No. 78 [77], 524).

15 Hamilton, *Federalist* (No. 9, 51).

16 In detail Brunhöber (2010a, chapter 1, I.).

17 E. g. Beard (1998).

18 E. g. Pocock (2003); also see Wood (1998).

19 E. g. Pangle (1988).

20 See Brunhöber (2010a, chapter 4, II. 1. a.; III. 1. b.).

21 Cf. Madison, *Federalist* (No. 39 [38], 250); see also Madison, *Federalist* (No. 10, 58). This will later be impressively scaffolded theoretically by Kant: from man's freedom it follows that the

turned out not to be sufficient to draw on Aristotelian democracy in order to realise the idea of popular sovereignty. The democracies of Antiquity rarely lasted long—due to external weakness and internal instability. The *Federalist* suggests that both problems can be overcome in a large body politic, because size guarantees external independence and internal peace. The size makes immediate decisions by all, however, practically impossible and thus requires the delegation of decision-making.[23] The democratic character of the procedure by which representation is allocated, nonetheless, ties the decision back to the will of the people and makes decision-makers accountable for their actions to the people.[24] Representation at the same time sets citizens free to become productive economically and to pursue egoistic interests, since they do not have to reign themselves on a daily basis. This task is transferred to the elected representatives.[25] At the same time the procedure of representation guarantees an orientation towards the common good in *political* decisions and thus contributes to internal stability. Representation furthermore enables the delegation of deliberative competence to experts and thus ensures a people's ability to decide rationally despite the complexity of political states of affairs in a developed society.[26] Finally, only representation enables the separation of powers, which in turn prevents despotism. If the people themselves held all powers of government, there could be no powers mutually controlling one another.

The core thought of the *Federalist* is a re-conception of the idea of representation. Thus, the American Revolution is not a mere reception of European ideas,[27] but a total renewal of them. This is very clear in the particular conception of the principle of representation. It is taken out of its hereditary-corporate con-

---

right to self-determination is intrinsic to any constitution as an ideal. Self-legislation thus is a principle of reason for him. Cf. Kant (1968a, 86 f.).

22 Hamilton, *Federalist* (No. 11, 72).

23 Madison [Hamilton], *Federalist* (No. 52 [51], 355). Cf. also Hamilton, *Federalist* (No. 76 [75], 510). By theories of direct democracy, representation is often reduced to this surrogate function; cf., e.g., Kelsen (1981, 26 ff.). On the other hand, in the theory of the *Federalist* representation has further essential functions.

24 Cf. Madison, *Federalist* (No. 48 [47], 337); Madison [Hamilton], *Federalist* (No. 57 [56], 384); Madison [Hamilton], *Federalist* (No.63 [62], 424); Hamilton, *Federalist* (No. 70 [69], 472, 476, 478); Hamilton, *Federalist* (No. 77 [76], 520). See Brunhöber (2010, chapter 4, II. 3. c.), Epstein (1984, 31).

25 Hamilton, *Federalist* (No. 76 [75], 510).

26 Cf. Madison [Hamilton], *Federalist* (No. 62 [61], 415 ff.), Madison, *Federalist* (No. 47 [46], 333 f.), Jay, *Federalist* (No. 64 [63], 432 f.).

27 This assumption seems to be the reason why European political theory concentrates on French and British roots when analysing democratic representation. See also Dreier (1988, 450 ff., 464), Fraenkel (1991, 153 ff., 185).

text and is given a democratic character. Representation is no longer—as in British theory—virtual, but actual (see below 2). Representation is no longer rooted in the identity of representatives and represented, but in the wilful transferral of power by the represented. And political decisions are not seen as mere recapitulation of a pre-existing common good, anymore. Political decisions are seen as finding compromises that can always be altered (see below 3). The traditional British theory of corporate representation is turned into a democratic idea of the separation of powers.

2 Real representation

The democratic turn is first noticeable in the representative mandate: it changes from a paternalistic to a democratic mandate. The *Federalist* leaves behind the British idea of virtual identity-representation and demands true representation. The representative is no longer an independent trustee of the people but is authorised by the people. The most prominent proponent of the British theory of the time, Edmund Burke, defined virtual representation as a fiduciary relationship:

> Virtual representation is that in which there is a communion of interests and a sympathy in feelings and desires between those who act in the name of any description of people and the people in whose name they act, though the trustees are not actually chosen by them.[28]

Here representatives need not to be elected (by all). While a procedure of selection is required, the legitimacy of representation follows from the natural order, the 'constitution' of society. Everyone has their natural position from which may result active and passive suffrage. Representation is legitimate because and if it adequately represents the organic body politic and there is an identity of interests between representatives and represented.[29] Accordingly, representation cannot, in principle, fail and therefore does not necessarily need to be controlled.[30] At most, corruption and partisanship[31] need to be suppressed in order not to disturb the natural process of representation.[32]

---

28 Burke (1975, 293).
29 Burke (1975, 293).
30 See Reid (1989, 48 f.).
31 At the time, the problem of partisanship was called the problem of factions. Today the term 'factions' is neither used in English nor in German. On the conceptual history see Beyme (1978, 677 ff.).

In contrast, representation in the British colonies in North America had developed to real delegation by an act of will.[33] This factual change is ultimately retraced legally by the United States Constitution (1787). The development was fuelled by the colonial structures of self-administration: elected representatives were the decision makers in town meetings as well as in parliaments. The independence efforts were finally sparked by the dispute whether Americans were represented in British parliament in such a manner that collecting taxes in the colonies was warranted. The slogan used in the campaigns against the Stamp and Sugar Acts was "No taxation without representation!"[34] Americans demanded actual representation through directly elected representatives. The British countered that the Americans were naturally represented in British parliament due to the natural order and the natural identity of interests.[35] After independence the Americans gave themselves a federal constitution which guarantees general, free and equal elections of all powers.[36]

The *Federalist* develops the theoretical foundation of this shift. It is a collection of papers written to promote the ratification of the United States Constitution in 1787/88. Against the idea of identity representation[37] Hamilton argues that the people shall decide freely whom they take to be best suited for their representation.[38] He argues further, even though this will commonly result in identity of interests the legitimacy of representation follows from electorate authorisation.[39] And Madison argues that there is no need for an identity of interests. Rather, in a republic the people are to choose the ones who they think best promote the common good. Their free vote is not to be restricted by any

---

32 Cf. Burke (1996, 658f.).

33 See Brunhöber (2010a, chapter 3, III.).

34 Slaughter (1984, 566ff.).

35 Cf., e.g., the speech by the British Joint Secretary of Treasury, Thomas Whately, on the defense of the Sugar Act of 1765, in: Morgan/Morgan (1962, 106f.).

36 Cf. Art. I, § 2, cl. 1, 2; § 3, cl. 1, Art. II, § 1, cl. 2 USConst. American voting rights were the most egalitarian of the time, Potter (2002, 115). On more detail see Brunhöber (2010, chapter 4, II. 1. a.).

37 The idea of identity representation was brought forward against the House of Representatives as constituted in the Federal Constitution, see e.g. Brutus (1981, 369), Smith (1981, 157ff.).

38 Hamilton, *Federalist* (No. 35 [33], 219ff.).

39 Ibid. Wood reads Hamilton as transposing the idea of virtual representation to the representation of interest groups (1969, 51ff.). But the mere identity of interest would have been sufficient for legitimate representation. This stands in contrast to the fact that, for Hamilton, the free act of authorisation is to guarantee that the representatives are responsive to all societal concerns, cf. Hamilton, *Federalist* (No. 35 [33], 222f.). See also Brunhöber (2010a, chapter 4, II. 2. b.).

qualifications: "No qualification of wealth, of birth, of religious faith, or of civil profession is permitted to fetter the judgement or disappoint the inclination of the people."[40] The people are to keep the control by means of periodic elections. These elections—and not some kind of identical interests—ensure that the representatives will govern in the interest of the people.[41]

The shift in meaning can also be seen in how the relation of representatives and people is understood. In Great Britain it was seen as a fiduciary relationship. The *Federalist* rather perceives it as a contract. In British constitutional theory of the time, representation could not be a relationship based on a free, wilful act, because the will was seen as result of the natural position of an individual in society. For the *Federalist*, however, man was not born into a pre-determined social order, anymore. In his eyes social order can be structured by the people themselves.[42] Hamilton thus sees representation as agency.[43] The representatives are agents who act on behalf of the represented. The constitution is seen as the framework of agency. If the agents exceed their authority as funded in the constitution their acts are not binding. This idea calls for an independent institution which controls the constitutionality of governmental acts.[44] Hence the constitution provides for a supreme court which has the power to declare void governmental acts. Madison also sees the representatives as agents of the people.[45] Government is an authorisation by mandate. The mandate is held by elected office holders for a limited period of time.[46]

The *Federalist* bases his ideas on Burke's and Locke's concept of fiduciary representation, but gives them a democratic twist.[47] The *Federalist* no longer sees representation founded in the natural identity of interests as Burke did,

---

40 Madison [Hamilton], *Federalist* (No. 57 [56], 384).
41 Madison [Hamilton], *Federalist* (No. 57 [56], 385 f.). See Brunhöber (2010, chapter 4, II. 2. b.).
42 Cf. Madison [Hamilton], *Federalist* (No. 51 [50], 352), Madison, *Federalist* (No. 43 [42], 295; No. 44 [43], 301), Locke (1964, chapter 11, § 142). The theory of the social contract was common coin at the time of the debate about the US constitution to such an extent that the *Federalist* naturally presupposed it. See Dietze (1957/58, 21 ff., 24; 1957, 307 ff., 311 ff.). On the social contract theory of the *Federalist* see Rosen (1999, 26 ff.), Potter (2002, 30 ff.). However, Locke's influence on the *Federalist* is contested. See section 1 above and also Brunhöber (2010a, chapter 1, I., chapter 3, I. 4.).
43 Hamilton, *Federalist* (No. 78 [77], 524).
44 Ibid. See Brunhöber (2010a, chapter 4, II. 5.).
45 Cf. Madison, *Federalist* (No. 46 [45], 315).
46 Madison, *Federalist* (No. 39 [38], 251), also see *Federalist* (No. 14, 84).
47 Cf. Madison, *Federalist* (No. 46 [45], 315), Madison [Hamilton], *Federalist* (No. 57 [56], 385), Madison [Hamilton], *Federalist* (No. 62 [61], 418), Hamilton, *Federalist* (No. 66 [65], 451; No. 68 [67], 458; No. 70 [69], 476, 478; No. 71 [70], 482). See *von Bose* (1989, 120 f.).

but in a wilful act of delegation. Different from Locke[48], confidence is sustained not by the right to dissolve government in case of misrepresentation but by periodic elections.[49] The continuous control by the people is also ensured by structuring the representative decision making process in a manner which allows for holding responsible the specific decision-makers as well as for public control.[50]

Against this background, assumptions previously taken to be self-evident become questionable in the context of an analysis of the concept of 'representation'. Many commentators argue that popular representation has its fundament in the representation of the estates.[51] Representation of the estates is based on the idea that representatives and represented have identical interests: peasants are to represent the peasantry etc. However, the North American elected rulers were seen as agents of the people just like the British monarch.[52] There did not need to be an identity of interests. Rather, it was important that the rulers acted on behalf of the people. The only difference is the source of power. The British monarchs derive their power from hereditary succession or the like whereas the American rulers derive their power form periodic (re-)elections. This is relevant, in particular, for the question of what representation is to achieve. If the end of representation is to reproduce all social interests parliaments need to consist of the several social, racial and religious groups etc. If representation means decision on behalf of the people there only need to be mechanisms that ensure that magistrates act in the interest of the people. If one wants to use the *Federalist* to argue for the latter, then it does not matter so much that the representatives come from all classes and interest groups. They could very well be recruited from a political elite. What matters is, rather, the mechanisms used to tie their decisions to public opinion. The *Federalist* takes this to be guaranteed by regular elections at short intervals and a public process of will-formation.

3 A procedural notion of the common good

The democratic turn is also seen in the decision making process. Just as before the goal was to find the common good. In contrast to British theory of the time,

---

48 Cf. Locke (1964, chapter 19, §§ 222, 232).
49 This difference is overlooked by Buchstein (1997, 376 ff., 392).
50 Cf. Madison, *Federalist* (No. 48 [47], 337), Madison [Hamilton], *Federalist* (No. 57 [56], 384; No. 63 [62], 424; No. 70 [69], 472, 476, 478); *Federalist* (No. 77 [76], 520). See Brunhöber (2010a, chapter 4, II. 3. c.).
51 Scheuner (1968, 386 ff., 394 f.); cf. Stern (1984, 946 ff.).
52 Hofmann (2003, 406 ff.); see also Brunhöber (2010a, chapter 4, II. 3. a.).

the *Federalist* no longer conceived of the common good as a substance, but as the result of a process of transformation that has to constantly be found anew. In principle all citizens are to be involved in it. At the same time the democratic delegation of deliberative power leads to a rationalisation of political decisions.

Burke still assumed that the common good is determined primarily by the organic, hereditary-corporate 'constitution' of society.[53] This requires suitable representatives who are capable of recognising the common good and bringing it to bear in their decisions. He finds them in the dignitaries who, in virtue of their governmental rank, naturally represent society in political decisions in parliament.

The *Federalist*, however, sees the common good as the "permanent and aggregate interests of the community".[54] The common good thus is a new manifestation of the sum of interests. The common good can only be determined in a political procedure that involves everyone.[55] It is not possible to rely on one or a few 'good rulers' for two reasons: First, there are no impartial rulers since everyone is affected by political decisions.[56] Second, one cannot hope for entirely reasonable statesmen, since the human cognitive faculties are fallible and there is no objective authority that could independently verify their decisions.[57]

On the one hand, with his idea of the aggregation of interests the *Federalist* does not equate the common good with the mathematical sum of interests as Thomas Paine and Jeremy Bentham did.[58] The common good cannot be calculated by summing up all the interests within a society. On the other hand, the common good is not just seen as the result of a horse-trading negotiation among interest groups. It essentially is an evaluation by the elected representatives.[59] It is determined in expanded, repeated and public debates and double-checked by several elected powers. The general perspective taken in this procedure is hoped to exclude any opinions which infringe upon individual rights or the com-

---

53 Cf. Burke (1996, 64 ff.; 1975, 241 ff.). See also Hofmann (2003, 457 ff.).
54 Madison, *Federalist* (No. 10, 57).
55 Madison, *Federalist* (No. 10, 59). Cf. also *Federalist* (No. 51 [50], 351, 353). See Gebhardt (1968, 75 ff., 84 ff.).
56 Epstein (1984, 83), White (1987, 28). Locke argues in a similar manner (1964, ch. 7, § 87).
57 Madison, *Federalist* (No. 10, 58). See also Hamilton, *Federalist* (No. 1, 5), Madison, *Federalist* (No. 37 [36], 232 f.), Hamilton, *Federalist* (No. 65 [64], 444).
58 Gebhardt (1968, 75 ff., 85). Cf. Paine (1995, 433 ff., 568), Bentham (1907, chapter 1, IV). Zehnpfennig (1999, 1 ff., 26), however, interprets the *Federalist*'s common good as the mathematical sum of interests. White (1987, 120) equates it with Bentham's concept.
59 Madison, *Federalist* (No. 10, 59).

mon interest.[60] This requires a corresponding structure of government, e. g. two houses of parliament. The determined common good is neither objectively true nor random. It is the relative best decision (for the moment). In *Federalist* No. 10, Madison argues that representation leads to a refinement and expansion of public opinion in the described manner:

> The effect of the [delegation of government] is [...] to refine and enlarge the public views, by passing them through a chosen body of citizens [...].[61]

So representation plays a decisive role for the opinions put forward. Representative government not only guarantees the election of the best,[62] but also the best possible decisions. The procedure of representation leads, first, to a refinement of opinions,[63] for the immediate particular interests of the citizens need to be articulated in a public discourse. Since opinions can only win in the public discourse if they are put forward in general terms, individual interests are channelled and oriented towards the common good.[64] The process requires independent decisions by the elected magistrates. Independent decisions are ensured institutionally by free, rather than fixed mandates[65] as well as de facto by the distance to the voters due to the size of the governed territory.[66]

Second, the *Federalist* expects rationalization by enlarging the basis for discussion. The size leads to greater input through which particular interests become less important and new coalitions of interests keep forming.[67] The governmental structure expands the horizon of discourse. Multilevel representation as

---

60 In the wake of Hume (1994, 33 ff., 34) the *Federalist* identifies this problem as a problem of the influence of factions, Madison, *Federalist* (No. 10, 57). On the concept of 'faction' see fn. 31 above.

61 Madison, *Federalist* (No. 10, 62).

62 The *Federalist* describes the best as virtuous. Some commentators interpret this as an adoption of the classical idea of virtuous leaders, e. g. Pocock (2003, 506 ff.). However, the *Federalist* is not content with founding the stability of self-government merely in the virtuousness of the representatives. Rather, he emphasises the separation of powers (see section 4 below). More detail in Brunhöber (2010a, chapter 4, III. 3. a. [2]).

63 Madison draws here on Hume's system of multi-layered government. However, while Hume's system is strictly hierarchical, Madison develops a multi-level system with coequal representative organs. This is neglected by Adair (1974, 93 ff., 106).

64 Cf. Madison, *Federalist* (No. 10, 64). Cf. Epstein (1984, 100), Haller (1992, 135 ff.).

65 The free mandate is presupposed as given by the *Federalist*. More detail in Brunhöber (2010a, chapter 4, II. 3. b.).

66 Cf. Gregg (1997, 57).

67 Madison, Federalist (No. 10, 62). Cf. Diamond (1992a, 17 ff., 33 f.).

well as separation of powers also do so. [68] Debates are constantly repeated on different levels and by different representatives with multiple electorates.

Third, the procedure of representation ensures a "reflexive loop"[69]: By transferring political decisions to elected magistrates the people's will can be re-examined. The representatives not only bring up the urgent political topics, but also develop decisive solutions. Public debate of these topics and solutions enable the people to form distinguished opinions on them. Still, the magistrates decide independently. Their solutions are tried in practice. If the people are not content with the results they can elect new magistrates who can alter previous decisions.[70]

At the end of this procedure there stands a preliminary, generally accepted balance of interests that takes into account as many points of view as possible.[71] Best results are ensured by the specific procedure. The end is not a singular common good, anymore, but a plurality: the *interests* of the community.[72] The notion of the common good as a substance is thus completely abandoned.

4 Separation of powers by multilevel representation in a federal state

The idea of separation of powers, too, undergoes a democratic turn in the *Federalist*.[73] The *Federalist* draws on the British idea of a mixed constitution as interpreted by Montesquieu[74] but overcomes the hereditary-corporate basis. Therefore, he calls his notion of a constitution an unmixed republic.[75] As with

---

68 Cf. Madison, *Federalist* (No. 10, 62 f.); idem [Hamilton], *Federalist* (No. 57 [56], 388).

69 Buchstein (1997, 376 ff., 396).

70 Cf. Madison, *Federalist* (No. 63, 425), Hamilton, *Federalist* (No. 71 [70], 482). Similarly Haller (1992, 121). These considerations put forward in the *Federalist* are partly read quite differently as having the aim of preventing interventionist legislation, e.g. Pitkin (1967, 195 ff.), Lazare (1996, 5), Möllers (2008, 31). On more detail see Brunhöber (2010a, chapter 4, III. 3. b.).

71 The result is not a rational truth as with Sieyès (1975, 239 ff., 251), who assumes a similar process of refinement. The Federalist knows that the decisions of representative assemblies are not always the best or the most rational decisions, cf. Madison (No. 10, 62).

72 Madison, *Federalist* (No. 10, 57).

73 See Brunhöber (2010a, chapter 4, II. 3. c.).

74 Some commentators argue the *Federalist* draws here on Harrington (see above section 1 and for more detail Brunhöber (2010a, chapter 1, I. 2)). The *Federalist* rather calls Montesquieu his oracle with regard to the separation of powers, Madison, *Federalist* (No. 47 [46], 324).

75 Madison, *Federalist* (No. 14, 84). For this reason, Riklin takes the *Federalist* to be an opponent of a mixed constitution (2006, 382 ff.).

Montesquieu,[76] in the *Federalist* the primary function of the separation of powers is to guarantee individual freedom. Only secondary separation of powers aims at preventing individual rulers from encroaching power.[77] The latter is mainly achieved by periodic elections. The *Federalist* inverts Montesquieu's line of argument on the separation of powers. [78] In the case of Montesquieu, distribution of power is the result of a corporate structure of society.[79] All social forces are to be involved in the political order by combining democratic (many), aristocratic (few) and monarchic (one) constitutional elements. Then the functions of the state (legislative, executive, judicative) need to be distributed to different institutions. In each institution the social corporations—people (many), hereditary nobility (few) and hereditary monarch (one)—are to be represented in a manner that protects them from encroachments by the others.[80] Separation of powers restraints the corporations from infringing the freedom of each other. In short, the idea to represent the several societal corporations in government calls for separation of powers.

Inversely, for the *Federalist* the principle of separation of powers requires separate representative institutions. Any non-divided government, independent of the form of government,[81] leads to arbitrariness, for it lacks sufficient control of tendencies opposing the common good and negating individual rights.[82] Even though the influence of such tendencies can be limited by delegating political decisions and by expanding the governed territory.[83] The accumulation of power is also to be prevented by the separation of powers, by checks and balances and by a balanced government.[84] If the people immediately governed themselves, however, all powers were held in one hand and could not be distributed. Therefore the *Federalist* demands that while all governmental power resides with the people, it be enacted by different representative organs which are each to be

---

76 Montesquieu (1992, Book XI, chapter 4, chapter 6). More detail in: Riklin (2006, 275 f., 279 ff.).

77 See Madison [Hamilton], *Federalist* (No. 57 [56], 384). More detail in Brunhöber (2010a, chapter 4, III. 2.). Different views are found in Diamond (1992b, 58 ff.) and Buchstein (1997, 376 ff.).

78 More detail in Brunhöber (2010a, chapter 4 II. 3.c.)

79 Montesquieu (1992, book XI, chapter 6).

80 Montesquieu (1992, book XI, chapter 6).

81 This is overlooked by Buchstein (1997, 376 ff., 394 f.).

82 Madison, *Federalist* (No. 46 [47], 324).

83 See section 3 above.

84 The *Federalist* speaks of secondary auxiliaries; Madison [Hamilton], *Federalist* (No. 63 [62], 425). For the concept of balanced government see Madison, *Federalist* (No. 49 [48], 341).

involved in the separate[85] governmental functions.[86] For example, not only the House of Representatives (many) and the Senate (few) are equally involved in legislation,[87] but also the president (one) participates due to his veto right[88].

For Montesquieu, the mutual control of the governmental institutions was ensured by the fact that they had their bases in the corporations and thus each had an individual will.[89] The *Federalist*, too, demands that in order to establish a balance of power, each power to have a foundation[90] as well as a will of its own[91]. But since he abandons prevalent hereditary-corporate notions of government and demands the sovereignty of the people[92], he can only achieve this through the internal structure of government.[93] The diverging foundations and wills are created by different modes of election and constituencies.[94] The individual wills are ensured by the fact that in principle no governmental organ is to be dependent on any other with regard to appointment, term of office and pay.[95] Furthermore, since each office holder has authorities to limit the other offices, individual ambitions will keep the others from encroaching powers.[96]

---

85 Madison [Hamilton], *Federalist* (No. 51 [50], 348), Hamilton, *Federalist* (No. 9, 91). This is also provided for by the US Constitution (cf. Art. I, § 1; Art. II, § 1, cl. 1; Art. III, § 2, cl. 1 USConst.).

86 Cf. Madison, *Federalist* (No. 47 [48], 332; No. 48 [47]; No. 49 [48]), Hamilton, *Federalist* (No. 69 [68]; No. 71 [70]).

87 See Madison [Hamilton], *Federalist* (No. 63 [62], 425).

88 Hamilton, *Federalist* (No. 73 [72], 494).

89 Montesquieu (1992, book XI, chapter 6).

90 Madison [Hamilton], *Federalist* (No. 55 [54], 377).

91 Madison [Hamilton], *Federalist* (No. 51 [50], 348).

92 Precisely for this reason the *Federalist* calls for an unmixed republic; Madison, *Federalist* (No. 14, 84).

93 Madison [Hamilton], *Federalist* (No. 51 [50], 347). But the constitution is not an automatic clockwork (as for Arendt 1963, 241) that determines political agents because they can alter the constitution (Art. V USConst.). See Brunhöber (2010a, chapter 4, III. 2.).

94 Madison [Hamilton], *Federalist* (No. 55 [54], 377), Hamilton, *Federalist* (No. 60 [59], 405). The House of Representatives, the Senate and the President are elected at different times in different constituencies according to different laws (cf. Art. I, § 1, cl. 1; § 3, cl. 2; Art. II, § 1, cl. 2 USConst.). There are different provisions for passive suffrage, too (cf. Art. I, § 2, cl. 2; § 3, cl. 3; Art. II, § 1, cl. 5 USConst.).

95 Madison [Hamilton], *Federalist* (No. 51 [50], 348 f.).

96 Madison [Hamilton], *Federalist* (No. 51 [50], 349). See also Hamilton, *Federalist* (No. 73 [72], 494). Cf. Montesquieu's parallel line of argument (1992, book XI, chapter 4). But neither private, as for Beard (1998, 14 ff.), nor lobby interests, as for Dahl (2006, 25 ff.), are to be used, but merely the individual ambitions. More detail in Brunhöber (2010a, chapter 4, III. 2.). Similarly Epstein (1984, 137 ff.), Pangle (1988, 109 f.), White (1987, 159 ff.).

Finally, the horizontal separation of powers is complemented by a vertical one between the Union and the individual states.[97] The federal structure is seen as an important element of separation of powers. The various federal institutions are mirrored in the state institutions. Each state institution has its own foundation and its own will and thus is able to check the federal government. Today it is commonly accepted that distinction of governmental functions prevents abuse of power. However, the additional idea of the *Federalist* has disappeared from continental European constitutional theory: Accumulation of power may also be prevented by various governmental institutions each having their own foundation (e. g. constituency) and each participating in the distinct governmental functions (e. g. presidential veto). Seen in this light, overlapping powers do not contradict separation of powers, but complement it.

5 Conclusion

The *Federalist*'s version of democratic representation is a mostly convincing and proven-in-practice system through which collective democratic decisions become possible not despite but because of pluralism. Two objections are to be mentioned, though:[98] the absence of fundamental rights and the question of a basic consensus as a precondition for democratic representation.

The objection of a missing charter of liberties seems obvious from a modern perspective. This absence is, however, systemic. Taking the lead from Locke's theory of the social contract, the *Federalist* took for granted inalienable natural rights that required no further mention.[99] Infringements of freedom were to be prevented by the governmental structure, in particular, the separation of powers.[100] But the Americans were soon to learn that this was not sufficient and passed the Bill of Rights in 1791. In the years to follow, various Supreme Court rulings ensured that the fundamental rights were not only written on paper but legally enforceable. The idea of an independent judiciary that can enforce fundamental rights is grounded in the agency concept of the *Federalist*: Since the constitution was seen as action-guiding framework for the representa-

---

97 Cf. Madison [Hamilton], *Federalist* (No. 51 [50], 350f.). On this see also Buchstein (1997, 376ff., 394f.).
98 In more detail Brunhöber (2010a, chapter 5, I., III.).
99 Cf. esp. Hamilton, *Federalist* (No. 84, 578).
100 See section 4 above.

tives there needed to be an independent institution such as the judiciary to check governmental actions.[101]

The *Federalist* did not deal with the question whether democratic representation needs some kind of common political basic consensus in order to make majority decisions generally acceptable. However, if the consensus is not framed as substantial identity (i.e. ethnic identity)[102] the *Federalist* was justified in assuming that a basic consensus existed at the time. A general consensus was based in mutual experiences with self-government in the states, the united fight for independence and the shared liberal-revolutionary ideas.[103] The theory of the *Federalist* makes it possible to conceive of democratic representation without state, ethnic people or nation, and without a predetermined common good. The *Federalist* steers a middle course between the two extremes of representation theories. The one extreme degrades individuals to just being parts of the whole to ensure unity. The other extreme forces individuals to subordinate their selfish interests to a common good. In the *Federalist*'s theory the individuals remain the origin of political decision. At the same time, people can freely pursue their particular interests since elected representatives discuss and decide political question on behalf of them. The *Federalist* finds the middle ground between the two extremes of representation theory in a procedural turn of the theory.

The *Federalist* does not focus on a substantial unity or a substantive common good, but on the procedure of decision making. In contrast to modern ideas of governance[104], however, the *Federalist* does not believe in the free play of forces or networks. In his eyes the political game needs a framework and safeguards that all participants jointly adopt. A free play without such safeguards would re-enforce existing power imbalances. The decision making procedure is to be structured in a manner that ensures as much plurality as possible.

The *Federalist* abandons notions of representation that require a pre-existent unity, that aim at embodiment of a substance or that are limited to reproducing an objectively given common good. He paves the way for an idea of democratic representation that can be realised without a nation state, without an ethnically homogeneous people and without a notion of a singular common good—a fundament for thinking democratic representation on the European as well as on the World stage.

---

101 Cf. Hamilton, *Federalist* (No. 78 [77], 524, 527).
102 Cf. Habermas (1990, 147 ff.).
103 Cf. Hamilton, *Federalist* (No. 11, 72 f.; No. 84, 580).
104 See e.g. Mayntz (2006, 11 ff.), Kooiman (2006, 149 ff.), Slaughter (2004, 261 ff.), Ladeur (2005, 89 ff.).

Bibliography

Adair, Douglass (1974): That Politics May Be Reduced To Science: David Hume, James Madison, And the Tenth *Federalist*, in: Colbourne, Trevor (ed.): Fame and the Founding Fathers: Essays by Douglass Adair, New York, pp. 93 – 106.

Adams, Angela/Adams, Willi Paul (1994): Einleitung—Die Federalist-Artikel und die Verfassung der amerikanischen Nation, in: Hamilton, Alexander/Madison, James/Jay, John: Die Federalist-Artikel. Politische Theorie und Verfassungskommentar der amerikanischen Gründerväter, Paderborn, xxvii–xciii.

Adams, Willi Paul (1973): Republikanische Verfassung und bürgerliche Freiheit, Darmstadt, Neuwied.

Arendt, Hannah (1963): On Revolution, London.

Aristoteles (2003): Politik, Olof Gigon (trans. & ed.), 9th ed., München.

Beard, Charles A. (1998): An Economic Interpretation of the Constitution of the United States, New Brunswick, London.

Bentham, Jeremy (1907 [1789]): Introduction to the Principles of Morals and Legislation, Oxford.

Beyme, Klaus (1978): Artikel 'Partei, Faktion', in: Geschichtliche Grundbegriffe, Historisches Lexikon zur politisch-sozialen Sprache in Deutschland, Bd. 4, Brunner, Otto/Conze, Werner/Koselleck, Reinhart (eds.), Stuttgart, pp. 677 – 734.

Böckenförde, Ernst-Wolfgang (1982): Mittelbare/repräsentative Demokratie als eigentliche Form der Demokratie, Bemerkungen zu Begriff und Verwirklichungsproblemen der Demokratie als Staats- und Regierungsform, in: Staatsorganisation und Staatsfunktion im Wandel, Festschrift für Kurt Eichenberger zum 60. Geburtstag, Müller, Georg/Rhinow, René A./Schmid, Gerhard/Wildhaber, Luzius (eds.), Frankfurt a. M, pp. 301 – 328.

Böckenförde, Ernst-Wolfgang (1991): Demokratie und Repräsentation, in: idem: Recht, Staat, Freiheit. Studien zu Rechtsphilosophie, Staatstheorie und Verfassungsgeschichte, Frankfurt a. M., pp. 379 – 405.

Böckenförde, Ernst-Wolfgang (2004): Demokratische Willensbildung und Repräsentation, in: Handbuch des Staatrechts. Demokratie—Bundesorgane, 2. Aufl. Bd. III, Isensee, Josef/Kirchhof, Paul (ed.), Heidelberg, § 34, pp. 31 – 54.

von Bose, Harald (1989): Republik und Mischverfassung: Zur Staatsformenlehre der Federalist Papers, Frankfurt a. M.

Brunhöber, Beatrice (2008): Recht als Potenz. Agambens 'Homo Sacer' und eine (postmoderne) Rechtsgeltungstheorie des potentiellen Rechts, in: Archiv für Rechts- und Sozialphilosophie 94, pp. 111 – 130.

Brunhöber, Beatrice (2010a): Die Erfindung 'demokratischer Repräsentation' in den Federalist Papers, Diss. Humboldt-Universität zu Berlin, 2010.

Brunhöber, Beatrice (2010b): Die Erfindung 'demokratischer Repräsentation' in den Federalist Papers, in: Roland Lhotta (ed.), Staatsverständnisse. Die hybride Republik. Die Federalist Papers und die politische Moderne, Baden-Baden, pp. 59 – 80.

Brutus (1981): Letter from Brutus to the New York Journal (Oktober 18, 1787), in: Storing, Herbert J. (ed.): The Complete Anti-Federalist, Vol. II, Chicago, London, pp. 369 ff.

Buchstein, Hubertus (1997): Repräsentation ohne Symbole—die Repräsentationstheorie des ‚Federalist' und von Hanna F. Pitkin, in: Göhler, Gerhard et al. (eds.): Institution—Macht

—Repräsentation: Wofür politische Institutionen stehen und wie sie wirken, Baden-Baden, pp. 376–432.

Burke, Edmund (1975): Letter to Sir Hercules Langrishe, On the Subject of the Roman Catholics of Ireland and the Propriety of admitting them to the elective Franchise, consistently with the Principles of the Constitution, as established at the Revolution (1792), in: idem, The Works, Twelve Volumes in Six, 1887, reprint, Vol. IV, pp. 241ff.

Burke, Edmund (1996): Speech at Bristol, Previous to the Election (September 6, 1780), in: idem, The Writings and Speeches of Edmund Burke, Vol. III: Party, Parliament, and the American War, 1774–1780, Langford Paul/Elofson W.M/Woods, John A. (eds.) Oxford, pp. 623ff.

Cooke, Jacob E. (1961): The Federalist, Middletown, Connecticut.

Dahl, Robert A. (2006): A Preface to Democratic Theory: How does popular sovereignty function in America? Expanded Edition, Chicago.

Derrida, Jacques (1991): Gesetzeskraft. Der "mystische Grund" der Autorität, Frankfurt a. M.

Diamond, Martin (1992a): Democracy and The Federalist: A Reconsideration of the Framers' Intent, in: Schambra, William A. (ed.): As Far as Republican Principles Will Admit, Essays by Martin Diamond, Washington, D.C., pp. 17–36.

Diamond, Martin (1992b): The Separation of Powers and the Mixed Regime, in: Schambra, William A. (ed.): As Far as Republican Principles Will Admit, Essays by Martin Diamond, Washington, D.C., pp. 58–67.

Dreier, Horst (1988): Demokratische Repräsentation und vernünftiger Allgemeinwille, Die Theorie der amerikanischen Federalists im Vergleich mit der Staatsphilosophie Kants, in: Archiv des öffentlichen Rechts 113, pp. 450–483.

Duso, Giuseppe (2006): Die moderne politische Repräsentation: Entstehung und Krise des Begriffs, Paschke, Peter. (trans.), Berlin.

Epstein, David F. (1984): The Political Theory of Federalist. Chicago.

Fraenkel, Ernst (1991): Die repräsentative und die plebiszitäre Komponente im demokratischen Verfassungsstaat, in: von Brünneck, Alexander (ed.): Deutschland und die westlichen Demokratien, mit einem Nachwort über Leben und Werk Ernst Fraenkels, Frankfurt a. M., pp. 153–203.

Gebhardt, Jürgen (1968): The Federalist, in: Maier, Hans/Rausch, Heinz/Denzer, Horst (eds.), Klassiker des politischen Denkens, Bd. 2: Von Locke bis Max Weber, München, pp. 75–103.

Grawert, Rolf (2004): Staatsvolk und Staatsangehörigkeit, in: Isensee, Josef/Kirchhof, Paul (eds.), Handbuch des Staatsrechts der Bundesrepublik Deutschland. Bd. II: Verfassungsstaat, 3rd ed., Heidelberg, § 16, pp. 107–141.

Gregg, Gary L. II (1997): The Presidential Republic, Executive Representation and Deliberative Democracy, Lanham, Maryland.

Habermas, Jürgen (2006): Faktizität und Geltung. Beiträge zur Diskurstheorie des Rechts und des demokratischen Rechtsstaats, 3rd ed., Frankfurt a. M.

Haller, Benedikt (1992): Repräsentation in Politik und Recht, in: Ritter, Joachim/Gründer, Karlfried/Eisler, Rudolf (eds.): Art. Repräsentation, Historisches Wörterbuch der Philosophie. Bd. 8, Darmstadt, col. 812–826.

Hamilton, Alexander (1961): The Papers of Alexander Hamilton, Syrett, Harold C./Cooke, Jacob E. (eds.) 9 vol., New York.

Hamilton, Alexander/Madison, James/Jay, John (1961): The Federalist, Cooke, Jacob E. (ed.), Middletown, Connecticut.

Hofmann, Hasso (2003): Repräsentation, Studien zur Wort- und Begriffsgeschichte von der Antike bis ins 19. Jahrhundert, 4th ed., Berlin.

Hofmann, Hasso/Dreier, Horst (1989): Repräsentation, Mehrheitsprinzip und Minderheitenschutz, in: Schneider, Hans-Peter/Zeh, Wolfgang: Parlamentsrecht und Parlamentspraxis, Berlin, pp. 165–197.

Horkheimer, Max/Adorno, Theodor W. (1955): Dialektik der Aufklärung, Amsterdam.

Hume, David (1994): Political Essays, Haakonssen, Knud (ed.), Cambridge.

Kant, Immanuel, (1968a [1798]): Der Streit der Facultäten, in: Kants Werke. Akademie-Textausgabe 7, Berlin, pp. 1–116.

Kant, Immanuel (1968b [1797]): Metaphysik der Sitten, in: Kants Werke. Akademie-Textausgabe 6, Berlin, pp. 203–494.

Kelsen, Hans (1981 [1929]): Vom Wesen und Wert der Demokratie, 2nd ed., Aalen.

Kielmannsegg, Peter Graf von (1985): Die Quadratur des Zirkels. Überlegungen zum Charakter der repräsentativen Demokratie, in: Matz, Ulrich (ed.), Aktuelle Herausforderungen der repräsentativen Demokratie, Köln, pp. 9–42.

Kooiman, Jan (2006): Governing as Governance, in: Schuppert, Gunnar Folke (ed.): Governance-Forschung: Vergewisserung über Stand und Entwicklungslinien, 2nd ed., Baden-Baden, pp. 149–172.

Ladeur, Karl-Heinz (2005): Globalization and the Conversion of Democracy to Polycentric Networks: Can Democracy survive the End of the Nation State, in: Ladeur, Karl-Heinz (ed.), Public Governance in the Age of Globalization, 2nd ed., Aldershot, pp. 89–120.

Landi, Alexander (1976): Madison's Political Theory, in: Political Science Reviewer 6, pp. 73–111.

Landshut, Siegfried (1968 [1964]): Der politische Begriff der Repräsentation, in: Rausch, Heinz (ed.), Zur Theorie und Geschichte der Repräsentation und Repräsentativverfassung, Darmstadt, pp. 482–497.

Leibholz, Gerhard (1967): Der Strukturwandel der modernen Demokratie, in: idem (ed.): Strukturprobleme der modernen Demokratie, 3rd ed., Karlsruhe, pp. 78–131.

Locke, John (1964 [1690]): Two Treatises of Government, Laslett, Peter (ed.), Cambridge.

Loewenstein, Karl (1972): Ketzerische Betrachtungen über die amerikanische Verfassung, in: Saladin, Peter/Wildhaber, Luzius (eds.), Der Staat als Aufgabe. Gedenkschrift für Max Imboden, Basel, pp. 233–254.

Lyotard, Jean-François (1989): Der Widerstreit, 2nd ed., München.

Madison, James (1978): The Papers of James Madison, in: Hutchinson, William T./Rachal, William M. E./Rutland, Robert A./Hobson, Charles F. (eds.), vol. 12, Charlottesville, Virginia.

Mason, Alpheus Thomas (1952): The Federalist—A Split Personality, in: American Historical Review 57, pp. 625–643.

Mayntz, Renate (2006): Governance Theory als fortentwickelte Steuerungstheorie?, in: Schuppert, Gunnar Folke (ed.): Governance-Forschung: Vergewisserung über Stand und Entwicklungslinien, 2nd ed., Baden-Baden, pp. 11–20.

McLean, John/McLean, Archibald (eds.) (1788): The Federalist: A collection of essays, written in favour of the new Constitution, as agreed upon by the Federal convention, September 17, 1787, New York.

Meyer, Hans (2005): Repräsentation und Demokratie, in: Dreier, Horst (ed.), Rechts- und staatstheoretische Schlüsselbegriffe: Legitimität—Repräsentation—Freiheit, Symposion für Hasso Hofmann zum 70. Geburtstag, Berlin, pp. 99–112.

Möllers, Christoph (2005): Netzwerk als Kategorie des Organisationsrechts—Zur juristischen Beschreibung dezentraler Steuerung, in: Janbernd Oebbeke (ed.), Nicht-normative Steuerung in dezentralen Systemen, Stuttgart, pp. 285–302.

Möllers, Christoph (2008): Die drei Gewalten. Legitimation der Gewaltengliederung in Verfassungsstaat, Europäischer Integration und Internationalisierung, Weilerswist.

Morgan, Edmund S./Morgan, Helen M. (1962): The Stamp Act Crisis: Prologue to Revolution, 2nd ed., New York.

Paine, Thomas (1995): Rights of Man, in: Collected Writings. Common Sense, The Crisis, and Other Pamphlets, Articles, and Letters, Rights of Man, The Age of Reason, Foner, Eric (ed.), New York, pp. 431–662.

Pangle, Thomas L. (1988): The Spirit of Modern Republicanism, The Moral Vision of the American Founders and the Philosophy of Locke, Chicago.

Pitkin, Hanna F. (1967): The Concept of Representation, Berkeley, Los Angeles.

Pocock, John G.A. (2003): The Machiavellian Moment: Florentine Political Theory and the Atlantic Tradition, 2nd ed., Princeton, New Jersey.

Potter, Kathleen O. (2002): The Federalist's Vision of Popular Sovereignty in the New American Republic, New York.

Reid, John Phillip (1989): The Concept of Representation in the Age of the American Revolution, Chicago.

Riklin, Alois (2006): Machtteilung. Geschichte der Mischverfassung, Darmstadt.

Rosen, Gary (1999): American Compact, Lawrence, Kansas.

Rousseau, Jean-Jacques (1966): Du contrat social ou principes du droit politique, Paris.

Scheuner, Ulrich (1968): Das repräsentative Prinzip in der modernen Demokratie, in: Rausch, Heinz (ed.): Zur Theorie und Geschichte der Repräsentation und Repräsentativverfassung, Darmstadt, pp. 386–418.

Schmitt, Carl (1970): Verfassungslehre, 5th ed., Berlin.

Sieyès, Emmanuel Joseph (1975): Politische Schriften 1788–1790, Schmitt, Eberhard/Riechhardt, Rolf (ed.), Darmstadt.

Slaughter, Anne Marie (2004): A New World Order, Princeton, New Jersey.

Slaughter, Thomas P. (1984): The Tax Man Cometh: Ideological Opposition to Internal Taxes, 1760–1790, in: William and Mary Quarterly 41, pp. 566–591.

Smith, Melancton (1981): Speech by Melancton Smith to the Convention of the State of New York (June 21, 1788), in: Storing, Herbert J. (ed.), The Complete Anti-Federalist, Vol. 6, Chicago, pp. 157 ff.

Stern, Klaus (1984): Das Staatsrecht der Bundesrepublik Deutschland, Bd. 1: Grundbegriffe und Grundlagen des Staatsrechts, Strukturprinzipien der Verfassung, 2nd ed., München.

Sternberger, Dolf (1971): Die Erfindung der Repräsentativen Demokratie. Eine Untersuchung von Thomas Paines Verfassungs-Ideen, in: idem: Nicht alle Staatsgewalt geht vom Volke aus, Stuttgart, pp. 59–81.

Thomas von Aquin (1943): Summa Theologica. Deutsche Thomas-Ausgabe, Salzburg.

Waschkuhn, Arno (2005): Regimebildung und Netzwerke: neue Ordnungsmuster und Interaktionsformen zur Konflikt- und Verantwortungsregulierung im Kontext politischer Steuerung, Berlin.

Welsch, Wolfgang (1987): Vielheit ohne Einheit? Zum gegenwärtigen Spektrum der philosophischen Diskussion um die 'Postmoderne', in: Philosophisches Jahrbuch 94, pp. 111–141.

White, Morton Gabriel (1987): Philosophy, The Federalist, and the Constitution, Oxford.

Wood, Gordon S. (1969): Representation in the American Revolution, Jamestown Essays on Representation, Howard, E. Dick (ed.), Charlottesville, Virginia.

Wood, Gordon S. (1998): The Creation of the American Republic 1776–1786. Reprint. Williamsburg, Virginia.

Zehnpfennig, Barbara (1999): Einleitung, in: Hamilton, Alexander/Madison, James/Jay, John. Die Federalist Papers, Darmstadt, pp. 1–44.

Norbert Campagna
E timore unum: When Fear Invites Itself at the Birth of the Federal Republic of America

Introduction

According to Lord Acton, federalism is "[t]he only barrier to Democracy" and "the best curb to democracy"[1]. Democracy is here understood in the sense of absolute democracy, i.e. the unlimited or unchecked sovereignty of a popular majority. In a federal state where the federated entities have kept at least part of their sovereignty there is a check on the sovereignty of a national popular majority. If the federated entities had not kept at least a part of their initial sovereignty, the whole formed by these entities would not be a federal, but, to use a term *en vogue* in late eighteenth century America, a consolidated state. Federalism, if anything, is a form of association in which, according to Pierre-Joseph Proudhon, "the federal attributions may never exceed in number or in reality those of the federated authorities"[2], i.e. in which the central state may never do anything which the federated entities had or have no right to do. This leads Proudhon to say that the federal authority is *strictu sensu* not a government, but merely an agent acting on behalf of the federated entities[3]. These have kept their full sovereignty and one of the major tasks of the federal state, a task defined by the federative compact, is precisely to guarantee that sovereignty. And in this context it may interesting to note that the self-claimed anarchist Proudhon also thinks that by dividing the people, a federal constitution is an efficacious barrier against democratic absolutism, a form of government to which the people naturally tend.

The felt and proclaimed need for guarantees, barriers or curbs reveals a fear of something which needs to be curbed, stopped or controlled. An entity X is afraid lest an entity Y does some real or imagined harm to it, and the guarantees, etc. are a means to prevent, as much as possible, the entity Y from doing that

---

1 Acton (1985, 558).
2 Proudhon (1999, 107). All translations from non-English sources are by the author, N.C.
3 This seems to correspond to how Senator Rowan from Kentucky understood American federalism in a speech held in 1830, when he said of the Constitution that it was "an agreement between the sovereign states to *exert jointly* their respective powers, through the agency of the General Government, for the purposes and in the manner delineated in that instrument of compact", cited in: Belz (2000, 278).

harm. Such a fear presupposes, at the very least, a form of defiance of X towards Y. Of course, if X and Y could lead perfectly separate lives with no interactions occurring between them, such a defiance would not exist. Things are different, however, if we suppose that X needs Y, that without Y, X would run the risk of destruction, or at least of a life that would be, in Hobbes's famous words, "nasty, solitary, poor, brutish and short". According to Hobbes, rational creatures will prefer anything to such a life and thus they will voluntarily submit to a sovereign who will protect them against each other. The Hobbesian sovereign is the only barrier to anarchy and the best curb to destructive human passions. Yet in Hobbes's scheme, there is no barrier protecting the subjects against the sovereign, because the existence of such a barrier would lead to conflicts between the subjects and the sovereign and thus open the possibility of civil war and a return to a "nasty, solitary, poor, brutish and short" life. For Hobbes, writing in the seventeenth century, the priority was to safeguard individuals against each other, and an absolute state was the only means Hobbes saw for allaying, as much as possible, the fear and mutual defiance individuals knew in the state of nature. The individuals had to surrender all their rights to the sovereign—excepting their right to life.

Though they were, for obvious chronological reasons, ignorant of the writings of Lord Acton and Proudhon, the American founding fathers were familiar with Hobbes. But they were also familiar with the writings of John Locke, for whom it was better to remain among pole-cats than to let a lion enter the scene. Whatever harms pole-cats could inflict on each other, they were at least more or less equal in their destructive potential and this rough equality could act as a curb on their aggressiveness. Of course, even Locke had to admit that an anarchic life among pole-cats was far from ideal and that something more than the rough equality was necessary to curb the aggressiveness of the cats. A political authority had to be established, but at the same time one needed a guarantee against this authority, lest it become an all-devouring lion.

If Hobbes and Locke, as philosophers, went back to what they thought were the most fundamental elements of social life, i.e. independent individuals—with Locke already bringing in some forms of sociability among these individuals—, the founding fathers, as politicians, were confronted to a reality which knew already a developed social and political organization. One such form of organization were the ex-colonies, which, in 1776, cut the link with Great Britain and proclaimed themselves sovereign states. Before 1776, the relation between the colonies and Great Britain could be described as being of a federal nature, because most of the colonists accepted the British King as executive power and judge, but rejected the legislative power of the British Parliament.[4] It was only when they saw that the King was not willing to protect them against Parliament that they abandoned their allegiance to the King and declared themselves to be sovereign in all and every respect.

Here our story begins: Thirteen independent states, jealous of their sovereignty, have to organize not only their peaceful coexistence, but also their defense against Great Britain—as well as against other potential or actual enemies. But what is more, at least at a symbolical level, they want to give an example to the world, an example of liberty. In a letter to Joseph Priestley from 1802, Jefferson writes that America has the "duty of proving what is the degree of freedom and self-government in which a society may venture to leave its individual members"[5], a duty which was not only felt in 1802, but right from the start. The thirteen states were all very proud to call themselves republics and one of their great fears was to become something else.

So here's the question: Can sovereignty, peace, security and republican liberty coexist or is any tentative to make them coexist something like the tentative to square the circle, i.e. an impossible task? And if something must, at least partially, be given up, what should it be and to what extent? For the founding fathers, the solution to these questions lay in federalism, i.e. in having between the thirteen ex-colonies something like the same kind of relation as existed before 1776 between these ex-colonies and Great Britain, the only difference being that the executive authority was not the King in London, but an entity sitting somewhere in America. If the thirteen ex-colonies had not been afraid of anything, that entity would probably never have come to existence.[6] If they had not been afraid of that very entity, the American Constitution would have been very different from what it looks like today.

In a letter to George Washington, James Madison writes that "[n]othing but the peculiarity of our circumstances could ever have produced these sacrifices of sovereignty on which the federal government now rests".[7] These lines were written in 1785, i.e. three years before the Articles of Confederation were replaced by the Constitution, and so three years before even greater sacrifices of sovereignty were accepted.

---

4 One of the major reasons being the fact that the colonies were not represented in Parliament.
5 Jefferson (1999, 372).
6 There was also another difference. The relation between the ex-colonies was to be founded upon a compact, whereas such a compact did not exist with England. On this point, see Bennett (1967, 36).
7 Madison (1999, 48)

In my contribution, I will look more closely at this "peculiarity of our circumstances" alluded to by Madison, and I want to focus on a specific element, *viz.* fear. After the ratification of the Constitution, Madison could have written: "Nothing but the conjunction of many particular fears could ever have produced these sacrifices and retentions of sovereignty characteristic of the constitution on which the federal government now rests"[8].

I will begin with the anthropological premises from which the founding fathers started, because these form the root for all the rest. If man were not afraid of man, groups of men would probably not be afraid of groups of men. But since man has reasons to fear man, groups of men have also reasons to be afraid of groups of men. And all these fears will lead to barriers, curbs and guarantees. The Union is primarily designed as a guarantee against non-member states. But it can also guarantee the integrity of one member against possible encroachments from other members. Each of the members needs guarantees against possible encroachments stemming from the entity acting as the agent of the union. Pole-cats have to be protected against the lion they have erected. Federalists and anti-federalists have, with some nuances, the same basically pessimist view of human nature. The main difference between the two camps was that whereas federalists were more eager to have a secure guarantee against foreign dangers and a dissolution or dislocation of the union, which would have massively increased these foreign dangers, anti-federalists were more eager to have secure guarantees against that very entity which was supposed to protect the states against foreign forces. These external and internal fears will make up the second and third parts of my contribution. In the last part, I will discuss the so-called guarantee clause of the American constitution. It says that the federal government will guarantee the republican character of the federated states. In 1788, some states feared that they might lose that republican character. But some states also feared that the federal entity might give a more comprehensive interpretation to the notion of republicanism, a fear which was not without its object and which led, among other things, to the abolition of slavery.

The four parts of my contribution may thus be summarized very briefly: (1) fearing man, (2) fearing foreigners, (3) fearing dislocation and consolidation, (4) fearing republicanism.

---

8 In that same year 1785, Richard Price wrote in his *Observations on the importance of the American Revolution:* "The present moment [...] though apparently the end of all their dangers, may prove the time of their greatest danger" (1991, 151). He should have written that the end of the danger to be exploited by the British Parliament might prove the time to be exposed to many other dangers.

1 Fearing man

The American founding fathers had a largely negative anthropology, and this anthropology is at the root of many of the fears that will be discussed in this contribution. If this anthropology had been more positive, the American constitutional history would probably have taken another turn and America might have become a unitary rather than a federal state.[9] But such a unitary state might also have emerged if Americans had been less optimistic, and thus, so to say, more Hobbesian, regarding the possibilities of taming man's nature, and especially the nature of those in charge of exercising power,[10] *via* institutional means. In this context, it is interesting to quote George Washington, who, in a letter to John Jay of 1786, writes: "We have probably had too good an opinion of human nature in forming our confederation".[11] In the same letter, though in another context, Washington warns against the danger of running from one extreme into another.[12] A look at the anthropological premises of the participants to the constitutional debate of 1787–88 might give the impression that the Americans have moved from too good an opinion of human nature to too bad an opinion of that nature.

Without striving for exhaustiveness, I will content myself with some select quotations establishing the point I want to make in this first part of my contribution, i.e. that the founding fathers, on both sides of the divide, had a largely negative anthropology. Let us begin with the federalist camp, and more precisely with the *Federalist Papers*, the series of articles written by Alexander Hamilton, James Madison and John Jay and designed to convince the people of New York to accept the constitutional project. In the 6th Letter, Hamilton describes men as "ambitious, vindictive and rapacious" (*Federalist*, 20) and sees them as being still far away from perfect wisdom and virtue. In 'The Farmer refuted', a text published in 1775, i.e. one year before the Declaration of Independence, Hamilton had already spoken of the fondness of power implanted in most men.[13] In the

---

9 Whatever John Rawls may have written to the contrary, no political theory can dispense with comprehensive doctrines.
10 As Bailyn writes, "what turned power into a malignant force, was not its own nature so much as the nature of man—his susceptibility to corruption and his own lust for self-aggrandizement" (1992, 59). No society can do without power, yet that power has always to be placed into the hands of human beings who, though they may use it for good purposes, are also often prone to use it for merely egoistical purposes.
11 Washington (2011, 246).
12 Ibid. (2011, 247).
13 Hamilton (2008, 93).

10th Letter, Madison stresses the "propensity of mankind to fall into mutual animosities" (*Federalist*, 43). Hamilton takes up the cue in the 34th Letter, when he observes that the violent passions reign stronger in men's hearts than the peaceful passions (*Federalist*, 161). Man, so we could sum up, is more prone to be ruled by passions than by reason, and he is more prone to be ruled by bad than by good passions.

In the so-called anti-federalist camp, we find the same negative anthropological premises. During the debates in the ratification convention of North Carolina, a speaker opposing the constitutional project said: "We ought to consider the depravity of human nature, the predominant thirst of power which is in the breast of every one [...]"[14]. In a contribution of 1788, an author opposing the constitutional project and writing under the pseudonym of Philadelphiensis mentions the "lust of dominion"[15], and John de Witt speaks of a "passionate thirst for power"[16]. In *The address and reasons of dissent of the minority of the convention of the state of Pennsylvania to their constituents*, the future representatives are described as "harpies of power" attracted by "the sweets of power"[17]. To add a further passage from Agrippa: "If we endeavour to be like other nations we shall have more bad men than good ones to exercise extensive powers. That circumstance alone will corrupt them"[18]. Patrick Henry, one of the leading anti-federalists, thinks it a folly to rests one's fate "upon the contingencies of our rulers being good or bad"[19].

Yet it is to be noted that in the federalist camp, the negative tone is sometimes nuanced. Thus Hamilton writes in the 76th contribution of the *Federalist* that "[t]he supposition of universal venality in human nature is little less an error in political reasoning than the supposition of universal rectitude", and he adds that the institution of delegation "implies that there is a portion of virtue and honor in mankind, which may be a reasonable foundation of confidence" (*Federalist*, 389). The same idea is expressed by James Madison in the 55th contribution of the *Federalist*, when he writes that

> [...] there is a degree of depravity in mankind which requires a certain degree of circumspection and distrust: So there are other qualities in human nature, which justify a certain portion of esteem and confidence. Republican government presupposes the existence of these qualities in a higher degree than any other form (*Federalist*, 286).

---

14 Cited in Mason (1972, 169).
15 Cited in Kenyon (1966, 80).
16 Ibid. (1966, 106).
17 Ibid. (1966, 56).
18 Ibid. (1966, 151).
19 Ibid. (1966, 257).

In a speech in the Virginia Ratification Convention, Madison asks the question: "Is there no virtue among us?" He pursues by saying that absent virtue, even the most elaborate political institutions cannot secure liberty and happiness for long.[20] Federalists sensed that they could not rest content with framing ideal institutions. As Alexis de Tocqueville will rightly point out some decennia later, good institutions may be temporary checks against the loss of liberty, but when the individuals acting within these institutions do not have a certain quantum of civic virtue, then even the best institutions cannot protect liberty for a long time.[21] Against the anti-federalist discourse stressing a "predominant thirst for power", federalists had to stress the existence of civic virtue. Unless the individuals exercising political and judicial offices were thought of as being capable of holding their thirst for power in check by their civic virtues, it would be imprudent, not to say foolish, to subject oneself to them.

2 Fearing foreigners

Though America was separated from Europe by the Atlantic Ocean, the thirteen states were not secure against possible military interventions by European powers, and first among them the British, who were not ready to give up their former colonies without fighting. Another possible danger was Spain, which could try to grapple some territory in the South. Then there were the many Indian tribes, which, though they were not necessarily eager to reconquer the territories taken from their ancestors by the colonists, could nevertheless be instrumentalized by the British or Spaniards. As to the French, they were favorable to the American cause, though not necessarily because of a peculiar love for Americans. In helping the Americans against the English, they scored important points against the latter.

It is mainly in federalist discourse that we find allusions to the threat posed by foreigners. Already in 1781, writing under the pseudonym of "The Continentalist", Alexander Hamilton pointed to the example of Greece, explaining its loss of liberty by the lack of a solid federal union, which made it an easy prey for the Turks.[22] Thus, if America wants to have a different future and not be the prey of the English, the thirteen states must consolidate their tie. In a speech in 1787, Hamilton even goes so far as to say that "all federal governments are

---

20 Madison (1999, 398).
21 Tocqueville (1952, 64).
22 Hamilton (2008, 171).

weak and distracted".[23] Such a weakness would leave open the door for foreign invaders. And in the 8th letter of the *Federalist*, again by the pen of Hamilton, we read:

> The violent destruction of life and property incident to war—the continual effort and alarm attendant on a state of continual danger, will compel nations the most attached to liberty, to resort for repose and security, to institutions, which have a tendency to destroy their civil and political rights. To be more safe they, at length, become willing to run the risk of being less free (*Federalist*, 32).

Four years earlier, in a circular to state governments, George Washington saw "the existence of the United States as an Independent Power" in jeopardy, if the Articles of Confederation were not amended so as to give stronger powers to the Continental Congress.[24] If the thirteen new sovereign states forming the United States of America wanted to remain together and thus deter possible conquerors much more efficiently than if each was to rest on its own, they had but one solution: Create a stronger tie, which is inseparable from giving up a larger part of their sovereignty. In Hamilton's view, if America wants to escape the situation he describes, i. e. loss of civil and political rights attendant on being constantly on one's guards against foreign invaders, it has to unite. As the Belgians say, "L'Union fait la force", to which one could add that union also makes dissuasion and thus render unnecessary liberticidal institutions.

In 1798, under the presidency of John Adams, Congress adopted the Alien and Sedition Acts, which curtailed civil and political rights in the name of national security. Madison, who was, with Jefferson, at the front of the opposition to the Acts, wrote to the latter: "Perhaps it is a universal truth that the loss of liberty at home is to be charged to provisions agst. danger real or pretended from abroad".[25] This universal truth had already been adumbrated by the Antifederalists ten years ago, during the debates surrounding the adoption of the constitution. In their eyes, those whom Philadelphiensis calls the "monarchymen in the convention" (in Kenyon 1966, 77), are just, to quote Centinel, trying "to terrify and alarm the people out of the exercise of their judgment"[26] by, as we would say in Luxembourg, drawing the devil on the wall. According to William Grayson, another anti-federalist author, the federalists are only agitating "phantoms and ideal dangers"[27], thus obfuscating the real dangers which lie

---

23 Hamilton (2001, 162).
24 Washington (2011, 208).
25 Madison (1999, 588).
26 In: Henry et al. (2010, 24).
27 Ibid. (2010, 11).

in a too strong central federal government. In the 8th letter of the *Federalist*, Hamilton had defended a radically different thesis, opposing the real dangers of disunion to the merely imaginary dangers of union (*Federalist*, 36). Brutus Junior, for his part, draws attention to the fact that tyrants used to create fear in the population in order to establish their tyranny.[28]

From this opposition it becomes apparent that behind discussions concerning the fear one should have of foreign nations, another debate goes on, with other fears, i. e. the fear of dislocation and that of consolidation.

3 Fearing dislocation and consolidation

When they declared themselves independent in 1776, the thirteen colonies became thirteen sovereign states and what they had in common was first and foremost their will not to be subject to England, neither to its Parliament, nor, and this was the novel claim, to the king. They were of course also united by a common history, going back to the first settlement in Jamestown, the arrival of the Mayflower and the beginnings of colonization. Yet very soon, the united colonists were to separate, mainly on religious grounds, so that by 1776, the original colony had become a plurality of thirteen colonies. Already in his 'General Orders' of 1775 George Washington expressed the hope that "all Distinctions of Colonies will be laid aside"[29], thus giving to understand that the task at hand required, beyond the declaration of independence, which was to come one year later, a declaration of unity, which had yet to come. In 1788 Washington, in a letter addressed to the president of the federal congress and accompanying the text of the constitution, mentioned the difficulties engendered by "a difference among the several states as to their situation, extent, habits, and particular interests"[30]. Hamilton was more optimistic, when after a speech held in the New York Ratification Convention he affirms that "the local interests of the states are in some degree various; and that there is some difference in their habits and manners: But this I will presume to affirm; that from New Hampshire to Georgia, the people of America are as uniform in their interests and manners, as those established in Europe"[31]. Eight years later, in his *Farewell Address*, Georges Washington seems to have joined into that optimism, when he mentions merely "slight

---

28 Ibid. (2010, 108).
29 Washington (2011, 69).
30 Cited in Madison (2007, 639).
31 Hamilton (2001, 501).

shades of difference", and says that Americans have "the same Religion, Manners, Habits and political Principles"[32].

In the anti-federalist camp, this optimism was far from prevailing in 1788. One of the most radical statements is to be found in John de Witt, who speaks of "the different states, whose interests differ scarcely in nothing short of everything"[33]. A group of Albany County Gentlemen mentions "people of different laws, customs, and opinions".[34] This is what George Clymer, a delegate from Pennsylvania to the Philadelphia Convention, said: "If the states have such different interests that they cannot be left to regulate their own manufactures without encountering the interests of other states, it is a proof that they are not fit to compose one nation".[35]

The thirteen states were, to say the least, suspicious of each other, with some being more suspicious of some others. I'm not sure that in 1783 the Abbé de Mably adequately captured the situation of America when he wrote in his *Observations sur le gouvernement et les lois des États-Unis d'Amérique* that it is a great advantage that the thirteen colonies have renounced establishing a unitary state, as such a state would have been the expression of "a certain fear, a defiance against themselves, which would have been a bad augury"[36]. Mably's statement makes sense in a Hobbesian framework, i.e. if we suppose that the states, like the Hobbesian individuals, would think themselves in need of protection against each other. The Abbé's syllogism can be put as follows:

P1: Only entities mistrusting each other will submit to a unitary government.

P2: The thirteen colonies did not submit to a unitary government.

C: Hence the thirteen colonies do not mistrust each other.

The syllogism adequate to the American situation is however the following:

P1*: Entities mistrusting a unitary government will not submit to a unitary government.

P2*: The thirteen colonies mistrusted a unitary government.

C*: Hence the thirteen colonies did not submit to a unitary government.

---

32 Washington (2011, 367).
33 Cited in Kenyon (1966, 97).
34 Ibid. (1966, 361).
35 Cited in Madison (2007, 480).
36 Mably (1789, 291).

Mably's *modus tollens* must thus be replaced by a *modus ponens*. The absence of a unitary government is not a proof of deep mutual sympathies, but of fear. For the anti-federalists, fear of a unitary government, of what came to be called 'consolidation', was stronger than fear of a possible dislocation. While the federalists feared a return to an anarchic state of nature, with a war of every state against every state[37], anti-federalists feared a return to monarchy, with an American king replacing the British king.

The specter of a state of nature is evoked by George Washington in his Circular to state Governments of 1783. In a letter to Benjamin Harrison written the following year, Washington laments the disinclination of states to yield necessary power to Congress and says that one should be more afraid of the weakness of Congress than of its power.[38] The specter of a war of all against all is evoked by John Jay in the 5th letter of the *Federalist*, when he writes that absent a true union, the states will be "like most other *bordering* nations, they would always be either involved in disputes and war, or live in the constant apprehension of them" (*Federalist*, 17), i.e. they will be in a situation exactly like that of the individuals in Hobbes's state of nature. In his above-mentioned Circular to state governments of 1783, Washington prophesies that if the states fall back to a state of nature, there is the danger that a tyranny will emerge.[39] In other words, everything would happen as Hobbes had predicted in his thought experiment. The only means to avoid tyranny is to avoid dislocation. In 1787–88, the only means to avoid dislocation was, in the eyes of the federalists, the adoption of the constitutional project elaborated in Philadelphia.

In the writings of the anti-federalists—who, by the way, should not be designated by what Candidus calls "the cant term of antifederalism"[40], but should rather be called *alter-federalists* since they promoted another form of federation and were not opposed to the idea of a federation as such[41]—the fear of monarchy and aristocracy are paramount, monarchy being associated with a consolidated, as opposed to a—at least in the eyes of the anti-federalists—truly federal union. Philadelphiensis prognosticates that "thirteen free commonwealths are to be

---

37 Berkin even speaks of "a political limbo more frightening than any state of nature" (2003, 75).

38 Washington (2011, 208).

39 Washington (2011, 210).

40 Cited in Henry (2010, 62).

41 As Howard writes, so-called Federalists had better be called Nationalists (Howard 2004, 240). As a consequence, their opponents would have to be called Antinationalists. On the Antifederalists, see for example Turner Main 1974.

consolidated into one despotic monarchy"[42]. Melancton Smith rather dreads an aristocracy when he asks the following rhetorical question: "Can the liberties of three millions of people be securely trusted in the hands of twenty-four men?"[43] To explain the number: The legislative encompassed 91 representatives. The quorum was 46 and the majority of the quorum was 24. Robert Yates saw the danger of another kind of aristocracy when he fustigates the American judges as "independent of the people, of the legislature, and of every power under heaven".[44]

Let me close this third part by quoting Jefferson, who in a letter to Madison of 1789 writes:

> The tyranny of the legislatures is the most formidable dread at present, and will be for long years. That of the executive will come in its turn, but it will be at a remote period (1999, 368).

4 Fearing republicanism

The specters of anarchy, aristocracy, monarchy, despotism and tyranny were not only specters that could wreak havoc in the Union as such, but also in the single states. Even if the federal government did not interfere with the republican character of the single states, forces within these states could bring about a change in a state's constitution and the union of thirteen republics would then transform itself into a union of twelve republics plus something else. Such a union would not be stable, at least if one believed theoreticians of federalism, who thought that a federation could only thrive among states with the same type of government. So if the union were to remain stable, the republican character of the federated entities had to be secured. The so-called guarantee clause was to bring this security. This clause—it is section 4 of Article IV—reads as follows: "The United States shall guarantee to every state in this Union a Republican Form of Government [...]".

During the debates in the constitutional convention, governor Morris of Pennsylvania was, as reported by Madison, "very unwilling that such laws as exist in R. Island should be guaranteed"[45]. Mr. Houston, who represented Georgia, was, according to Madison's report, "afraid of perpetuating the existing Constitutions of the states. That of Georgia was a very bad one, and he hoped would

---

42 Cited in Kenyon (1966, 71).
43 Ibid. (1966, 387).
44 Ibid. (1966, 352).
45 Madison (2007, 280).

be revised and amended".[46] Rhode Island was to remain a lasting topic in the decennia to follow, notably with Dorr's rebellion in 1841. To make matters brief: By 1841, Rhode Island still lived under a royal charter from 1663 which had a very narrow suffrage and everything but an equitable representation— which explains Governor Morris's view just exposed. Thomas Dorr, a lawyer, set out to frame a new constitution, organized illegal elections and was elected governor. Since the established governor did not recognize Dorr, the latter instigated an armed attack against the arsenal at Providence. The attack failed, the rebellion was quashed and Dorr was sentenced to life imprisonment and hard labor. He was amnestied in 1845.[47]

The case of Rhode Island confronts us with the question: What is a republican government? If we go back to Roman history, the Republic is the period between Monarchy and Empire. Hence the common assumption since about the second half of the eighteenth century that a republican government stands in opposition to a monarchical and to a despotic government, a common assumption illustrated for example by Montesquieu. As is well known, Montesquieu distinguishes between republics, monarchies and despotic regimes, subdividing republics in aristocracies and democracies. During the Middle Ages, the notion of a republic was wider and tended to designate any form of government which cared for the *res publica*, i.e. the common good. Republics of any sort were opposed to tyrannies, the tyrant—at least the tyrant by exercise—looking only after his own personal good.

So how did the founding fathers define a republican government? The Federal Convention did not try to give a definition. Those who wanted to make matters short just presupposed that a republican government was the kind of government established in any of the thirteen states, whatever the differences between these governments. This presupposition did not only make matters short, but it also permitted states to ward off a possible application of the guarantee clause against them. Call the *status quo* a republic, do not change it, and there is no danger that the guarantee clause will be applied.

Whatever the pragmatic merits of such a solution may be, some authors nevertheless tried to give a more substantial definition of what is to be understood by the word 'republic'. A republican government, so Agrippa, is a government in which "every citizen has an influence in making the laws, and thus they are conformed to the general interest of the state". Brutus, for his part, tells us that "[i]t is the true republican principle to diffuse the power of making the laws among

---

46 Cited in Madison (2007, 281).
47 On this episode, see May Mowry (2009).

the people and so to modify the forms of the government as to draw in turn the well informed of every class into the legislature"[48]. Last but not least, Thomas Jefferson[49], in a letter to Isaac Tiffany dated 1819, defines a pure republic as "a state of society in which every member, of mature and sound mind, has an equal right of participation, personally in the direction of the affairs of the society"[50]. In a letter to John Taylor written three years before, Jefferson had lamented that in America there was much less republicanism than ought to have been expected.[51] Twenty years before, in 1797, in a letter to James Sullivan, Jefferson had blandly admitted that the US constitution was a mix of monarchy and republicanism.[52] As can be gathered from a letter of 1816 to Samuel Kercheval, Jefferson thought it was up to every state to determine who was to be admitted to suffrage and who was not.[53] At least three categories were to be excluded. Children formed the first category, and their exclusion was justified by their age and, as a natural consequence, their lack of intellectual and moral maturity. The second category is made up of women. The exclusion of women was, some authors like Condorcet in France apart, a normal matter in those days. The usual justifications for exclusion were either lack of reason or lack of independence, as women were generally dependent of their husband or father. Jefferson has another rationale, as he wants to exclude them "to prevent depravation of morals and ambiguity of issue"[54]. Some decennia later, James Fenimore Cooper, in his *American Democrat*, justifies the exclusion of women by arguing that it is necessary to remove from the home "the strife of parties, and the fierce struggle of political controversies"[55]. When Jefferson speaks of "ambiguity of issue", he is not, as everybody will have guessed, speaking of uncertain electoral results, but is alluding to the consequences of a promiscuous sexuality which, for reasons known only to Jefferson, follow the admission of women to the suffrage. The fear of a depravation of morals sounds more interesting, at least if one takes morals not to mean only sexual morals. If politics is a game of power and if those entering the game cannot remain long without succumbing to the rules of the game, whatever their moral purity at the beginning, then letting women participate would in fact lead to a depravation of morals, unless women were, to use

---

48 Cited in Henry (2010, 190).
49 Cited in Kenyon (1966, 139).
50 Jefferson (1999, 224).
51 Ibid. (1999, 209).
52 Ibid. (1999, 417).
53 Ibid. (1999, 220).
54 Washington (1999, 220).
55 Cooper (1969, 38).

Kant's famous formula, made of a lesser crooked wood than men. As to Cooper's rationale, it presupposes the distinction between the public and the private and insists on keeping public issues out of the private sphere, for fear that the polemogeneous aspects of the public sphere contaminate the private sphere and thus cause a disruption of the family.

Besides children and women, Jefferson excludes a third category from the suffrage, i.e. slaves, the rationale being that slaves have no property nor will of their own. The question that should be asked here is not whether a republican form of government can tolerate that slaves be excluded from the suffrage, but whether a republican form of government can tolerate the institution of slavery. Already in 1787, in a short piece called *Vices of the political system of the U.S.*, James Madison had clearly and unambiguously stated that "[w]here slavery exists the republican Theory becomes still more fallacious"[56]. What solution does Madison propose? In his *Memorandum on colonizing freed slaves* of 1789 as well as in a letter to Robert Evans dated 1819, Madison takes for granted an insuperable prejudice of whites against blacks, so that an integration of blacks is for him out of the question. His proposed solution consists in transporting freed slaves back to where their ancestors came from, i.e. back to Africa, and to let them do there whatever they want to do with their lives. He goes even thus far as to propose that the government should sell vacant territories and use the money to buy off slaves from their masters. In this context he writes: "And if in any instances, wrong has been done by our forefathers to people of one colour, by dispossessing them of their soil, what better atonement is now in our power than that of making what is rightfully acquired a source of justice & of blessings to a people of another colour?"[57] So, first Indians are unjustly dispossessed of their soil, then these territories are rightfully sold to colonists, then the money from that transaction is used to rightfully buy off slaves from their masters, and by this buying off, justice is done to "a people of another colour" and this people is invited to enjoy the blessings of crossing the Atlantic and going back *en masse* to a Continent which was about to be colonized by the Europeans.

Can someone be of a mature and sound mind if he cannot free himself of his prejudices against a certain class of the population when these prejudices are merely based on skin-color? In his definition of a pure republic, Jefferson sees a mature and sound mind as a sufficient condition for participation. Had he also seen it as a necessary condition, and had the prejudice against the blacks been incompatible with a mature and sound mind, then many an American citi-

---

56 Madison (1999, 72).
57 Ibid. (1999, 731).

zen would have had to be deprived of his right to vote. In these debates concerning republicanism and slavery, Southerners, eager to protect an institution on which a large part of their economy rested, retorted by saying that since slavery and republicanism were seen by most as compatible in 1788, they just were compatible. Some, drawing on the examples of Ancient Greece, went even so far as to argue that slavery fostered republicanism, as it permitted a greater equality among free citizens, as it freed these of harassing labor, thus making possible their political participation.

The question of the compatibility of slavery and republicanism was to pop up several times in the nineteenth century, for example during the Missouri crisis of 1819. As it was to be decided whether Missouri was to be admitted to the Union, Northern states refused that admission, arguing that slavery, legal in Missouri, was incompatible with republicanism. The question reached its climax with the War of Secession, but this is another story.

Conclusion

In this contribution, I have highlighted four major fears which were present at the birth of the United States of America and which help to explain, better than any abstract and high-flowing philosophical theory, the form the Constitution and, hence, the United States of America took. There is no doubt that those who expressed these fears tended to exaggerate, so as to draw as many Americans as possible towards their proposed solution. What the birth of America shows, is thus an ideological use of fear. This ideological use of fear is still present today and tends rather to grow than to diminish.

The most problematic of these fears is without doubt the fear of radical republicanism. It threw a rather dark light on the republican discourse. Yet the Constitution provides for an instrument which, if taken seriously, could have made America a true example of republicanism. The guarantee clause, so Charles Sumner, is a "sleeping giant"[58]. If this giant were to be taken seriously, American institutions would undergo an earthquake, however. Not so much on the merely formal level—suffrage is universal for all American citizens, whether white or black, male or female. The earthquake would rather touch the dimension of publicity and empowerment. In a true republic, everything relating to the public should be open to scrutiny, and money should not influence any public decision whatsoever. Yet transparency and what Michael Walzer would call

---

58 Quoted in Wiecek (1972, 168).

the separation of spheres is not only necessary at the level of federated states, but also at the level of the federal government. What if, at all of these levels, there is a fear of radical and substantial republicanism, i. e. if all authorities, federated and federal, were afraid of acting on the principles of radical republicanism? Who will then face the dilemma mentioned by Wiecek, i. e. the "dilemma of depriving a state of republican government temporarily in order to assure its restoration permanently"[59]?

In the United States of America, the Supreme Court has an important role in implementing the principles of a true republic. In the past, it has sometimes had the courage to assume this role, for example in *Brown vs. Board of Education*. If it were to give a radical reading of the notion of republic, it would be acting on behalf of the sleeping giant in the Constitution. If it would so, fear would spread among those who profit from the present system, in which it is money, and not so much virtue or talent, which determines American politics. And that would no doubt be a very wholesome fear.

Bibliography

Acton, John E. E. (1985): Selected writings. Volume III. Essays in religion, politics and morality, Indianapolis.

Bailyn, Bernard (1992): The ideological origins of the American Revolution, Cambridge, Mass.

Belz, Hermann (ed.) (2000): The Webster-Hayne debate on the nature of the union, Indianapolis.

Berkin, Carol (2003): A brilliant solution, Boston, Mass.

Cooper, James Fenimore (1969): The American Democrat, Baltimore, Maryland.

Hamilton, Alexander/Jay, John/Madison, James (1978): Federalist (Papers), London.

Hamilton, Alexander (2001): Writings, New York.

Hamilton, Alexander (2008): The revolutionary writings, Indianapolis.

Hartwell Bennett, Walter (1967): American theories of federalism, Tuscaloosa, Alabama.

Henry, Patrick/Yates, Robert/Byron, Samuel (2010): The Anti-federalist Papers, Lexington.

Howard, Dirk (2004): Aux origines de la pensée politique américaine, Paris.

Jefferson, Thomas (1999): Political writings, Cambridge.

Kenyon, Cecelia M. (ed.) (1966): The Antifederalists, Indianapolis.

Mably, Gabriel Bonnot, Abbé de (1789): Œuvres complètes, Tome 8. Observations sur le gouvernement et les loix des États-Unis d'Amérique, Londres.

Madison, James (1999): Writings, New York.

Madison, James (2007): The debates in the Federal Convention of 1787: which framed the Constitution of the United States of America. Amherst, New York.

Mason, Alpheus Thomas (ed.) (1972): The States Rights Debate, New York.

---

59 Wiecek (1972, 173).

May Mowry, Arthur (2009 [OCR automated reprint from the 1901 edition]): The Dorr War; or the constitutional struggle in Rhode Island, s.l.

Price, Richard (1991): Political writings, Cambridge.

Proudhon, Pierre-Joseph (1999): Du principe fédératif et de la nécessité de reconstituer le parti de la révolution, Paris.

Tocqueville, Alexis de (1952): Œuvres complètes. Tome II, volume 1. L'Ancien Régime et la Révolution, Paris.

Turner Main, Jackson (1974): The Antifederalists, New York.

Washington, George (2011): Selected writings, New York.

Wiecek, William M. (1972): The guarantee clause of the U.S. constitution, Ithaca, N.Y., and London.

Heinz-Gerd Schmitz

Wie man der Tugend aufhelfen kann. Zur philosophischen Begründung einer föderalen Organisation des Gemeinwesens

Einleitung

Vor der erfolgreichen Wiederbelebung des Kontraktualismus durch John Rawls Anfang der siebziger Jahre des letzten Jahrhunderts konnten Vertragstheorien nur ein müdes Lächeln bei politischen Theoretikern erzeugen. Schließlich schien festzustehen, dass Vereinbarungen, wie Hobbes, Locke, Rousseau sie kennzeichnen, niemals stattgefunden hatten; denn die Menschen werden in der Regel in bereits bestehende staatliche Gebilde hineingeboren und können diese bestenfalls durch Auswanderung wechseln, nicht aber *ex nihilo* durch Verhandlungen erzeugen. Daher gestand man dem Kontraktualismus, wenn man ihn überhaupt ernst nahm, lediglich einen gewissen heuristischen Wert zu. Auch die Rawlssche Konstruktion geht darüber nicht hinaus; man könnte von einem vertragstheoretischen Gedankenexperiment sprechen.

Allerdings ist eine solche Einschätzung des Kontraktualismus insofern etwas voreilig, als sie die historisch-faktischen Verhandlungen außer Acht lässt, durch welche Föderationen entstehen. Zwar handelt es sich auch hier nicht um Kreationen *ex nihilo*, aber man schafft hier doch etwas Neues. Dies kann in zwei gleichsam gegenläufigen Richtungen geschehen: Entweder finden sich ehemals souveräne Staaten zu einer Verbindung zusammen, welche ihnen eine gemeinsame Regierung beschert, die – neben anderen Tätigkeitsfeldern in der Regel – völlige Kontrolle insbesondere über die Außenpolitik besitzt, eine einheitliche Währung reguliert, gesetzliche Bedingungen des Wirtschaftens und seiner Finanzierung schafft, Streitkräfte aufstellt und unterhält.[1] Auf allen diesen Feldern verzichten die sich zusammenschließenden Staaten auf ihre Souveränität, ihnen verbleiben dann lediglich solche Aufgaben, die – gemäß dem Subsidiaritäts-

---

1 Eine Orientierung gewinnt man hier, wenn man einen Blick in die amerikanische Verfassung wirft: Artikel 1, Sektion 8 sowie das 10. Amendment. Von philosophischer Seite kommt die Aufzählung der Aufgaben der Zentralregierung, die Sidgwick liefert (1919, 475).

prinzip[2] – von ihnen besser ausgeführt werden können als von einer Zentralregierung.

Was ich soeben beschrieben habe, ist die föderale Bewegung von mehreren Einzelstaaten zu einer Union, die als ein neues politisches Subjekt die Weltbühne betritt. Es finden sich aber auch historische Beispiele für die gegenläufige Entwicklung, für die föderale Aufspaltung eines ehemals zentralistischen Gebildes.[3] Hier entstehen neue, auf die Bundesstaaten begrenzte Regierungen, welche durch eigene Parlamente und eine für sie zuständige Judikative kontrolliert werden. Auch in diesem Falle gilt das Subsidiaritätsprinzip.

Eine philosophisch beflissene Politiktheorie, welche den Kontraktualismus bestenfalls als ein Gedankenexperiment hat zulassen wollen, hat sich um den Föderalismus wenig gekümmert. Zwei große Ausnahmen kann man benennen – einmal die Theoretiker der amerikanischen Verfassung, die sich mit den sogenannten *Federalist Papers* zu Wort melden,[4] und zum anderen Immanuel Kant, der die Möglichkeit eines Weltstaates erörtert und eine ausgesprochen lockere Form des föderalen Zusammenschlusses, im Grunde nur eine Allianz[5] von Staaten vorschlägt. Beide Ansätze stehen insofern gegeneinander, als sie in verschiedene Richtungen weisen – die Federalists wollen den Zentralismus stärken,[6] Kant will ihn, was das Postulat eines Weltstaates angeht, ganz erheblich begrenzen. Daher

---

2 Es handelt sich hier ursprünglich um ein Gebot der katholischen Soziallehre, das dann politisch bedeutsam geworden ist. Vgl. Artikel 3 b des Maastricht-Vertrages, Artikel 23 des Grundgesetzes der Bundesrepublik Deutschland, Artikel 3 der Schweizerischen Bundesverfassung.

3 Unterhalb dieser Schwelle bleiben Entwicklungen, welche man gerne als ,Devolution' bezeichnet. Ein Beispiel hierfür sind gewisse Maßnahmen in Großbritannien, die z. B. zu walisischen, nordirischen und schottischen Parlamenten geführt und gewisse Exekutivorgane geschaffen haben. Alle drei Landesteile bleiben freilich so Teil des Einheitsstaates, dass von einem föderalen Aufbau nicht gesprochen werden kann.

4 Man hat in diesem Zusammenhang davor gesprochen, dass es nicht so sehr der gerne ins Feld geführte Althusius als vielmehr die Amerikaner gewesen seien, welche den Föderalismus erfunden haben, vgl. Elazar (1995, xxxviii).

5 Vgl. hierzu Sidgwick (1919, 473). Sidgwick will den Begriff des Föderalismus fassen, indem er diejenigen Staatsformen, die ihn begrenzen, benennt – einerseits den Einheitsstaat, andererseits eine Liga oder lockere Konföderation unabhängiger Staaten.

6 Der von ihnen verteidigte Verfassungsentwurf soll die *Articles of Confederation* – ratifiziert 1781 – ersetzen, welche den dreizehn Einzelstaaten Souveränität garantieren und deshalb nur einen sehr schwachen Kongress zulassen, der – etwa im Felde der Besteuerung – gar nicht unmittelbar auf die Bürger zurückgreifen kann, sondern auf Kontributionen der Einzelstaaten angewiesen ist. Zudem fehlt eine zentrale Exekutive, Ausschüsse übernehmen die Implementierung von Gesetzen; Bundesgerichte werden lediglich *ad hoc* gebildet.

scheint es sinnvoll, diese gegenläufigen Ansätze ins Zentrum zu stellen, wenn man die philosophischen Grundlagen des Föderalismus erörtern will.[7]

Ich will dies im Folgenden tun und dabei die These vertreten, dass der Föderalismus in philosophischer Perspektive als eine Antwort auf das Problem der Hinfälligkeit politischer Tugend verstanden werden kann.[8] Er stellt nämlich eine zweite Art der Gewaltenteilung dar, die keinen horizontalen,[9] sondern vertikalen Charakter hat. Andererseits ist es aber so, dass alles föderale Bestreben am Postulat der Souveränität seine Schranke findet. Will man dieses Postulat nicht aufgeben, dann ist man auf das Prinzip der Subsidiarität verwiesen, das freilich nur in einzelnen Staaten, nicht für eine Weltrepublik gelten kann.

Um diese These zu begründen, will ich zunächst kurz auf den Begriff der politischen Tugend eingehen, sodann die Position der Federalists umreißen, um schließlich in einem dritten Abschnitt Kant zu thematisieren.

1 Der Begriff der politischen Tugend

Die Bedeutung eines politiktheoretischen Konzeptes eruiert man häufig am einfachsten, wenn man an den Anfang des historischen Fadens zurückkehrt. Dort steht in vielen Fällen Aristoteles. An seiner Konzeption der Polis lässt sich ablesen, was unter politischer Tugend zu verstehen und wie sie gefährdet ist.

Die Polis ist für Aristoteles ein Ganzes aus Teilen. Die *politeia*, i.e. die Verfassung der Polis, bestimmt, wer als Teil anzusehen ist – in Athen z.B. nur freie, in der Stadt von athenischen Eltern geborene Männer. Obendrein legt die Verfassung fest, in welchem Verhältnis die Teile zueinander stehen; die Verfassung selektiert und korreliert also die Elemente, aus welchen die Polis besteht[10].

Aristoteles beantwortet die Frage, wer ein Bürger ist, zunächst so, dass er angibt, wozu jemand, der als Bürger selektiert wird, denn bestimmt ist; er liefert

---

7 Praktisch-politisch sind die Gründe, die für einen föderalen Zusammenschluss sprechen, sie sind schnell aufgezählt: Es geht um militärische Sicherheit, um ökonomische Prosperität (Schlagworte sind: Binnenmarkt, Währungsunion), um eine wirksame Außenpolitik. Für eine föderalen Zerlegung eines Zentralstaates führt man folgende Argumente ins Feld: Ethnische, religiöse, historische, auch sprachliche Besonderheiten gewisser Bevölkerungsgruppen können bezüglich des in ihnen schlummernden Konfliktpotentials dadurch neutralisiert werden, dass man in einem gewissen Umfang Selbstbestimmung gewährt; vgl. in diesem Zusammenhang Horowitz (2007, 985 ff.).
8 Ein – wenn auch vager – Hinweis auf den Zusammenhang des seit Platon und Aristoteles erörterten Tugendproblems mit dem Föderalismus findet sich bei Scott (2011, 1–39).
9 Zur horizontalen Gewaltenteilung vgl. exemplarisch Amar (1987).
10 Aristoteles, Pol. 1274b39 f.

also eine funktionale Kennzeichnung des Bürgers. Dies tut er, ohne dass er bereits auf bestimmte Verfassungen eingeht. Es wird also eine sehr allgemeine Angabe zu erwarten sein.

Die ersten beiden Bestimmungen sind negativ: Bürger ist man nicht schon dadurch, dass man auf dem Gebiet der Polis seinen Wohnsitz hat, und auch nicht dadurch, dass man vor Gericht gezogen werden kann oder selber einen Prozess anstrengen darf.[11]

Eine positive Formel bestimmt dann: Bürger ist, wer an Entscheidungen und an der Herrschaft beteiligt ist.[12]

Inhaltlich gefüllt wird diese Bestimmung dadurch, dass Aristoteles zwischen dem guten Mann und dem tugendhaften Bürger unterscheidet. Beide dürfen nicht identifiziert werden, weil die Differentialität der Bürger es nicht erlaubt, auf die Frage nach politischer Tugend nur eine Eigenschaft zu benennen. Wie die Mannschaft eines Schiffes verschiedene Aufgaben wahrnimmt, so füllen auch die Bürger verschiedene Funktionen aus. Das, was sie gemeinsam bewirken, ist das, woran die Tugend der Bürger abgelesen werden kann. Für jeden einzelnen gilt hingegen die ethische Bestimmung des guten Menschen.

Aus diesen Angaben lässt sich auf das Verhältnis von Ethik und Politik schließen. ‚Moralisch gut' ist eine Qualität, die man individuellem Handeln zuschreibt, ‚politisch gut, i. e. tugendhaft' ist eine Qualität der gemeinsamen Aktivitäten, welche durch die Korrelation der Bürger zustande kommen. ‚Politisch tugendhaft' ist daher letztlich eine Qualität der Verfassung. Die Ethik hat es also mit dem Individuum und seinen Handlungen zu tun, die Politik hingegen mit der Frage nach der Beschaffenheit der Bedingungen, welchen das Zusammenwirken der Bürger untersteht. Damit ist die Tugend der Bürger eine Qualität, die von der Verfassung abhängig ist. Diese gibt an, wer wann herrscht und beherrscht wird. Der politisch tugendhafte Bürger muss über das Wissen und die Fähigkeit verfügen, sowohl beherrscht zu werden als auch zu herrschen, und so ruht die Tugend des Bürgers auf dem Wissen über die Herrschaft über Freie aus beiden Perspektiven.

Die so gekennzeichnete Polis wird so lange gut regiert, wie die jeweils Herrschenden bzw. Beherrschten ihre Tugend wahren; sollten sie dies nicht tun, sich also dazu entschließen, nur noch zu herrschen, nicht aber, sich beherrschen zu lassen, dann wandelte sich die Polis entweder in eine Pöbelherrschaft (die Aristoteles Demokratie nennt), in das Regiment einiger Oligarchen oder gar in eine Tyrannis. Mittel, die sie davor bewahren, gibt es im Aristotelischen Aufriss nicht.

---

11 Pol. 1275a6f.
12 Pol. 1275a23.

Man ist halt auf die Tugend der Bürger in ihrer Gesamtheit angewiesen, aber natürlich auch auf die moralischen Qualitäten der Individuen.

2 Die Position der *Federalists*

Die Leistung der Väter der amerikanischen Verfassung besteht darin, dieses Übel klar gesehen und ihm abgeholfen zu haben. Wenn die Menschen Engel wären, heißt es recht lapidar in den *Federalist Papers*, dann brauche man keine Regierungen; wenn Engel die Menschen regierten, dann wären interne und externe Kontrollen der Regierungen überflüssig. Beide Fälle sind nicht gegeben, sondern es sind Menschen, die Menschen regieren;[13] und deren Tugend muss aufgeholfen werden.

Man hat auf der Grundlage dieser Einsicht – durchaus im Bewusstsein, eine Novität in die Welt zu setzen[14] – eine konstitutionelle Konstruktion ersonnen, welche die Hinfälligkeit politischer Tugend kompensieren soll. Ich will im Folgenden die besonderen historischen Umstände, unter denen die *Federalist Papers* entstanden sind, weitgehend abblenden und mich auf die systematisch bedeutsamen Aspekte der in ihnen vertretenen Auffassungen konzentrieren.

Jay, einer der drei Autoren, formuliert die Prämisse: Menschen brauchen eine Regierung, an die sie einen Teil ihrer natürlichen Rechte abtreten müssen, damit diese handlungsfähig wird.[15] Die Aufgabe der Regierung besteht darin, innere und äußere Sicherheit zu schaffen.[16] Hamilton präzisiert die Gefahren, die im Inneren drohen. Ihre Quelle sind ,domestic factions', welche unter dem Vorwand, dem Land zu dienen, ihre partikularen Interessen verfolgen.[17] Diese Bestimmung führt dann unmittelbar zur Frage nach der politischen Tugend. Hamilton konstatiert, man müsse den trügerischen Traum von einem goldenen Zeitalter aufgeben; denn

---

13 Ich belege und zitiere nach folgender Ausgabe: Hamilton, A./Madison, J./Jay, J. (1965), *The Federalist or, The New Constitution. With an Introduction by W.R. Brock*, London/New York (= *F.* nebst Seitenangabe), hier: *F.* 264.

14 Vgl. Madison im 37. Artikel – *F.* 177. Die Forschung hat dieser Auffassung zum Teil zugestimmt, vgl. Kielmannsegg (2007, 356). Der Novitätsanspruch ist freilich nicht ganz gerechtfertigt, wenn man einen Blick in Montesquieus *De l'esprit de lois* wirft (1979, 266 [1748]). Hier heißt es, eine föderative Republik könne einerseits äußeren Feinden widerstehen, andererseits innere Korruption verhindern; denn wenn einer der Teilstaaten korrumpiert werden sollte, dann würden die anderen dem Spuk schnell ein Ende machen und ihn reformieren.

15 *F.* 5. Hamilton nennt als Grund für die Schaffung von Regierungen die Leidenschaften der Menschen, die mit den Geboten der Vernunft nicht konform gehen. Vgl. *F.* 71/72.

16 *F.* 9.

17 *F.* 20/ 21.

von einer vollkommenen politischen Weisheit und von perfekter politischer Tugend sei man weit entfernt.[18]

Mit deutlicher Anspielung auf Montesquieu nennt Hamilton dann in einem späteren Artikel die Gegenmaßnahmen, die konstitutionell ergriffen werden können:

- Gewaltenteilung,[19]
- ‚balances and checks', die auf diesem Wege erreicht werden können,
- die Einrichtung von Gerichtshöfen, deren Richter auf Lebenszeit bestallt werden und daher Unabhängigkeit gewinnen,
- Abgeordnetenwahl durch das Volk, das dann auf seinen jeweiligen Repräsentanten und sein Abstimmungsverhalten Einfluss nehmen kann, ohne dass von einem imperativen Mandat die Rede wäre,
- schließlich ein föderativer Staatsaufbau.[20]

Freilich ist sehr genau zwischen einer Konföderation und einem föderal organisierten Staat zu unterscheiden. Erstere stellt einen lockeren Staatenverbund dar, wie er zur Zeit der Verfassungsdiskussion besteht. Das Hauptmerkmal ist hier eine schwache Zentralregierung, die nicht die Möglichkeit eines direkten Zugriffs auf die Bürger der Einzelstaaten besitzt,[21] sondern lediglich einen Bezug zu den Mitgliedsstaaten hat.[22] Eine Föderation hingegen besitzt diese Möglichkeit[23]. Den in ihr vereinigten Staaten gewährt sie eine direkte Repräsentation in einer zweiten Parlamentskammer sowie gewisse Souveränitätsrechte. Damit untersteht der Bürger zwei Regierungen, die beide den Regulaturen der Gewaltenteilung unterworfen sind. Dadurch entsteht eine Verdopplung der Sicherheitsmechanismen. Denn beide Regierungen – die des Einzelstaates und die der Union – kontrollieren einander und werden ihrerseits durch die Gewaltenteilung innerhalb ihrer selbst kontrolliert.[24] Man hat es also mit einer horizontalen und vertikalen Gewaltenteilung zu tun – horizontal auf der Ebene der einzelnen Regierungen. Daraus folgt die Erkenntnis: Föderalismus ist eine Form vertikaler Gewaltenteilung.

---

18 *F.* 25
19 Vgl. *F.* 245. Das Prinzip der Gewaltenteilung lautet: „Ambition must be made to counteract ambition" (*F.* 264).
20 *F.* 37.
21 Vgl. Hamilton im 15. Artikel, *F.* 71; Sidgwick (1919, 479) greift dieses Kriterium auf. Zuvor hat J. S. Mill es quasi kanonisch gemacht – vgl. dessen *Considerations on Representative Government* (1862, 322 f.).
22 Vgl. Madison im 9. Artikel, *F.* 194.
23 Vgl. ebd.
24 Vgl. *F.* 266.

Hier leuchtet das Subsidiaritätsprinzip auf. Es gewinnt seine Bedeutung durch die Größe eines Gemeinwesens, dessen Ausdehnung weit über die Begrenzungen der griechischen Stadtstaaten hinausgeht, also nicht im engeren Sinne demokratisch,[25] sondern republikanisch, i. e. qua Repräsentation regiert werden muss. Es geht darum, eine Balance zwischen der Nähe der Politiker zu ihrer Wählerschaft und dem nötigen Abstand zu finden, der ein freies Urteil im Blick auf das große Ganze erlaubt. Aufgelöst wird dieses Paradoxon der fernen Nähe durch ein föderales Gebilde, das durch die lokalen Regierungen die Nähe und durch die Zentralgewalt den nötigen Abstand herstellt.[26]

Madison nennt dann den Föderalismus auch ein Mittel gegen den Parteienstaat, in seiner Sprache: gegen die ‚factions'; denn gegen die einzelnen parteipolitisch organisierten Interessengruppen treten jetzt die Interessen einzelner Mitgliedsstaaten, in denen zwar auch Parteien existieren mögen, vielleicht sogar als Dependancen der Parteien im Bunde, aber sie sind aufgrund ihrer größeren Bürgernähe den Vorstellungen der Menschen in ihrem Bundesstaat näher als die Großorganisation der gesamten Union.

Fasst man die Überlegungen zusammen, dann lässt sich sagen: Die Väter der amerikanischen Verfassung erfinden den föderalen Staat[27] als eines der Mittel, eine despotische Entartung ihrer Republik zu verhindern, welche dadurch entsteht, dass mit durchaus tugendhaften Bürgern kaum zu rechnen ist – oder: Der Föderalismus soll, neben anderen, außenpolitischen Funktionen, die er hat, im Inneren der hinfälligen Tugend der Menschen auf die Beine helfen.

3 Kants Argumentation gegen einen Weltstaat

Wenn denn die Vorteile einer föderativen Staatenorganisation – was die inneren Verhältnisse angeht – so groß sind, wie eben beschrieben, dann stellt sich unmittelbar die Frage, warum man nicht einen föderal organisierten Weltstaat ins Auge fassen sollte. Dieser könnte alles Militär abschaffen und durch eine Art Weltbundespolizei ersetzen. Tyrannische, jeder politischen Tugend Hohn spre-

---

25 Madison definiert: „[...] in a democracy the people meet and exercise the government in person; in a republic, they assemble and administer it by their representatives and agents" (*F.* 62).
26 Vgl. *F.* 46.
27 Proudhon hat gewiss Unrecht, wenn er den Vätern der amerikanischen Verfassung vorwirft, hinter ihrem vermeintlichen Föderalismus stecke ein übler Zentralismus (vgl. *Du principe fédératif et de la nécessité de reconstituer le parti de la révolution* (1863, 106)): Der Grund für diese Vorhaltungen liegt darin, dass er als Föderation ausgibt, was die Verfassungsväter gerade abschaffen wollten, nämlich die lockere Konföderation der Einzelstaaten.

chende Regime träten nicht mehr auf. Aufgrund zwischenstaatlicher Transferleistungen ließen sich Wohlstandsdifferenzen endlich effizient einebnen – also letztlich Hunger und Elend beseitigen, die heute noch weite Teile der Welt beherrschen.

Um diese Idee zu erörtern, will ich – wie angekündigt – auf Kants Überlegungen zu einem Weltstaat zurückgreifen. Staaten befinden sich untereinander trotz aller Verrechtlichungsversuche nicht nur zu Kants Zeiten, sondern auch heute noch in einem Verhältnis, welches von potentieller Gewalttätigkeit überschattet oder gar durch tatsächliche Gewaltausübung vergiftet ist. Kant hat zur Zivilisierung dieses völlig unbefriedigenden Zustandes die Regeln eines *ius ad bellum*[28] und *in bello*[29] vorgelegt und – über die Tradition hinausgehend – ein Recht nach dem Kriege.[30] Was er nicht versucht hat, ist dem Treiben dadurch ein Ende zu machen, dass er einen föderalen oder gar zentralistischen Weltstaat postuliert hat, der – analog zur politischen Vereinigung der Individuen – die einzelnen Staaten zur Anerkennung einer sie bändigenden Obrigkeit zwingt.

Für diese Haltung finden sich in den verschiedenen Schriften Kants ganz unterschiedliche Begründungen. Man stößt (a/b) auf einen zweifacher Impraktikabilitätseinwand, (c) auf den Despotismusverdacht und (d) auf einen Inkonsistenzvorwurf.

a) Hier stellt Kant einmal fest, die Staaten seien einfach nicht dazu bereit, ihre wilde Freiheit aufzugeben; „[...] einen [...] Völkerstaat (*civitas gentium*), der zuletzt alle Völker der Erde befassen würde", wollten die Staaten durchaus nicht.[31] Daher möge eine solcher Vorschlag „in der Theorie eines Abbé von St. Pierre, oder eines Rousseau noch so artig klingen", für die Praxis gelte er nicht, „wie er denn auch von großen Staatsmännern, mehr aber noch von Staatsoberhäuptern als eine pedantisch-kindische aus der Schule hervorgetretene Idee jederzeit ist verlacht worden".[32] Kant mag sich dieser Einschätzung nicht vollends anschließen, ihre politische Wirksamkeit zu unterschätzen, wird man ihm aber gewiss nicht vorhalten können.

b) Zum anderen heißt es, „bei gar zu großer Ausdehnung eines solchen Völkerstaats über weite Landstriche" müsse „die Regierung desselben, mithin

---

28 Vgl. *Metaphysik der Sitten – Rechtslehre* (= *MdSR* § 56), in: Kant AA 6: 346; *MdSR* § 57, in: AA 6: 347.

29 *MdSR* § 57, AA 6: 347.

30 *MdSR* § 58, AA 6: 348 f.

31 *Zum ewigen Frieden* (= *ZeF*), AA 8: 357; vgl. auch die Angaben in der *Kritik der Urteilskraft* (= *KdU*), AA 5: 432 f.).

32 *Über den Gemeinspruch* (= *Gem*), AA 8: 313; vgl. auch: *Die Religion innerhalb der Grenzen der bloßen Vernunft* (= *Rel*), AA 6: 34.

auch die Beschützung eines jeden Gliedes endlich unmöglich werden". Wolle man hingegen mehrere solcher ‚Corporationen' zulassen, dann sei nichts gewonnen.[33]

c) Hier lautet der Einwand: übergroße Staaten werden der Freiheit gefährlich, weil sie „den schrecklichsten Despotismus" hervorrufen.[34] Eine nähere Erklärung findet diese These im *Ewigen Frieden:* Der durch die Absonderung der Staaten voneinander heraufbeschworene Zustand sei immer noch besser als ihre Zusammenschmelzung „[...] durch eine die andere überwachende und in eine Universalmonarchie übergehende Macht, weil die Gesetze mit dem vergrößerten Umfange der Regierung immer mehr an ihrem Nachdruck einbüßen, und ein seelenloser Despotism, nachdem er die Keime des Guten ausgerottet hat, zuletzt doch in Anarchie verfällt".[35] Die Idee eines Weltstaates enthüllt sich – dieser Überlegung zufolge – als der Großmachttraum eines einzelnen Landes, das alle anderen in sich aufzusaugen begehrt, um „durch Schwächung aller Kräfte" einen ‚Kirchhof der Freiheit' zu errichten.[36]

d) Hier heißt es: In der Idee eines Weltstaates liegt ein Widerspruch, „weil ein jeder Staat das Verhältniss eines Oberen (Gesetzgebenden) zu einem Unteren (Gehorchenden, nämlich dem Volk) enthält, viele Völker aber in einem Staate nur ein Volk ausmachen würden, welches (da wir hier das Recht der Völker gegen einander zu erwägen haben, so fern sie so viel verschiedene Staaten ausmachen und nicht in einem Staat zusammenschmelzen sollen) der Voraussetzung widerspricht".[37]

Es ist leicht zu sehen, dass hier auf ganz unterschiedlichen Niveaus argumentiert wird. Die ersten beiden Einwände (a/b) haben politisch-praktischen Charakter. Sie zeigen deutlich, dass Kant durchaus um die Schwierigkeiten weiß, welche mit der Zumutung eines Souveränitätsverlustes der Einzelstaaten verbunden sind. Überdies wird klar, dass die rein technischen Probleme einer Überdehnung von Verwaltungseinheiten ins Kalkül gezogen werden. Diese Überlegungen sprechen nicht nur gegen einen zentralen, sondern auch gegen einen föderalen Weltstaat; denn das bereits erwähnte ausgewogene Verhältnis von Nähe und Ferne, welches herbeizuführen der Föderalismus ersonnen werden ist, dürfte sich in einem Weltstaat kaum herstellen lassen.

---

33 *MdSR* § 61, AA 6: 350.
34 *Gem*, AA 8: 311.
35 *ZeF*, AA 8: 367.
36 *ZeF*, AA 8: 367.
37 *ZeF*, AA 8: 354.

Die letzten beiden Einwände (c/d) dient dem Abweis einer Universalmonarchie, i. e. einer solchen weltstaatlichen Konstruktion, die Einzelstaaten nicht übergreift, sondern sie – zwecks imperialer Erweiterung – in sich aufsaugt, also nichts mit einer Föderation zu tun hat; (c) argumentiert dabei aus den Konsequenzen, i. e. mit dem Despotismusverdacht, (d) hingegen erhebt den Vorwurf, jede über eine lockere, man könnte sagen, subföderale Allianz hinausgehende Vereinigung sei in sich selbst widersprüchlich.

Angesichts dieser Argumente lässt sich die Position, welche Kant bezieht, so kennzeichnen: Abgewiesen werden die beiden denkbaren Extremfälle einer Beibehaltung des außenpolitischen Naturzustandes einerseits, einer Universalmonarchie andererseits. Vorgeschlagen wird eine Vereinigung von Staaten, welche genau so weit reicht, dass ein Souveränitätsverzicht unterbleibt.

Man hat Kant vorgehalten, ohne Souveränitätsverzicht lasse sich sein Plan einer Zivilisierung der internationalen Beziehungen nicht in Angriff nehmen – ganz gleichgültig, ob man nun einer Weltinnenpolitik das Wort redet oder lediglich den Kantischen ‚ultraminimalen‘ in einen ‚extrem minimalen Weltstaat‘ verwandeln will.[38] Trifft diese Kritik zu, dann wäre in der Tat die von Kant ins Auge gefasste lockere Allianz durch einen föderalen Weltstaat zu ersetzen.

Warum der Gedanke eines Souveränitätsverzichtes der Kantischen Rechtsphilosophie unvorstellbar ist, muss abschließend behandelt werden.

Kant stellt fest, dass die Rede vom Völkerrecht unterschiedliche staatliche Quasi-Subjekte voraussetze. Seien diese nicht mehr vorhanden, dann könne auch nicht mehr vom Völkerrecht gesprochen werden. Die Schwäche dieser Überlegung scheint darin zu liegen, dass Kant hier ein Alles-oder-nichts-Argument konstruiert, welches auf den ersten Blick nicht zwingend ist. Denn anarchische Handlungsfreiheit und universalmonarchische Despotie bilden keine vollständige Disjunktion, vielmehr sind durchaus Zwischenformen partiellen Souveränitätsverzichtes denkbar – man hat hier natürlich alle Formen eines föderalen Zusammenschlusses vor Augen, i. e. die eine oder andere Spielart eben des ‚Föderalism‘, von welchem Kant selbst spricht.[39]

Da Kant keine ausreichende Erklärung für sein Beharren auf vollständiger einzelstaatlicher Souveränität zu geben scheint, sieht man sich gezwungen, sie gleichsam aus der Gesamtheit seiner politiktheoretischen Bemerkungen zu extrahieren. Hier bieten sich folgende Überlegungen an: Einzelstaaten verwandeln provisorisches in peremptorisches Recht. Ist dies erfolgt, dann ist der grundlegende Freiheitsanspruch einer Pluralität von Individuen verwirklicht. Darüber

---

38 Vgl. Höffe (1995, 109–132).
39 Vgl. den Titel des zweiten Definitivartikels in *ZeF*, AA 8: 354; *Gem*, AA 8: 311.

hinausgehende Einschränkungen lassen sich nur so rechtfertigen, dass die einzelstaatliche Rechtssicherung als unzulänglich erwiesen würde.[40] Ein solcher Nachweis, sollte er denn gelingen, führte freilich nicht dazu, einen Staatenstaat zu postulieren, sondern man hätte aus ihm vielmehr den Schluss zu ziehen, dass die defizitäre Begründung von Einzelstaaten so zu revidieren wäre, dass sie ihrer Aufgabe schließlich nachzukommen in der Lage wären.

Kurz: Jede Rechtsgemeinschaft, die nach einer sie überwölbenden Organisation eines Staatenstaates verlangt, gesteht damit zugleich ein, die Aufgabe, welche zu lösen sie geschaffen worden ist, nicht erfüllen zu können. Hier ist dann aber nicht dadurch Abhilfe zu schaffen, dass man diese defizitären Quasi-Subjekte durch eine metastaatliche Konstruktion saniert, sondern nur dadurch, dass sie sich selbst in eine Gestalt bringen, welche dem Freiheitsanspruch der Individuen gerecht wird. Geht man hingegen davon aus, dass der Unzulänglichkeitsbeweis scheitert, dass also die Einzelstaaten genau die Aufgabe erfüllen, zu welcher sie geschaffen worden sind, dann bedeutete jede metastaatliche Organisation einen Souveränitätsverlust, der – wie gering oder wie umfangreich er auch immer ausfallen mag – ihren Status als freie Republiken aufhebt.[41]

Es ist also letztlich immer wieder der Gedanke unteilbarer einzelstaatlicher Souveränität, der im Zentrum der Kantischen Ablehnung einer supra-nationalen politischen Organisation steht, die über die von ihm konzeptualisierte lockere Allianz hinausgeht. Freilich ist der Kern des Gedankengangs damit noch nicht erreicht; denn hinter der Rede von Souveränität steht die Idee des allgemeinen gesetzgebenden Willens. Erst wenn man ihn genauer ins Auge fasst, wird deutlich, dass es die Substanz des Einzelstaates ist, welche in Gefahr gerät, wenn er einen wie auch immer gearteten Souveränitätsverlust in Kauf nimmt.

In einer Nachlassnotiz Kants findet sich die Feststellung, eine uneingeschränkte oberste Gewalt, i.e. Souveränität, sei unabdingbar. Diese könne aber nur der ‚gemeinschaftliche Wille' besitzen.[42] Dieser ist es, welcher genau dann Sicherheit schafft, wenn er „collectiv allgemeiner (gemeinsamer) und machthabender Wille"[43] ist. Die Staatsgründung ist mithin deshalb Pflicht, weil nur sie es erlaubt, den allgemeinen Willen in einen machthabenden allgemeinen Willen zu verwandeln; sie ist genau dann misslungen, wenn es nur partikulares Wollen ist, welches sich in das Gewand des allgemeinen Willens kleidet.

Souveränität meint also nichts anderes als die Herrschaft des Rechts als des allgemeinen Willens. Gestünde Kant nun zu, dass diese Souveränität zugunsten

---

40 Vgl. Kyora (1996, 99f.).
41 Vgl. Flikschuh (2000, 185).
42 Nachlassnotiz Nr. 7713, AA 19: 498.
43 *MdSR* § 8, AA 6: 256.

supra-nationaler politischer Entitäten beschnitten oder gar ganz aufgehoben werden muss, dann hätte er zugleich eingeräumt, dass es vor dieser Verzichtleistung nicht der allgemeine Wille war, der hier die Kodifikation des Rechts betrieben hat, sondern das lediglich partikulare Wollen eines nur einzelstaatlichen Quasi-Subjektes. Es ist also die Dignität der *res publica*, welche auf dem Spiel steht, wenn sie in eine Föderation mit fremden Staaten gebracht werden soll.

Treffen diese Überlegungen zu, dann wird unmittelbar einsichtig, warum Kant das Alles-oder-nichts-Argument präsentieren muss. Denn partikulares Wollen und allgemeiner Wille stehen in der Tat im Verhältnis einer vollständigen Disjunktion. Daher bedeutet nun das Zugeständnis der Notwendigkeit eines Metastaates zugleich das Eingeständnis der Partikularität der Einzelstaaten. Diese in ihrem außenpolitischen Verhalten zu zivilisieren, kann deshalb nur einer lockeren Allianz, nicht einem föderalen Weltstaat oder gar einer weltstaatlichen Zentralorganisation anvertraut werden.

Der Blick in die Kantische Philosophie hat gezeigt, dass der Wunsch, mit Hilfe föderaler Strukturen der politischen Tugend der Bürger aufzuhelfen, in einem klaren Spannungsverhältnis zur Konzeption eines souveränen Staates steht. Man kann diese Spannung innerhalb einzelner Nationen austarieren, wie die Verfassung der Vereinigten Staaten zeigt, im globalen Maßstab dürfte man daran scheitern. Denn eines der nicht unwesentlichen Argumente für den Föderalismus ist nicht nur die innere Sicherheit vor despotischen Politikern, es war immer der Hinweis auf eine Außenpolitik, welche mit einer Pluralität fremder Staaten zu interagieren hat. William Riker hat gewiss Recht, wenn er eine föderale Welt eine Chimäre nennt: Um sich zusammenzuschließen – so sein Argument – brauche man einen Feind.[44] Der könnte dann nur extraterristisch sein.

Bibliographie

Amar, Akhil Reed (1987): Of Sovereignty and Federalism, in: The Yale Law Journal 96, pp. 1425–1520.

Aristoteles, Politik.

Elazar, Daniel J. (1995): Foreword, Althusius' Grand Design for a Federal Commonwealth', in: Johannes Althusius, Politica, edited and translated by Frederick S. Carney, Indianapolis, pp. xxxv–xlvi, http://oll.libertyfund.org/titles/692 (2016/02/12).

Flikschuh, Katrin (2000): Kant and Modern Political Philosophy, Cambridge.

Hamilton, Alexander/Madison, James/Jay, John (1965): The Federalist or, The New Constitution. With an Introduction by W. R. Brock, London, New York.

---

44 Riker (1995, 513).

Höffe, Otfried (1995): Völkerbund oder Weltrepublik?, in: Kant, Immanuel. Zum ewigen Frieden. Klassiker auslegen, Bd. 1, Höffe, Ottfried (Hg.), Berlin, S. 109 – 132.

Horowitz, Donald L. (2007): The Many Uses of Federalism, in: Drake Law Review 55, pp. 953 – 966.

Kant, Immanuel (1968 [1797]): Metaphysik der Sitten – Rechtslehre (= MdSR), in: ders.: Werke. Akademie-Textausgabe. Unveränderter photomechanischer Abdruck des Textes der von der Preußischen Akademie der Wissenschaften 1902 begonnen Ausgabe von Kants gesammelten Schriften. Berlin (= AA 6).

Kant, Immanuel (1968 [1795]): Zum ewigen Frieden (= ZeF), in: AA 8.

Kant, Immanuel (1968 [1790]): Kritik der Urteilskraft (= KdU), in: AA 5.

Kant, Immanuel (1968 [1793]): Über den Gemeinspruch: Das mag in der Theorie richtig sein, taugt aber nicht für die Praxis (= Gem), in: AA 8.

Kant, Immanuuel (1968 [1793]): Die Religion innerhalb der Grenzen der bloßen Vernunft (= Rel), in: AA 6.

Kielmannsegg, Peter Graf (2007): Alexander Hamilton/James Madison/John Jay, Der Federalist (1788), in: Manfred Brocker (Hg.): Geschichte des politischen Denkens. Ein Handbuch, Frankfurt a. M., S. 349 – 363.

Kyora, Stefan (1996): Kants Argumente für einen schwachen Völkerbund heute, in: Volker Bialas/Hans-Jürgen Häßler (Hg.): 200 Jahre Kants Entwurf ‚Zum ewigen Frieden'. Idee einer globalen Friedensordnung, Würzburg, S. 96 – 107.

Mill, John Stuart (1862): Considerations on Representative Government, New York.

Montesquieu, Charles Louis de Secondat, baron de La Brède et de (1979 [1748]): De l'esprit des lois, 2 Bde., Paris.

Proudhon, Pierre-Joseph (1863): Du principe fédératif et de la nécessité de reconstituer le parti de la révolution, Paris.

Riker, William H. (1995): Federalism, in: Robert E. Goodin/Philip Pettit (Hg.): A Companion to Contemporary Political Philosophy, Oxford/Cambridge, Mass., S. 508 – 514.

Scott, Kyle (2011): Federalism. A Normative Theory and its Practical Relevance, New York.

Sidgwick, Henry (1919): The Elements of Politics, 4. Aufl., London.

Nineteenth Century Reception and Criticism of Federalist Ideas

Michael Wolff

Naturzustand und Völkerrecht. Hegel über Kants Idee eines Föderalismus freier Staaten, auf den das Völkerrecht zu gründen sei

1 Einleitung

Hegel hat die Ansicht vertreten, es bestehe zwischen souveränen und militärisch gerüsteten Staaten ein „Verhältnis der Gewalt" und ein *„Zustand* des *Krieges"* (*E* § 545). Er nennt diesen durch Austragen militärischer Konflikte unterbrochenen, als „Abwechselung" von Vertragstreue und Vertragsbruch erscheinenden Zustand, in dem sich solche Staaten dauerhaft befinden, „Naturzustand" (*R* § 333), von dem, als einem „Zustand der Gewaltthätigkeit und des Unrechts", nicht „Wahreres gesagt werden" könne, „als daß *aus ihm herauszugehen ist"*.[1] Mit dieser Ansicht steht Hegel in einer Tradition, die auf Hobbes zurückgeht.

Auf den ersten Blick scheint es so, als sei Hegel auch darin Hobbes gefolgt, dass dieser aus dem zwischenstaatlichen Naturzustand keinen wirklichen Ausweg gesehen hatte. Hegel wird meist so gelesen, als habe er einen solchen für unmöglich gehalten. Kant hatte angenommen, dass ein „ewiger Friede" den zwischenstaatlichen Naturzustand zu beenden habe, und diese Annahme war so zu verstehen, dass dieser Friede der Zustand einer Rechtsordnung sein müsse, die in Analogie zur staatsbürgerlichen Verfassung das Recht jedes einzelnen Staates sichern und durch einen zwanglos geschlossenen Bund freier Staaten dauerhaft garantiert werden könne. Hegel hat in seinen *Grundlinien der Philosophie des Rechts* gegen die so verstandene Annahme den folgenden Einwand erhoben:

> Die *Kantische* Vorstellung eines *ewigen Friedens* durch einen Staatenbund, welcher jeden Streit schlichtete, und als eine von jedem einzelnen Staate anerkannte Macht jede Mishelligkeit beilegte, und damit die Entscheidung durch Krieg unmöglich machte, setzt die *Einstimmung* der Staaten voraus, welche auf moralischen, religiösen oder welchen Gründen und Rücksichten, überhaupt immer auf besonderen souverainen Willen beruhte, und dadurch mit Zufälligkeiten behaftet bliebe. (*R* § 333 *Anm.*)

---

1 *E* § 502 *Anm.* (Hervorhebung im Original). Vgl. *RPR*, 400 und 403.

Man hat diesen Einwand als Polemik bezeichnet.[2] Nach verbreiteter Meinung hätte sich Hegel den Blick auf den von Kant beschriebenen Ausweg aus dem Naturzustand nicht so leichtfertig verbauen sollen.

Aber die Bezeichnung als Polemik ist verfehlt. Es handelt sich bei dem zitierten Einwand vielmehr um ein sachliches Argument, das auf eine problematische Voraussetzung in Kants Idee eines weltfriedensstiftenden Staaten- oder Völkerbundes (*foedus pacificum*, *ZeF* 356) hinweist. Der Hinweis bezieht sich darauf, dass ein solcher Bund auf Verträgen zwischen souveränen Staaten beruht und diese Verträge *„Einstimmung"* voraussetzen, daher Krieg zwischen ihnen nur so lange „unmöglich" ist, wie unter ihnen diese Einstimmung herrscht.[3] Da Verträge gebrochen oder gekündigt werden können, ist die Errichtung eines Staatenbundes kein zuverlässiges Mittel zur dauerhaften Verhinderung von Kriegen.[4]

---

2 Ilting (1978, 305). Nach Ilting „polemisiert" Hegel in der Anmerkung zu *R* § 333 gegen Kant und Fichte, „die auf das Völkerrecht ihre Lehre vom Völkerbund folgen ließen." Fulda (2003, 231) betrachtet dieselbe Anmerkung als „Polemik gegen das Ideal Ewigen Friedens". – Eine Parallelstelle zu *R* § 333, die in der Mitschrift einer Heidelberger Vorlesung Hegels zu finden ist und in der es heißt: „Kant und andere haben nun von einem ewigen Frieden gesprochen. Dies ist ein wohlmeinender Gedanke, der auch moralisch gut ist; [...]" (*RV 1817/18*, 194), bestätigt, dass mit der *„Kantische[n]* Vorstellung eines *ewigen Friedens"* die Vorstellung von Autoren mit gemeint ist, die wie Fichte unter dem Einfluss von Kants Schrift *Zum ewigen Frieden* von 1795 standen.
3 Bereits Kants Schüler Friedrich Gentz hatte in seinem Aufsatz ‚Über den ewigen Frieden' von 1800 gegen die Ansicht argumentiert, ein auf Verträgen beruhender Staatenbund sei imstande, Krieg unmöglich zu machen: „Ein freier Vertrag unter Staaten wird immer nur so lange beobachtet werden, als keiner von denen, welche ihn schlossen, zugleich den Willen und die Macht ihn zu brechen besitzt, d. h. mit anderen Worten, solange auch ohne einen solchen Vertrag der Friede, welchen er gründen soll, bestehen würde." (Gentz 1953, 479).
4 Im *Zusatz* zu *R* § 259 heißt es: „Es können Staatenverbindungen eintreten, wie z. B. die Heilige Allianz, aber diese sind immer nur relativ und beschränkt, wie der ewige Frieden" (*RZ*, 405). Der *Zusatz* zu *R* § 324 erläutert dies: Die Heilige Allianz habe „die Absicht" gehabt, „ungefähr ein solches Institut zu sein", wie Kant es mit einer Föderation von Staaten zur Schlichtung ihrer Streitigkeiten vorgeschlagen habe (*RZ*, 493 f.). Hiermit bezieht sich Hegel auf die Präambel des Allianzvertrages vom 26. September 1815, in der der Kaiser von Österreich, der König von Preußen und der Zar von Russland erklären, dieser Vertrag habe „lediglich den Zweck", „vor aller Welt ihren unerschütterlichen Entschluß zu bekunden, als die Richtschnur ihres Verhaltens in der inneren Verwaltung ihrer Staaten sowohl als auch in den politischen Beziehungen zu jeder anderen Regierung allein die Gebote [...] der Gerechtigkeit, der Liebe und des Friedens" anzusehen, „damit sie den menschlichen Einrichtungen Dauer verleihen und ihren Unvollkommenheiten abhelfen." (Der vollständige Text ist im französischen Original abgedruckt in *CJCG*, 290 f.) Hegel behauptet nicht, der mit diesem Vertrag geschlossene Bund entspreche dem von Kant geforderten *Foedus pacificum*, sondern nur, die „Absicht" der Heiligen Allianz habe „ungefähr" auf der Linie des von Kant an die Fürsten Europas und die französische Republik adressierten Friedensplans gelegen. „Das Jahr 1815, in dem die Herrscher der Restauration mit dem Wiener Kongreß die eigentliche Epoche des strikt zwischenstaatlichen Völkerrechts einleiteten, ist zugleich das Ge-

Alternativen zur „Idee der Föderalität", die nach Kants Friedensschrift von 1795 zum ewigen Frieden hinführt (*ZeF*, 356), hat Hegel in seiner Rechtsphilosophie nicht in Betracht gezogen, auch nicht die beiden Alternativen, die schon Kant selbst in seiner Schrift *Zum ewigen Frieden* diskutiert und verworfen hatte: die der „Universalmonarchie", in der alle Einzelstaaten aufgelöst sind, und die des „Völkerstaats" (oder der „Weltrepublik"), in der sich die Einzelstaaten öffentlichen Zwangsgesetzen zu unterwerfen haben.[5] Deshalb hat es den Anschein, als habe Hegels Rechtsphilosophie nur für die These argumentiert, ein Ausweg aus dem Naturzustand und der Eintritt in einen dauerhaften öffentlich-rechtlichen Zustand sei für souveräne und militärisch gerüstete Staaten unmöglich.

Bei genauerem Hinsehen zeigt sich indessen, dass Hegels Argumentation differenzierter ist und dass nicht die Rede davon sein kann, er gebe sich zufrieden mit der Annahme, der Zustand, in dem sich solche Staaten im Verhältnis zueinander befinden, sei nichts anderes als ein Hobbesianischer *status naturalis*. Auch auf die Staatenwelt (und nicht nur auf die Welt des „abstrakten" Privatrechts) ist deshalb Hegels Aussage zu beziehen, „Wahreres" könne nicht gesagt werden als: *Exeundum esse e statu naturali*.

Welchen Ausweg aus diesem Zustand hat Hegel gesehen? – Um auf diese Frage eingehen zu können, ist es nötig, die Rede vom Naturzustand etwas genauer zu erläutern.

2 Militärischer Zustand und militärische Konflikte

Welchen Sinn hatte es anzunehmen, unabhängige und militärisch gerüstete, d. h. auf militärische Konflikte vorbereitete Staaten befänden sich schon wegen ihrer Unabhängigkeit voneinander in einem Naturzustand und dieser Zustand sei ein Zustand des Unrechts, der Gewalttätigkeit und des Krieges? Widerspricht diese Annahme nicht schon in trivialer Weise der gewöhnlichen Art, zwischen Krieg und Frieden zu unterscheiden? – Sagt man nicht mit Recht, dass man im Frieden lebt, wenn kein Krieg ist, und dass kein Krieg ist, solange Friedensverträge eingehalten

---

burtsjahr der Friedensbewegungen, die dieses Recht teils überwinden, zumindest aber in seiner Friedensfunktion stärken möchten" (von Bogdandy und Venzke (2014, 68 f.)); vgl. van der Linden (1987, 31 – 38) und Fried (1905, 229 – 231).

5 *ZeF*, 367, 354 und 357; zur Universalmonarchie siehe auch *TP*, 310 f. und *RGV*, 34, zur Weltrepublik (als „Republik freier verbündeter Völker") auch *RGV* 34. – Zu Kants Diskussion der drei Modelle eines öffentlich-rechtlichen Friedenszustandes siehe Byrd und Hruschka (2010, 196 – 203).

werden? Und ist der Zustand, in dem man lebt, wenn kein Krieg ist, nicht eher das genaue Gegenteil eines Zustandes der Gewalttätigkeit und des Unrechts?

Hobbes hat diese Fragen auf eine sehr einfache Weise beantwortet. In seinem *Leviathan* von 1651 hat er den Grund genannt, aus dem nach seiner Ansicht Krieg nicht einfach gleichzusetzen ist mit dem Austragen von Schlachten und Kampfhandlungen.

> For as the nature of Foule weather, lyeth not in a showre or two of rain; but in an inclination thereto of many dayes together: So the nature of War, consisteth not in actuall fighting; but in the known disposition thereto, during all the time there is no assurance to the contrary. All other time is peace. (*L* 1, 13. 62)

Wie also schlechtes Wetter nicht im Regnen besteht, sondern in einer Neigung dazu, so besteht Krieg nicht im Austragen von Schlachten, sondern in einer Bereitschaft dazu. Nach dieser leicht faßlichen Erläuterung des von Hobbes gebrauchten Begriffs des Krieges befindet sich ein Staat bereits im Kriegszustand, wenn er sich an die Maxime des römischen Kriegstheoretikers Flavius Vegetius hält: *Si vis pacem, para bellum.* Was man gewöhnlich Frieden nennt, unterscheidet sich von dem, was Hobbes Krieg nennt, nur durch einen geringeren Grad der Neigung zur Anwendung von Waffengewalt. Hobbes hat daher angenommen, dass

> though there had never been any time, wherein particular men were in a condition of warre one against another; yet in all times, Kings, and Persons of Soveraigne authority, because of their Independency, are in continuall jealousies, and in the state and posture of Gladiators; having their weapons pointing, and their eyes fixed on one another; that is, their Forts, Garrisons, and Guns upon the Frontiers of their Kingdomes; and continuall Spyes upon their neighbours; which is a posture of War. (*L* 1, 13. 63)

Dieser Zustand, in dem sich souveräne Machthaber im Verhältnis zueinander befinden, gleicht nach Hobbes dem Zustand, in dem sich Menschen befinden, wenn es keine „gemeinsame Macht" (*common power*) gibt, die über ihnen steht und fähig ist, sie „einzuschüchtern" (*to keep them all in awe*) (*L* 1, 13. 8 und 11–12). Diesen Zustand nennt Hobbes Naturzustand.[6]

Kant hat gleichfalls seinen Wortgebrauch so eingerichtet (siehe *RL* § 54), dass er vom („beständigen") Krieg als „Zustand" schon dann spricht, wenn der Zustand der Kriegsbereitschaft gemeint ist, in dem sich unabhängige Staaten im Verhältnis zueinander befinden (*RL* § 53); „wirklichen" Krieg nennt er den offenen mit Waffengewalt ausgetragenen Streit unabhängiger Staaten (*RL* § 54). Seine Un-

---

6 Was Hobbes in *De Cive* und anderswo Naturzustand (*status naturae*) nennt, heißt in seinem *Leviathan* „natural condition of mankind" (s. die Überschrift zu *L* 1, 13).

terscheidung zwischen dem *Zustand* (*status*) des Krieges und dem *wirklichen* Krieg rechtfertigt Kant folgendermaßen:

> Hobbes' Satz: *status hominum naturalis est bellum omnium in omnes*, hat weiter keinen Fehler, als daß es heißen sollte: *est status belli etc.* Denn wenn man gleich nicht einräumt, daß zwischen Menschen, die nicht unter äußern und öffentlichen Gesetzen stehen, jederzeit wirkliche Feindseligkeiten herrschen: so ist doch der Zustand derselben (*status iuridicus*), d.i. das Verhältniß, in und durch welches sie der Rechte (des Erwerbs oder der Erhaltung derselben) fähig sind, ein solcher Zustand, in welchem ein jeder selbst Richter über das sein will, was ihm gegen andere recht sei, aber auch für dieses keine Sicherheit von andern hat oder ihnen giebt, als jedes seine eigene Gewalt; welches ein Kriegszustand ist, in dem jedermann wider jedermann beständig gerüstet sein muß. Der zweite Satz desselben: *exeundum esse e statu naturali*, ist eine Folge aus dem erstern: denn dieser Zustand ist eine continuirliche Läsion der Rechte aller andern durch die Anmaßung in seiner eigenen Sache Richter zu sein und andern Menschen keine Sicherheit wegen des Ihrigen zu lassen, als bloß seine eigene Willkür. (*RGV*, 97)

Demnach besteht Frieden (gemeint als Zustand, der dem Kriegszustand entgegengesetzt ist,) erst dann, wenn die Bereitschaft zur Anwendung von Waffengewalt und die Anmaßung, in seiner eigenen Sache Richter zu sein, auf allen Seiten ein Ende hat. Insofern ist der Ausdruck „ewiger Friede" für Kant ein Pleonasmus (*ZeF*, 343). In der *Metaphysik der Sitten* gebraucht er das Wort „Frieden", wenn nicht ausdrücklich vom ewigen Frieden die Rede ist, allerdings regelmäßig so, dass er mit ihm nur diejenigen Phasen im Verhältnis zwischen Staaten bezeichnet, die durch „wirkliche" Kriege unterbrochen werden.

Was nach diesem Wortgebrauch ein Zustand des Krieges (oder ein Naturzustand) ist, unterscheidet sich nach Kant von („wirklichen") Kriegen, die geführt und durch Friedensverträge beendet werden, im wesentlichen dadurch, dass unsere Kenntnis von ihm nicht bloß empirisch ist, sondern darauf beruht, dass es

> *a priori* in der Vernunftidee eines solchen [...] Zustandes [liegt], daß, bevor ein öffentlich gesetzlicher Zustand errichtet worden, vereinzelte [...] Völker und Staaten niemals vor Gewaltthätigkeit gegen einander sicher sein können, und zwar aus jedes seinem eigenen Recht zu thun, *was ihm recht und gut dünkt*, und hierin von der Meinung des Anderen nicht abzuhängen. (*RL* § 44)

Hegel bringt denselben Sachverhalt mit folgenden Worten zum Ausdruck: Im

> *Verhältnisse* [der Staaten] zu einander hat die Willkühr und Zufälligkeit statt, weil das *Allgemeine* des Rechts um der autonomischen Totalität dieser Personen [d.h. der Staaten] willen, zwischen ihnen nur seyn soll, nicht *wirklich* ist. Diese Unabhängigkeit macht den Streit zwischen ihnen zu einem Verhältnisse der Gewalt, [zu] einem *Zustand* des *Krieges* [...]. (*E* § 545)

Die Unabhängigkeit der Staaten voneinander besteht darin, sich das Recht anmaßen zu können, in jeder sie selbst betreffenden Angelegenheit darüber zu entscheiden, was ihnen im Verhältnis zu anderen Staaten als rechtmäßig erscheint. Dass jedem Staat *dasselbe* als rechtmäßig erscheinen *sollte*, bleibt eine Forderung, deren Durchsetzung wegen des Fehlens einer übergeordneten und mit hinreichender Zwangsgewalt ausgestatteten Macht nicht erzwingbar ist. Die bloße Möglichkeit der Nichtübereinstimmung enthält daher schon die Möglichkeit der Anwendung von militärischer Gewalt und ruft Kriegsbereitschaft hervor.

Bis zu diesem Punkt stimmen die Überlegungen Kants und Hegels überein. Auch Hegels Wortgebrauch, was die Rede von Krieg und Kriegszustand angeht, stimmt mit demjenigen Kants überein (siehe *E* §§ 545–547). Da diese Rede vom gewöhnlichen Wortgebrauch abweicht und leicht mißverstanden werden kann, werde ich im Folgenden das, was bei Kant und Hegel („wirklicher") Krieg" heißt, *militärischen Konflikt* nennen, und vom *militärischen Zustand* sprechen, wenn der Zustand der Bereitschaft zur Austragung militärischer Konflikte gemeint ist.

Will man verfolgen, an welcher Stelle die Überlegungen Kants und Hegels auseinandergehen, so muß man darauf achten, dass sie den militärischen Zustand in unterschiedlicher Weise als *Naturzustand* beurteilen, und daher auch zu unterschiedlichen Ansichten darüber gelangen, wie aus diesem Zustand herauszukommen ist.

3 Ideen des Friedensföderalismus

Was zunächst Kant angeht, so setzt er wie Hobbes den militärischen Zustand mit dem zwischenstaatlichen Naturzustand gleich. Das heißt, er nimmt an, dass *aus dem zwischenstaatlichen Naturzustand herauszugehen* dasselbe bedeutet wie den militärischen Zustand zu verlassen. Dies liegt daran, dass er unter dem Naturzustand ganz allgemein einen Zustand versteht, in dem eine äußere Macht fehlt, die in der Lage wäre, durch Rechtszwang eine öffentlich gesetzliche Ordnung herzustellen, d. h. Frieden zu stiften. Nach diesem Verständnis besteht eine genaue Analogie zwischen dem beim Fehlen eines öffentlichen Rechts bestehenden Zustand der Gewaltanwendungsbereitschaft von Privatpersonen gegen Privatpersonen und dem militärischen Zustand unabhängiger Staaten. Der Ausweg aus dem Naturzustand kann in beiden Fällen nur als *Beendigung* dieses Zustandes gedacht werden. Diesbezüglich unterscheidet sich Kant von Hobbes im wesentlichen nur darin, dass er die Ansicht vertritt, die Beendigung des militärischen Zustandes müsse als Staatsziel weltweit an die Stelle des „Hauptzwecks" treten, auf den „bisher alle Staaten ohne Ausnahme ihre innere Anstalten gerichtet haben" (*RL*, ‚Beschluß', 354). Denn der „Zustand des Krieges" sei ein Zustand „des

Rechts des Stärkeren", der „an sich selbst im höchsten Grade unrecht ist" und aus dem „die Staaten, welche einander benachbart sind, auszugehen verbunden sind" (*RL* § 54).

Sowohl in seiner Friedensschrift von 1795 als auch in seiner Rechtslehre von 1797 betrachtet Kant den Föderalismus „freier Staaten", auf den das Völkerrecht „gegründet sein" solle, als notwendiges Mittel zur Beendigung des zwischenstaatlichen Naturzustandes.[7] Die Rede von freien Staaten entspricht dabei der Terminologie des zeitgenössischen Naturrechts, nach der ein Staat (*civitas*) „frei" heißt, dessen Oberherrscher (*summus imperans*) keiner menschlichen Herrschaft (*imperium humanum*) unterliegt.[8] Mit der Freiheit der Staaten ist insofern dasselbe gemeint, was Hegel ihre „Souverainetät gegen außen" nennt.[9] Kant unterscheidet einen Staaten- oder „Völkerbund" von einem (aus vereinigten Staaten bestehenden) „Völkerstaat" dadurch, dass die ihm zugehörigen Staaten keinem öffentlichen Zwangsgesetz und keiner ihnen übergeordneten „souveränen Gewalt" unterworfen sind, sondern eine „*fortwährend-freie* Association" oder „Genossenschaft" bilden und in einer „Verbindung" stehen, die nicht „auf einer Staatsverfassung gegründet" ist.[10] Eine *genaue* Analogie zwischen dem Ausgang aus dem privatrechtlichen Naturzustand und dem aus dem zwischenstaatlichen Naturzustand kann es nicht geben, weil dieser schon die Existenz innerstaatlicher Rechtszustände voraussetzt, die entweder despotisch oder republikanisch sein können. Während der bloß privatrechtliche Naturzustand nach Kants Ansicht als Zustand zu denken ist, in dem jeder das Recht hat, den anderen zu zwingen, in einen öffentlich rechtlichen Zustand zu treten, d. h. sich einem öffentlich gesetzlichen Zwang zu unterwerfen, widerspricht es dem Anspruch der Staaten auf „Freiheit" (d. h. auf ihre Souveränität nach außen), sich von irgendeinem anderen (republikanischen oder despotischen) Staat zwingen zu lassen, in einen völkerrechtlichen Zustand zu treten, der nicht „ihrer Idee vom Völkerrecht" entspricht (*ZeF*, 357).[11] Weil also Staaten „innerlich schon eine rechtliche Verfassung haben" und deshalb

> dem Zwange anderer [Staaten], sie nach ihren Rechtsbegriffen unter eine erweiterte gesetzliche Verfassung zu bringen, entwachsen sind,

---

7 Siehe die Überschrift des ‚Zweiten Definitivartikels zum ewigen Frieden' in *ZeF* 354.
8 So lautet die Definition bei Achenwall und Pütter in § 895 ihrer *Elementa Iuris Naturae* von 1750. Auch in Kants Vorlesungen zur Rechtsphilosophie ist von freien Staaten im Sinne dieser Definition die Rede. Hingegen meint Höffe (1995, 113), Kant fordere mit seinem „Föderalism freier Staaten" einen Bund von Republiken.
9 Siehe die Überschrift des aus den §§ 321 – 329 bestehenden Abschnitts der *Grundlinien* (*R*, 264).
10 Siehe *ZeF*, 356 f. und 383 sowie *RL* § 54 und § 61.
11 Vgl. Kleingeld (2012, 50 – 58).

kann für sie

> nach dem Völkerrecht nicht eben das gelten [...], was von Menschen im gesetzlosen Zustande nach dem Naturrecht gilt, ,aus diesem Zustande herausgehen zu sollen'. (*ZeF*, 355 f.)[12]

Aus diesem Grund kann „eine erweiterte gesetzliche Verfassung", deren Errichtung zur Beendigung des zwischenstaatlichen Naturzustands erforderlich ist und auf die sich das Völkerrecht gründen lässt, nicht von der gleichen Art sein, wie die Vernunft sie zur Beendigung des privatrechtlichen Naturzustands fordert. Das heißt, sie kann keine Staatsverfassung sein. Die Forderung, aus dem Naturzustand herauszugehen, kann deshalb für Staaten nicht bedeuten, sich zu einem Völkerstaat zusammenzuschließen. Vielmehr muss sie fordern, einen „Bund von besonderer Art" zu schließen, nämlich einen Staatenbund,

> den man den *Friedensbund* (*foedus pacificum*) nennen kann, der vom *Friedensvertrag* (*pactum pacis*) darin unterschieden sein würde, daß dieser bloß *einen* Krieg, jener aber *alle* Kriege auf immer zu endigen suchte. Dieser Bund geht auf keinen Erwerb irgend einer Macht des Staats, sondern lediglich auf Erhaltung und Sicherung der *Freiheit* eines Staats für sich selbst und zugleich anderer verbündeten Staaten, ohne dass diese doch sich deshalb (wie Menschen im Naturzustande) öffentlichen Gesetzen und einem Zwange unter denselben unterwerfen dürfen. (*ZeF*, 356)[13]

Kant hat an der Idee eines freien Föderalismus, „den die Vernunft nothwendig mit dem Begriffe des Völkerrechts verbinden muß" (*ZeF*, 356), sowie an der Ablehnung eines (sich allmählich über die ganze Erdkugel ausbreitenden und zuletzt alle Völker befassenden) Völkerstaats als eines Mittels zur Beendigung des zwischenstaatlichen Naturzustands in seiner *Rechtslehre* von 1797 festgehalten: Die zur Friedenserhaltung geeignete „Verbindung" dürfe, so sagt er hier (*RL* § 54), „keine souveräne Gewalt (wie in einer [staats]bürgerlichen Verfassung), sondern nur eine *Genossenschaft* (Föderalität) enthalten." Allerdings hat er in der *Rechtslehre* die in der Friedensschrift vertretene Ansicht aufgegeben, die „Ausführbarkeit der Idee der Föderalität" lasse sich darstellen durch die Aussicht auf ein einziges weltweites Geschehen, das, „wenn das Glück es so fügt," damit beginne, dass

---

12 In seiner *Rechtslehre* von 1797 weist Kant auf denselben Umstand hin, indem er sagt, „im Völkerrecht" komme „nicht bloß ein Verhältniß eines Staats gegen den anderen im Ganzen, sondern auch einzelner Personen des einen gegen einzelne des anderen, imgleichen gegen den ganzen anderen Staat selbst in Betrachtung" (*RL* § 53, 343 f.).
13 Kants Ausdruck „ohne daß [...] diese sich [...] unterwerfen dürfen" bedeutet in heutigem Deutsch: „ohne daß [...] diese sich [...] unterwerfen müssen".

ein mächtiges und aufgeklärtes Volk sich zu einer Republik (die ihrer Natur nach zum ewigen Frieden geneigt sein muß) bilden kann,

so dass „diese einen Mittelpunkt der föderativen Vereinigung für andere Staaten" abgibt,

> um sich an sie anzuschließen und so den Freiheitszustand der Staaten gemäß der Idee des Völkerrechts zu sichern und sich durch mehrere Verbindungen dieser Art nach und nach immer weiter auszubreiten. (*ZeF,* 356)

Von dieser Ansicht eines einzigen sich allmählich auf der Erdkugel ausbreitenden Friedensbundes und von der mit ihr verbundenen Überzeugung, der „ewige Friede" sei „keine leere Idee, sondern eine Aufgabe, die, nach und nach aufgelöst, ihrem Ziele (weil die Zeiten, in denen gleiche Fortschritte geschehen, hoffentlich immer kürzer werden) beständig näher kommt" (*ZeF,* 386), findet sich jedenfalls in der *Rechtslehre* keine Spur mehr.

Im Gegenteil, Kant deklariert nun selbst den (als „das letzte Ziel des Völkerrechts" vorgestellten) ewigen Frieden als eine „unausführbare Idee" (*RL* § 61). Unausführbar ist sie in seinen Augen nunmehr, weil für ihre Ausführung nur zwei Alternativen in Frage kommen: Entweder ist der „*Staatenverein*", der den „wahren *Friedenszustand*" schließlich herzustellen hätte, ein einziger Verein, oder es gibt „eine Menge solcher Corporationen"; im ersten Fall muß die Ausführung am notwendig werdenden Umfang der „Ausdehnung" des Staatenvereins scheitern, weil, wenn diese zu groß wird, die „Beschützung" jedes Mitgliedstaates „endlich unmöglich werden muß"; im zweiten Fall befinden sich die Staatenvereine in einem Zustand, der dem „Kriegszustand" gleicht, der zwischen nicht verbündeten Einzelstaaten besteht (*RL* § 61). Ausführbar ist aus diesem Grund nicht die Idee des ewigen Friedens, ausführbar sind vielmehr nur „die politische[n] Grundsätze", die „darauf abzwecken, [...] solche Verbindungen der Staaten einzugehen, als zur continuirlichen *Annäherung* zu demselben dienen" (*RL* § 61).[14] Nicht den ewigen Frieden selbst, sondern die Annäherung an ihn bezeichnet Kant jetzt als („auf der Pflicht, mithin auch auf dem Recht der Menschen und Staaten gegründete") Aufgabe (*RL* § 61).

Deshalb schreibt er in der *Rechtslehre*, es sei nun

---

14 Nach der (nicht ganz korrekten) englischen Übersetzung von Byrd und Hruschka (2010, 203) bezeichnet Kant in § 61 nicht *politische Grundsätze* (*political principles*), nach denen Staatenverbindungen einzugehen sind, sondern die Annäherung (*approximation*) an den ewigen Frieden als „ausführbar" (*executable*).

> nicht mehr die Frage: ob der ewige Friede ein Ding oder Unding sei, und ob wir uns nicht in unserem theoretischen Urtheile betrügen, wenn wir das erstere annehmen, sondern wir müssen so handeln, als ob das Ding sei, was vielleicht nicht ist, auf Begründung desselben und diejenige Constitution, die uns dazu die tauglichste scheint (vielleicht den Republicanism aller Staaten sammt und sonders) hinwirken, um ihn herbei zu führen und dem heillosen Kriegführen, worauf als den Hauptzweck bisher alle Staaten ohne Ausnahme ihre innere Anstalten gerichtet haben, ein Ende zu machen. Und wenn das letztere, was die Vollendung dieser Absicht betrifft, auch immer ein frommer Wunsch bliebe, so betrügen wir uns doch gewiß nicht mit der Annahme der Maxime dahin unablässig zu wirken; denn diese ist Pflicht; [...]. (*RL* („Beschluß'), 354 f.)[15]

Mit der Unausführbarkeit der Idee des ewigen Friedens ist nicht etwa gemeint, es handele sich um eine leere, praktisch unbrauchbare Idee. Dass sie unausführbar ist, bedeutet für Kant lediglich, dass sie nicht durch *Institutionen* wie Völkerbund, Staatenbünde, Völkerstaat und Universalmonarchie *exekutierbar* ist. Die Nichtexekutierbarkeit dieser Idee schließt für Kant aber keineswegs aus, dass der ewige Friede als „höchstes *politisches* Gut" zu betrachten ist (*RL*, ‚Beschluß', 355). Dementsprechend ist es Sache der *Politik*, Grundsätzen zu folgen, nach denen in *inneren* und *äußeren* Verhältnissen der Staaten die Voraussetzungen dafür zu schaffen sind, den Ausbruch von Kriegen zu verhindern. Was die *inneren* Verhältnisse anlangt, sind Grundsätze gemeint, nach denen Despotien in friedliebende, d.h. an Abrüstung und Entmilitarisierung (z. B. an der Abschaffung „stehender Heere") interessierte Republiken umzuwandeln sind. Was die *äußeren* Verhältnisse anlangt, sind Grundsätze gemeint, nach denen Bündnisverträge einzugehen sind, die nur der allgemeinen Friedenssicherung durch Abrüstung und Entmilitarisierung zwischenstaatlicher Konflikte dienen.

Während Kant 1795 den „Friedensbund" als ein einziges, sich kontinuierlich auf der Erdkugel ausbreitendes Staatensystem beschreibt (*ZeF*, 357), schreibt er 1797 jedem Staat das Recht zu, seine zum Zweck dauerhafter Friedenserhaltung einmal eingegangene „Verbindung" mit anderen Staaten „zu aller Zeit" wieder aufzukündigen (*RL* § 54).[16] Um ein Recht handelt es sich hier nach Kant insofern, als es (ebenso wie das Recht zur Verbündung) „ein Recht *in subsidium* eines anderen und ursprünglichen Rechts" ist, „den Verfall in den Zustand des wirklichen Krieges derselben untereinander von sich abzuwehren" (*RL* § 54). Kant berücksichtigt damit den Umstand, dass auch verbündete Staaten nicht unter allen Umständen bereit sind, die aus ihren Verträgen folgenden Verpflichtungen immer und ewig einzuhalten. Aus diesem Grund muß auch ein Staatenverein, der

---

15 Mit dem „Republicanism aller Staaten" kann hier nicht die Weltrepublik, sondern nur die republikanische Staatsverfassung als Verfassung jedes Einzelstaats gemeint sein.
16 Die zweite Auflage von 1798 ersetzt hier „Verbündung" durch „Verbindung".

der Friedenserhaltung dienen soll, „von Zeit zu Zeit erneuert werden" (*RL* § 54). Daher sollte die Organisationsform eines solchen Vereins nach Kants Ansicht nicht die Form eines unauflöslichen und mit Zwangsgewalt ausgestatteten Bundesstaates sein, sondern die eines Staatenkongresses, „zu welchem sich zu gesellen jedem benachbarten [Staat] unbenommen" bleibe:

> Unter einem Congreß wird hier aber nur eine willkürliche, zu aller Zeit auflösliche Zusammentretung verschiedener Staaten, nicht eine solche Verbindung, welche (so wie die der amerikanischen Staaten) auf einer Staatsverfassung gegründet und daher unauflöslich ist, verstanden; – durch welchen allein die Idee eines zu errichtenden öffentlichen Rechts der Völker, ihre Streitigkeiten auf civile Art, gleichsam durch einen Proceß, nicht auf barbarische (nach Art der Wilden), nämlich durch Krieg, zu entscheiden, realisirt werden kann. (*RL* § 61, 350 f.)[17]

Als Vorbild für den als *„permanenten Staatencongreß"* organisierten Verein dient Kant nicht die Verfassung der USA, sondern („wenigstens was die Förmlichkeiten des Völkerrechts in Absicht auf Erhaltung des Friedens betrifft") die „Versammlung der Generalstaaten" in den Haag, soweit sie „in der ersten Hälfte dieses [des 18.] Jahrhunderts noch statt fand",

> wo die Minister der meisten europäischen Höfe und selbst der kleinsten Republiken ihre Beschwerden über die Befehdungen, die einem von dem anderen widerfahren waren, anbrachten und so sich ganz Europa als einen einzigen föderirten Staat dachten, den sie in jener ihren öffentlichen Streitigkeiten gleichsam als Schiedsrichter annahmen, statt dessen späterhin das Völkerrecht bloß in Büchern übrig geblieben, aus Cabinetten aber verschwunden, oder nach schon verübter Gewalt in Form der Deductionen der Dunkelheit der Archive anvertrauet worden ist. (*RL* § 61, 350)[18]

Mit diesem Rückblick auf eine vergangene Epoche deutet Kant zugleich die *politische* Forderung an, das Völkerrecht aus der Dunkelheit der Archive in die Kabinette zurückzuholen, das heißt: den zwischenstaatlichen Naturzustand dadurch

---

17 Die beiden Originaldrucke enthalten statt „zu aller Zeit auflösliche Zusammentretung" den Ausdruck „zu aller Zeit ablösliche Zusammentretung". Dies entspricht § 54, in dem es von der (als permanentem Staatenkongress zu organisierenden) Verbindung heißt, sie könne „zu aller Zeit aufgekündigt" und müsse „mithin von Zeit zu Zeit erneuert", d. h. im Falle ihrer Auflösung, durch eine entsprechende Nachfolgeorganisation *abgelöst* werden.
18 Nach Byrd und Hruschka (2010, 203 – 205) entspricht Kants Beschreibung der Haager Generalstaatenversammlung als gesamteuropäischen Verhandlungszentrums der Darstellung in François Michel Janiçons *État Présent de la République des Provinces-unies* von 1729 ebenso wie die Vorstellung von „ganz Europa" als föderiertem Staat der Darstellung in den *Anfangs-Gründen der Wissenschafft von der heutigen Staats-Verfassung von Europa* des Staatsrechtslehrers Johann Jacob Moser aus dem Jahr 1732.

zu überwinden, dass jede Regierung ihr Handeln an der „Idee eines zu errich-
tenden Rechts der Völker" ausrichtet, ihre Streitigkeiten untereinander „auf civile
Art, gleichsam durch einen Proceß" zu entscheiden, zu dessen Durchführung ein
permanenter Staatenkongreß („gleichsam" als Schiedsgericht) notwendig ist.[19]

4 Friedensbündnispolitik

Es ist nach dem soeben vorgenommenen Vergleich der Friedensschrift von 1795
und der Rechtslehre von 1797 leicht zu erkennen, dass Kant seine Ansicht über den
Zusammenhang zwischen ewigem Frieden und Völkerbund so modifiziert hat,
dass ihn die oben beschriebene Kritik Hegels nicht mehr trifft. Der Völkerbund,
von der die Rechtslehre handelt, kann nicht mehr so verstanden werden, wie noch
Fichte (als Rezensent der Friedensschrift) ihn verstanden hatte, nämlich als einen
„Mittelzustand", durch dessen allmähliche Ausbreitung auf der Erdkugel ein
Endzustand der Staatenwelt herstellbar wäre, der den Streit zwischen Staaten
unmöglich machen würde.[20] Man sollte Hegels Kritik an der „*Kantischen* Vorstellung eines *ewigen Friedens*" in *R § 333 Anm.* so auffassen, dass sie sich auf
nichts anderes als den so verstandenen Völkerbund bezieht.[21]

Hegel bezweifelt keineswegs, dass Staatenverbindungen oder internationale
Schiedsgerichte nützlich sein können zur Verhinderung militärischer Konflikte.
„Schiedsrichter und Vermittler zwischen Staaten" sieht Hegel in *R § 333 Anm.*

---

19 Kants Vorsicht („gleichsam") beim Vergleich des Vorgehens des permanenten Staatenkongresses mit dem Prozeß eines Schiedsgerichts entspricht seiner Orientierung an der Haager Generalstaatenversammlung insoweit, als diese mehr mit Diplomatie als mit Gerichtsbarkeit zu tun
hatte. Die „Idee", dass das Verfahren internationaler Schiedsgerichte sich „qualitativ von Pro-
zessen der politischen Verhandlung" unterscheiden und „einer juristischen Methodik folgen"
solle, „gewann" erst am Ende des 19. Jahrhunderts mit den Haager Friedenskonferenzen, die der
Entwicklung von Grundsätzen für die friedliche Regelung internationaler Konflikte durch einen
internationalen Schiedsgerichtshof dienen sollten, „an Gewicht" (von Bogdandy und Venzke
(2014, 47)).
20 Fichte schreibt in seiner Rezension: „[D]er von Kant vorgeschlagene Völkerbund zur Erhaltung
des Friedens ist lediglich ein Mittelzustand, durch welchen die Menschheit zu jenem großen Ziele
[nämlich zum ewigen Frieden] wohl dürfte hindurchgehen müssen; so wie ohne Zweifel die
Staaten auch erst durch Schutzbündnisse einzelner Personen unter sich entstanden sind." (*RZeF*,
433)
21 Dass sich Hegel in *R § 333 Anm.* nicht auf Kants Rechtslehre, sondern auf dessen Friedensschrift (und deren Verständnis durch andere) bezieht, zeigt die Nachschrift zu einer Vorlesung von
1819/20, in der Hegel diese Anmerkung so kommentiert hat: „Kant in seinem ‚Ewigen Frieden'
stellt es als ein Vernunftgebot dar, einen Staatenbund zu schließen. Ein solcher Bund beruht aber
immer nur auf der besonderen Gesinnung derer, die ihn schließen." (*RV 1819/20, 279*)

ausdrücklich vor.[22] Hegel bestreitet nur, dass es denkbar sei, militärische Konflikte mit Hilfe eines Staatenbundes unmöglich zu machen. Dieser müßte eine Zwangsgewalt haben, die nicht in Frage kommt, da souveräne Staaten miteinander nur Verträge schließen, folglich weder einzeln noch gemeinsam öffentliche Zwangsgesetze von justitiabler allgemeiner Geltung geben können.

Dies besagt Hegels Satz: „Es gibt keinen Prätor [...] zwischen Staaten" (*R* § 333 *Anm.*). Mit diesem Satz spielt er auf die alt-römische Gerichtsverfassung an; nach ihr hatte der Prätor als oberster Richter die letzte Entscheidung über Rechtsstreitigkeiten zu treffen und dabei für die Tatsachenfeststellung einen besonderen Judex zu bestellen, während er selbst für die Subsumtion des Einzelfalles unter gegebene Gesetze zuständig war (vgl. *R* § 225 *Anm.*). Bezogen auf das Völkerrecht bedeutet das Fehlen einer *überstaatlichen Legislative* und das Fehlen einer *ihr verpflichteten letzten gerichtlichen Instanz*, dass die Idee des ewigen Friedens als einer öffentlich-gesetzlichen internationalen Rechtsordnung unausführbar ist.

Hegel setzt sich mit den das Völkerrecht betreffenden Einzelheiten der Kantischen Friedensschrift nicht sehr ausführlich auseinander. Dies dürfte damit zusammenhängen, dass er schon die naturrechtlichen Voraussetzungen nicht ausnahmslos akzeptiert, von denen Kant dort ausgeht. Er teilt nämlich nicht die auf Hobbes zurückgehende Ansicht, der militärische Zustand unabhängiger Staaten sei *schon als solcher* dasselbe wie der zwischenstaatliche *Naturzustand*. Der Ausgang aus diesem ist nach Hegel deshalb keineswegs dasselbe wie die Beendigung des militärischen Zustands. Nach seiner Ansicht sind Staaten nur „insofern im Naturzustande gegeneinander", als ihr jeweiliges Verhältnis unter dem „Prinzip der Souveränität" steht:

> Der Grundsatz des *Völkerrechts*, als des *allgemeinen*, an und für sich zwischen den Staaten gelten sollenden Rechts, zum Unterschiede von dem besondern Inhalt der positiven Traktate, ist, daß die *Traktate*, als auf welchen die Verbindlichkeiten der Staaten gegeneinander beruhen, *gehalten werden* sollen. Weil aber deren Verhältnis ihre Souverainetät zum Princip hat, so sind sie insofern im Naturzustande gegeneinander, und ihre Rechte haben nicht in einem allgemeinen zur Macht über sie constituirten, sondern in ihrem besondern Willen ihre *Wirklichkeit*. (*R* § 333)

---

22 Keineswegs entspricht es Hegels Ansicht, wenn Ilting (1983, 349) schreibt: „Die Notwendigkeit von Kriegen folgt für Hegel, ebenso wie für alle Vertreter des rationalen Naturrechts, aus der Koexistenz souveräner Staaten [...]: Wenn es kein Gericht gibt, das die Konflikte zwischen Staaten schlichten kann, so ist immer mit Kriegen um die Durchsetzung von Rechtsansprüchen zu rechnen; wenn es aber ein solches Gericht gäbe, so wären die Staaten nicht mehr souverän, sondern Teile eines universalen Bundesstaats."

Vom zwischenstaatlichen Naturzustand wird hier offensichtlich nicht angenommen, dass er „unmittelbar aus dem Begriff staatlicher Souveränität" folge.[23] Wenn diese Annahme Hegels Ansicht entspräche, könnte es für ihn keinen Ausweg souveräner Staaten aus ihrem Naturzustand geben. Von diesem Zustand nimmt Hegel vielmehr an, dass er ein Zustand sei, in dem die „Rechte" selbständiger Staaten nicht in einem *allgemeinen Willen*, und zwar genauer,

> nicht in einem allgemeinen zur Macht über sie konstituierten [Willen], sondern in ihrem besonderen Willen ihre *Wirklichkeit* (R § 333)

haben. Dieser Zustand (des Fehlens *eines machthabenden allgemeinen Willens*) folgt nach Hegel *nicht* unmittelbar daraus, dass selbständige Staaten *souverän sind*, sondern daraus, dass sie ihre Souveränität als oberstes „*Prinzip*" ihres Verhältnisses zueinander gelten lassen, statt sie dem „Grundsatz" des allgemeinen Völkerrechts unterzuordnen, nach dem Verträge einzuhalten sind.[24]

Dieser Grundsatz (*pacta sunt servanda*) kann mit der Geltung des Souveränitätsprinzips in zwischenstaatlichen Verhältnissen dann kollidieren, wenn die Verwirklichung der Rechte, die Staaten gegeneinander zu haben meinen, von „ihrem besonderen Willen" abhängig ist und dieser Wille keinem *allgemeinen Willen* entspricht (R § 333). Bei einer solchen Abhängigkeit und Nichtübereinstimmung mit einem *allgemeinen Willen* bleibt der Grundsatz *pacta sunt servanda*, wie Hegel schreibt, „beim *Sollen*"; und dieser Umstand hat zur Folge, dass der zwischenstaatliche Zustand eine „Abwechselung" von Zuständen des Friedens und des militärischen Konflikts (d. h. von Zuständen vertragsgemäßer Beziehungen und der „Aufhebung" solcher Zustände) ist.[25]

Die Aussage, der völkerrechtliche Grundsatz ‚*Verträge sind einzuhalten*', bleibe „beim *Sollen*", bedeutet nun nicht, dieser Satz habe keine verpflichtende

---

23 Nach Ilting (1983, 348) gehört diese Annahme zu den Voraussetzungen, von der Hegels Rechtsphilosophie ausgeht.

24 Dementsprechend ist nach *E* § 545 der militärische Zustand eine Folge daraus, daß „das *Allgemeine* des Rechts um der autonomischen Totalität dieser Personen [d. h. der individuellen Staaten] willen zwischen ihnen nur seyn *soll*, nicht *wirklich* ist." Zum Verhältnis der Begriffe der Souveränität und Totalität siehe *R* § 275 *Zusatz*, § 330 *Zusatz* sowie *E* § 523.

25 Hegel formuliert diesen Gedanken im Zusammenhang wie folgt: „Weil aber deren [d. h. der Staaten] Verhältnis ihre Souverainetät zum Princip hat, so sind sie insofern im Naturzustande gegeneinander, und ihre Rechte haben nicht in einem allgemeinen zur Macht über sie constituirten, sondern in ihrem besonderen Willen ihre *Wirklichkeit*. Jene allgemeine Bestimmung [d. h. der Grundsatz des *Völkerrechts*, als des *allgemeinen*, an und für sich zwischen den Staaten gelten sollenden Rechts,] bleibt daher beym *Sollen*, und der Zustand wird eine Abwechselung von dem den Traktaten gemäßen Verhältniße, und von der Aufhebung desselben." (*R* § 333)

Geltung und bringe nur eine leere Forderung zum Ausdruck. Sie bedeutet nur, dass dessen Befolgung nicht durchsetzbar ist durch Staaten, die das Souveränitätsprinzip als oberstes Prinzip politischen Handelns in internationalen Beziehungen gelten lassen. In diesem Falle beruht die Vertragseinhaltung „auf *unterschiedenen souveränen Willen*" (*R* § 330) bei gleichzeitigem Fehlen eines machthabenden allgemeinen Willens, das auf Verträgen beruhende positive Recht in allgemein geltendes Recht zu verwandeln (*R* § 333).

Dementsprechend besteht nach Hegels Darstellung das „äußere Staatsrecht" aus zwei Teilen (s. *E* § 547). *Einesteils* handele es sich um (positives) Recht, das auf „positiven Traktaten" (d. h. auf Verträgen) beruht. Was diesen Teil betrifft, enthalte das äußere Staatsrecht „nur Rechte, denen die wahrhafte Wirklichkeit" abgehe. *Andernteils* beruhe das „äußere Staatsrecht" „auf dem sogenannten *Völkerrechte*, dessen allgemeines Prinzip das vorausgesetzte *Anerkanntseyn* der Staaten" sei.[26] Hegel spricht diesem allgemeinen Prinzip sowie dem Völkerrecht (das mit seinem Grundsatz *pacta sunt servanda* auf ihm beruht) keineswegs „die wahrhafte Wirklichkeit" ab, die dem positiven Teil des äußeren Staatsrecht „abgeht" (*E* § 547). Um seine Ansicht in diesem Punkt genauer zu verstehen, muß man den Unterschied einsehen, der zwischen dem „allgemeinen Prinzip" des Völkerrechts (dem „Anerkanntsein") einerseits und dem „Grundsatz des *Völkerrechts*" (*R* § 333) (*pacta sunt servanda*) besteht.

Hierzu findet sich eine interessante Bemerkung unter Hegels ‚Notizen zum dritten Teil der *Encyklopädie*' von 1817:

> Im Völkerrecht [ist] erster Grundsatz: die Tractaten sollen gehalten werden – erstes Prinzip aber [ist], das Fürsichseyn[, die] Selbständigkeit des Staates – wer den Tractat bricht, soll als allgemeiner Feind behandelt werden. (*EN*, 485.12–14)

Mit „erster Grundsatz" meint Hegel (hier wie in *R* § 333) einen ersten Satz im Sinne eines zitierfähigen, fest eingebürgerten und am Anfang einer Satzfolge stehenden Ausdrucks, nämlich den Satz *pacta sunt servanda*, während „erstes Prinzip" zu verstehen ist im Sinne eines logisch vorausgesetzten, implizit enthaltenen Grundgedankens. Kant hatte in seiner *Rechtslehre* geschrieben, man könne von einer einzelnen „Verletzung öffentlicher Verträge" „voraussetzen",

---

[26] Vom „sogenannten" Völkerrecht spricht Hegel, da das „Anerkanntseyn der Staaten", das es als „Prinzip" voraussetzt, ein wechselseitiges Verhältnis eigentlich nicht von Völkern, sondern von Staaten ist. Bereits Kant hat in *RL* § 53 darauf hingewiesen, dass das „Recht der *Staaten* in Verhältniß zu einander [...] nicht ganz richtig im Deutschen das Völkerrecht genannt wird, sondern vielmehr das Staatenrecht (*ius publicum civitatum*) heißen sollte".

daß sie die Sache aller Völker betrifft, deren Freiheit dadurch bedroht wird, und die dadurch aufgefordert werden, sich gegen einen solchen Unfug zu vereinigen und ihm [sc. dem ungerechten Feind, der dieser Verletzung schuldig ist] die Macht dazu zu nehmen; – aber doch *nicht, um sich in sein Land zu teilen*, [...] sondern es eine neue Verfassung annehmen zu lassen, die, ihrer Natur nach, der Neigung zum Kriege ungünstig ist. (*RL* § 60)

Kant meint also, dass, wenn ein Staat den Satz ‚*pacta sunt servanda*' (in Worten oder Taten) nicht gelten lässt, er dann von allen als „ungerechter Feind" zu behandeln sei, was soviel heißt wie: dass ein solcher Staat es nicht verdiene, als Staat anerkannt und entsprechend behandelt zu werden. Sinngemäß folgt daraus: Wenn ein Staat als solcher anerkannt zu werden verdient, so wird er den Satz *pacta sunt servanda* gelten lassen. Genau diesen Grundgedanken der Kantischen Völkerrechtstheorie greift Hegel auf, wenn er in *E* § 547 annimmt, das Völkerrecht beruhe mit seinem Grundsatz, dass Verträge einzuhalten sind, auf dem „Prinzip des vorausgesetzten Anerkanntseyns der Staaten".[27]

Allerdings ist Hegel zugleich weit davon entfernt, mit Kant die Forderung aufzustellen, alle Völker sollten sich gegen einen vertragsbrüchigen Staat verbünden, um ihn als gemeinsamen („allgemeinen") „ungerechten Feind" zu behandeln und seine Verfassung außer Kraft zu setzen. Vielmehr vertritt er die Ansicht, dass wegen der „vielseitigen Beziehungen", die ein einzelner Staat (z. B. aufgrund von Handels- und Wirtschaftsinteressen) mit anderen Staaten oder mit auswärtigen privaten und öffentlichen Einrichtungen unterhält, es eine „Menge" von „Verletzungen" gebe, denen er ausgesetzt sein kann, ohne dass es „an sich" (aufgrund positiver Gesetze und gerichtlicher Untersuchungen) bestimmbar wäre, welche von diesen Verletzungen wirklich ein „bestimmter Bruch der Traktate" und welche eher als „Verletzung der Ehre und Anerkennung" anzusehen ist.[28] Gerade mächtige Staaten, Staatenbündnisse und Imperien neigen diesbezüglich, wie Hegel betont, zur „Reizbarkeit": sie können nach dem Souveränitätsprinzip ihren schrankenlosen Willen und ihre Ehre in jede sie betreffende „Einzelheit" legen auf der Suche nach Gelegenheiten, sich militärisch zu betätigen und lösbare

---

27 Hegel dürfte Kant darin zugestimmt haben, dass die Geltung des Grundsatzes *pacta sunt servanda* sowohl im Privat- als auch im Völkerrecht *apriorischen* Charakter hat und auf einem allgemeinen Rechtsprinzip beruht. Nach Kant lautet das allgemeine Rechtsprinzip: „Eine jede Handlung ist recht, die oder nach deren Maxime die Freiheit der Willkür eines jeden mit jedermanns Freiheit nach einem allgemeinem Gesetze zusammen bestehen kann." (*RL* § C, 230). Hegel führt dieses Rechtsprinzip in *R* § 21 auf ein allgemeineres „Prinzip des Rechts, der Moralität und der Sittlichkeit" (*R* § 21 Anm.) zurück. Nach Kant lassen öffentliche Vertragsbrüche „eine Maxime" erkennen, „nach welcher, wenn sie zur allgemeinen Regel gemacht würde, kein Friedenszustand unter Völkern möglich, sondern der Naturzustand verewigt werden müßte." (*RL* § 60)

28 Siehe *R* § 334 in Verbindung mit *EN*, 485.

Rechtsstreitigkeiten in scheinbar unlösbare Rechtskonflikte zu verwandeln. Es gibt daher Fälle, in denen es Staaten, auch wenn sie beiderseits im Recht sind, nicht gelingt, ihre gegenseitigen Verletzungen durch „Übereinkunft" zu überwinden, so dass ihr Streit „nur durch Krieg entschieden werden" kann (*R* § 334). Eine solche Entscheidung entscheidet nicht über Rechte, sondern nur über die Durchsetzbarkeit von Ansprüchen auf Rechte. Hegel weist hier indirekt darauf hin, dass auch der Krieg gegen „ungerechte Feinde" keine Rechtsentscheidung herbeiführen könne. Darum hält er Kants Prinzip, vertragsbrüchige Staaten als allgemeine Feinde zu behandeln und mit Krieg zu bekämpfen, für verfehlt.

Nach seiner Ansicht läßt sich also die Befolgung des völkerrechtlichen Grundsatzes *pacta sunt servanda* und das in ihm „vorausgesetzte Prinzip des *Anerkanntseyns* der Staaten" (*E* § 547) weder durch Krieg noch durch eine überstaatliche Institution durchsetzen. Staaten, die dem Souveränitätsprinzip Vorrang vor diesem Grundsatz geben, lassen sich in einen gesetzlichen Zustand, wie Kant ihn gefordert hat (*RL* § 61), gar nicht bringen, auch wenn es möglich ist, internationale Institutionen zu schaffen, die hin und wieder in der Lage sind, als Schiedsgerichte oder Vermittler Konflikte zwischen Staaten aufzulösen.

Welcher Ausweg aus dem zwischenstaatlichen Naturzustand steht nach Hegels Ansicht aber dann noch offen?

5 Friedenspolitisch relevante Rechtsgrundsätze

Offensichtlich ist es dieser: Da nach seiner Ansicht der Naturzustand, in dem sich souveräne Staaten befinden, darin seinen Grund hat, dass sie dem Souveränitätsprinzip Vorrang vor dem Grundsatz des allgemeinen Völkerrechts (und damit vor allen aus ihm folgenden Rechten) geben, können sie nur dadurch aus dem Naturzustand herausgehen, dass sie auf eben diesen Vorrang verzichten. Dies bedeutet nicht, dass souveräne Staaten auf ihre Souveränität verzichten, es bedeutet vielmehr nur, dass sie darauf verzichten, die fortgesetzte Geltung des Rechts, soweit es auf zwischenstaatlichen Verträgen beruht, ausschließlich von der eigenen souveränen Entscheidung abhängig zu machen. Nur insoweit dieser Verzicht zu einer Sitte geworden ist, ist der zwischenstaatliche Naturzustand (als Zustand der Gewalt und des Unrechts) aufgehoben. Die Aufhebung dieses Zustandes ist demnach ein gradueller Vorgang. Von einer vollständigen Aufhebung dieses Zustandes könnte man nur sprechen, wenn der beschriebene Verzicht zur allgemeinen, weltweiten Sitte geworden ist.

Hegel hat, soweit ich weiß, nirgendwo diesen Ausgang aus dem zwischenstaatlichen Naturstand deutlich beschrieben. Aber es scheint mir außer Zweifel zu stehen, dass er in ihm die endgültige Auflösung des von Hobbes aufgeworfenen

Problems gesehen hat. Dies deutet sich schon darin an, dass er den zwischenstaatlichen Naturzustand bestimmt als Zustand, in dem die Rechte souveräner
Staaten nicht in einem machthabenden allgemeinen Willen („nicht in einem
allgemeinen zur Macht über sie konstituierten Willen"), sondern nur „in ihrem
besonderen Willen" *Wirklichkeit* haben (*R* § 333). Denn damit deutet Hegel an, dass
er zwar noch an Kants Ansicht festhält, nur ein allgemeiner und machthabender
Wille könne den Ausgang aus dem Naturzustand herbeiführen, aber im Unterschied zu Kants Friedensschrift nimmt er an, dieser Wille lasse sich nur als Wille
derjenigen „absoluten Macht auf Erden" (*R* § 331) exekutieren, die der souveräne
Staat schon als solcher ist. Mit anderen Worten: Nur dadurch, dass der besondere
Wille der einzelnen Staaten den allgemeinen Willen, nämlich den *Grundsatz*, das
allgemeine Völkerrecht als wirkliches Recht gelten zu lassen, in sich aufnimmt,
kann der internationale Naturzustand überwunden werden. Hegel beschreibt
diese Aufnahme eines allgemeinen Willens in den besonderen Willen der Staaten
als einen epochalen weltgeschichtlichen Vorgang, bei dem „im Geiste der Regierungen und Völker [...] die Weisheit über das, was in der Wirklichkeit an und für
sich recht und vernünftig ist", erwacht (*E* § 552 A.).[29]

Man kann hier fragen, worauf sich Hegels Überzeugung stützt, dieses Erwa-
chen von Rechtsbewußtsein und Vernunft könne wirklich im „Geiste" der Regierungen und Völker stattfinden. Die Antwort hierauf scheint mir zu sein, dass
diese Überzeugung auf einem Grundgedanken beruht, der in Hegels Darstellung
des äußeren Staatsrechts eine zentrale Rolle spielt, den man aber leicht übersieht.
Nach dieser Darstellung führt nämlich der Vorrang, den souveräne Staaten dem
Souveränitätsprinzip vor dem Grundsatz des allgemeinen Völkerrechts geben, in
einen manifesten Widerspruch. Denn der Umstand, dass Staaten ihrer Souveränität die Stelle eines höchsten Prinzips einräumen, führt dazu, dass der militärische Zustand, in dem sie sich befinden, ihre „Selbständigkeit" und damit eben
ihre Souveränität „aufs Spiel" setzt (*E* § 547). Mit ihrer Selbständigkeit wird sogar
„das sittliche Ganze selbst [...] der Zufälligkeit ausgesetzt" (*R* § 340). Das heißt,
dass *alles*, was von staatlicher Selbständigkeit abhängt, nämlich alles geltende
private und öffentliche Recht und alles zu schützende private und öffentliche
Wohl durch den zwischenstaatlichen Naturzustand bedroht wird. Dieser ist nur
deshalb möglich, weil Staaten ihrer eigenen souveränen Entscheidungsmacht
Priorität vor der Geltung der Prinzipien internationalen Rechts einräumen. Dieser

---

29 „[...] es erwacht die Weltweisheit im Geiste der Regierungen und der Völker, d. h. die Weisheit
über das, was in der Wirklichkeit an und für sich recht und vernünftig ist. Mit Recht ist die
Production des Denkens und bestimmter die Philosophie Weltweisheit genannt worden, denn das
Denken vergegenwärtigt die Wahrheit des Geistes, führt ihn in die Welt ein, und befreit ihn so in
seiner Wirklichkeit und an ihm selbst." (*E* § 552 *Anm.*)

manifeste Widerspruch im äußeren Staatsrecht macht den Grundwiderspruch dessen aus, was Hegel die „Dialektik der besonderen Volksgeister" (*E* § 548) oder die „Dialektik der Endlichkeit dieser Geister" (*R* § 340) nennt: Es ist derjenige Widerspruch, den Völker und Staaten aufzulösen haben, um den Naturzustand, der zwischen ihnen herrscht, zu überwinden.[30]

Da es sich hier um einen Widerspruch in den subjektiven Einstellungen von Regierungen und Völkern handelt, bedarf es aus Hegels Sicht eigentlich nur des Denkens, um ihn zu bemerken und durch seine Auflösung zur Vernunft zu kommen. Da Recht, Moralität und Sitte ohne Denken nicht möglich ist, sieht Hegel – in weltgeschichtlicher Perspektive – in der (noch so beschränkten) „Sittlichkeit" der Völker einen *„denkenden* Geist" am Werk, der in der Lage ist, seine eigene Widersprüchlichkeit und damit „die Endlichkeit, die er als Volksgeist [...] hat," in sich aufzuheben (*E* § 552). Den so durchs „Denken" in die „Welt" eingeführten „Geist" nennt Hegel „allgemeinen Geist" (auch „Weltgeist", *E* § 549, oder „Weltweisheit", § 552 *Anm.*). Für die Aufhebung und Erhebung der (besonderen) Volksgeister in den allgemeinen Geist gilt, was Hegel ganz allgemein vom „Aufheben" und „Erheben [des Willens] ins Allgemeine" sagt, nämlich: Es sei „Thätigkeit des *Denkens*", dessen Durchsetzung im Willen „das Prinzip des Rechts, der Moralität und aller Sittlichkeit" ist (*R* § 21 *Anm.*). Nach seiner Ansicht ist es denn auch der denkende Geist, der sich in nationalen und internationalen Sitten zur Geltung zu bringen hat und darüber hinaus das Recht hat, in letzter Instanz über Staaten und Völker zu richten. Deshalb nennt Hegel den Weltgeist den „höheren Prätor" (*R* § 339 *Zusatz*)[31] oder den „absoluten Richter" (*R* § 259 *Zusatz.*).[32] Dieser Richter wirkt nicht als äußere Macht und überstaatliche Rechtsinstitution, son-

---

30 Hegel beschreibt den Widerspruch des äußeren Staatsrechts – nach dem Vorbild von Kants „Antinomie" der rechtlich-praktischen Vernunft (*RL* § 7 *Anm.*) – in der folgenden Weise: „Das Verhältnis von Staaten ist das von Selbständigkeiten, die zwischen sich stipulieren, aber zugleich über diesen Stipulationen stehen" (*R* § 330 *Zusatz*, *RZ*, 498). Nach Hennis folgt dieser Satz aus einer These, mit der Hegel den „Begriff der völkerrechtlichen Souveränität" geschaffen habe; dies sei die These, dass der Staatswille „als höchstes Gesetz nur das eigene Wohl anerkenne", so dass „die Verträge mit anderen Staaten nur so lange gelten" können, „als sie jenem Gesetz entsprechen" (Hennis 2003, 93). Hennis hat nicht bemerkt, dass der in Rede stehende Satz nicht daraus folgt, dass der Staatswille nur das eigene Wohl als höchstes Gesetz anerkennt, sondern daraus, dass Staaten sich zu einander als Richter in eigener Sache verhalten. Man findet bei Hegel auch nicht die Behauptung, das eigene Wohl sei höchstes Gesetz für *den Staatswillen*, sondern nur die Aussage, das eigene Wohl sei höchstes Gesetz für Staaten „als *besondere* Willen gegen einander" (*R* § 336).

31 Siehe auch *RV 1818 – 1831*, Bd. 4, Nachschrift Griesheim, 743 f.

32 Der Text stimmt auch hier überein mit der Nachschrift Griesheim, *RV 1818 – 1831*, Bd. 4, 633 f.

dern als „Geist, der sich im Prozesse der *Weltgeschichte* seine Wirklichkeit gibt" (*R* § 259; vgl. § 339 *Zusatz*).[33]

6 Schluss

Kant hatte in seiner Friedensschrift von 1795 gefordert, dass das Völkerrecht auf einen Föderalismus souveräner Staaten „gegründet sein" solle (‚Zweiter Definitivartikel'). Mit Föderalismus war hier das „Surrogat" eines Völker- oder Staatenstaats, d.h. einer überstaatlichen öffentlich gesetzlichen Zwangsgewalt gemeint, die „nach der Vernunft" eigentlich notwendig sei, um (in Analogie zur Beendigung des privatrechtlichen Naturzustandes und zur Herstellung eines öffentlich rechtlichen Zustandes) den zwischenstaatlichen Naturzustand zu beendigen und einen öffentlichen Rechtszustand zwischen den Staaten herzustellen (*ZeF*, 356 und 357). Eine solche Forderung wird in Hegels Rechtsphilosophie nicht erhoben. Dies bedeutet aber keineswegs, dass zwischen Kants und Hegels Auffassungen, sofern sie die Grundlagen des Völkerrechts betreffen, eine tiefe, unüberbrückbare Kluft bestünde. Schon Kant selbst hat dafür, dass eine solche nicht wirklich besteht, mit seiner *Rechtslehre* von 1797 gesorgt. Sein Gedanke, dass das Völkerrecht in die Kabinette, aus denen es „verschwunden" sei, zurückgeholt werden müsse und, wenn auch nicht der ewige Friede selbst, so doch die auf dauerhafte Friedenserhaltung zielenden politischen Grundsätze exekutierbar seien, stimmt mit Hegels Ansichten überein. Nach diesen hat das Völkerrecht durchaus internationale Institutionen vorzusehen, die (wie der von Kant vorgesehene „permanente Staatenkongreß", *RL* § 61) als „Schiedsrichter und Vermittler" (*R* § 333 *Anm.*) zur Demilitarisierung von Konflikten beitragen. Allerdings können solche Institutionen nur unter der Voraussetzung wirksam sein, dass souveräne Staaten aufhören, in Konfliktfällen Richter in eigener Sache zu sein. Darum sind die Fundamente des Völkerrechts tiefer zu legen als es der Zweite Definitivartikel in Kants Friedensschrift gefordert hatte. Dessen *Rechtslehre* und die in Hegels *Grundlinien der Philosophie des Rechts* und in seiner *Enzyklopädie* enthaltene Rechtsphilosophie sind in wesentlichen Hinsichten gleichartige Versuche, diese Aufgabe zu lösen. Man kann nicht sagen, sie hätten im Zeitalter der

---

33 Das in *R* § 340 vorkommende Zitat „Die Weltgeschichte ist das Weltgericht" aus Schillers Gedicht ‚Resignation' (Schiller 1992, 168) gehört zum Kontext des Gedankens, dass die Weltgeschichte ein *Prozeß* sei, in dem der denkende Geist über die besonderen Volksgeister richtet. Hingegen meint Geismann (2010, 156), dem Text von *R* § 333 – 340 entnehmen zu dürfen, nach Hegel übernehme der Krieg „die Rolle des mittelalterlichen Gottesgerichts" und mache die Weltgeschichte zum Weltgericht.

Massenvernichtungswaffen, Kampfdrohnen und Privatarmeen, deren Zulassung mit humanitärem Völkerrecht schlechthin unvereinbar ist, ihre Aktualität verloren.

Bibliographie

Achenwall, Gottfried und Pütter, Johann Stephan (1995): Anfangsgründe des Naturrechts (Elementa Iuris Naturae) (1750): Jan Schröder (Hg. und Übers.), in: Hans Maier und Michael Stolleis (Hg.), Bibliothek des deutschen Staatsdenkens Bd. 5, Frankfurt am Main.

Byrd, B. Sharon und Hruschka, Joachim (2010): Kant's Doctrine of Right. A Commentary, Cambridge.

CJCG | Corpus Juris Confoederationis Germanicae, oder Staatsacten für Geschichte und öffentliches Recht des Deutschen Bundes. (1858), Nach officiellen Quellen hg. von Philipp A. G. von Meyer. Erster Theil. Staatsverträge. Dritte Auflage, Frankfurt am Main.

Fichte, Johann Gottlieb (1796): RZeF | Rezension zu Immanuel Kant, Zum ewigen Frieden, Nachdruck in: Immanuel Hermann Fichte (Hg.): Fichte's sämmtliche Werke. Bd. 8, Berlin 1846, S. 427–436.

Frank, Martin (2011): Kant und der ungerechte Feind, in: Deutsche Zeitschrift für Philosophie 59, S. 199–219.

Fried, Alfred H. (1905): Handbuch der Friedensbewegung, Wien.

Fulda, Hans Friedrich (2003): Georg Wilhelm Friedrich Hegel, München.

Geismann, Georg (2010): Warum Kants Friedenslehre für die Praxis taugt und warum die Friedenslehren von Fichte, Hegel und Marx schon in der Theorie nicht richtig sind, in: Georg Geismann (Hg.), Kant und kein Ende, Bd. 2, Würzburg, S. 147–163.

Gentz, Friedrich (1953): Über den ewigen Frieden, in: Historisches Journal 2 (1800), S. 710–790. Nachdruck in: Kurt von Raumer (Hg.): Ewiger Friede: Friedensrufe und Friedenspläne seit der Renaissance, Freiburg, S. 461–497.

Hegel, Georg W. F.: *GW* | Gesammelte Werke, Hamburg, 1968 ff.

Hegel, Georg W. F.: *EN* | ‚Notizen zum dritten Teil der Encyklopädie [von 1817]', in: Enzyklopädie der philosophischen Wissenschaften im Grundrisse (1817), GW 13, S. 251–543.

Hegel, Georg W. F.: *E* | Enzyklopädie der philosophischen Wissenschaften im Grundrisse (1830), in: GW 20.

Hegel, Georg W. F.: *R* | Grundlinien der Philosophie des Rechts, in: GW 14.

Hegel, Georg W. F.: *RPR* | „Unterklasse Rechts-, Pflichten- und Religionslehre aus den Schuljahren 1809/10 bis 1815/16." in: Nürnberger Gymnasialkurse und Gymnasialreden (1808–1816), GW 10, S. 367–420.

Hegel, Georg W. F.: *RV 1817–1820* | Die Philosophie des Rechts. Die Mitschriften Wannenmann (Heidelberg 1817/18) und Homeyer (Berlin 1818/19), hg., eingeleitet und erläutert von Karl-Heinz Ilting, Stuttgart, 1983.

Hegel, Georg W. F.: *RV 1818–1831* | Hegels Vorlesungen über Rechtsphilosophie 1818–1831. Vier Bände, Hg. von Karl-Heinz Ilting, Stuttgart–Bad Cannstatt, 1973 ff.

Hegel, Georg W. F.: *RV 1819/20* | Philosophie des Rechts, Die Vorlesung von 1819/20 in einer Nachschrift, hg. von Dieter Henrich, Frankfurt, 1983.

Hegel, Georg W. F.: *RZ* | Grundlinien der Philosophie des Rechts oder Naturrecht und Staatswissenschaft im Grundrisse, Mit Hegels eigenhändigen Notizen und den mündlichen Zusätzen, in: Hegel, Werke in zwanzig Bänden, Bd, 7, Frankfurt am Main, 1970.

Hegel, Georg W. F.: *T* | Theses, in: Texte zur Habilitation (1801), GW 5, S. 227–228.

Hegel, Georg W. F.: *WBN* | Ueber die wissenschaftlichen Behandlungsarten des Naturrechts (1803), in: GW 4, S. 415–485.

Hennis, Wilhelm (2003): Das Problem der Souveränität. Ein Beitrag zur neueren Literaturgeschichte und gegenwärtigen Problematik der politischen Wissenschaften, Tübingen.

Hobbes, Thomas, (1957): L | Leviathan or the Matter, Forme and Power of a Commonwealth Ecclesiastical and Civil, Michael Oakeshott (ed.), Oxford.

Höffe, Otfried (1995): Völkerbund oder Weltrepublik, in: Otfried Höffe (Hg.): Immanuel Kant, Zum ewigen Frieden. Klassiker auslegen. Band 1, Berlin, S. 109–132.

Ilting, Karl-Heinz (1978): Naturrecht, in: Otto Brunner und al. (Hg.): Geschichtliche Grundbegriffe. Historisches Lexikon zur politisch-sozialen Sprache in Deutschland, Stuttgart, Band 4.

Ilting, Karl-Heinz (1983): Erläuterungen, in: Hegel (RV 1817–1820), S. 287–363.

Janiçon, François Michel (1729): État Présent de la République des Provinces-Unies, et des Pais qui en dependent, Tome Premier, La Haye.

Kant, Immanuel: AA | Kant's gesammelte Schriften, Akademie-Ausgabe, Berlin, 1902ff.

Kant, Immanuel: *KU* | Kritik der Urteilskraft (1790), in: AA 5.

Kant, Immanuel: *RGV* | Die Religion innerhalb der Grenzen der bloßen Vernunft (1793), in: AA 6, S. 1–202.

Kant, Immanuel: *RL* | Metaphysik der Sitten. Erster Theil. Metaphysische Anfangsgründe der Rechtslehre (1797), in: AA 6, S. 203–372.

Kant, Immanuel: *TP* | „Über den Gemeinspruch: Das mag in der Theorie richtig sein, taugt aber nicht für die Praxis" (1793), in: AA 8, S. 273–314.

Kant, Immanuel: *ZeF* | Zum ewigen Frieden (1795), in: AA 8, S. 341–386.

Kleingeld, Pauline (2012): Kant and Cosmopolitanism. The Philosophical Ideal of World Citizenship, Cambridge.

Moser, Johann Jacob (1732): Anfangs-Gründe [der] Wissenschafft von der heutigen Staats-Verfassung von Europa und dem unter den Europäischen Potenzien üblichen Völcker- oder allgemeinen Staats-Recht. Erster Theil, Tübingen.

Schiller, Friedrich (1992): Gedichte in der Reihenfolge ihres Erscheinens, 1776–1799, in: Schillers Werke. Nationalausgabe. Bd. 1, Weimar.

van der Linden, Wilhelmus H. (1987): The International Peace Movement 1815–1874, Amsterdam.

von Bogdandy, Armin und Venzke, Ingo (2014): In wessen Namen? Internationale Gerichte in Zeiten globalen Regierens, Berlin.

Katja Stoppenbrink
Representative Government and Federalism in John Stuart Mill

> When the conditions exist for the formation of efficient and durable federal unions, the multiplication of them is always a benefit to the world.
> (Mill, CW 19, 559[1])

Introduction

Federalism and its compatibility with representative government is a *leitmotiv* in eighteenth and nineteenth century scholarship on political authority and its legitimacy conditions. While in traditional (republican) democratic theory in the Aristotelian vein the advent of concepts of representation poses a challenge and is first seen as alien and incompatible with democracy, the 'invention' of representative government in the *Federalist Papers*[2] paves the way for a broader understanding of political legitimacy. However, in a structural analogy to representative government, a *federal* organization of political authority is just as well considered a challenge to traditional views on democratic legitimacy. The 'mediation' of legitimacy relations through either representatives ('*horizontal mediation*') or institutional sub-units which are 'inserted' between a central authority and individual citizens ('*vertical mediation*') is both from a historical and a theoretical point of view neither self-evident nor self-explanatory but in need of explanation and justification.

In the aftermath of the innovative and practically relevant contributions of the authors of the *Federalist Papers* one of the most important works on political theory are the—often ignored and unappreciated—*Considerations on Representative Government* (= *Considerations*) by John Stuart Mill (1861). In its Chapter XVII Mill specifies his perceptions and views "Of Federal Representative Government" (chapter title) which is presented as a particular case of representative government. Mill's *Considerations* currently do not receive the kind of attention they deserve as an original contribution to the history of political theory. They propose a

---

1 Mill's works are cited by volume and page of The Collected Works of John Stuart Mill (= CW) in thirty-three volumes edited by J.M. Robson, Toronto and London, 1963–1991.
2 See Brunhöber (2010) and in this collection.

decidedly democratic—in the sense of deliberative or even participatory—form of legislation and offer a treatise of federalism *in nuce*.

In a first part of the chapter on federal government Mill spells out *three necessary conditions*—however not for there to be a federal order in the first place but for a federal order to be *advantageous* ("advisable", CW 19, 553) for the populations concerned (1). In what follows I will enumerate and discuss these necessary conditions made out and proposed by Mill and then focus on the two most distinctive and—from a contemporary point of view—remarkable features argued for by Mill: first, the importance of the implementation of a constitutional court within a (any) federal order (2), second, the argumentation in favor of a bicameral system (3). I will then regard Mill's further discussion of the overall benefits related to the different types of federal orders (4) and come to a conclusion in which I attempt to assess Mill's place in the history of political thinking on federalism (5). More specifically, I will ask whether Mill is a mere epigone with regard to the authors of the *Federalist Papers* and, say, Alexis de Tocqueville, to all of whom he frequently[3] refers to himself.

Following Mill, there are two principal arguments for the advantage of a federalist order over a unitary structure:

(1) the chain of legitimacy under conditions of representative government is closer to citizens if 'mediated' by territorial sub-units ⇨ political/institutional justification;

(2) the sub-units constitute each an individual 'object of identification' for their citizenry and population and thus better allow for and foster a 'sense of belonging' to the political entity ⇨ psychological justification.

Both are in accordance with the principle of participation which is a central element of Mill's political philosophy and in particular his democratic theory as set out in the *Considerations*.

1 Necessary conditions of federalism

Mill distinguishes three conditions "[T]o render a federation advisable" (ibid.). These are (i) sufficient mutual sympathy among the populations concerned, (ii) dependency of the sub-units on the aggregated, united power ("not too pow-

---

3 The "Federalist" is said to be "the most instructive treatise we possess on federal government" (CW 19, 555), for reference to Tocqueville (1835) see also CW 19, 557 and Mill (1835; 1840).

erful individual units"[4]) and (iii) an adequate balance of power between the sub-units ("equality of strength"[5]). In other words, Mill proposes an emotional, a power-related and an equality condition which each refer to the relations between sub-units and their populations respectively.

1.1 On the sympathy condition

Mill does not specify what would be "sufficient" in terms of "mutual sympathy among the populations" (CW 19, 553). Still, this is a subsistence and compliance condition for any federal arrangement. The pivotal element is defensive cooperation and 'comradeship in arms'.[6] ("The federation binds them always to fight on the same side [...]"; ibid.) If "they would generally prefer to fight on opposite sides" [...] (ibid.), federal unity and coherence are at stake.

Even if not quantified, the "sympathies"[7] Mill has in mind are substantially determined as "race, language, religion" and, both in addition and resulting from these, a "feeling of identity of political interest" (ibid.). Furthermore, and this is astonishing, Mill mentions a commonality of "political institutions" (ibid.); this latter aspect may, e. g., refer to legal or political culture. The example *ex negativo* discussed by Mill, who publishes his *Considerations* on the brink of the American Civil War, is slavery—for Mill the only[8] apple of discord threatening the North American federal union "where all the conditions for the maintenance

---

4 Føllesdal (2014).

5 Føllesdal (ibid.).

6 Empirically the import of this criterion may perhaps be better appreciated with reference to a more recent example than the Swiss Confederation (originally: comrades by oath) invoked by Mill: *Nota bene* that this touchstone was not reached by the European Defence Community proposed by French prime minister René Pleven in 1950—which failed ratification by the French parliament in 1954.

7 Cf. also *Considerations*, chapter XVI (CW 19, 546) where Mill discusses various causes of "[T]his feeling of nationality", scil., "identity of race and descent [...] [C]ommunity of language, community of religion [...] [G]eographical limits [...][,] identity of political antecedents; the possession of national history, and consequent community of recollections; collective pride and humiliation, pleasure and regret, connected with the same incidents in the past. None of these circumstances, however, are necessarily sufficient by themselves". This passage is referred to by Rawls in order to justify why his "Law of Peoples" deals with "Peoples and Not States" (1999, 23 and 23 n. 17). The latter problem cannot be enlarged upon here, but see, e.g. Føllesdal (2006).

8 Mill emphasizes "the sole drawback of difference of institutions in the single but most important article of slavery, this one difference goes so far [...] as to [...] effecting the disruption of a tie of so much value to [the two parties in the then forthcoming civil war]" (CW 19, 553).

of union existed at the highest point" (ibid.). The sympathy condition may be alleviated since even if there are different religious allegiances, there may be a sufficiently "common interest" (ibid.) derived from external threat and the motive to preserve one's liberty which seems only feasible by a union. The paradigmatic example given by Mill is Switzerland.

1.2 On the mutual dependency condition

For Mill, "the stability of a federal government" (CW 19, 554) is a resultant of the mutual dependency of the federated entities. The characteristics and in particular the magnitude of military power of the sub-units may not be such that the sub-unit in question could survive self-sufficiently and autarkic. As a second necessary however not sufficient condition for a durable federation Mill thus spells out that "the separate states be not so powerful as to be able to rely for protection against foreign encroachment on their individual strength" (ibid.).

This is *not* a genuine holistic argument since it does not positively claim that 'the sum of the sub-units must be stronger than the individual sub-units added together' but that each sub-unit be 'too weak' to live and defend itself on its own. The prospective advantage of joining the union makes the sub-unit *in spe* inclined to partially give up its own freedom of action—however, given this second condition, it could be argued that the entity which is to become a sub-unit does not even have any significant freedom of action prior to joining and that it *therefore* has a strong motive to become part of the union. The first underlying premise of Mill's second condition is that the sub-units must be *sustainably motivated* to join and stay in the federal union for the federation to be stable and durable. The fact that a sub-unit is not powerful enough to defend itself is a sufficient motivation according to this condition. Hence, the stability and cohesion of the federation can (only) be maintained if the sub-units are in themselves not strong enough to continue to exist separately.

However, here a problem for the legitimacy of the federal union arises: Can it still be deemed a *voluntary association* based on free consent if the sub-unit would at any rate not be able to survive on its own, i.e. if its independence is threatened anyway? Does this reveal a general dilemmatic structure of federalist reasoning in Mill such that (first horn of the dilemma) if there is a possibility for self-reliance of the sub-units the federation cannot durably be maintained, and (second horn) if the states cannot survive on their own they are not free in their decision to join? This suspicion may be countered by analogy to economic incentives: If a cost benefit analysis yields a clear result in favor of one of the options compared we generally do not take this to be a flawed decision-making process.

A 'free' decision against the economically most beneficent option is conceivable in such a situation. Admittedly, this question would have to be dealt with in a theory of *consent* spelling out the conditions of adequately free consent (more particularly in collective actors) rather than federalist theory. However, the economic incentive does not generally put pressure on an agent such that the voluntariness of the decision to be taken would be removed. So, structurally pursuing the analogy, if an independent state rationally compares the alternatives and opts for an association with other free and equal states in a federal arrangement, this bears resemblance to decision-making in the face of economic incentives and can be taken to be the product of a rational weighing process rather than a desperate move out of an impasse. This voluntarist picture corresponds to the ideal-type of a bottom up construction of a 'coming together' union.— Then, subsequently, Mill's (economic or power-related) mutual dependency condition works as a factor of 'holding together' the union since any secession would require a safe and sound prognosis as to future (economic or military) self-reliance and autarky.[9]

Unfortunately, Mill does not straightaway distinguish a "confederation" (CW 19, 554) from other kinds of federal arrangement, such as "federations" and "federal unions" with an "internal government" (ibid.). 'Federation' can be taken to serve as a generic term covering federal arrangements of any kind. With respect to the second condition Mill specifies that even individual policy differences[10] between the levels can provoke the dissolution of federal bonds.

1.3 On the relative equality condition

Mill requires "that there be not a very marked inequality of strength among the several contracting states" (CW 19, 554). Unlike the second this third condition does not refer to a member's *individual* strength but its strength (military power, population, access to resources, 'cultural capital' and the like) *in relation to* other members. An imbalance in power is problematic when it gives rise to hegemonic ambitions[11] of one of the contracting states. While any 'exact' equal-

---

9 Mill refers indeed to a kind of weighing of interests when he explains the implications of his second condition.
10 "[...] whenever the policy of the confederation [...] is different from that which any one of its members would separately pursue, the internal and sectional breach will [...] be in danger of going so far as to dissolve it" (CW 19, 554).
11 In Mills terms: "there should not be any one state so much more powerful than the rest as to be capable of vying in strength with many of them combined" (CW 19, 554).

ity of resources is not attainable among the members of a federation ("some will be more populous, rich, and civilized than others", ibid.), the inequality should not exceed a reasonable amplitude.

Historically, this problem may be at the origin of the slow-moving unification process of German territories in the nineteenth century. In the German Confederation (*Deutscher Bund* 1815–1866) the numerous autonomous German states were dominated by the Kingdom of Prussia on the one hand, the Austrian Empire on the other. Any 'solution' to what was being discussed as the 'German Question' would have included either one or two hegemonic powers. According to Mill's third condition this ensemble could not result in a stable and viable federation. As a contemporary, Mill even cites and amplifies the example of Germany; his quintessence is that the inequality and imbalance of power "is alone enough to reduce the German Bund to almost a nullity" (CW 19, 554). He even reiterates the fact that the German Customs Union (*Zollverein*) of 1834 was *not* a creation of the *Bund*[12] but a separate project of economic unification under the auspices of Prussia.

2 Constitutional courts as guarantors of federalist orders

If we take a federal order to be the "territorial division of power between constituent units"[13], a taxonomic dividing line is the extent to which the central unit has legislative powers and its decisions have direct effect vis-à-vis the individual citizens in the sub-units. In a mere confederation, such as formed by the North American states (and former British colonies) from 1776 to 1787 there is a common government by delegation of local representatives. In an integrated federal state the central government has power on all individual citizens.[14] Thus, in the aftermath, the US Constitution directly involves the sub-units' citizens, mediation of power via the federated sub-units is not necessary anymore. Mill takes up this demand for direct authority of the central government over citizens in

---

12 The *Bund* "never bestowed on Germany a uniform system of customs, nor so much as a uniform coinage" (ibid.).
13 Føllesdal (2014).
14 Cf. *The Federalist Papers* No. 39, attributed to Madison, Hamilton/Madison/Jay (2003, 241 [1787–1788]): "The idea of a national government involves in it not only an authority over the individual citizens [...]".

all sub-units, however, on his account, the federal level does not have the *Kompetenz-Kompetenz* to decide over the powers attributed to it.

In a federation

> [...] it is evidently necessary [...] that the constitutional limits of the authority of each [sub-unit] [...] be precisely and clearly defined" and that "the power to decide between them in any case of dispute should not reside in either of the governments [...] but in an umpire independent of both. (CW 19, 556)

Mill thus deduces the necessity of a constitutional court from the exigencies of a federal arrangement with its vertical division of powers:

> There must be a Supreme Court of Justice, and a system of subordinate courts in every state of the Union [...] (CW 19, 556)

One may object that this is but a descriptive reiteration of the then state of the art in the North American federal state of which Mill is so fervently an advocate.[15] Even if the credit for having 'invented' and implemented a constitutional court system does not go to Mill, he does make a theoretical point here in that he both demands and justifies the implementation of an institutional adjudication of constitutional issues pertaining to the federal organization of powers. Functionally, to prevent internal wars as a means of dispute settlement, a court is needed at the federal level "whose judgment [...] shall be final" (ibid.) There shall not be any immunity from its jurisdiction, but

> [E]very state of the Union, and the federal government itself [...] must be liable to be sued in those courts for exceeding their powers, or for non-performance of their federal duties, and must in general be obliged to employ those courts as the instrument for enforcing their federal rights. (ibid.)

Mill calls it a "remarkable consequence [...] that a court of justice [...] is supreme over the various governments" and even has the right to declare that a law or an act issued by either level of government "has no legal validity" (ibid.). Both from the perspective of a non-federal state (e. g. France) and from the perspective of a strong version of parliamentary sovereignty (e. g. England) this constitutional

---

15 Mill affirmatively refers to "this great national institution", "[T]he main pillar of the American Constitution" (both CW 19, 557), relates "[T]he discussions on the American Constitution" and, again relying on testimony by Tocqueville, comes to the conclusion that the practice of constitutional jurisdiction had by then (the publication of Tocqueville's reports in 1835 and 1840) been well implemented (CW 19, 556).

control even of outcomes of democratic decision-making indeed seems innovative and outrageous.[16] However, it is not only factually endorsed by Mill but theoretically defended as a necessary feature of a well-functioning 'strong' federal order. Constitutional control and judicial review both of the rule of law (in the sense of *ultra vires* control based on the federal attributions of powers) and compliance with federal duties is thus introduced and justified as 'a by-product' or an implication of a vertical federal structure.

Referring to Tocqueville's 'case study' (1835) at hand, Mill even states success conditions ("grounds of confidence", CW 19, 557) for constitutional jurisdiction:

(i)   *ex post* instead of *ex ante* control,[17]
(ii)   control of individual cases in dispute between (private) individuals ("between man and man", CW 19, 557),
(iii) constitutional 'closure' and settlement of the dispute as *'ultima ratio'*,[18]
(iv)   deliberative character of the proceedings and involvement of the public,[19]
(v)   adversarial nature of proceedings,[20]
(vi)   parsimony of decision-making,[21]
(vii) impartiality and political independence of judges who are under an obligation to render justice, i.e. they may not leave a question brought before them undecided, and finally,
(viii) "intellectual pre-eminence of the judges" (ibid.).

Confidence both in the judges and via the judges and in the other characteristics of the institution of the constitutional court is a necessary prerequisite for "the

---

16 In a similar vein, see Mill's commentary on Tocqueville (1835, 66): "They cannot, indeed, punish a legislature for having overstepped its authority, but they can set aside its acts. They are avowedly empowered to refuse to enforce any law, whether enacted by the federal or by the state legislatures, which they consider unconstitutional."

17 The court "does not declare the law *eo nomine* and in the abstract, but waits until a case [...] is brought before it judicially, involving the point in dispute" (CW 19, 557). This is vaguely reminiscent of the later 'default and challenge model of justification' in contextualist epistemology according to which, to put it simply, there is no need to give reasons for one's beliefs unless there is (external) demand to do so.

18 The court's "declarations are not made in a very early age of the controversy" (ibid.).

19 Mill emphasizes "that much popular discussion usually precedes" the court's judgment (ibid.).

20 Here this is but meant to imply judgment on the merits upon careful argumentation by lawyers of both sides.

21 It is decided "only as much of the question at a time as is required by the case before it" (ibid.).

stability of federal institutions" (CW 19, 557).[22] The *topos* of the judiciary—judicial review of constitutional issues—as a necessary confidence-building mechanism in the rule of law certainly does not commence in Mill (but arguably in the *Federalist Papers* and the practice implemented subsequently to the adoption of the US Constitution), but Mill deserves credit for reinforcing, restating and transmitting these insights which are both theoretically renewed and refined and practically contested up until today. While traditionally, in a federal structure, control of constitutionality serves as a protection of sub-units against undue usurpation of power by the center, today the shift is towards individual fundamental and human rights which have to be safeguarded against encroachments and violations by both center and sub-units in a multi-level political arrangement. Thus, it is the judiciary implemented at the federal center which is a guarantor of individual liberties rather than a defender of sub-unit powers.

Mill's analysis is farsighted in that he regards the federal constitutional judiciary as a replacement of war and diplomacy by the rule of law to settle disputes, the replacement of international law by internal legal relations. His *Considerations* can be taken to be elements of a theory and justification of both judicial review at a federal constitutional and a supranational or international level since he adds a cosmopolitan hope:

> The Supreme Court of the federation dispenses international law, and is| the first great example of what is now one of the most prominent wants of civilized society, a real international tribunal. (CW 19, 557 f.)

Mill is here way ahead of his time.

The constitutional court envisaged by Mill is "an umpire independent of both"[23], the federal and the decentralized levels. The division of powers between the center and the sub-units serves to protect individuals from encroachments at either level. In Mill, who is—unlike, e. g., Jeremy Bentham—skeptical[24] of excessive cen-

---

22 This is why the ruling holding unconstitutional a federal statute, the so-called Missouri Compromise, prohibiting slavery in certain territories, had such an impact and such disruptive repercussions on the trust basis of the court that—according to Mill—the court was deemed "scarcely strong enough to bear many more such shocks" (CW 19, 557). See *Dred Scott v. Sandford*, 60 U.S. 393 (1856), http://caselaw.findlaw.com/us-supreme-court/60/393.html (2015/10/12); cf. also on "[T]he court's most dreadful case" Finkelman (2007).
23 Føllesdal (2014).
24 See, e. g., Mill (1862) and Buchstein/Seubert (2013, 304) who argue that chapters XV to XVII in the *Considerations* are to be read as "Plädoyers für politische Dezentralisierung, Föderalismus

tralization, the core idea is to defend individual citizens from encroachments originating at the central level. His discussion of the control of constitutionality shows that federalism implies a "high level of constitutional politics"[25].

However, if not unforeseen, then at any rate undiscussed by Mill, a tendency towards centralization and the specter of a 'government of the judges' come as a challenge for federal constitutional courts. On empirical grounds, Watts (2008, 159) argues that

> [I]f courts are to be accepted within a federation as impartial and independent adjudica-
> tors, there appear to be two requirements: (1) independence from influence on the court
> by any particular level of government, and (2) proportional representativeness of member-
> ship on the court. The first of these raises the issue of the method and security of appoint-
> ment. In relation to the second of these issues, in most federations some provision is made
> either by constitutional requirement or in practice for the constituent unit governments to
> have a role in the appointment of judges adjudicating the constitution.

While Mill describes in great detail (see the list above) the conditions of well-functioning constitutional courts and assesses their institutional value as guarantors of trust and confidence, this is but a downstream view focusing on the courts' powers and outputs. Mill does not waste any words on the judges' appointment and thus omits to take up the upstream perspective. This is a patent lacuna.[26]

3 Federalist bicameralism

In the chapter on federal government Mill submits an argument in favor of bicameralism. In line with his general concern about expertise in government,[27]

---

und kommunale Selbstverwaltung", a triad meant to counter alienation from government by means of public deliberation and participation.

25 Føllesdal (2014). This diagnosis is close to the discussion on 'Constitutionalism and Federalism', see Lenaerts (1990); it is not challenged but rather reinforced by the developments in the European Union, cf. Weiler (2001).

26 Mitigated however by Mill's *in extenso* discussion of Tocqueville's report on various aspects of the judiciary in the North American democracy (1835, 66–68).

27 Mill's usage of 'government' is meant to include legislation and administration, a "fitting constitution of a federal government [...] of course consists of a legislative branch and an executive" (CW 19, 559).

he departs from the assumption that the 'principle of competence'[28] has to be respected along with the 'principle of participation'. The challenge for any well-designed institutional arrangement of government is to combine both, hence the introduction of a second parliamentary chamber. He judges that "the provision of the American Constitution seems exceedingly judicious, that Congress should consist of two houses" (CW 19, 559).

While Mill cites again this example of the North American union, his point is of a general theoretical nature. The first chamber is to be the *locus* of representative democracy, the second is to represent state governments[29], and Mill emphasizes that "every state, whether large or small, should be represented in it by the same number of members" (ibid.). The second chamber is thus an instrument to operationalize the equality condition, Mill's third necessary condition of a federal representative government.

According to Mill there is and should be a double majority requirement (majority of the citizens *plus* majority of the states) of each act of legislation. Neither is this a necessary provision in any federalist setting nor does it render bicameralism specific to federal orders—but there are specific features, purposes and advantages of bicameralism in a federal framework.[30] Apart from implementing further checks and balances within the parliamentary system combining a horizontal and a vertical dimension, for Mill, based on probabilistic reasoning the second chamber has the likely effect "of raising the standard of qualifications in one of the houses" (ibid.). If there is direct popular election of the members of the second chamber, this is an empirically untenable argument since "generally they tend to vote along party lines rather than strictly for the regional interests they represent"[31]. However, in Mill's time, the US state legislatures indeed tended to select what Mill refers to as "eminent men" (CW 19, 559). Mill's 'principle of competence' is thus respected by selection practices for the second chamber the objectives of which are to raise the intellectual and other qualities of deliberation processes.

---

28 These are the guiding themes of Thompson's landmark book on "John Stuart Mill and Representative Government" (1976, 13 – 53, 54 – 90; first chapter on "[T]he Principle of Participation", second chapter on "[T]he Principle of Competence").

29 At the time of the *Considerations* the members of the United States Senate were still elected by the legislatures of each state. Popular election of senators was only introduced by the Seventeenth Amendment to the Constitution in 1912 – 13.

30 In his empirical study Watts (^{3}2008, 147) mentions two former federations with unicameral legislatures, Pakistan and Serbia-Montenegro, "neither of which proved stable".

31 Watts (^{3}2008, 151).

While it is controversial whether second chambers are in contradiction with the democratic principle of "one person one vote"[32], democratic majority rule comes as a challenge for heterogeneous citizenries since the domination (or rather: subjugation) of minority groups can only be prevented by institutional safeguards—this refers back to judicial review including a constitutional court *and* speaks in favor of the implementation of a second chamber to represent the different constituent units of the federation. So how does Mill relieve the tension between representation of the people and a—preferred?—more 'élitist' version of representative government—or doesn't he? It can be argued that in the combined horizontal and vertical representation constituted by the bicameral system the tension is in a dialectical way '*aufgehoben*' in the joint legislative authority of the two chambers, one being reserved for representatives of the federal subunits, the other being directly elected by the citizenry. The second chamber with its additional, 'reflective' element is thus a further source of stability and trust in the political authority which in any federal system must be a 'split' authority—if not by the 'expertise' of its members then by the very fact that a further deliberative step is added to the legislative procedure.

The second chamber is an additional link in the chain of accountability watching over decision-making at the central level—by participating in it. Often intricate and complex interlocking arrangements[33] are put in place to allow for this additional oversight of decision-making at the central level. Thereby, second chambers can—provided they represent sub-units at the central federal level—operationalize a certain reading of a principle of subsidiarity in that they guard against over-active, *ultra vires* law-making at the federal level and watch over the vertical allocation of powers. Thus, there is a constant explicit

---

32 See, e.g., the discussion related to in Watts (^{3}2008, 152–155); for the US Senate see Lee/Oppenheimer (1998).
33 Cf. for instance the complex attributions of the *Bundesrat* in the German legislative process at the federal level. While itself being involved in federal legislative decision-making, the *Bundesrat* watches over the attributions of power and can challenge alleged usurpations of competences by the federal level by commencing proceedings before the constitutional court. See, e.g., Article 93 (1) of the German Basic Law regarding the jurisdiction of the Federal Constitutional Court: The court shall rule "1. on the interpretation of this Basic Law in the event of disputes concerning the extent of the rights and duties of a supreme federal body [...]" If affected as such a "supreme federal body" the *Bundesrat* can challenge legislation before the court. There are other procedures giving the *Länder* a right of recourse to the court, e.g. Art. 93 (1) (3): "[...] in the event of disagreements concerning the rights and duties of the Federation and the Länder, especially in the execution of federal law by the Länder and in the exercise of federal oversight" there is jurisdiction by the federal constitutional court; http://www.gesetze-im-internet.de/englisch_gg/englisch_gg.html#p0559 (2015/10/12).

or tacit institutional interplay between second chambers and constitutional courts, like communicating pipes, the more active second chambers are in controlling legislation at the federal level, the less likely the constitutional court will have to intervene—unless the second chamber itself goes to court. At any rate, Mill comes to the same conclusion as nowadays, e.g., Watts (2008, 157) in his comparative study, scil. that

> [...] [A] recognition of the supremacy of the constitution over all orders of government and a political culture emphasizing the fundamental importance of respect for constitutionality are [...] prerequisites for the effective operation of a federation.

4 Differences, functions and effects of federal unions

Taxonomy and advantages of the federation. Following the North American constitutional development, Mill distinguishes two modes of organizing a federal union (CW 19, 554):

- a confederation ("a mere alliance"[34] between governments) such as the Old Swiss Confederacy (before 1847), the then contemporary German Confederation and the North American States after independence and before the entry into force of the US Constitution, in which "federal authorities may represent the governments solely, and their acts may be obligatory only on the governments as such" on the one hand, and
- a federal government the decisions of which have 'direct effect', i.e. which typically will "have the power of enacting laws [...] binding directly on individual citizens" (all ibid.) on the other.

Mill stresses the vertical interconnectedness[35] of the two levels of government, "the only principle [...] ever likely to produce an *effective* federal government" (ibid.; my emphasis, K.S.). The decisive features of such a strong federal government are then characterized as follows:

i.   federal legislation on the legal basis of conferred powers ("[W]ithin the limits of its attributions"),

---

34 CW 19, 554. It is susceptible to contingencies and precarious alliances.
35 "The Federal Congress [...] is a substantive part of the government of every individual state." (CW 19, 555)

ii. direct effect of federal legislation on citizens ("laws [...] obeyed by every citizen individually"),

iii. enforcement of federal law by federal officers ("executes them through its own officers"[36] otherwise "no mandates [...] disagreeable to a local majority would ever be executed"[37]),

iv. federal adjudication ("enforces them [the federal laws] by its own tribunals"[38]).

Hence, there is a duplication of powers on the federal level (legislative—executive—judiciary); state-making properties are attributed to the federal level as well. The problem of dual allegiance of citizens arises since "every citizen of each particular state owes obedience to two governments, that of his own state and that of the federation" (CW 19, 556).

Mill leaves open the possibility that an effective federal *government* may not *eo ipso* provide for an effective federalism; it is certainly a necessary feature but may not be sufficient for a well-functioning federal order. *E contrario*, without direct effect and its own means of enforcement, a central unit is considered part of a *weak* federal arrangement. Even if there is a federal army there is but the option to resort to war ("no other sanction or means of enforcement than war", CW 19, 555). However, according to Mill, this is contrary to the purpose of the federation. The assumed pacifying function (see *infra*) of a federal union is questioned if the center is too weak to implement its laws and orders to the effect that "[S]uch a federation is more likely to be a cause than a preventive of internal wars" (ibid.).

At the very beginning of his chapter on federal representative governments Mill sets out to examine the advantages of a federal system over a unitary system as follows:

> Portions of mankind who are not fitted or not disposed to live under the same internal government may often, with advantage, be federally united as to their relations with foreigners, both to prevent wars among themselves, and for the sake of more effectual protection against the aggression of powerful states. (CW 19, 553)

---

36 CW 19, 555.
37 Ibid. Empirically, the picture is more diverse. While Tocqueville was first to introduce the theoretical distinction of legislative and administrative federalism, the German Basic Law, e. g., provides for the execution of federal laws on federal commission by the *Länder*, whereby "establishment of the authorities shall remain the concern of the Länder". See Article 85 (1); http://www.gesetze-im-internet.de/englisch_gg/englisch_gg.html#p0439 (2015/10/12).
38 CW 19, 555.

There seem to be objective ("not fitted") or subjective ("not disposed") accepta-bility conditions of the combination of groups of people (or rather—without any ethnic connotation—peoples; in Mill's own words "[P]ortions of mankind") under a, i. e. one and the same, government in a unified or unitary political sys-tem. If these are not met, an alternative combination may be a federal system which constitutes but a 'partial' union, scil. as regards "their relations with for-eigners" where "foreigners" are then but individuals who do not belong to any of the sub-units having become "federally united". Entering a federal system thus changes the scope of the national/foreign ascription. On this view, even if they "do not [...] live under the same internal government" (ibid.) federally united people(s) are not 'foreigners' vis-à-vis each other. What would otherwise be an international belligerent collision then becomes an internal affair, a 'civil war' at the utmost. However, the central advantages of a federal system, as Mill em-phasizes as his very point of departure, are the pacifying effects both among the sub-units (internally) and—by way of deterrence—as regards third parties (exter-nally).

Pacifying effect and 'federal peace'. A federal union is an instrument "through which the weak, by uniting, can meet on equal terms with the strong" (CW 19, 559), "it weakens the temptations to an aggressive policy" (ibid.)—inter-nally and externally since it acts as a deterrent—and be it through its increased military strength. According to Mill

> [A] federal government has not a sufficiently concentrated authority to conduct with much efficiency any war but one for self-defense, in which it can rely on the voluntary| co-oper-ation of every citizen [...] (CW 19, 559 f.).

Federations are deemed to be less aggressive than unitary states, they do not only *not* wage wars among themselves but are also said to be more peaceful vis-à-vis external powers. Warfare is thus restricted to defensive wars, the general idea is that federations serve to prevent wars and promote peace. What in the Kantian[39] tradition has been discussed as the 'democratic peace'[40] theory, the hy-pothesis that democracies do not start wars, do not act aggressively towards other states but at the utmost react in a defensive posture towards external ag-gressors and thereby enter into wars, may be termed an allegation of 'federal peace' on the basis of Mill's *Considerations*. Here, it is not the moment to exam-

---

39 Thomas Paine and Tocqueville have also put forward similar claims, Mill will thus have been well familiar with it.
40 Subsequently taken up, e. g. by Rawls (1999) and most prominently studied by Michael W. Doyle (1983a; 1983 b) as a more specific "liberal peace theory".

ine the theory in either of its formulations for its empirical merits, but underline the (alleged) pacifying function as one of Mill's central arguments in favor of federalism.

Representative democracy, welfare and liberty. For Mill, an effective, well-functioning federation in which the pacifying effect pertains has to be a *representative* democracy. He claims that "among monarchical states" (CW 19, 556) only a weak and precarious kind of (con-)federation "seems possible" (CW 19, 555 *in fine*). Several characteristics of a monarchy prevent a king from wholeheartedly entering a federation: he derives his power from "inheritance [instead of] delegation" (CW 19, 556), does neither assume (what would under international law today be termed) 'state responsibility' nor accept any direct effect ("exercise of sovereign authority", ibid.) on his subjects (who are not 'citizens' in the modern sense of the term), is likely to maintain and stick to his separate army and not be loyal to the federal level.[41]

Interestingly, in Mill as one of the intellectual founding fathers of utilitarianism the dimension of economic prosperity and welfare comes less to the fore among the reasons for federalism. Of course, there are other purposes of a federation, such as a customs union, free interstate trade ("mutual commerce should be free, without the impediment of frontier duties and custom houses", CW 19, 558). But this is not Mill's first and foremost occupation. His central concern in the *Considerations* is not the utilitarian's interest in welfare but the justification of a participatory *democratic* government, a *representative* government and—in addition—a *federal* representative[42] government. Mill advances an argument on the federal attribution of competences *natura rei*[43]. Besides, there are federal powers by convenience ("it is convenient [...] that all post-offices should be under the federal government", ibid.), however, these do not follow 'logically'[44] or 'naturally' from the federal arrangement but may be in the community interest to be regulated at a more local level. Central powers are justified "in transactions with foreign powers" (ibid.), while in other matters

---

41 Mill ponders, however not affirmatively, the United Kingdom as an exception to this claimed rule (CW 19, 556).

42 Mill explicitly states that "the constitution of [a federal government] is amenable to the same principles as that or representative government generally" (CW 19, 559).

43 For instance, for Mill, "[T]he powers of a federal government *naturally* extend not only to peace and war [...] [but, for instance,] all custom duties and trade regulations [...]" (CW 19, 558; my emphasis, K.S.). Again, the example of the United States is given.

44 Mill seems to have been aware of the US constitutional doctrine of *implied powers*.

[...] the question depends on how closely the people in general wish to draw the federal tie; what portion of their local freedom of action they are willing to surrender, in order to enjoy more fully the benefit of being one nation. (CW 19, 558).

Thus, the attribution of powers is not discussed in terms of a principle of subsidiarity but as an upshot of democratic theory and its principle of participation. The construction is bottom-up; apart from the powers which are 'naturally federal' only limited attributions of power are envisaged. In theory, Mill's argumentation would allow for a very 'rugged' and asymmetric picture of attributions of power in which different sub-units would transfer different powers upon the central unit.[45]

5 Epigonism or progressive political philosophy? From the authors of the *Federalist Papers* to Tocqueville and Mill

In the *Considerations* we are given an impression of a modern-day ideal-type federal union which had been put into practice in North America for more than half a century at the time of Mill. While a first widely received report on North American constitutional practice had been given by Alexis de Tocqueville around thirty years before (1835/1840), Mill presents a 'consolidated' and theoretically refined version of the development of federalism, heavily drawing on Tocqueville and the *Federalist Papers* as further sources. We are thus justified in asking for the status of Mill's discussion of federalism. Are his mere footnotes in the history of federalist ideas such that he merely counts as a descriptive *rapporteur*, an epigone of his predecessors whom he frequently cites in his work? In these concluding remarks I will go on a brief *tour d'horizon* of Mill, the political theorist, the reader of Tocqueville, and the advocate of federalism in order to argue that these suspicions are unfounded.

Mill political theorist. At present Mill's political philosophy seems underrated, especially his *Considerations*[46] and even more so his discussion of *federal*[47]

---

45 This resembles the principle of conferral (*Prinzip der begrenzten Einzelermächtigung*) in Art. 5 (1) TEU (Treaty on European Union).
46 Cf. the review to the new German translation published in 1971 by Wallner (1972) with the qualification that [Mill's] "Konzeptionen auf der Grundlage der englischen Situation im 19. Jahrhundert interpretiert werden [müssen]." Today there is a renewed interest in the *Considerations* from a genuine theoretical perspective in both political science and political philosophy, see, e.g., the German publications mentioned in Buchstein/Seubert (2013, 293, n. 11).

representative government. Mill scholarship is either mainly historical or narrowly focused on the utilitarian tradition and its tension with Mill's conception of liberty. Accordingly, his political writings are often dismissed as mere practical observations of little theoretical interest. Indeed, the stance Mill takes in his chapter on federalism is at the outset one of a political counsellor interested in practical outcomes ("render a federation *advisable*", CW 19, 553; my emphasis, K.S.). His approach is from empirical observations, historical examples and contemporary political discussions. Deductions from *a priori* principles or other principled considerations do not play a role in his political thought. However, his is a normative theory of political institutions ("a better doctrine must be possible", CW 19, 373); even if Mill goes through the positive constitutional institutions of the United States and compares the confederation to the later constitution of the union this is done with the objective of spelling out the necessary and sufficient conditions of a sustainable federal order. The object of interest is not primarily each particular federalist institution but the aim is to carve out a kind of Weberian ideal-type following the most advanced and theoretically exacting empirical example of the time, the US.

A federal order allows for local variation—even in a cooperative arrangement competition is implicitly admitted and spurred between sub-units competing for 'best' solutions for problems which—in spite of the respective local character—will be structurally equivalent in the different sub-units. Even if there are constitutional equalization requirements at the central level (such as, e.g. in the Basic Law of the Federal Republic of Germany[48]) there will in practice be considerable differences between member units and—*de facto*—accepted inequalities between sub-units even in symmetric federal arrangements (i.e. in federal orders in which the sub-units have the same attributions of powers). In comparison to uni-

---

47 In his portray of Mill as 'founder of modern political and social thought' Rosen (2013) omits the discussion of federalism amid Mill's concerns for liberty and representative democracy. The diagnosis is similar for the *Cambridge Companion to Mill* edited by Skorupski (1998) and even the anthology by Urbinati and Zakaras (2007) in which the focus is on "Making Sense of Liberal Imperialism" (Holmes) and "Some Unanswered Questions in Mill's Politics" (Ryan), both referring to the subsequent chapter of the *Considerations* (CW 19, 562–577) in which Mill asks for "the best way of governing colonies" (Ryan 2007, 150) and offers a justification of colonialism and imperialism of which it is—*contra* Holmes?—indeed hard to make sense. In his encyclopedia entry on federalism, Føllesdal (2014) lists Mill as part of the intellectual history of Western federalist thought.

48 The German Basic Law provides for concurrent legislative powers of the federal level to the extent this is required for the "establishment of equivalent living conditions throughout the federal territory", see Art. 72 (2), https://www.gesetze-im-internet.de/englisch_gg/englisch_gg.html (2015/10/12).

tary states there is also an increased opportunity for participation in (local, decentralized) decision-making in federal arrangements. This general theme of Mill's discussion of representative government, his principle of participation, is again taken up in his treatment of federal government.

Mill reader of Toqueville. In Mill's discussion of democracy, the 'principle of participation'[49] is complemented by a 'principle of competence'[50]. Throughout the *Considerations* Mill is concerned with the guarantee of an adequate basis of knowledge and expertise for decision-making at any level. Mill is inspired by the socially rather conservative Alexis de Tocqueville[51] and his reports and analyses in *Democracy in America* (two volumes 1835 and 1840). Just like Tocqueville Mill fears the 'tyranny of the majority'[52], a *topos* not uncommon in (early) modern thought on democracy[53]. In Mill it is the specter of majority rule by the English working classes of his time which is the reason why Mill's political philosophy is commonly said to have an ambivalent posture towards democracy. However, Urbinati (2002) has claimed that this view is mistaken, that Mill was not hostile towards democracy but in search of 'realistic' ways to achieve more inclusive participation while maintaining competence[54] in government. In the aftermath of the Federalists and their "invention of representative democracy"[55] Mill can be taken as an early explorer of possible avenues to combine representation and participation. For Mill—and this is the gist of Urbinati's reconstruction of Mill's political thought—politics is essentially deliberative. Al-

---

49 Cf. Thompson (1976, 132).

50 This is the second grand theme of Thompson (1976, 54–90).

51 Tocqueville is rightly credited for his innovative method of comparative political science, see, e. g., Mansfield/Winthrop (2006, 98–103) citing Tocqueville's famous statement at the beginning of *Democracy in America I*: "A new political science is needed for a world altogether new" (translated by Mansfield/Winthrop 2006, 81). Tocqueville correctly predicts the forthcoming generalized advent of democracy but does not wholeheartedly endorse it.

52 *Democracy in America* I, chapter XV: Unlimited Power Of Majority, And Its Consequences, Part II: Tyranny Of The Majority (translation Henry Reeve). Cf. Richter (2006, 251 f.).

53 Montesquieu (1748, Book VIII, Chapter 2, 351): "Il se forme de petits tyrans qui ont tous les vices d'un seul. Bientôt ce qui reste de liberté devient insupportable; un seul tyran s'élève; et le peuple perd tout [...] La démocratie a donc deux excès à éviter: [...] l'esprit d'égalité extrême, qui la conduit au despotisme d'un seul [...]." For the influence of Montesquieu on Tocqueville cf., e. g., Richter (1970).

54 However, this can be 'technically' understood as in a patient-general practitioner-relation; see Urbinati (2002, 48) on this example on expert government given by Mill ("A man's control over his physician is not nugatory, [...] he does not direct his physician what medicine to administer. He either obeys the prescription of his physician, or, if dissatisfied with him, takes another", CW 18, 72); Mill first calls this 'rational democracy' (CW 18, 71).

55 Brunhöber (2010) and in this volume.

though this idea cannot be further explored here, Mill can be read as a forerunner of deliberative democratic theory[56] rather than as a mere advocate of political 'liberalism'. This is what Mill may have had in mind when he fervently argued in favor of representative government. The participation principle is at the core of Mill's political thought—and federalism is just another instrument to achieve self-determination, high rates of participation and a government close (closer) to citizens than distant, centralized, unitary political authorities.[57]

Mill advocate of federalism as an avenue to participation and recognition. With respect to the federal/unitary distinction and the problem of whether "a country which is determined to be united should form a complete or a merely federal union" (CW 19, 560) Mill discusses several aspects such as the size of the territory and the question of how distant provinces are to be reached by a central government. Mill does not at all deny that humans live together in groups and communities—his point of departure is that "portions of mankind" (CW 19, 553) may come together in federations. Federalism thus appears to be a third way (the *'tertium datur'*[58]) between outright universal cosmopolitanism and unitary nation states. Thus, in his first necessary condition of federalism Mill presupposes what may be termed 'the argument from identity politics': A federalist structure allows for the recognition of particular identities; ethnic, cultural, linguistic, religious and other allegiances and groups may best be respected and preserved

---

56 If in the Habermas (1992)—Pateman (1970)—Barber (²2004 [1984]) debate on participatory vs. deliberative politics Mill had to be situated he could be taken to be a defender of the participatory nature of the political process—and still be concerned with the 'quality' and substance of deliberation processes and decision-making. In his philosophy he thus exemplifies the tensions which—under a different guise—also occupied the twentieth century thinkers: the *de facto* exclusionary character of the deliberative process while participatory democracy *de jure* should be as inclusive as possible. In his *Considerations* Mill presupposes both (i) the value of participation and (ii) the claim that participation can best be achieved by way of a representative government (see especially chapter III of the *Considerations*). Yet he never explicitly gives reasons for this claim. (This has lucidly been shown in a recent paper by Marco Schnieder (Münster); unpublished manuscript 2015.)

57 From today's perspective unacceptably exclusionary or élitist views are complemented in Mill by demands for general education and gradual access to the right to vote, cf. his vindication of women's suffrage, etc. Still it has to be admitted that the problem of expertise in democratic government persists: experts are to be found in the executive, in technocratic government and— even more problematic—in the external expertise offered by and commanded from consultancies, interests groups and lobbyists. Democratic control is *de facto* made impossible in these cases, one of the principal challenges for today's democracies and far from, say, Barber's ideas of 'strong democracy'.

58 In a similar vein cf. Härtel (2012, 3): "Zwischen Nachtwächter- und Zentralstaat: Föderalismus als 'tertium datur'".

in federal arrangements. He recognizes the problem of minority protection in the face of majority decision-making at the central level; however, for Mill,

> [...] it is always practicable to reconcile minor diversities with the maintenance of unity of government. All that is needful is to give a sufficiently large sphere of action to the local authorites. (CW 19, 561)

This is both an argument for a federal order and an instrumental proposition of how even in a unitary state unity can be reconciled with diversity: there must be sufficient room for self-governance at a local level. Institutionally this may be implemented by specific autonomous powers of provinces and the like—all "[U]nder one and the same central government" (CW 19, 561). This is even possible in an ideal-type unitary state such as France's *ancien régime*. However—and this is Mill's own conclusion—the preservation of diversity is conceivable both in a unitary and a federal arrangement as long as the approach is bottom up and constitutionally protected. There should be, first, "the guaranty of a constitutional provision against any attempt at assimilation", and secondly, no institutional change should be implemented "except by the voluntary act of those who would be affected by the change" (ibid.).[59]

Diversity and the cultural needs of minorities should be constitutionally protected—both in a unitary and a federal state. A federal state, however, has the advantage that these groups may cluster in individual sub-units and their interests may additionally be protected by centralized decision-making and fundamental rights safeguards provided for at the central level. Hence, judicial review at the constitutional level does not only ensure and control vertical attribution of powers but also offers safeguards of individual and group rights, especially minority rights. This is perhaps the most important and enduring lesson to be learnt from Mill's characterization of federalism: Sub-units may serve identity functions. The dual[60] or multiple allegiance required in federal orders may be a point of reference for defenders of 'communitarian' ideas in politics.

To conclude: Mill is a forerunner of present-day federalist taxonomy and description. In Lijphart's federal/unitary distinction of democracy the 'secondary characteristics' of federalism are specified: bicameralism, constitutionalism in the sense of a stable, written constitution forming a center-piece of the rule of

---

59 Cf. also Mill's plea for local self-determination in chapter XV of the *Considerations* "Of Local Representative Bodies".

60 The dual allegiance of citizens and the 'split' political authority is a contested issue in political theory. Many thinkers deny the possibility of double loyalty (e.g. Carl Schmitt, nowadays Roger Scruton?).

law, constitutional courts to watch over the constitutionality of legislation.[61] All of this is reflected in Mill.

Bibliography

Barber, Benjamin R. ([2]2004 [1984]): Strong Democracy: Participatory Politics for a New Age, Berkeley.

Brunhöber, Beatrice (2010): Die Erfindung "demokratischer Repräsentation" in den Federalist Papers, Tübingen.

Buchstein, Hubertus/Seubert, Sandra (2013): Nachwort, in: John Stuart Mill, Betrachtungen über die Repräsentativregierung [German translation], Berlin, pp. 289–326.

Doyle, Michael W. (1983a): Kant, Liberal Legacies, and Foreign Affairs, in: Philosophy and Public Affairs 12, 205–235.

Doyle, Michael W. (1983b): Kant, Liberal Legacies, and Foreign Affairs, Part 2, in: Philosophy and Public Affairs 12, 323–353.

Finkelman, Paul (2007): Scott v. Sandford: The Court's Most Dreadful Case and How it Changed History, in: Chicago-Kent Law Review 82, pp. 3–48.

Føllesdal, Andreas (2006): Justice, Stability and Toleration in a Federation of Well-Ordered Peoples, in: Rex Martin/David A. Reidy (eds.), Rawls's Law of Peoples: A Realistic Utopia?, Oxford, pp. 299–317.

Føllesdal, Andreas (2014): Federalism, in: Edward N. Zalta (ed.), The Stanford Encyclopedia of Philosophy (Spring 2014 Edition), http://plato.stanford.edu/archives/spr2014/entries/federalism/ (retrieved 2015/10/12).

Habermas, Jürgen (1992): Chapter 7: Deliberative Politik—ein Verfahrensbegriff der Demokratie, in: idem: Faktizität und Geltung. Beiträge zur Diskurstheorie des Rechts und des demokratischen Rechtsstaates, Frankfurt a. M., pp. 349–397.

Härtel, Ines (2012): Alte und neue Föderalismuswelten, in: idem (ed.): Handbuch Föderalismus—Föderalismus als demokratische Rechtsordnung und Rechtskultur in Deutschland, Europa und der Welt. Band I: Grundlagen des Föderalismus und der deutsche Bundesstaat, Berlin/Heidelberg, pp. 3–22.

Hamilton, Alexander/Madison, James/Jay, John (2003 [1787–1788]): The Federalist Papers, edited by Clinton Rossiter, with an introduction and notes by Charles R. Kesler, New York.

Holmes, Stephen (2007): Making Sense of Liberal Imperialism, in: Urbinati, Nadia/Zakaras, Alex (eds.): J. S. Mill's Political Thought. A Bicentennial Reassessment, Cambridge, pp. 319–346.

Lee, Frances E./Oppenheimer, Bruce I. (1998): Sizing Up the Senate: The Unequal Consequences of Equal Representation, Chicago.

Lenaerts, Koen (1990): Constitutionalism and the Many Faces of Federalism, in: The American Journal of Comparative Law (AJCL) 38, pp. 205–263.

Lijphart, Arend ([2]2012): Patterns of Democracy: Government Forms & Performance in Thirty-six Countries, New Haven.

---

61 Lijphart ([2]2012, ch. 10 on federalism).

Mansfield, Harvey C./Winthrop, Delba (2006), Tocqueville's New Political Science, in: Welch, Cheryl B. (ed.): The Cambridge Companion to Tocqueville, New York, pp. 81–107.

Mill, John Stuart (1835): De Tocqueville on Democracy in America I, in: The Collected Works of John Stuart Mill, Volume XVIII—Essays on Politics and Society Part I, ed. John M. Robson, Toronto and London, pp. 47–90, http://oll.libertyfund.org/titles/233 (2015/10/12).

Mill, John Stuart (1840): De Tocqueville on Democracy in America II, in: The Collected Works of John Stuart Mill, Volume XVIII—Essays on Politics and Society Part I, ed. John M. Robson, Toronto and London, pp. 153–204, http://oll.libertyfund.org/titles/233 (2015/10/12).

Mill, John Stuart (1977 [1862]): Centralisation, in: The Collected Works of John Stuart Mill, Volume XIX—Essays on Politics and Society Part 2, edited by J.M. Robson, Toronto and London, pp. 579–613, http://oll.libertyfund.org/titles/mill-the-collected-works-of-john-stuart-mill-volume-xix-essays-on-politics-and-society-part-2 (2015/10/12).

Mill, John Stuart (1977 = [3]1865 [1861]): Considerations on Representative Government, in: The Collected Works of John Stuart Mill, Volume XIX—Essays on Politics and Society Part 2, edited by J.M. Robson, Toronto and London, pp. 371–577, http://oll.libertyfund.org/ti tles/mill-the-collected-works-of-john-stuart-mill-volume-xix-essays-on-politics-and-soci ety-part-2 (2015/10/12).

Montesquieu, Charles Louis de Secondat, baron de La Brède et de (1951 [1748]): De l'Esprit des Lois, in: Œuvres complètes, vol. II, Paris, pp. 227–995.

Pateman, Carol (1970): Participation and Democratic Theory, Cambridge.

Rawls, John (1999): The Law of Peoples, Cambridge and London.

Richter, Melvin (1970): The Uses of Theory: Tocqueville's Adaptation of Montesquieu, in: Essays in Theory and History. An Approach to the Social Sciences, ed. by Melvin Richter, Cambridge/Mass., pp. 74–102.

Richter, Melvin (2006): Tocqueville on Threats to Liberty in Democracies, in: Welch, Cheryl B. (ed.): The Cambridge Companion to Tocqueville, New York, pp. 245–275.

Rosen, Frederick (2013): Mill (Series Founders of Modern Political and Social Thought), Oxford.

Ryan, Alan (2007): Bureaucracy, Democracy, Liberty: Some Unanswered Questions in Mill's Politics, in: Urbinati, Nadia/Zakaras, Alex (eds.): J. S. Mill's Political Thought. A Bicentennial Reassessment, Cambridge, pp. 147–165.

Skorupski, John (ed.) (1998): The Cambridge Companion to Mill, Cambridge.

Thompson, Dennis Frank (1976): John Stuart Mill and Representative Government, Princeton/New Jersey.

Tocqueville, Alexis de (1835 and 1840): De la démocratie en Amérique, 2 vol., Paris.

Tocqueville, Alexis de (2003 [1838]): Democracy in America, translated by Henry Reeves, New York.

Urbinati, Nadia (2002): Mill on Democracy. From the Athenian Polis to Representative Government, Chicago.

Wallner, Ernst M. (1972): [Review of] John Stuart Mill, Betrachtungen über die repräsentative Demokratie, in: Das Historisch-Politische Buch 20, p. 123.

Watts, Ronald L. ([3]2008): Comparing Federal Systems, Montreal et al.

Weiler, Joseph H. H. (2001): Federalism Without Constitutionalism: Europe's Sonderweg, in: Nicolaidis, Kalypso/Howse, Robert (eds.): The Federal Vision: Legitimacy and Levels of Governance in the United States and the European Union, Oxford, pp. 54–70.

**Contemporary and Systematic Approaches
to Federalism**

Volker Gerhardt

Föderalismus und Subsidiarität. Über horizontale und vertikale Verteilung politischer Lasten in der Demokratie

1 Ein Ausgangspunkt in der Antike

Meine mir selbst beinahe langweilig werdende, seit mehr als vierzig Jahren in verschiedenen Zusammenhängen zunächst gegen die vorherrschende Meinung in meinem Umfeld erarbeitete,[1] dann an zentralen Fragen exemplarisch verstärkte[2] und inzwischen stets im Munde geführte Überzeugung, dass die politische Philosophie ihren uns bis heute prägenden Ursprung in der Antike hat, könnte sich auch mit Blick auf die Organisationsprinzipien der *Föderalität* und der *Subsidiarität* bestätigen lassen. Denn nicht nur die Sachverhalte kommen bei Griechen und Römern vor, sondern auch durchaus treffende und teils schon terminologisch verwendete Begriffe.

Das *Bündnis* von als gleichrangig angesehenen Partnern, das bei den Griechen noch *symmachia* hieß, und das die Römer *foedus* nannten, spielte bereits im *Attischen Seebund* eine exponierte Rolle. Wann immer es um die Fragen der *Zuständigkeit* und der *Lastenverteilung* zwischen den beteiligten *poleis* im Krieg wie im Frieden ging, war die Bereitschaft, sich wechselseitig zu helfen und auch die Konsequenzen gemeinsam zu tragen, essenziell.[3] *Koinōnia*, also die über die Grenzen einer *polis* hinausreichende Gemeinschaft in einem Bund, die auch „Teilnahme" und „Hilfeleistung" bedeutet, dürfte der erste Terminus für das gewesen sein, was wir heute als *Subsidiarität* bezeichnen.

Dazu gab es, soweit ich weiß, keine ausformulierte Theorie. Aber es scheint eine pragmatische und aus dem Selbstverständnis der beteiligten Parteien folgende Regelung zu sein, dass man sich im Bündnis, nach den jeweils gegebenen eigenen Möglichkeiten, gegenseitig hilft. Damit wäre bereits unter den frühen Bedingungen des politischen Handelns eine bis heute gültige Voraussetzung erfüllt, die heute unter den Titeln von *Föderalismus* und *Subsidiarität* ihren programmatischen Ausdruck findet.

---

1 Vgl. vom Verf. (1976 [1974]; 1996 [1983]).
2 Vgl. vom Verf. (1999; 2002; 2007; 2012).
3 *pálai de koinōsantas tēn dynamin koina* (Thukydides, Geschichte des Peloponnesischen Krieges, I, 39).

Solange sich keine gegenteiligen Belege finden, behaupte ich daher, dass sich unter politischen Handlungsträgern, die auf wechselseitige Anerkennung bedacht sind, bereits in der griechischen Antike eine der *Föderalität* und der *Subsidiarität* wie von selbst nahekommende Verteilung von Zuständigkeiten ergeben hat. Solange das Ziel einer politischen Absprache nicht in der Unterwerfung oder gar der Auflösung der Institutionen der anderen Beteiligten liegt, ergeben sich *Kooperationsformen*, welche die Eigenständigkeit der Partner gelten lassen und ihnen auch die Möglichkeit bieten, die sie vorrangig betreffenden Maßnahmen, wann immer sie können, mit den eigenen Mitteln durchzuführen.

In den historisch dokumentierten Großereignissen der griechischen Politik hat es dafür freilich nur geringen Spielraum gegeben. Schon das demokratische Athen hat der Versuchung nicht widerstehen können, seine Verbündeten zu majorisieren. Und nach dem Zusammenbruch der Athenischen Demokratie waren die politischen Verhältnisse in Griechenland teils so unsicher, teils durch den Dominanzanspruch einzelner Mächte, zunächst Spartas, dann Makedoniens und schließlich Roms, derart einseitig ausgerichtet, dass der föderale Gedanke wohl nur in Ausnahmen Anwendung finden konnte. Also gibt es mit Blick auf die Politik im klassischen Griechenland, wenn ich richtig sehe, wenig Anlass, von einem politisch praktizierten und theoretisch elaborierten Charakter der Prinzipien von *Föderalität* und *Subsidiarität* zu sprechen.

Gerade weil beide eng mit einander verbundenen Handlungsformen so nahe lagen, wann immer man auf Bündnispartner angewiesen war, muss man hervorheben, dass es offenbar schon den Griechen nicht leichtgefallen ist, ihnen auch Geltung zu verschaffen. Man braucht Respekt vor denen, mit denen man kooperiert, muss deren eigene Verfassung in Rechnung stellen und auch zur realistischen Einschätzung ihrer Kräfte bereit sein – alles Fähigkeiten, die den jeweils eigenen Machtinteressen der beteiligten Parteien nur zu leicht entgegen stehen. Daraus können wir bereits die grundsätzliche Lehre ziehen, dass zur Wahrung von Föderalität und Subsidiarität ein gewisses Maß an *Selbstbeschränkung in den eigenen Machtinteressen* gehört.

Doch damit greife ich vor. Für den Anfang mag genügen, dass es spätestens mit dem Eintritt der Griechen in den Raum des Politischen die Sache, den Geist und die Begrifflichkeit dessen gegeben hat, worüber hier zu sprechen ist. Die Pluralität der Machtverteilung im Siedlungsgebiet der Griechen hat dies gewiss begünstigt. Schon die *Ilias* führt uns vor, dass sich die Macht der Griechen im Kampf gegen äußere Feinde nur in der *Form von Bündnissen* entfalten konnte. Und sie lehrt uns, wie sehr die *Streitlust* und das *Streben nach Vorherrschaft* der Stämme und Städte der Kontinuität der Bündnispolitik entgegenstanden.

Dennoch möchte ich mit meinem Hinweis nicht behaupten, dass die Griechen *Föderalismus und Subsidiarität* erfunden haben. Christian Meier hat inzwischen

klargestellt, dass sein Buchtitel „Die Entstehung des Politischen bei den Griechen"
nicht so gelesen werden darf, als hätte das Politische im Klassischen Griechenland
seine weltgeschichtliche Premiere gehabt.[4]

In Rom steht der von der Stadt ausgehende Dominanzanspruch nicht in Frage:
Zwischen der verfügenden Macht im Zentrum und den als *foederati* anerkannten
Stammeseinheiten in den Kolonien gibt es, trotz einer zum Teil beachtlichen Li-
beralität im Umgang mit den eingebundenen Kulturen, ein so beträchtliches
Machtgefälle, dass es selbst bei der ausdrücklichen Zusicherung eigener Hand-
lungsräume nicht vergessen wird.

2 Neue Chancen in der Moderne

Erst der Zerfall der imperialen Übermacht bringt den Gedanken einer *gleichbe-
rechtigten horizontalen Kooperation* verschiedener staatsförmiger Gebilde und
ihrer *vertikal gestuften Kompetenz* auf die Tagesordnung des politischen Handelns
in Europa. Erst hier findet sie, erneut mit einiger Verspätung, die Aufmerksamkeit
der politischen Theorie.

Abgesehen von ersten Ansätzen in der spätmittelalterlichen Rezeption des
platonisch-aristotelischen Partizipationsgedankens, für den man insbesondere in
den italienischen Stadtrepubliken empfänglich ist,[5] kommen die ersten innova-
tiven Impulse für eine Befassung mit *Föderation* und *Subsidiarität* aus der *nach-
reformatorischen Theologie*. Man benötigt *Regularien für den Aufbau* der sich neu
erfindenden protestantischen Kirchen. Die Kritik an der zentralistischen Organisation der römisch-katholischen Kirche lässt nach Formen suchen, die den Gemeinden selbst mehr Raum für eigene Entscheidungen bieten. In der Wahl der
Pfarrer üben die Gläubigen selbst Einfluss auf die Hierarchie der Kirche aus; sie

---

4 Vgl. dazu Meier (1981). In einer Berliner Akademie-Debatte hat Christian Meier die These seines
Buches relativiert: Er habe nicht behaupten wollen, dass die Griechen die Erfinder des Politischen
seien, sondern nur zu zeigen versucht, wie die Griechen zu ihrer Form des Politischen gefunden
haben. Die mir von Meier inzwischen zur Verfügung gestellte Korrespondenz zwischen ihm und
Siegfried Unseld über den Titel des Buches bestätigt die Aussage des Autors. Inzwischen hat er sie
auch ausgeführt: Christian Meier (2011, 15 ff.). In der Sache bestätigend: Dihle (2009).
5 Vgl. Aristoteles, Politik, III. Buch: „Ein Bürger ist einfach und direkt durch nichts anderes zu
definieren, als durch die Art und den Umfang seiner Teilnahme an der Rechtssetzung und
Rechtsprechung sowie an den Leistungen der Verwaltung." (1275a 22 – 24) Wenig später wird,
nach erneuter Betonung der Definition (1275a33) hervorgehoben, dass die Demokratie den
Bürgern die besten Chancen gibt, auf die beschriebene Weise, nämlich durch „Teilhaben" (*metéchein*), an der Politik mitzuwirken. Die ersten Übersetzer der Aristotelischen Politik verwenden
für *to metéchein: participatio*. Zu der Rolle Platons vom Verf. (2008, 14 – 31).

übernehmen das, was sie nach ihrem Glauben weder als Individuen noch als Gemeinschaft von sich weisen können: *Sie tragen Verantwortung für sich und ihre Kirche*. Damit ist ein institutioneller Anspruch gestellt, der auch politische und staatsrechtliche Folgen hat. Die Namen, die hier zu nennen wären, reichen von Althusius und Grotius über Pufendorf und Montesquieu bis hin zu Kant.

Sieht man auf die theologischen Anfänge im 16. Jahrhundert und nimmt die ebenfalls wesentlich von spanischen Theologen geführten Debatten über die Rechte der sogenannten Indios in den Kolonien hinzu, dann kann es nicht wundern, dass die seit dem Niedergang Athens nahezu ganz aus der Theoriedebatte verschwundene *Demokratie* wieder Erwähnung und zaghafte Zustimmung findet. So geschieht es bei dem Jesuiten Francisco Suarez 1604 und findet sein Echo zunächst bei den anglikanischen Separatisten, die um Anerkennung in ihrer von Rom nicht anerkannten Staatskirche ringen.[6] Bleibenden Erfolg haben die sogenannten „Sekten" erst, nachdem ihre führenden Vertreter England verlassen haben und mit dem aus Europa mitgenommen Theoriegepäck zunächst das *Recht, ihrem eigenen Glauben zu leben*, erstreiten. Und wenn sie sich dabei auf die Schriften des *Neuen Testaments* berufen, können sie sich dem Anspruch nicht entziehen, dem Paulinischen Toleranzgebot zur politischen Anerkennung zu verhelfen. Nicht ohne Grund führt der in den neuenglischen Kolonien geführte Streit zwischen verschiedenen christlichen Glaubensgemeinschaften zu einer praktizierten Duldung verschiedener Bekenntnisse.[7]

Dazu passt, dass man auf dem europäischen Kontinent die administrativen Zuständigkeiten in den reformierten Kirchen so weit wie möglich nach „unten", also in die Gemeinden verlagert, und sie dort auch zu *entscheiden* sucht. Erst im Konfliktfall müssen sie auf die nächst höhere Beratungsebene gehoben werden. So „helfen" sich die verschiedenen Einrichtungen auch über Hierarchiestufen hinweg. Deshalb ist der Begriff des *subsidiums* (also der *Hilfe* und des *Hilfsmittels*) durchaus angemessen. *Aus der Aktivität von unten und der Koordination von oben wird ein Verfahren gemeinsamer Verantwortung in vertikaler Kooperation.*

Angesicht der in der Politischen Wissenschaft verbreiteten Neigung, die politische Theorie erst bei Thomas Hobbes oder, wenn es hoch kommt, bei Machiavelli beginnen zu lassen, muss man auch mit Blick auf *Föderalismus und Subsidiarität* Einspruch gegen die absurde historische Verkürzung erheben. Es ist vielmehr so, dass diese so spät ins politische Bewusstsein rückenden, eng miteinander verschwisterten Gedanken ihren Ursprung mindestens in der *Antike* haben. Es ergeht ihnen lediglich ganz ähnlich, wie auch der – ebenfalls mit ihnen

---

6 Dazu im Ganzen: Ottmann (2006).
7 Dazu des Näheren: Forst (2003).

auf das Innigste verbundenen und in den phönizischen und hellenischen Städten erfundenen – *Demokratie*.[8]

Sehen wir einmal von der absurden *Lehre vom Naturzustand* und von der ins politische Abseits führenden absolutistischen *Idee der Souveränität* ab, so haben wir eine durchaus überschaubare Anzahl weiterführender neuzeitlicher Innovationen: Es sind die *Gewaltenteilung*, die *Rechtsstaatlichkeit* und das *Menschenrecht*.[9] In Verbindung mit den *vier Grundprinzipien der Politik:* der *Partizipation*, der *Konstitution*, der *Repräsentation* und *Öffentlichkeit*[10] führen die überkommenen und aufeinander angewiesenen Ideen der *Demokratie*, der *Föderalität* und der *Subsidiarität* zu einer *erweiterten Konzeption von Politik*, ohne die es nicht möglich sein dürfte, die Probleme regionaler und globaler politischer Kooperation zu bewältigen.

3 Der Anteil der Kirchen

Mit Blick auf die Emanzipationsgeschichte der neuzeitlichen Politik haben wir uns angewöhnt, die Religionen und ihre Theologien als die wesentliche Quelle aller Streitigkeiten anzusehen, die spätestens mit dem Dreißigjährigen Krieg derart selbstzerstörerische Formen annehmen, dass der Schlichter in der Form des modernen *Rechtsstaats* als historisch-politische Notwendigkeit erscheint.

Davon muss man nichts zurücknehmen, wenn man daran erinnert, dass es bereits in Athen und Rom gelungen ist, die priesterlichen Funktionen in eine dienende Leistung gegenüber der Politik zu überführen. Der politische Machtanspruch der römisch-katholischen „Kirchenfürsten" hat diese Einbindung erschwert und der Absolutismus der spätmittelalterlichen Theologie hat sie nahezu unmöglich gemacht. Also musste wohl erst die *Kirchenspaltung* mit der nachfolgenden *Kirchenzersplitterung* bei gleichzeitiger *Selbstverabsolutierung des Staates* hinzukommen, um zu einer Befriedung zu gelangen, die der Selbstdestruktion der europäischen Mächte Einhalt gebot.

Darin liegt bekanntlich das große Verdienst des *Westfälischen Friedens*.[11] Es wird aus der Sicht der nachfolgenden Jahrhunderte freilich dadurch geschmälert,

---

8 Wer in Umlauf kommen, etwas durchaus Modernes namhaft machen möchte, der kann auf Föderalismus und Subsidiarität verweisen. Hier bietet sich der bestenfalls noch bis Hobbes oder Machiavelli zurückblickenden Politischen Wissenschaft der Gegenwart die Chance, auch einmal über etwas sprechen zu können, das sich tatsächlich wesentlich ihrer eigenen Zeit verdankt.
9 Dazu vom Verf. (2007; 2012; 2013, 62 – 68).
10 Dazu inzwischen auch vom Verf.: Demokratie als politische Form der Menschheit (Vortrag).
11 Dazu vom Verf. (1998, 485 – 489).

dass sich nunmehr die autonomisierten Nationalstaaten als Sachwalter eines rein politisch verstandenen Absolutismus aufspielen und sich gegenseitig in die Vernichtung treiben.

Im letzten Jahrzehnt des vergangenen Jahrhunderts hätten wir vielleicht zu dem Urteil geneigt, dass auch diesem Treiben endlich ein Ende gesetzt ist. Doch heute wissen wir, dass es ein voreiliges Urteil gewesen wäre. Gleichwohl lehren uns die zahllosen durch religiöse Gegensätze befeuerten Konflikte auf der Welt, dass es prinzipiell richtig war und auch künftig als unumkehrbar gelten muss, die Religionen grundsätzlich aus den politischen Konflikten herauszuhalten. Dass ihnen allein dadurch die Chance eröffnet wird, ihrer genuinen Aufgabe nahe zu bleiben, nämlich zum *Glauben* und zum *Gottesdienst* anzuleiten, kann uns zusätzlich versichern.

Die Zwischenbemerkung zur Stellung der Religion dient dem Zweck, die Aufmerksamkeit darauf zu lenken, dass uns *Föderalität* und *Subsidiarität* daran erinnern, dass die Politik der Religion und ihren Theologien auch einiges verdankt – was wir freilich nur zu schätzen wissen, solange die irreführende These der *Politischen Theologie*, die alle Politik für ein *Säkularisat des Glaubens* ansieht, nicht jede kategoriale Unterscheidung zunichte macht.

Schon *symmachia* und *koinōnia* haben im griechischen Sprachraum sowohl für politische wie auch geistliche Einheiten Gültigkeit gehabt. Mit der nach Jahrhunderten der Verfolgung endlich gewonnenen Selbständigkeit hat die römische Kurie allein mit der für sich selbst übernommenen staatsförmigen Verfassung und dem kanonischen Recht viel zur geschichtlichen Transformation des römischen Rechts beigetragen. Zwar hat sie sich dadurch weit vom sie begründenden Evangelium fortbewegt, aber sie hat eine politisch essenzielle Erbschaft der Antike gesichert, die es heute allererst möglich macht, etwas zum „Weltkulturerbe" zu erklären: Vor diesem Hintergrund hätten wir beste Gründe, das *Recht* selbst zum vermutlich wichtigsten Weltkulturerbe zu erklären.

Als es der Römischen Kirche zu dämmern begann, dass sie im Konzert der politischen Mächte, die sich als Nationalstaaten zu etablieren suchten, nicht mehr mithalten konnte, hat sie sich als *kulturelle* Großmacht zu etablieren versucht. Darin wurde sie bekanntlich von Luther gestört, der aus naheliegenden Gründen dafür kein Verständnis aufbringen konnte. Gleichwohl hat die Kurie durch den Wiederaufbau der „ewigen Stadt" und als wohlhabende Förderin der Künste ein welthistorisches Beispiel gegeben, das heute niemand mehr missen möchte – selbst die außereuropäischen Völker nicht.[12]

---

12 Jeder Besuch in Rom führt das vor Augen.

Das sind nicht die einzigen Leistungen, die wir den christlichen Kirchen verdanken. Zu erinnern wäre an die mit zunehmendem Aufwand betriebene Sicherung der antiken Literatur. Bedenken wir, dass dazu neben der literarischen, philosophischen und juridischen Überlieferung auch die großen medizinischen Schriften des Altertums gehören, dann wird augenblicklich klar, dass wir ohne die Kirchen wohl keine Universitäten hätten und somit wohl auf die wichtigste Institution zur Entfaltung und Verbreitung der Wissenschaften in Europa verzichten müssten. Dieses *subsidum* ist auch für die Staaten, die sich laizistisch nennen, von einiger Bedeutung; es fördert von sich aus die unter säkularen Bedingungen unverzichtbare kulturelle *Föderalität*.

Auch die Juristen, die vom späten 15. Jahrhundert an zu Hauptakteuren des politischen Handelns geworden sind, sind auf Universitäten ausgebildet worden. Die erst später nach Platonischem Vorbild hinzugekommenen Akademien haben die Universität vorausgesetzt und tun dies bis heute.

Der kirchengeschichtliche Exkurs sollte nicht ablenken, sondern im Gegenteil die Aufmerksamkeit darauf verstärken, dass wir in *Föderalität* und *Subsidiariät* zwei organisatorische Vorleistungen aus dem Raum des Glaubens vor uns haben, die der Politik allein dadurch nahe kommen, dass sie die *kulturelle Vielfalt* einüben, ohne die der moderne Territorialstaat gar nicht möglich ist. Das mag im Fall der Föderation gelegentlich unfreiwillig geschehen sein, weil der Glaubensstreit zur verschärften Abgrenzung von benachbarten Staaten beigetragen hat. Die gemeinsamen Überlebensproblemen wäre man besser durch Absprache und Zusammenarbeit angegangen. Hier wäre das christliche Gebot der Nächstenliebe auch das politisch Vernünftige gewesen. Doch man unterschätze nicht die produktive Kraft der Vielfalt. Sie wurde durch die Organisationen des Glaubens gefördert, die ja nicht nur stets ihre nichtgläubigen Widersacher haben, sondern aus sich selbst heraus unablässig abtrünnige Widersacher erzeugen. So sind die Kirchen historische Generatoren einer religiösen und kulturellen Vielfalt, die oft von sich aus einen politischen Ausgleich forden, der nur unter Bedingungen von Föderalität und Subsidarität erbracht werden kann.

Doch da insbesondere die großen Kirchen sowohl in ihrer räumlich und geistlich weit verzweigten Organisation, mit ihren große Unterschiede überbrückenden supranationalen Aufgaben, mit der Vielfalt ihrer kirchlichen und klösterlichen Einrichtungen sowie mit der Heterogenität ihrer politischen, sozialen und kulturellen Aktivitäten nur im Rahmen einer *internen föderalen Ordnung* zusammen zu halten waren, so gaben sie auch durch ihre Organisation Anregungen für die politische Bewältigung der vielfältigen Aufgaben in einem Staat. Zugleich spricht es, so meine ich, für sich, dass die abgespaltenen Kirchen sogleich selbst nach einer föderalen Ordnung suchen, obgleich sie im Schutz ihrer Landesherren bereit sind, sich eine zentralistische Verfassung zu geben. Mit Vorblick auf das Jubiläum von 2017 wäre es hilfreich, auch darauf zu achten, welche evolutionären Impulse die Reformation dem Glauben als einer kulturellen Produktivkraft gegeben hat.

4 Der tradierte außenpolitische Primat der Föderation

Die scheinbar abschweifenden Überlegungen zur Kirchenorganisation führen mich ins Zentrum meiner kurzen Ausführungen zu den beiden Themabegriffen dieser Tagung: In politischen Bündnissystemen, wie es sie seit der griechischen und römischen Antike gegeben hat, gehört der *föderale Gedanke* zur Substanz vertraglicher Abmachung zwischen staatsförmigen Partnern; er schließt die *wechselseitige Hilfeleistung* mit den jeweils gegebenen Kräften der beteiligten Subjekte ein.

Insofern sind *symmachia* und *koinōnia, foedus* und *subsidium,* also die durch Absprachen vereinbarte *Föderation* mit der aus ihr entspringenden *Subsidiarität* ein *altes Geschwisterpaar* der politischen Organisation. Sie sind jedoch auf das Feld außerstaatlicher Aktivitäten beschränkt, setzen von einander ursprünglich unabhängige Partner voraus und bleiben somit in ihrem politischen Zweck begrenzt. So kann es nicht wundern, dass überall dort, wo auch unter nachantiken Bedingungen von politischen Bündnissen eigenständiger Staaten die Rede war und ist, die Idee der Föderation, mit den von ihr in der Sache geforderten Beistandsverpflichtungen, selbstverständlich ist.

Diese – wie wir heute sagen: auf *Außenpolitik* gegründete und sie auch weitestgehend tragende – Tradition tritt in ihrer Bedeutung und Reichweite in den großen *Friedensentwürfen der Neuzeit* hervor und ist inzwischen zu einer *Leitidee des internationalen* Rechts geworden. Auf diesem Feld kann der föderale Gedanke weltumspannend werden – so wie es Kant, der ja nicht mehr bloß einen „Fürstenbund" im Blickfeld hat und weit davon entfernt ist, nur von christlichen Staaten zu sprechen, in seinem Entwurf einer föderalen Weltordnung konzipiert.[13]

Wer diese Konzeption einer globalen Weltföderation gering schätzt, hat sich von einer Anteilnahme an den politischen Fragen der Gegenwart verabschiedet. Alle die Gemeinschaft der Menschen betreffenden Fragen stellen sich längst in einem *globalen Zusammenhang;* ihre Anlässe und ihre Bedeutung lassen sich in der Regel nur noch in ihrer wechselseitigen Verschränkung erkennen; und Antworten oder gar Lösungen sind so gut wie in allen Fällen nur auf dem Weg

---

13 Kant, Immanuel (1971 [1795]): *Zum ewigen Frieden.*

grenzüberschreitender Kooperationen ausmachen. Wo immer Staaten tätig sind, auch dort, wo sie nicht in vorgegebenen Bahnen eines geplanten, vereinbarten oder schon weitgehend realisierten Staatensystems (wie der *Europäischen Union*) eingebunden sind, haben sich auf föderale Zusammenhänge einzulassen, die im *regionalen Kontext* zwangsläufig besonders dicht sein dürften, dennoch teils faktisch, teils tendenziell allein aus sachlichen Gründen[14] eine *globale Dimension* erfordern.

Wer unter diesen Bedingungen meint, er könne durch Austritt aus einer ihm in ihren Pflichten lästigen gewordenen Organisation eine, ohnehin nur in fragwürdigen Theorien beschriebene nationalstaatliche Eigenständigkeit zurückgewinnen, der weiß nicht, wovon er spricht. Und wenn er tatsächlich die Konsequenz zieht, den bestehenden Staatenbund zu verlassen, wird er die meiste Zeit nach seinem Austritt damit verbringen, Anschluss an andere Organisationen zu finden. Welche Vorteile dann damit verbunden sind, kann man schwer prognostizieren; zu vermuten ist allerdings, dass der Neuling weniger gute Bedingungen vorfinden wird, als er in seiner alten Beziehung hatte.

5 Eine neue weltpolitische Konstellation

Die Präferenz für die außenpolitische Perspektive geht von der Prämisse aus, dass es die *Einzelstaaten* sind, die sich durch eigene souveräne Entscheidung in eine Föderation von Staaten einbinden lassen und darin, wenn auch durch eine größere Zahl von vertraglichen Regelungen eingeschränkt, weiterhin *selbst* entscheiden können, wie weit sie ihr in *föderativer Beziehungspflege* und *subsidiärer Eigenleistung* bestehendes Engagement treiben möchten.

Doch so geht es in der bereits zu einem politischen *Gesamtsystem* zusammengewachsenen globalen Welt schon lange nicht mehr zu! Wir befinden uns längst in einem *Realsystem globaler Verflechtungen*, über die vermutlich kein Staat in unumschränkter Souveränität befinden kann. „Vermutlich" sage ich hier nur, um mich der Beweispflicht zu entziehen, ob es auch nur den *Vereinigten Staaten von Amerika* möglich wäre, aus dem *Weltpostverein*, der *Weltbank*, der *UNO*, der *NATO*, der *WHO*, der *OECD* oder auch nur aus einer größeren Zahl von Vereinbarungen über die *Flugsicherheit*, über *Interpol*, den *Zahlungsverkehr*, das *Erdbeben-* und *Tsunami-Warnsystem*, das international gültige *Maßsystem* oder das *IOC* auszusteigen.

---

14 Denen die Politik zu folgen hat, wenn sie ihre Versprechen gegenüber den Menschen erfüllen will. Das ist die demokratische Prämisse, denen meine Überlegungen folgen.

Natürlich gibt es Ausnahmen wie Nordkorea, Weißrussland, den Tschad oder eine Reihe von Zwergstaaten, die vornehmlich darauf zu achten haben, dass ihre Grenzen offen und ihre Steuern extrem niedrig bleiben, dass ihre Casinos nicht zahlungsunfähig werden und ihre Briefmarken weiterhin Interessenten finden. Gewiss ist es auch richtig, dass ein nicht geringer Teil der wachsenden globalen Verbindlichkeiten auch über staatliche Grenzen hinweg bewältigt werden kann; doch der Anteil der nicht verhandelbaren technischen Anteile steigt so rasch an, dass die früher so genannten „Sachzwänge" der Politik immer geringere Spielräume offen lassen. Man kann auch, wie man weiß, den Umweltschutz sträflich vernachlässigen. Aber kein entwickelter Staat kann es sich erlauben, den globalen Konferenzen fernzubleiben. Und gesetzt, es gibt effiziente und ökonomisch vertretbare Technologien, wird sich keine Regierung, die Wahlen gewinnen will, erlauben, die normierenden Absprachen zu missachten.

Alle technisch, militärisch und zivilrechtlich entwickelten Länder befinden sich untereinander in einem derart hohen Zustand gegenseitiger Vernetzung, dass es allenfalls noch eine theoretische Chance gibt, den *politischen Realverbund* zu verlassen. Sowenig es einem Staat möglich ist, auf ein *Gesundheits-* und *Bildungssystem*, auf den grenzüberschreitenden *Straßen-, Schienen-* und *Luftverkehr* oder einen *Energieverbund*, zu verzichten, so unbedingt ist seine Verpflichtung, sich für *Handel* und *Geldverkehr* offen zu halten, den *Sport*, den *Tourismus*, die *mediale Kommunikation* zu pflegen und die Kontrolle der *Kernreaktoren*, der *Waffenproduktion* und der *epidemischen Erkrankungen* zuzulassen und, dies vor allem, den *wissenschaftlichen Austausch* zu fördern.

Aus gegebenem Anlass wollen wir die *Sicherheitsinteressen* nicht vergessen, zu denen auch die *Geheimdienste*, nicht nur in den USA, sondern auch bei uns in Europa gehören. Um es noch einmal etwas grundsätzlicher zu sagen: Die *Technik*, die – bislang weitgehend *unbenannt* und gewiss in vielem noch *unbekannt* – seit ihren Anfängen die politische Organisation sowohl *erfordert* wie *ermöglicht*,[15] die der Politik in Athen und Rom eine neuartige auf *öffentliche Kenntnisse, individuelle Freiheit* und *rechtliche Konstitution* gegründete *kulturelle Dynamik* gegeben hat und der kein geringer Anteil an der *Herausbildung des neuzeitlichen Nationalstaats*

---

15 „Pharao" bedeutet ursprünglich „Herr der Kanäle". Man musste also Bewässerungssysteme bauen können, ehe ihr Schutz und die Bewältigung der durch sie geschaffenen Erträge ebenso wie die mit ihnen entstehenden Konflikte nötig wurden. Offenkundig ist der Zusammenhang zwischen militärischer und politischer Organisation, in der Entstehung der frühen Staaten im vorderasiatischen Raum. Die Verarbeitung von Erzen und die Waffenproduktion machen die Technik sogar zur treibenden Kraft der politischen Entwicklung. Doch schon bei den Leistungen der Institutionen, vornehmlich natürlich der politischen Administration ist der technische Anteil nicht zu übersehen.

zukommt – diese den Menschen bis in sein Inneres konstituierende *Technik* wird uns angesichts der *dichten Besiedlung der Erde*, der immer noch *wachsenden Erdbevölkerung* und (das kann hier nicht mehr als eine Abkürzung sein) der *digitalen Innovation* zu *neuen Formen der politischen Organisation* gleichermaßen nötigen wie befähigen.[16]

6 Die neue Form der weltpolitischen Organisation

Um aus der geschilderten Lage in aller Kürze eine organisatorische Konsequenz zu ziehen, stelle ich abschließend *zwei Thesen* auf, die ich nur kurz kommentiere, um sie im letzten Punkt meiner Überlegungen mit einer Konsequenz für die, wie ich meine, konstitutive Rolle von *Föderation und Subsidiarität* zu verbinden:

Die *erste* These bietet eine Entscheidung in der von Immanuel Kant prominent verhandelten Alternative zwischen einer zentralistischen *Weltrepublik* und einer dezentralen *Föderation* aller friedensfähigen Staaten. Ich bin nicht sicher, ob darin für Kant ein echter Gegensatz bestanden hat. Jedenfalls hat er ihn in derart *salomonischer Weise* erörtert, dass man schon herauszuhören vermeint, dass er nicht wirklich an eine echte politische Entscheidungsfrage glaubt. In neuerer Zeit aber ist das Problem wiederholt kontrovers und mit Optionen für jeweils eine der beiden Seiten erörtert worden.

In seiner Friedensschrift von 1795 sagt Kant, „*in thesei*" spräche alles für die zentralstaatliche Organisation einer Weltrepublik, denn nur in ihr könne es das staatsrechtlich unerlässliche Gewaltmonopol geben, das eine einheitliche Rechtsprechung und ein in sich konsequentes politisches Handeln ermöglicht. Wenn ein rechtlich verbindlicher Frieden herrschen solle, dann habe es ein *Frieden* zu sein, wie ihn nur ein *Staat im Inneren* schaffen könne. Damit wäre der alle Menschen umfassende *Weltstaat* die durch die Theorie als zwingend anzusehende Perspektive allen politischen Handelns. Alle Politik wäre dann, wie Luhmann gerne sagte, „Weltinnenpolitik".

„*In hypothesi*" hingegen muss man nach Kant von der Trägheit der bestehenden Einzelstaaten ausgehen, die auf ihr Machtmonopol mit der zugehörigen Handlungskompetenz nicht freiwillig verzichten möchten. Also spreche mit Blick auf den realen Gang der kommenden Geschichte alles für eine *Weltföderation* republikanischer Staaten, die sich auf die drei Definitivartikel der internationalen Friedenssicherung verständigen und gemeinsam Frieden wahren.

---

16 Dazu vom Verf. (2014).

Sofern man nach zwei Jahrhunderten schrecklichster Kriege überhaupt davon sprechen kann, hat Kant mit seiner skeptischen Annahme *in hypothesi* Recht behalten. Ohne Not werden die Staaten ihre Selbständigkeit nicht aufgeben. Es hat zwar lange gedauert, bis man seine Friedensidee überhaupt ernst genommen hat; aber *Völkerbund* und *Vereinte Nationen* haben sich in ihrer Gründungsphase als Organisation im Vorfeld einer auf die Menschenrechte gegründeten Föderation verstanden. Die Bemühungen um die kontinentalen Zusammenschlüsse von Staaten in Europa, Lateinamerika und Ostasien, vielleicht auch im westasiatisch-osteuropäischen Raum mit einem Zentrum in Moskau, sprechen nicht gegen eine solche Entwicklung, auch wenn es eines Tages die *Vereinigten Staaten von Europa* geben sollte. Ein Weltstaat, gar eine Weltrepublik, ist nicht in Sicht. Das kann man – angesichts der mit ihm in seinem Inneren drohenden totalen Machtentfaltung – als sehr beruhigend ansehen.

Meine *erste These* ist nun, dass der *Weltstaat*, ob republikanisch oder nicht, politisch gar nicht mehr nötig ist. Denn, wie bereits angedeutet, gibt es längst *reale Verbindungen der Staaten*, die sich um ein Lebensniveau auf dem Stand der erreichten technischen, ökonomischen und kulturellen Entwicklung bemühen. Durch die bestehenden Verbindungen in Handel und Verkehr, in Wissenschaft und Kultur sind sie, *nicht nur faktisch*, sondern in der Regel auch durch *rechtverbindliche Verträge und Absprachen* so eng vernetzt, dass sie sich selbst massiv gefährden würden, wenn sie auch nur einen Teil der Vereinbarungen aufkündigen würden. Denn dadurch gingen nicht nur die materialen Vorteile verloren: Durch das zunehmend international gültige Recht gibt es eine *steigende Verbindlichkeit*, die unter Berücksichtigung der wachsenden internationalen Gerichtsbarkeit, ein *unilaterales Gewaltmonopol* eines Weltstaats entbehrlich machen könnte.

Man braucht also die *in thesei* postulierte, schon im weitesten Vorfeld mit zahlreichen politischen Befürchtungen befrachtete *Weltrepublik* nicht, um eine *gesicherte politische Weltordnung* für möglich zu halten. Es genügt, die bestehenden Staaten rechtlich zunehmend enger an einander zu binden und sie auf gemeinsame Grundsätze einer humanen Lebensordnung zu verpflichten. Eine föderale Organisation aller Staaten könnte vollauf genügen, um alle Aufgaben, die zu erledigen man von einem Weltstaat erwartet, zu bewältigen. Gleichzeitig bietet nur die Pluralität der beteiligten Kräfte eine Chance, die Gefahr einer Tyrannei durch ein Machtmonopol zu mindern. Hier wäre es der *Föderalismus*, der einer demokratischen Organisation einer globalen politischen Einheit zu Hilfe käme.

Überdies gehört nur wenig Phantasie dazu, sich das Kräftegleichgewicht innerhalb der globalen politischen Körperschaft unter Bedingungen der *Subsidiarität* vorzustellen. Denn nur sie kann unter den Konditionen einer föderalen politischen Organisation die Kräfte eines lebendigen Wettbewerbs entfachen, ohne den es keine Leistungsgerechtigkeit im Weltmaßstab geben kann. Denn ohne

Subsidiarität gäbe es nur abstrakte Verteilungsprobleme, mit deren Lösung eine zentrale Instanz definitiv überfordert wäre.

Meine *zweite These* schließt an die erste an und bringt lediglich die Einsicht zum Ausdruck, dass die Politik nicht nur auf *Pluralität*, sondern auch auf den *Antagonismus* der sie tragenden und fördernden Kräfte angewiesen ist. Um sich die Produktivität der politischen Konkurrenz zu erhalten, wäre es definitiv zu wenig, nur auf die *innere Opposition* in einem Weltstaat zu setzen, aber wohl auch zu viel, wenn es angesichts der Ungleichheit der Mächte an der *Kräfteverteilung* in der gegenwärtigen Staatenwelt bliebe. Deshalb wäre es von größtem Vorteil, wenn man den Großmächten *mit neu geschaffenen politischen Kräften* ökonomisch, technologisch, kulturell und damit auch *politisch opponieren* könnte.

Also bedarf es dort, wo dies geographisch, historisch und kulturell möglich ist, eines engeren Zusammenschlusses in einer *Vereinigung verschiedener* Staaten. Hier liegt, um es kurz zu machen, die historische Notwendigkeit der *Europäischen Union*.

Nach den Kriegen, die Europa in seiner Geschichte zerfetzt und im letzten Jahrhundert fast gänzlich vernichtet haben, war es ein elementares Gebot des *gesunden Menschenverstandes* und der *Humanität*, endlich ein *einiges Europa* zu schaffen. Jean-Claude Junckers Wort, dass, wer an der Notwendigkeit der europäischen Vereinigung zweifele, einen Soldatenfriedhof des Ersten oder des Zweiten Weltkriegs besuchen solle, gilt nach wie vor. Aber es gibt auch einen *politischen Imperativ* zu einer *eigenständigen* Europäischen Union, wenn man an die wirtschaftliche und wissenschaftliche Zukunft Europas denkt. Jedes einzelne Land hat nur dann eine Chance, sich in seiner Eigenart zu erhalten, wenn es sie selbstbestimmt in eine europäische Gemeinschaft einbringt. Das ist freilich nur der erste Aspekt meiner *zweiten These*. Denn über ihm sollte die global-politische Perspektive nicht vergessen werden: Wenn wir die Qualität und die Zukunft einer Politik im Weltmaßstab sichern wollen, brauchen wir ein Europa, das mit den *derzeitigen und künftigen* Weltmächten in Asien und Amerika wirksam konkurrieren kann.

7 Die konstitutive Rolle von Föderation und Subsidiarität

Nachdem die Ideen der *Föderation* und der *Subsidiarität* ihr realpolitisches Dasein wesentlich unterhalb der Schwelle politisch-theoretischer Wahrnehmung gefristet haben, ist es nun an der Zeit, auch ihre *konstitutive Aufgabe* theoretisch zu exponieren und praktisch umzusetzen. Dazu kann ich hier bestenfalls einen Anstoß geben, bei dem es mir wichtig ist, die mit beiden Ideen verbundene *prinzipielle Anerkennung* der *Gleichheit der Partner* hervorzuheben.

Dazu gehören das *Recht* und eine *politische Kultur*, die es bislang in der Politik nur stellen- und zeitweise geben hat. Sie gilt es zu schaffen und auf eine verlässliche Grundlage zu stellen. Das ist der *erste Punkt*.

Bislang hat die *Politik der dominierenden Mächte* derart im Vordergrund gestanden, dass dort, wo die *Föderation* überhaupt zum Thema werden konnte, lediglich das *Ob* im Vordergrund gestanden hat. Doch nun kommt es darauf an, über das *Wie* zu sprechen. Das ist der *zweite Punkt*.

Das *Ob*, so meine ich, kann angesichts der zahlreichen *ethnischen, religiösen, sprachlichen* und *regionalen* Konflikte in Europa und anderswo nicht strittig sein. Ich erinnere nur an die Bestrebungen der Katalanen und der Basken, der Nordiren und der Schotten oder an die Ukraine, die wohl nicht vor dem Ausbruch eines Bürgerkrieges stehen müsste, wenn es in Russland, in der Sowjetunion und schließlich in dem wieder selbständig gewordenen Land *föderale Strukturen* gegeben hätte.

An *dritter* Stelle wäre die *korrelative Stellung von Föderation und Subsidiarität* zu exponieren. Rein historisch erscheint das wenig plausibel, weil beide Prinzipien, nachdem man sie endlich zum Gegenstand der Aufmerksamkeit machte, in der Regel nur *für sich* beraten wurden. Jedenfalls gilt das für die amerikanischen *Federalists* und den zur Überwindung zwischenstaatlicher Gegensätze entworfenen *Föderalismus kooperierender Völker einerseits* und für die erwähnte *kirchenorganisatorische Debatte andererseits*.

Auch bei der Suche nach der im 19. Jahrhundert endlich auch politisch aufgenommenen *sozialen Frage*, in der *kirchliche Laienorganisationen* und *gewerkschaftsnahe Gruppen* sowie die theoretisch einflussreiche *Genossenschaftsbewegung* das *Subsidiaritätsprinzip* in Deutschland überhaupt erst bewusst gemacht haben, ging es um *innenpolitische Initiativen* mit einer sehr begrenzten internationalen Reichweite. Der föderale Gedanke kam dabei, wenn ich richtig sehe, nur am Rande vor.

Das würde ich zu den Besonderheiten rechnen, die durch die äußeren politischen Gegebenheiten unschwer zu erklären sind. Schauen wir auf die *Sache* (oder besser gesagt: auf das *Problemfeld*), auf die (oder das) sich beide politische Konzepte beziehen, dann geht es in beiden Fällen um die *Beförderung eines politischen Ganzen* unter angemessener Einschätzung der Leistung der einzelnen Partner: *Die Föderation bündelt die Kräfte zu Gunsten des Ganzen, und die Subsidiarität verfolgt das gleiche Ziel durch Entlastung des Ganzen durch größtmögliche Mobilisierung der Kräfte der jeweils Beteiligten.*

Dabei liegt der politische Kern, um den es an *vierter* Stelle gehen könnte, *im gemeinsamen Ursprung* beider Ideen, der in nichts anderem besteht als in der größtmöglichen *Selbstbestimmung der beteiligten Partner.* Der *Föderalist* möchte *aus eigener Einsicht* und nach *seinen besten Kräften* mitwirken, dabei aber seine *Identität* und seine *Entscheidungsmöglichkeit* nicht verlieren. Der *Subsidiarist*, will eben diese Eigenständigkeit soweit wie irgend möglich auch in den *materialen politischen Entscheidungen* wahren und denkt dabei nicht nur an die bloße Sicherung seiner Kompetenzen; ihm geht es vielmehr um deren *optimalen Einsatz* für das politische und soziale Ganze. Durch das Ziel der *Aktivierung und Mobilisierung seiner eigenen Kräfte* überbietet der Subsidiarist den Föderalisten. Während der eine auf dem *formalen Gesichtspunkt* ausgewogener Beteiligung unter prinzipiell Gleichen gerichtet ist, ist der Subsidiarist der *materiale Föderalist.*

Wie mein langer Anlauf zu diesem kurzes Abschluss schon erkennen lässt, läge mir an *fünfter Stelle*, an einer genauen historisch-systematischen Einordnung in den *Kontext der politischen Ideengeschichte.* Meine Neigung wäre, daran zu glauben, dass sich im Vordringen von *Föderalismus* und *Subsidarität* eine Wende in der Schwerpunktsetzung des politischen Denkens anzeigt. Meine Hoffnung zielt darauf, dass die Logik der Globalisierung eine *Ausweitung des rechtsstaatlichen Denkens* mit sich bringt, die eine *Domestizierung der Machtpolitik* einschließt.

Nach der Problemlage der Menschheit hat die *Machtpolitik der Staaten* nicht nur an Interesse, sondern auch an Bedeutung verloren. Die Menschen interessiert die *Kunst des Möglichen* inzwischen angesichts der scheinbaren Unmöglichkeit, die Erde als ein Ort zu erhalten, der dem menschlichen Leben eine *Perspektive* erhält. Dazu gehört nach wie vor an erster Stelle der *Frieden.* Aber schon mit Blick auf den Frieden sind die Fragen der *Ressourcen-* und der *Umweltsicherung* sowie die von Jahr zur Jahr *dramatisch anwachsenden sozialen Gegensätze* hinzugekommen.

Davon ist derzeit mit besten Gründen überall die Rede, so dass ich dazu am Ende nicht mehr sagen muss. Umso mehr hoffe ich, mit meiner abschließend exponierten Erwartung, dass sich mit dem Erstarken des *politiktheoretischen Zwillings von Föderalismus* und *Subsidiarität* eine *Wende in der Aufmerksamkeit* für die wahren Probleme der von uns allen benötigten und geforderten Politik anzeigt, eine Anregung zu geben.

Bibliographie

Aristoteles, Politik.

Dihle, Albrecht (2009): Hellas und der Orient. Phasen wechselseitiger Rezeption, Berlin/Boston.

Forst, Rainer (2003): Toleranz im Konflikt. Geschichte, Gehalt und Gegenwart eines umstrittenen Begriffs, Frankfurt a. M.

Gerhardt, Volker (1976): Vernunft und Interesse, Phil.-Diss. Münster 1974, Münster.
Gerhardt, Volker (1996): Vom Willen zur Macht. Anthropologie und Metaphysik der Macht am exemplarischen Fall Friedrich Nietzsches, Berlin/New York (Habilitationsschrift, Münster 1983).
Gerhardt, Volker (1998): Zur historischen Bedeutung des Westfälischen Friedens, in: Bussmann, Klaus/Schilling, Heinz (Hg.): 1648: Krieg und Frieden in Europa (Katalog zur Ausstellung 350 Jahre Westfälischer Frieden). Bd. 3, Münster/München, S. 485–489.
Gerhardt, Volker (1999): Selbstbestimmung. Das Prinzip der Individualität, Stuttgart.
Gerhardt, Volker (2002): Immanuel Kant: Vernunft und Leben, Stuttgart.
Gerhardt, Volker (2007): Partizipation. Das Prinzip der Politik, München.
Gerhardt, Volker (2008): Die erste Lehre von der Verfassung. Der Beitrag der Nomoi zur Theorie der Politik, in: Volker Gerhardt/Reinhard Mehring/Henning Ottmann/Martyn P. Thompson/Barbara Zehnpfennig (Hg.): Jahrbuch Politisches Denken 18, S. 4–31.
Gerhardt, Volker (2012): Öffentlichkeit. Die politische Form des Bewusstseins, München.
Gerhardt, Volker (2013): Die Quadratur der Politik. Bürger zwischen individueller Entfaltung und gesellschaftlicher Verpflichtung, in: Christoph Eichert/Roland Löffler (Hg. im Auftrag der Herbert Quandt-Stiftung): Die Bürger und ihr Staat. Ein Verhältnis am Wendepunkt?, 33. Sinclair-Haus-Gespräche 2013, Freiburg/Basel/Wien, S. 62–68.
Gerhardt, Volker (2014): Licht und Schatten der Öffentlichkeit. Zu Voraussetzungen und Folgen der digitalen Innovation, Wien.
Gerhardt, Volker (o. D.): Demokratie als politische Form der Menschheit, Vortrag.
Kant, Immanuel (1971 [1795]): Zum ewigen Frieden, in: Kants Werke. Akademie Ausgabe (1902). Bd. 8. Preussische Akademie der Wissenschaften (Ed.), Berlin/New York, S. 341–386.
Meier, Christian (1981): Die Entstehung des Politischen bei den Griechen, Frankfurt a. M.
Meier, Christian (2011): Griechen und Europa, Die großen Herausforderungen der Freiheit im fünften Jahrhundert v. Chr., Europavortrag am 20. Januar 2010, in: Universitätsreden Nr. 89, Universität Saarbrücken, Universaar, S. 15 ff.
Ottmann, Henning (2006): Geschichte des politischen Denkens, Bd. 3, Stuttgart.
Thukydides, Geschichte des Peloponnesischen Krieges.

Andreas Føllesdal

Subsidiarity to the Rescue for the European Courts? Resolving Tensions Between the Margin of Appreciation and Human Rights Protection

The empty phrases concerning the states' margin of appreciation—repeated in the court's judgments for too long already—are unnecessary circumlocutions, serving only to indicate abstrusely that the States may do anything the Court does not consider incompatible with human rights [...]
(Brauch 2005, 148)

Introduction

One of the constant tensions in multilevel legal and political orders concerns the allocation of authority among the bodies at different levels.[1] What scope of autonomy should they enjoy over various issue areas, and how should they be checked or balanced? One of the recent arenas for such tension and debate concerns the role of the European Court of Human Rights (ECtHR), which is entrusted the power of judicial review over the member states of the Council of Europe's compliance with the European Convention on Human Rights (ECHR, Convention). According to the 'Copenhagen Criteria' of accession to the European Union (EU), the ECtHR thus serves important gate keeper functions for applicant states to the European Union (European Council 1993). It also monitors the continual compliance with the Convention by existing members—which is of shared concern for all EU states. In exercising its powers, the Court must often combine apparently irreconcilable requirements: it must assess and sometimes criticize the states' legislation and policies—yet respect the sovereignty of those of the states which are well functioning democracies. Further controversies have

---

1 This article was written under the auspices of ERC Advanced Grant 269841 MultiRights—on the Legitimacy of Multi-Level Human Rights Judiciary, and the Research Council of Norway through its Centres of Excellence Funding Scheme, project number 223274—PluriCourts The Legitimacy of the International Judiciary. The present version has benefited from discussions at a conference on the Philosophical Foundations of Federalism—University of Luxembourg May 5, 2014. I am grateful for comments received at that occasion and from Stian Øby Johansen.

been fuelled by the EU member states' decision that the EU itself shall accede to the ECHR (European Council 2007, Art 6.2), especially by the Court of Justice of the European Union's (CJEU) rejection of the draft accession treaty (CJEU 2014). The CJEU was *inter alia* sceptical of subjecting the EU to supervision by the ECtHR.

Protests against how the ECtHR manages the dilemma between protecting human rights and respecting sovereignty came to a peak at a meeting of the Council of Europe's Committee of Ministers on the future of the European Court of Human Rights in Brighton 2012. The meeting *inter alia* agreed to subtle changes to the Convention. When Protocol 15 comes into force the Preface will conclude thus:

> Affirming that the High Contracting Parties, in accordance with the principle of subsidiarity, have the primary responsibility to secure the rights and freedoms defined in this Convention and the Protocols thereto, and that in doing so they enjoy a margin of appreciation, subject to the supervisory jurisdiction of the European Court of Human Rights established by this Convention. (Protocol No. 15 Amending the Convention on Fundamental Freedoms 2013)

This change introduces two new phrases into the Convention. The principle of subsidiarity is familiar from federal thought, expressing a rebuttable presumption to place authority as local as possible. The margin of appreciation doctrine was developed by the Court itself. The Court thereby grants a state the authority, within certain limits, to determine whether the rights of the ECHR are violated in a particular case.

Critics may fear that these two quite diffuse and contested phrases will further obfuscate rather than improve on the Court's response to the dilemma between human rights protection and respect for sovereignty. Subsidiarity is used in so many different ways that it may provide an intellectual guise to cover up the Court's complete abdication from the role of human rights protector in Europe by granting states broad discretion. EU accession—if it will indeed occur—will pose further challenges: does subsidiarity guide the decisions about which of the two European courts should be superior, and how they should exercise their authority? Should the EU enjoy a similar margin of appreciation as the member states of the Council of Europe? That might seem to follow from the general presumption in the treaty negotiations that the EU should be treated on an equal footing with the contracting states. For instance, the negotiation team behind the draft agreed inter alia that "current control mechanism of the Convention should, as far as possible, be preserved and applied to the EU in the same way as to other High Contracting Parties" (47+1 (2013), para 7).

This chapter seeks to reduce such fears. The margin of appreciation, duly specified in ways guided by the principle of subsidiarity, can contribute to alleviate this tension in a defensible way. A 'Principle of Subsidiarity' can alleviate some of the challenges posed by the margin of appreciation doctrine, in particular that it sacrifices human rights protection on the altar of respect for state sovereignty. Section 1 presents the Margin of appreciation doctrine and some criticism raised against it, section 2 sketches versions of the principle of subsidiarity relevant for this discussion. Section 3 seeks to bring subsidiarity to bear on the question of which authority the ECtHR should enjoy within a multi-level European legal order, and in particular why it should grant states a certain margin of appreciation. Section 4 considers how these arguments concerning a margin of appreciation applies to the European Union—leaving the many other aspects of accession aside.

1 The margin of appreciation and its critics

The margin of appreciation doctrine ('the Doctrine') is a practice whereby the Court sometimes defers to the state's own judiciary about whether the Convention rights have been violated. The Doctrine is often traced back to the 1958 *Cyprus case* where the then Commission asserted that the UK authorities "should be able to exercise a certain measure of discretion in assessing the extent strictly required by the exigencies of the situation" (*Greece v United Kingdom* 1958–1959). In this case the issue was a state of public emergency, an exemption clause in Art 15. A margin of appreciation is claimed by the Court to be appropriate for at least three main issue areas.

- 'Balancing' the rights against other urgent issues such as emergencies, public safety, the economic well-being of the country etc—as permitted for several rights to private life, religion, expression etc (Art 8, 9, 10).
- 'Balancing' or 'trade-offs' among different private human rights in the Convention—such as between freedom of expression (Article 10) and privacy (Article 8).
- How to apply the norms to the specific circumstances of a state, which may depend on shared values and traditions or perceived threats.

To grant a margin of appreciation, the Court often requires that the accused state has undertaken a 'proportionality test' to check if the rights violation could have been avoided by other policies in pursuit of the same social objectives.

The Doctrine has received much praise and much criticism, some of both are well deserved. It expresses some respect for sovereign democratic self-government but only within some limits: for instance, the Court has hardly ever granted a margin of appreciation concerning infringements to rights to life, or against torture or slavery (Art 2, 3, 4). Yet the 'Doctrine' is so vague and multifarious that even to refer to it in the singular, and to call it a 'doctrine' seems unduly charitable. More fundamentally, the margin of appreciation doctrine may grant both the ECtHR and powerful states too much discretion, and put human rights at risk, contrary to the purpose of the ECHR.

There are at least three kinds of concern. Firstly, the Doctrine creates legal uncertainty, because states are unable to predict and hence cannot avoid violations of the ECHR (Lester 2009; cf. Brauch 2005, 125, Macklem 2006, Arai-Takahashi 2013). Indeed, even the judges of the Court disagree about the Doctrine to such an extent that legal certainty seems at risk:

> I believe that it is high time for the Court to banish that concept from its reasoning. It has already delayed too long in abandoning this hackneyed phrase and recanting the relativism it implies. (*Z v Finland* (1997), Judge De Meyer partly dissenting)

To some extent the uncertainty is due to the legal norms, rather than the margin of appreciation doctrine itself. Consider Art 10 which protects freedom of expression—but

> [...] subject to such formalities, conditions, restrictions or penalties as are prescribed by law and are necessary in a democratic society, in the interests of national security, territorial integrity or public safety, for the prevention of disorder or crime, for the protection of health or morals, for the protection of the reputation or rights of others, for preventing the disclosure of information received in confidence, or for maintaining the authority and impartiality of the judiciary. (Art 10, para 2)

The Court often—but not always—grants states a margin of appreciation in determining whether such interests override the right. Thus in the *Sunday Times* case, a majority of eleven judges found against the UK, that Art 10 protected newspapers reporting on a case. But nine dissenting judges held that this should have been left to the domestic judiciary:

> The difference of opinion separating us from our colleagues concerns above all the necessity of the interference and the margin of appreciation which, in this connection, is to be allowed to the national authorities. (*The Sunday Times v United Kingdom* 1979).

Similar disagreements among judges are legio (*Observer and Guardian v United Kingdom* 1991, *Wingrove v United Kingdom* 1996). One upshot of this criticism is that the Doctrine should be made more precise, *and* more consistently applied, than is presently the case.

A second concern is that the vague Doctrine leaves too much discretion to the judges. Again, it would seem that one main response is to make the rules of the doctrine—including the consensus test—more precise.

A more precise Doctrine does not automatically avoid other objections: that such discretion entails a failure of the ECtHR to protect human rights in the short and long run. The Court thereby "side-step[s] its responsibility as the ultimate interpretative authority in the Convention system" (Yourow 1996, 181). Indeed, "[t]he essence of the international control mechanism may evaporate if there is in fact no effective check upon national power" (ibid).

Is this a correct criticism? If the Court is in the habit of granting all states a very wide margin, the value added of the ECtHR diminishes: it leaves each state to be judge in its own case. Yet as practiced, the margin is not granted to the non-derogable rights to life (Art 2), against torture (Art 3), slavery or forced labour (Art 4), though the ECtHR has referred to the margin of appreciation with regard to some aspects of Art 2 (cf. *Budayeva v Russia* 2008) and Art 3 (*M.C. v Bulgaria* 2003 and *Berganovic v Croatia* 2009).[2] Moreover, the margin of appreciation often concerns a 'balancing' among rights in the ECHR. Such 'balancing' does not entail *less stringent* human rights protection, but rather how the government gives some rights a certain weight compared to other rights. Finally, national courts enjoy such a margin only when the ECtHR is satisfied that the national court has duly considered several conditions, in the form of a proportionality test—in good faith (*Rasmussen v Denmark* 1988).

So I submit that a more specified margin of appreciation can reduce several of the concerns stemming from vagueness, and not risk its objective unduly. But such specification must be guided by an understanding of why a margin of appreciation should be accepted at all. This is the question for which a Principle of Subsidiarity may be thought to offer guidance.

How can the Doctrine help prevent domination in the form of human rights abuses over citizens from their own domestic authorities, without subjecting well-functioning democracies to undue constraints from international judges at the Court, as part of the multi-level European legal order? I submit that one way to limit the risk of domination is to specify the doctrine, in light of a general account of what the ECtHR should do—and guided by principle of subsidiarity.

---

2 Thanks to Oddný Mjöll Arnardóttir for these references.

2 Subsidiarity

Several authors claim that a principle of subsidiary supports 'the' margin of appreciation doctrine (Benvenisti 1999, Spielmann 2012, Kratochvil 2011, del Moral 2006, 614, Sweeney 2005). I submit that there is some truth to this claim, mainly in that appeals to subsidiarity indicate *the sorts of arguments* that may be made.

The 'principle of subsidiarity' has a variety of versions, each with long historical roots (Føllesdal 1998). In the history of political thought principles of subsidiarity address the issue of how to allocate or use authority within a political or legal order, typically amongst a centre and member units within some sort of federal structure. For our purposes what unites the various traditions is the assumption that the burden of argument lies with attempts to centralize authority. Various principles of subsidiarity express a commitment to leave as much authority to the more local authorities as possible, consistent with achieving the stated objectives. Different versions will argue that member units or the centre should have the final say for such decisions; or that central action should be permitted or instead required under certain conditions; some versions hold that central action should *replace* local decisions, others maintain that the centre should rather seek to bolster the local authority's ability to make correct decisions.

For our purposes, it may be helpful to distinguish a 'state centric' principle of subsidiarity from 'person-centred' versions of the principle. The former matches a standard presumption of international law that sovereign states are free to decide whether they have shared objectives which they judge are better secured by delegating some of their authority to some central body—such as an international court. Such arguments may be based on states' inability or unwillingness to achieve sufficient coordination absent some centralised body, or simply the need for mutual trust that each state actually do their share. Such pooling of sovereignty may thus differ across issue areas depending on the interests of states, the nature of their collective problem, and the new risks induced by a centralized authority.

From this perspective, the central puzzle of international human rights courts is: if they are the solution, what exactly is the problem states have? In light of the answer, what scope should a domestic court retain for adjudicating the state's compliance with the human rights treaty? One answer to the question is that a state may want to 'bind itself' or commit itself to a regional or international human rights court (Alter 2008). At least two audiences are important for states submitting themselves to the ECHR: they may thereby become more credible in the eyes of their citizens and thereby secure their more willing compliance.

And such credibility in the eyes of other states is important for states who pool sovereignty—such as in the EU.

It might seem odd that scrutiny and risks of vocal criticism and sanctions by an international body may enhance trust. The answer lies in authorities' need for credibility among the governed. We can draw on Margaret Levi's discussions of trust to understand this connection. She holds firstly that citizens' sense of political obligation helps elicit compliance:

> Empirically, political obligation rests on the citizen's perception that government actors and other citizens are trustworthy. The activation of obligation implies institutional arrangements that make promises and commitments credible, but it may also require extraordinary acts of compensation to overcome distrust based on past experiences. (Levi 1998, 208)

Second, an important component to secure such voluntary compliance with the law is general trust in the rule of law. Agents of the state must be trusted to use their powers for the common good, and be law abiding and law enforcing. Third, courts that are somewhat independent of the government can bolster such trust in several ways: both to maintain the rule of law, and to give citizens and officials reasons to believe that their rulers indeed uphold the rule of law.

The political leadership can express its commitment to the rule of law precisely by choosing to be monitored by independent courts:

> What defines its commitment to the rule of law is the willingness to be bound by the laws and to ensure that the laws are implemented and enforced universally. (Levi and Epperly 2010, 6)

By deciding to be subject to courts, the leadership ties its own hands and ensures some transparency about what they do. A desired effect is to gain credibility among subjects, by subjecting themselves to such scrutiny. Governing bodies thereby enhance citizens' trust that the authorities do indeed seek to respect and promote the best interests of the subjects. External actors in the form of independent international tribunals thus provide assurance to citizens and other authorities about the authorities' use of power and commitment to the rule of law.

Generally, one may think that a state-centred version of subsidiarity would support as broad a margin of appreciation as possible, consistent with these objectives of maintaining trust, so that the state retains maximal authority.

A 'person-centred' version of subsidiarity does not give such primacy to the state and the interests of states, but instead insists that subsidiarity goes 'all the way down.' The states are not the 'natural' reservoir of sovereign authority, but should only have such legal powers and immunities as needed to secure the shared interests of its members: the communities and municipalities—and ultimately the citizens whose states they are.

From this point of view, the important design challenge of international human rights courts and the margin of appreciation is to grant the state enough authority to promote the interests of its citizens and of foreigners, whilst preventing the abuse of such powers in the form of human rights violations—and generate trust that this is the case, when such trust is well deserved. Regional or international human rights courts can provide such protections—but at the same time, citizens run the risk that these courts misuse or even abuse their power from incompetence or ill will. In particular, the courts should not limit democratic self-governance unduly, insofar as such governments are sufficiently responsive to the best interests of their citizens.

For our purposes here, I submit that the 'person centric' principle of subsidiarity is more plausible. Such conceptions of subsidiarity will not support a broad margin of appreciation in general: that would indeed be contrary to the objectives of the ECHR (Kratochvil 2011, 332). Instead, the arguments for the Doctrine must show that certain interests of individuals require centralized authority above the state, e. g. human rights protected and promoted by the ECHR, but that a margin of appreciation is still permitted or even required.

Indeed, why should a person-centred principle of subsidiarity allow a margin of appreciation at all? It would seem to re-create the problems for which the ECtHR were the solution, namely to prevent the state from being judge in its own case—be it human rights violations or arbitration disputes. States use human rights treaties to bind themselves. Compare the treaties which primarily are to solve shared problems among states, where each state only binds itself as much as necessary to obtain those benefits. In contrast, a state binds itself to an international human rights court in order to enhance its own credibility as a "rule of law", human rights respecting political system. One implication is that treaty interpretations and adjudication should *not* minimize the curtailment of state sovereignty. Nor should a margin of appreciation be as broad as possible —to the contrary, why should states enjoy any margin? We now turn to consider why individuals' interests may require that international human rights judicial review be constrained by a margin of appreciation. This requires us to look at the ECtHR as part of a multi-level legal order.

3 Applying the Principle of Subsidiarity to the ECtHR and its Margin of Appreciation

To apply the principle of subsidiarity properly to the margin of appreciation doctrine involves several steps. We start with the objectives and other functions of the ECHR.

These objectives, stated in the Preamble, are, in short, to help secure "universal and effective recognition and observance of the Rights therein declared" and "to take the first steps for the collective enforcement of certain of the rights stated in the Universal Declaration." Note that this objective does not require harmonization across states, but rather to ensure certain thresholds of human rights protection. The abstraction of human rights may be amongst their virtues, since they can be specified in different ways to reflect such differing circumstances (Etinson 2013). Variation among institutions in different jurisdictions is thus not a threat to this objective—unlike treaties which explicitly aim at the harmonization of various rules, such as the EU.

Another important *de facto* function of the ECtHR concerns its role in the European Union. As per the Copenhagen Criteria it is a gate keeper for entry, in that all applicant states must become subject to the Court as members of the Council of Europe. Moreover, the Court contributes to monitor whether existing member states respect human rights. The latter is important not only for the citizens within the country being monitored, but arguably directly relevant for all in the EU. The Lisbon treaty allows secondary law making in many issue areas on the basis of complex qualified majority voting (European Council 2007, Art 16.3–4). Thus inhabitants are subject to decisions largely decided by politicians of other states than their own. They have good reason to insist that those politicians must be strongly committed to human rights if the subjects are to be able to trust the good will and competence of their new rulers. Suspected violations of human rights triggered reactions against Austria after elections there in 2000 (Føllesdal 2006; 2007). That experience led to the inclusion of a more cautious procedure for the EU in the *Treaty on European Union* (*Treaty on European Union, Nice Amendments* 2001, Art 7.1).

The next question is why, according to a person-centred principle of subsidiarity, should these objectives require the centralization of adjudication of human rights violations to a regional court at all? And which powers should it have—given that full harmonization is not an objective? The express role of the ECtHR is to assist states in securing these objectives: to "ensure the observance of the engagements undertaken by the High Contracting Parties" (Art 19 ECHR). The ECtHR is thus not authorised to promote and protect human rights by all means. Rather, the task of the ECtHR is 'subsidiary' or supportive and supplementary vis-à-vis the states, to *supplement and strengthen* the protection offered by domestic judiciary. States remain primary protectors of human rights. The state remains the primary responsible actor to respect human rights.

Note that to ascertain compliance with the convention requires local and counterfactual knowledge about avoidable abuse or neglect by means of the laws and policies of their government, familiarity about the local culture and circumstances, the risks individuals face due to complex interplay between majority culture and institutions—and about a range of feasible alternative policies which may avoid such violations. This is one reason why the chamber of the ECtHR which hears a case always includes the judge with respect to that particular country.

As regards the need for human rights assurances in a federation with qualified majority voting, international supervisory bodies seem necessary to protect citizens against other EU member state governments, who now share decision making authority over them. This role of human rights judicial review may become more important as the EU becomes more subject to majoritarian mechanisms where all member states can vote. It is then especially important that citizens can trust that all member state authorities exercise such powers responsibly. No political party should enjoy domestic political power that may lead them to favor EU policies that violate human rights. Human rights courts can give assurance to citizens and other member state governments that each of the state governments is committed to human rights—and that majority rule among them thus is not overly risky. Such concerns are arguably even more salient insofar as EU authorities undermine the democratic bases of legitimation in the member states (Føllesdal and Hix 2006).

The next question is then, given the multi-level system where the ECtHR plays this supportive, supplementary role: what contribution does a margin of appreciation doctrine provide? It essentially returns adjudication of the ECHR to the domestic courts of the very same member state accused of a violation.

From the perspective of a person-centred conception of subsidiarity, the state organs should retain the final authority to determine compliance with the Convention when the ECtHR *cannot* or is *unlikely* to provide extra protection. That is: a margin of appreciation should apply insofar and for those objectives, and under those conditions, where the domestic courts and other authorities are *at least as well suited* as the ECtHR to determine whether there is a breach. For instance, there should be a very low risk that the domestic court will skew its judgment unduly in favour of the state in its dispute with its citizens.

What arguments of this kind may be offered for the margin of appreciation doctrine?

Firstly, recall that the Court holds that the margin of appreciation is restricted in the rights it applies to. The Court hardly grants any margin of appreciation when certain rights are at risk under certain emergencies, regardless of what states claim, namely rights against torture or slavery.

Secondly, in the three main issue areas where the Court holds that domestic authorities are better placed than the ECtHR to judge due to local knowledge, this assessment seems plausible: balancing rights against certain urgent issues, balancing among rights, and applying the norms to specific circumstances where there are local traditions and culture at stake. The Court often claims that domestic authorities are in principle better placed than an international court to evaluate such local needs and conditions (*Hatton v the United Kingdom* 2003, 634). Thus the margin of appreciation may be interpreted and assessed as a way the Court expresses subsidiarity by giving the domestic judiciaries the benefit of any doubt. However, the person-centred conception of subsidiarity does not warrant such a general presumption. The Court must assess the risk of human rights abuses in a more nuanced way, as indeed it does.

The ability of local authorities to strike the balance right is not enough: Under which circumstances are local authorities *likely* to make decisions in ways that respect human rights appropriately? When, in short, will domestic laws and policies be sufficiently responsive to the best interests of all citizens, and when will the domestic authorities have mechanisms of self-correction in this regard? I submit that this is more likely under conditions of democratic rule under the rule of law. Such polities are likely to be more responsive to human rights and self-correcting than alternative modes of governance. Under functioning democratic mechanisms and the rule of law the population deliberates about alternative policies and legislative proposals in light of their implications for all affected parties, so as to promote broadly shared interests whilst avoiding harm to anyone; and an independent judiciary protects the human rights of the inhabitants.

On this line of reasoning, the ECtHR is unlikely to provide a better assessment of violations of the Convention than domestic judiciaries when the sort of deliberation has occurred in good faith. Insofar as this argument holds, the ECtHR should allow no margin of appreciation for rights concerning political participation, freedom of expression and other rights required for well-functioning democratic decision making. And indeed, this appears to be a pattern of the margin of appreciation practice:

> [...] taking into account the vital importance in a democratic society of freedom of expression and freedom of the press, the State's margin of appreciation in these cases is very nar-

row indeed. (*Observer and Guardian v United Kingdom* 1991, partly dissenting opinion of Judge Pekkanen; and cf. *Handyside v United Kingdom* 1976, § 49)

Furthermore, the majoritarian democratic mechanisms are not particularly reliable in securing the vital interests and equal respect for those who are likely to regularly find themselves outvoted. For this reason, international courts should not grant a wide margin of appreciation for the vulnerable interests of minorities —such as freedom of religion, even in well-functioning democracies. Again, this pattern appears to be in accordance with the current practice of the margin of appreciation doctrine.

Finally, even democratic deliberative majoritarian decision making is not always well functioning. While domestic authorities may know more about the domestic setting, they need not know much about which alternative policies may serve the legitimate interests and values sufficiently well. This requires comparative perspectives which domestic authorities may be too myopic to discern. Thus it makes sense for the Court to check whether the state has performed a proportionality test when certain human rights appear to be at stake. Such a test checks that state authorities have not overlooked less invasive alternatives, and have not ignored the impact on some groups—and at the same time ensure that the population can be ascertained that this is in fact the case. Such deliberation about alternatives and their impact is of course what well-functioning democratic decision making should be based on.

Insofar as such proportionality testing has not occurred, in well-functioning democracies and elsewhere, the presumption in favor of domestic democratic decision making no longer stands. Indeed, the ECtHR hesitates to grant a margin of appreciation unless there is evidence that the domestic authorities have undertaken such a proportionality test. Thus the Court often states that

> [...] from *Hirst v. the United Kingdom (no. 2)* it could be deduced that the margin of appreciation would be narrower when Parliament had not analysed and carefully weighed the competing interests or assessed the proportionality of blanket rules. (*Lindholm and Others v. Norway [Tomtefestesaken]* 2012, 85)

I submit that such statements by the Court may nudge states into more careful proportionality testing. The Court thereby performs its subsidiarity, supportive function, helping to improve the domestic democratic processes.

4 Should the European Union enjoy a margin of appreciation?

If the EU does become party to the ECHR, this will be an important challenge both for the EU and for the ECtHR. Ratification may reduce the substantive and institutional fragmentation of international human rights law in Europe. But conflicts will not disappear without trace.

One may wonder what value is added if the EU should accede to the ECHR. At first glance not much seems to be at stake, since all member states of the EU have already ratified the ECHR and are subject to review by the ECtHR. The EU— and hence the Union organs including the CJEU—are already treaty bound to respect the ECHR, and the Lisbon Treaty enhances the legal standing of the EU Charter on Fundamental Rights.

One important change wrought by EU's accession is that the EU will be subject to the judgments of the European Court of Human Rights (ECtHR). This court will also monitor, adjudicate and sanction any violations that might arise. They may be violations which the CJEU overlooks—and potential violations by the CJEU itself.[3] Such monitoring may achieve several benefits. Firstly, it helps reduce the risk of violations of the ECHR—violations that the CJEU might not have identified. Such protection is especially important insofar as the chain of delegation from national authorities to EU institutions is too long, and even more so when important EU bodies such as the European Central Bank and the European Commission explicitly or de facto operate beyond direct democratic control. Their treatment both of Union citizens and of their own employees will be held more closely to human rights standards both by the Charter and by ratification.

Human rights bodies may be especially important institutional mechanisms in the EU due to the pervasive mistrust characteristic of 'coming together' federations in general (Stepan 2000). Such political orders emerge when governments seek objectives beyond the reach of any single state, and that cannot be secured by treaty agreements alone. Examples of such objectives include external defense, or common regulations in response to a globalizing economy. A crucial concern for the joining states is to ensure such shared objectives without allowing undesired centralization or harmonization, or other abuse of central authorities. Human rights regulations and monitoring that apply to the centre of the federation reduce or remove some such fear.

---

3 I am grateful to Stian Øby Johansen for this reminder.

This review mechanism can also provide much needed trust *that* the EU does indeed respect these constraints. Such human rights review can serve as a valuable trust-building feature among citizens and authorities in an exceedingly complex multi-level political structure. This is of particular value in a political order where individuals have several sometimes conflicting political obligations, toward both their national and European legislation, and where such conflicts may give rise to understandable suspicions among other Union citizens and politicians. In the case of the EU, the national and Union authorities may thus want the domestic populations and national constitutional courts to trust their human rights compliance. By ratifying the ECHR the national authorities give evidence of such sincerity, since they thereby let independent international organs monitor and even sanction Union authorities.

These benefits notwithstanding, we can expect conflicts of interpretation between the ECtHR and the CJEU, and both about the EU's Charter of fundamental rights relationship to the ECHR and about interpretations of the ECHR. While our focus here is on whether the EU should enjoy a margin of appreciation, the arguments require a brief historical backdrop.

The 1999 Cologne European Council decided to consolidate the fundamental rights that applied to the EU level and make them more visible in a *Charter of Fundamental Rights* (European Council 1999, Art 44 and Appendix IV) (Heinz 2006). The Charter provided a much needed clarification of the legal human rights obligations of member states, and received full legal effect, after prolonged discussions, when the Treaty of Lisbon entered into force December 1, 2009.

The Charter includes a wide range of legal rights. It lists a range of civil, political, economic and social rights of European citizens and others resident in the EU. These legal rights are said to draw on the ECHR, and the case law of the ECtHR, as well as rights derived from the "constitutional traditions" common to the Member States; economic and social rights within the European Social Charter and the Community Charter of Fundamental Social Rights of Workers; and other international conventions to which the EU or its Member States are parties. However, the European Council made no explicit mention of any UN declarations or conventions, though they might be thought to express rights derived from the common 'constitutional traditions'.

Article 52(3) of the Charter seeks to alleviate any conflicts between it and the ECHR by insisting that where there are conflicts, "the meaning and scope of those rights shall be the same as those laid down by the said Convention." This presumably means that the judgments of the ECtHR will be binding on the CJEU. Hitherto the CJEU has seemed to accept the ECtHR's view that member states cannot avoid their obligations under ECHR even as members of the EU, and the CJEU has so far seemed to aim for consistency. But whose interpretation will be decisive is a matter that remains to be discovered—and this may become a contested issue. Indeed, one of the several objections the CJEU raised in its opinion concerning the draft ratification treaty was precisely this.[4]

Following accession the ECHR will become part of EU law (European Union 2007, Art 216(2)). This threatens the role of the CJEU as the ultimate authority on interpretation of EU law—unless the ECtHR always respects the CJEU's decisions. In particular, the ECtHR should not be able to bind the EU to the ECtHR's interpretation of the ECHR (CJEU 2014, para 183–4). In particular, the CJEU claimed that no member state should be allowed to maintain 'higher' human rights standards than the Charter where the EU has harmonized the relevant laws (*Melloni*). Thus the CJEU asserts that *its* interpretation of the ECHR—presumably interpreting it consistently with the Charter—should be authoritative, rather than deferring to the ECtHR's interpretation. ECHR organs should not bind the EU to a particular interpretation of rules of EU law. The point of ratification of the ECHR would however seem to be precisely to subject the EU to the independent control by the ECtHR, on the basis of its interpretation of the ECHR. A reservation to this effect by a state acceding to the ECHR would presumably be struck down as incompatible with the object and purpose of the treaty.[5]

May such differences of interpretation occur in practice? One important source of discrepancy is that the CJEU must weigh the various values and objectives of the EU against each other. While human rights are included among the Union's values in Article 2, Article 3 states several objectives of the Union. In particular, the four economic freedoms of the single market—the free movement of people, goods, services and capital—are on the same legal footing as the Charter of Fundamental Rights. Several cases indicate how the CJEU seeks to 'balance' human rights against these market enhancing freedoms when they conflict, e.g. by means of a proportionality test (de Vries 2013, discussing *inter alia* Laval 2007, Schmidberger 2003, Viking 2007, Omega 2004).[6] If the EU accedes to the ECHR on the ordinary terms, it will be for the ECtHR to decide when it is asked to judge the CJEU's weighing. Consider in particular that the ECtHR,

---

4 The opinion states several other objections. The opinion has received much attention, including at http://eulawanalysis.blogspot.com.br/2014/12/the-cjeu-and-eus-accession-to-echr.html, http://blogg.uio.no/jus/smr/multirights/content/opinion-213-a-bag-of-coal-from-the-cjeu, http://www.verfassungsblog.de/opinion-213-eu-accession-echr-christmas-bombshell-european-court-justice/#.VbD-VbPtmkp, http://echrblog.blogspot.com.br/2014/12/cjeu-rules-draft-agreement-on-eu.html, http://europeanlawblog.eu/?p=2731.
5 http://europeanlawblog.eu/?p=2731#sthash.Md1Swv9M.dpuf.
6 I am grateful to Stian Øby Johansen for nudging this expansion.

but not necessarily the CJEU, grants human rights priority over ordinary legislation and public policies.

On the other hand, the ECtHR grants a certain scope of discretion to the parties who have ratified the ECHR. Should the EU and the CJEU come to enjoy similar leeway?

Recall that the "Margin of Appreciation" is defended as a way to respect domestic democratic processes that are more attuned to local peculiarities and traditions, when the policies and legislation has been subject to a proper proportionality test by the authorities:

> By reason of their direct and continuous contact with the vital forces of their countries, State authorities are in principle in a better position than the international judge to give an opinion on the exact content of these requirements [of morals] as well as on the 'necessity' of a 'restriction' or 'penalty' intended to meet them. (*Handyside* 1976, para 48).

However, this justification does not hold for the EU bodies (Føllesdal and Hix 2006, Føllesdal 2014). The EU is widely criticized for being out of touch with local circumstances, and the democratic pedigree of EU decisions is contested. At best, the chains of delegation are too long. Furthermore, the legislative process is not clearly set up to provide the requisite proportionality test.

Some observers claim that the ECtHR uses the margin of appreciation as a 'double standard', e.g. to avoid conflicts with more powerful states (Benvenisti 1999, 844). If so we may suspect that present—and future—'harmony' with the CJEU simply reflect the power of the latter rather than a normatively defensible respect for the democratic processes behind EU rules. In defense, these flaws in the democratic quality of the EU may change—indeed, the ECtHR might nudge the EU toward a more satisfactory proportionality test, if the EU accedes to the ECHR. Furthermore, I submit that the ECtHR may contribute in many such ways to render rules, citizens and authorities more trustworthy. Assurance that European decisions will not threaten individuals' human rights, and that the national authorities who participate in joint decision making respect human rights domestically, may thus increase the likelihood that citizens and national authorities will accept the majoritarian decisions of the EU (Binder 1995, Weiler 1991).

If the complex EU order is to deserve compliance and support by its citizens and member states, it must have well developed policies to monitor and protect against suspected human rights violations committed by Union bodies. Such policies must also be trustworthy. The ECtHR may therefore play an especially valuable role in providing assurance that EU authorities actually comply with the ECHR. Note that also when EU authorities *actually* act within their mandate, they may benefit from such independent monitoring: Such monitoring helps assure citizens that the authorities do indeed act within their mandate.

Sceptics may still wonder how the ECtHR contributes to trust, given that it regularly finds states in violation of the ECHR. If this were indeed a correct description, the objection is correct: then, the ECtHR does not persuade citizens to support the EU—or their member states. Human rights norms and bodies will only contribute to assurance in these ways *if in fact* the institutions satisfy such human rights norms. Otherwise the focus on human rights will instead serve to bring even more attention to these failures—and lead to less compliance or at least greater discussion about whether to comply. I submit that it is precisely this risk that renders the ECtHR a trustworthy trust-building mechanism, which the member states—and the EU—can use strategically: The governments 'up the ante' by subjecting its own state and the EU to such review, and thus show that they are sincerely committed to enhance the human rights of its inhabitants. When the states or the EU do in fact generally comply with the ECHR, as assessed by the ECtHR, this monitoring does provide assurance that the state—and EU—authorities merit obedience.

5 Conclusion, criticisms reconsidered

In the debate about whether the margin of appreciation doctrine amounts to an abdication by the Court, the present arguments have come to the rescue of the Doctrine. With the features laid out here, applied within these scope conditions, the Doctrine seems compatible with and even required by the rationale for placing some authority with the ECtHR to adjudicate human rights—when this supplements review by domestic courts. When constrained in this way, a margin of appreciation doctrine serves the particular objectives of the ECtHR within the multi-level European legal order, including its role in monitoring human rights compliance by member states in the European Union. Note, however, that it is not obvious that similar features and scope conditions should be part of a 'margin of appreciation doctrine' for other international courts, with different relations to other actors in the multi-level global system, and with other objectives with different normative weight than human rights. Nor is it clear that the ECtHR should grant the EU such a margin, if the EU becomes subject to the ECHR. The margin of appreciation doctrine was originally meant to accommodate the legitimate diversity among national legislations and traditions due to local circumstances, and to defer to their familiarity concerning the local needs—as long as they perform a proportionality test. It remains an open question whether similar arguments count in favor of granting the EU discretion in how it chooses to respect and promote human rights, since it can hardly be said to have a 'national' tradition of its own, nor are Union authorities obviously 'closer' to or more sensitive to local circumstances than the ECtHR. To the contrary, the EU may be suspected of being insufficiently sensitive to human rights concerns relative to the other objectives and values laid down in the Lisbon Treaty.

Consider in conclusion, the criticisms voiced against the margin of appreciation doctrine and how a person-centred conception of subsidiarity can alleviate them. The defence presented here should not cast doubt that the current margin of appreciation doctrine of the ECtHR is vague and partially inconsistent. The implication is that the Doctrine should be improved, rather than be abolished. These arguments thus support the change to the Preamble of the ECHR wrought by Protocol 15. But the general and vague appeal to 'subsidiarity' will neither help settle the dilemmas between sovereignty and human rights protection, nor provide much guide to the Court's use of the margin of appreciation in the cases brought before it. We may hope that Protocol 15 and the possible accession of the EU to the ECHR will fuel more philosophically informed attention to the Court's interpretation of subsidiarity and its margin of appreciation doctrine, by philosophers, lawyers and political scientists alike. Indeed, we may hope that the Court draws on a well reasoned conception of subsidiarity to further develop its Doctrine. The Doctrine should be specified not in the light of a state centric conception of subsidiarity which would tend to grant all states a wide margin to be judge in their own case as long as other states would not stop cooperation with them. Rather, a person-centred subsidiarity principle should be a guide. It already supports several of the features of the current Doctrine. They must be further elaborated, so that the margin of appreciation doctrine becomes worthy of that name, and so that the member states of the Council of Europe, and the European Union become and remain worthy of their citizens' obedience.

Bibliography

47+1 (2013): Draft Explanatory Report to the Agreement on the Accession of the European Union to the Convention for the Protection of Human Rights and Fundamental Freedoms —Appendix V, in: Fifth Negotiation meeting between the CDDH ad hoc negotiation group and the European Commission on the Accession of the European Union to the European Convention on Human Rights, Final report to the CDDH 47+1(2013)008rev2

Alter, Karen (2008): Delegating to International Courts: Self-Binding vs. Other-Binding Delegation, in: Law and contemporary problems 71, pp. 37–76.

Arai-Takahashi, Yutaka (2013): The Margin of Appreciation Doctrine: A Theoretical Analysis of Strasbourg's Variable Geometry, in: The European Court of Human Rights, edited by Føllesdal, Andreas/Peters, Birgit/Ulfstein, Geir, Cambridge, pp. 62–105.

Benvenisti, Eyal (1999): Margin of Appreciation, Consensus, and Universal Standards, in: International Law and Politics 31, pp. 843–54.

Binder, Darcy S. (1995): The European Court of Justice and the Protection of Fundamental Rights in the European Community: New Developments and Future Possibilities in Expanding Fundamental Rights Review to Member State Action, Jean Monnet Working Papers 1995, no. 4.

Brauch, Jeffrey. A. (2005): The Margin of Appreciation and the Jurisprudence of the European Court of Human Rights: Threat to the Rule of Law, in: Columbia Journal of European Law 11, pp. 113–50.

Buyse, Antoine (2014): CJEU Rules: Draft Agreement on EU Accession to ECHR Incompatible with EU Law, http://echrblog.blogspot.com.br/2014/12/cjeu-rules-draft-agreement-on-eu. html, visited on: 6 January 2016.

CJEU, Court of Justice of the European Union (2014): Opinion Pursuant to Article 218(11) TFEU —Draft International Agreement—Accession of the European Union to the European Convention for the Protection of Human Rights and Fundamental Freedoms— Compatibility of the Draft Agreement with the EU and Feu Treaties, Curia.europa.eu, no. 2/13.

del Moral, Ignacio de la Rasilla (2006): The Increasingly Marginal Appreciation of the Margin-of-Appreciation Doctrine, in: German Law Journal 7, pp. 611–624.

Douglas-Scott, Sionaidh (2014): Opinion 2/13 on EU accession to the ECHR: a Christmas bombshell from the European Court of Justice, http://verfassungsblog.de/en/opinion-213-eu-accession-echr-christmas-bombshell-european-court-justice/, visited on: 6 January 2016.

Etinson, Adam (2013): Human Rights, Claimability and the Uses of Abstraction, in: Utilitas 25, pp. 1–24.

European Council (1993): Presidency Conclusions, Copenhagen Meeting, SN 180/1/93.

European Council (2007): Treaty of Lisbon Amending the Treaty on European Union and the Treaty Establishing the European Community, Signed at Lisbon, 13 December 2007, in: Official Journal of the European Union vol.50, no. 2007/C 306/01.

European Union (2007): Treaty on the Functioning of the European Union, in: Official Journal C 326, 26/10/2012, pp. 1–390.

Føllesdal, Andreas (2014): Democratic Standards in an Asymmetric Union, in: Democratic Politics in a European Union under Stress, Cramme, Olaf/Hobolt, Sara B. (eds.), Oxford, pp. 199–216.

Føllesdal, Andreas (2006): Justice, Stability and Toleration in a Federation of Well-Ordered Peoples, in: Rawls's Law of Peoples: A Realistic Utopia?, Martin, Rex/Reidy, David (eds.), Oxford, pp. 299–317.

Føllesdal, Andreas (1998): Subsidiarity, in: Journal of Political Philosophy 6, pp. 231–59.

Føllesdal, Andreas (2007): Toward Self-Sustaining Stability? How the Constitutional Treaty Would Enhance Forms of Institutional and National Balance, in: Regional and Federal Studies 17, pp. 353–74.

Føllesdal, Andreas, and Hix, Simon (2006): Why There Is a Democratic Deficit in the EU: A Response to Majone and Moravcsik, in: Journal of Common Market Studies 44, pp. 533–62.

Handyside v United Kingdom, App no 5493/72 European Court of Human Rights (1976) EHRR 24 523.

Hatton v the United Kingdom, ECtHR (2003) 611.

Heinz, Wolfgang (2006): The EU External Relations and Human Rights, in: Human Rights in Europe. A Fragmented Regime?, Brosig, Malte (ed.), Frankfurt, pp. 184–207.

International Transport Workers' Federation v Viking, ECJ (2007) ECR Case C-438/05 I-10779.

Johansen, Stian Øby (2015): Opinion 2/13: A bag of coal from the CJEU, http://blogg.uio.no/jus/smr/multirights/content/opinion-213-a-bag-of-coal-from-the-cjeu, visited on: 6 January 2016.

Kratochvil, Jan (2011): The Inflation of the Margin of Appreciation by the European Court of Human Rights, in: Netherlands Quarterly of Human Rights 29, pp. 324–57.

Laval Un Partneri Ltd v Svenska Byggnadsarbetareförbundet, ECJ (2007) ECR Case C-341/05 I-11767.

Lester (2009): The European Court of Human Rights after 50 Years, in: European Human Rights Law Review 4, pp. 461–78.

Levi, Margaret (1998): Consent, Dissent and Patriotism, New York.

Levi, Margaret and Brad Epperly (2010): Pricipled Principals in the Founding Moments of the Rule of Law, in: James Heckman et al. (eds.): Global Perspectives on the Rule of Law, London, pp. 192–209.

Lindholm and Others v. Norway [Tomtefestesaken], App no 13221/08 ECtHR (2012) Series B 13221/08.

Macklem, Patrick (2006): Militant Democracy, Legal Pluralism, and the Paradox of Self-Determination, in: International Journal of Constitutional Law 4, pp. 488–516.

Melloni, App no C-399/11 CJEU (2013).

Observer and Guardian v United Kingdom, App no 13585/88 ECtHR (1991).

Omega Spielhallen- und Automatenaufstellungs-GmbH v Oberbürgermeisterin der Bundesstadt Bonn, ECJ (2004) ECR Case C-36/02 I-9609.

Council of Europe. Protocol No. 15 Amending the Convention on Fundamental Freedoms.

Peers, Steve (2014): The CJEU and the EU's accession to the ECHR: a clear and present danger to human rights protection, http://eulawanalysis.blogspot.com.tr/2014/12/the-cjeu-and-eus-accession-to-echr.html, visited on 6 January 2016

Rasmussen v Denmark, ECtHR (1988) Ser B 71.

Reitemeyer, Stefan, and Pirker, Benedikt (2015): Opinion 2/13 of the Court of Justice on Access of the EU to the ECHR—One step ahead and two steps back, http://european lawblog.eu/?p=2731#sthash.Md1Swv9M.QvNAm6hm.dpuf, visited on: 6 January 2016.

Schmidberger, Internationale Transporte und Planzüge v Republik Österreich, ECJ (2003) ECR Case C-112/00 I-5659.

Spielmann, Dean (2012): Allowing the Right Margin. The European Court of Human Rights and the National Margin of Appreciation Doctrine: Waiver or Subsidiarity of European Review?, in: Cambridge Yearbook of European Legal Studies 14, pp. 381–418.

The Sunday Times v United Kingdom, ECtHR (1979).

Sweeney, James A. (2005): Margins of Appreciation: Cultural Relativity and the European Court of Human Rights in the Post-Cold War Era, in: International and Comparative Law Quarterly 54, pp. 459–474.

Treaty on European Union, Nice Amendments (2001). Official Journal of the European Communities.

de Vries, Sybe (2013): Balancing Fundamental Rights with Economic Freedoms According to the European Court of Justice, in: Utrecht Law Review 9, pp. 169–192.

Weiler, Joseph H. H. (1991): The Transformation of Europe, in: Yale Law Review 100, pp. 1–81.

Wingrove v United Kingdom, App no 19/1995/525/611 (1996).

Yourow, Howard Charles (1996): The Margin of Appreciation Doctrine in the Dynamics of European Human Rights Jurisprudence, Leiden.

Z v Finland, App no 22009/93 ECtHR (1997) European Human Rights Reporter 25 371.

List of Contributors

Privatdozentin Dr. **Beatrice Brunhöber**, Juristische Fakultät, Humboldt-Universität zu Berlin, Germany

Professor (assoc.) Dr. **Norbert Campagna**, Institute of Philosophy, University of Luxembourg, Luxembourg

Professor **Andreas Føllesdal**, Department of Philosophy, University of Tromsø, Norway

Seniorprofessor Dr. Dr. h.c. **Volker Gerhardt**, Institut für Philosophie, Humboldt-Universität zu Berlin, Germany

Professor **Robert Hanna**, Independent philosopher, Visiting research professor, The Pontifical Catholic University of Parana, Curitiba, Brazil.

Professor Dr. **Dietmar H. Heidemann**, Institute of Philosophy, University of Luxembourg, Luxembourg

Professor Dr. **Heiner F. Klemme**, Seminar für Philosophie, Martin-Luther-Universität Halle-Wittenberg, Germany

Professor Dr. **Bernd Ludwig**, Philosophisches Seminar, Universität Göttingen, Germany

Professor Dr. **Heinz-Gerd Schmitz**, Philosophisches Seminar, Universität zu Köln, Germany.

Professor Dr. **Lukas K. Sosoe**, Institute of Philosophy, University of Luxembourg, Luxembourg

Dr. **Katja Stoppenbrink**, LL.M., Philosophisches Seminar & DFG-Kolleg-Forschergruppe 1209 „Theoretische Grundfragen der Normenbegründung in Medizinethik und Biopolitik", Westfälische Wilhelms-Universität Münster, Germany

Professor em. Dr. **Michael Wolff**, Abteilung Philosophie, Universität Bielefeld, Germany

Index